Human Development in the Era of Globalization

Keith B. Griffin

Human Development in the Era of Globalization

Essays in Honor of Keith B. Griffin

Edited by
James K. Boyce
University of Massachusetts, Amherst, USA

Stephen Cullenberg
University of California, Riverside, USA

Prasanta K. Pattanaik
University of California, Riverside, USA

Robert Pollin
University of Massachusetts, Amherst, USA

Edward Elgar
Cheltenham, UK • Northampton, MA, USA

Published by
Edward Elgar Publishing Limited
The Lypiatts
15 Lansdown Road
Cheltenham
Glos GL50 2JA
UK

Edward Elgar Publishing, Inc.
William Pratt House
9 Dewey Court
Northampton
Massachusetts 01060
USA

Paperback edition 2009

A catalogue record for this book
is available from the British Library

Library of Congress Cataloging in Publication Data
Human development in the era of globalization : essays in honor of Keith B. Griffin / edited by James Boyce ... [et al.].
p. cm.
Includes bibliographical references.
1. Economic policy. 2. Poverty. I. Griffin, Keith B. II. Boyce, James K.

HD87.H88 2006
339.4'6'091734—dc22

2005050876

Mixed Sources
Product group from well-managed forests and other controlled sources
www.fsc.org Cert no. SA-COC-1565
© 1996 Forest Stewardship Council
FSC

ISBN 978 1 84542 593 7 (cased)
ISBN 978 1 84844 665 6 (paperback)

Typeset by Manton Typesetters, Louth, Lincolnshire, UK
Printed and bound by MPG Books Group, UK

Contents

Contributors

Albert Berry, University of Toronto

James K. Boyce, University of Massachusetts, Amherst

Mark D. Brenner, University of Massachusetts, Amherst

Anjan Chakrabarti, Calcutta University

Stephen Cullenberg, University of California, Riverside

Diane Elson, University of Essex

Mwangi wa Gĩthĩnji, Gettysburg College

Steven M. Helfand, University of California, Riverside

Azizur Rahman Khan, University of California, Riverside

John Knight, Oxford University

Edward S. Levine, University of California, Riverside

Victor D. Lippit, University of California, Riverside

Terry McKinley, United Nations Development Program

Prasanta K. Pattanaik, University of California, Riverside

Charles Perrings, University of York

Robert Pollin, University of Massachusetts, Amherst

Carl Riskin, Queens College, City University of New York

Binayak Sen, Bangladesh Institute of Development Studies

Li Shi, Institute of Economics, Chinese Academy of Social Sciences

Rehman Sobhan, Centre for Policy Dialogue, Dhaka

Lina Song, School of Sociology and Social Policy, University of Nottingham

Bob Sutcliffe, University of the Basque Country

Acknowledgements

Keith and Dixie Griffin

This volume collects the papers that were presented at the April 2004 Festschrift conference honoring the work of Professor Keith B. Griffin. The conference was held in Gordon Hall at the University of Massachusetts, Amherst, the home of the Political Economy Research Institute (PERI). PERI co-sponsored the conference. The other co-sponsor was the Department of Economics at the University of California, Riverside. UC, Riverside was Keith's academic home from the time of his stepping down as President of Magdalen College, Oxford University in 1988 until his retirement from classroom teaching – but not anything else – in 2004. (Professor Griffin's curriculum vitae as of 2005 is presented at the end of this volume, listing all of his academic appointments and major professional activities over a more than 40-year period).

Professor Griffin has been a mentor, colleague, teacher and friend to all of us. We therefore feel highly privileged to have had the opportunity to organize the 2004 Festschrift conference and to edit this volume. But of course, none of this would have been possible without the enthusiastic contributions of many other friends and co-workers. We must first mention Judy Fogg, the frighteningly capable, while still always warm, gracious and charming administrative manager of PERI. When we say 'we organized' the UMass conference, we really mean that we thought about how to organize it, and that Judy Fogg did virtually all the hard work to make things actually happen. We are very grateful for all of her contributions.

We are equally grateful to our colleagues who enriched the 2004 conference by presenting formal comments on the various papers. These discussants were Michael Ash, Jerry Epstein, Nancy Folbre, and Mohan Rao of UMass, Elissa Braunstein of Colorado State University (previously of UMass), Carmen Diana Deere of University of Florida (also previously of UMass), and Steve Marglin of Harvard. Gary Dymski and David Fairris of UC, Riverside also actively participated in the conference, offering typically trenchant and surprising observations. We were sorry that our other UC, Riverside colleague Howard Sherman was unable to come to the event. Professor Amy Ickowitz of Clark University was also an important contributor to the conference, presenting a preliminary version of her ongoing work about shifting cultivation patterns in Central and West Africa.

We were happy to work with Edward Elgar Publishing on this project. We wish to thank especially the US acquisitions editor Alan Sturmer, our copyeditor Cathrin Vaughan, and the typesetter David Manton. Lynda Pickbourn of UMass also provided us with important assistance in preparing the volume for publication.

There is only one logical place to end these acknowledgements, and that is by recognizing Keith's wife Dixie. Dixie and Keith met in their 12th-grade homeroom class in Texas, and have been a couple ever since. Dixie's name by itself gives a partial sense of who she is – a warm, generous, livewire from the heart of Texas. But Dixie is also an Oxford sophisticate and an unpredictable Californian. One cannot imagine Keith's persistent energy and originality proceeding as it has for decades without Dixie's own energy and originality keeping pace, every step of the way.

Jim Boyce, Steve Cullenberg, Prasanta Pattanaik and Bob Pollin

Introduction

James K. Boyce, Stephen Cullenberg, Prasanta K. Pattanaik and Robert Pollin

This volume honors Keith Griffin's more than 40 years of fundamental contributions to the discipline of economics. It is fitting, therefore, that each of the chapters in the volume reflects the influence of Griffin's own pathbreaking work, the hallmarks of which are a deep commitment to advancing the well-being of the world's poor majority, and an unflinching willingness to question conventional wisdom as to how this ought to be done.

Four overarching themes recur in both Keith Griffin's work and this volume. The first is the need not only to eradicate poverty but also to redress inequalities in the distribution of income and wealth within and among nations. The second is the impact of growth on inequality, and conversely of inequality on growth. The third is the political economy of policy-making – recognizing that policies are the result of contests amongst competing individuals, groups and classes, rather than an outcome of dispassionate optimization by technocrats insulated from political processes. The final theme is heterogeneity and its implications for development strategies.

INEQUALITY AND POVERTY

Long before it became fashionable to do so, Keith Griffin took poverty reduction to be the central objective of development. In the mid-1960s this normative stance was itself a radical departure from the prevailing view that economic growth was the overriding goal. But Griffin went further, insisting that poverty cannot be divorced from inequality. Hence the terms 'poverty' and 'inequality' are often paired in his writings, as in the title of the book *International Inequality and National Poverty* (1978) and in the title of the book he co-edited with Azizur Rahman Khan, *Poverty and Landlessness in Rural Asia* (1977), landlessness being a key dimension of asset inequality.

One advantage of this formulation is that in addition to underscoring a basic reason for persistent poverty – inequality in the distribution of income and wealth – it draws our attention to the other end of the spectrum, the rich. In so doing, it suggests that the problem is not just the poor, who need to be rescued somehow from poverty, but that the rich may be part of the problem, too.

Amongst economists who pay serious attention to distribution, the usual focus is the distribution of income. Griffin has devoted equal attention to the distribution of assets, or wealth. Thus in the introduction to *Poverty and Landlessness*, Griffin and Khan write: 'The only way to alter substantially the distribution of income is by altering the distribution of wealth in agrarian countries. This implies above all the need for land reform.' The reconfiguration and redistribution of rights to assets is an intellectual terrain where many economists fear to tread. Griffin has been among the intrepid exceptions.

INEQUALITY AND GROWTH

A second theme in Griffin's writings and this volume is the impact of growth processes and economic policies on inequality. The inequalities that have concerned Griffin include – again, far ahead of his time – not only vertical disparities of class but also horizontal disparities across regions, ethnic groups, and other social divides. In his landmark essay, 'Financing development plans in Pakistan' (1965), Griffin dissected the ways in which that country's development strategy systematically exacerbated the economic gap between its two wings, East Pakistan (now Bangladesh) and West Pakistan. In recent years, more economists have begun to recognize the importance of horizontal inequalities, among other reasons because they can be precursors of violent conflict and civil war – a link that the course of events in Pakistan illustrated a few years later.

In his work on the 'green revolution' in Asian agriculture – the introduction of highly fertilizer-responsive varieties of rice and wheat – Griffin focused on the impacts of technological change on inequality. He concluded, in contrast to conventional thinking then and now, that agricultural growth does not inevitably translate into improved well-being of the poor. Although agricultural growth may be necessary to reduce hunger, it is not sufficient. 'The reason,' Griffin wrote in *The Political Economy of Agrarian Change* (1974), 'lies not so much in inadequate technology, as in inappropriate institutions and policy. The explanation for the latter, in turn, lies not in the ignorance of those who govern but in the powerlessness of most of those who are governed.'

In this respect, Griffin's critique recalls Karl Marx's famous comments on the working man and the machine: 'It took both time and experience,' Marx wrote, 'before the workpeople learnt to distinguish between machinery and its employment by capital, and to direct their attacks not against the material instruments of production, but against the mode in which they are used.'[1] In the same vein, Griffin directed his attack not against the new agricultural technology *per se*, but against the agrarian structures in which the technology was introduced.

Turning the growth–equity linkage around, Griffin also has pointed to the ways in which inequality constrains economic growth. In an era when many economists assumed an axiomatic 'great trade-off' between growth and equity, this was a radical proposition. Today it has entered the mainstream of development economics.

Griffin extended this logic to critique foreign aid. In contrast to mainstream assumptions, he argued that aid (that is, inflows of external capital at below-market interest rates) does not necessarily promote more rapid growth. Instead it can depress domestic savings and reduce the efficiency of investment – particularly in countries with very unequal distributions of wealth and power.[2] Thirty years ago, this claim created a storm of controversy. Yet it now is accepted, albeit somewhat grudgingly, such as in 1998 publication of the World Bank itself, *Assessing Aid: What Works, What Doesn't, and Why*. The Bank study found that in countries with what the Bank calls 'poor policy,' a 1 percent increase in aid (as a fraction of national income) leads to a 0.3 percent decrease in the rate of growth. In reporting this remarkable conclusion, the authors of the Bank study should have exclaimed, 'Griffin was right!' Instead the findings are reported in an appendix, and the authors make no mention of Griffin's pioneering analysis.

THE POLITICAL ECONOMY OF ECONOMIC POLICY

A third theme is the importance of understanding the political economy of economic policy. Where do 'poor policies', however these may be defined, come from? Griffin consistently has rejected the notion that policy shortcomings are simply the result of mistakes. Instead he traces them to the distribution of wealth and power. 'Governments may claim to rule in the "national interest",' he wrote in *The Political Economy of Agrarian Change*, 'but in reality they act on behalf of their supporters.'

If so, we must ask what can be done to avoid an accumulation of advantages and disadvantages whereby the rich capitalize on their power and grow richer still, while the poor grow relatively (and perhaps absolutely) poorer. Griffin and the contributors to this volume uphold the view that there are alternatives, and that humankind is not trapped in an inexorable process of polarization from which there is no escape short of apocalyptic change. In this respect, their work echoes the maxim of the late Raymond Williams: 'To be truly radical is to make hope possible rather than despair convincing.'

Since the late 1980s Griffin's work on the transition from central planning to more market-guided economic systems in China and other low-income countries, such as Vietnam and Mongolia, has advanced alternatives to orthodox prescriptions for rapid privatization of state-owned enterprises and indiscriminate price liberalization.[3] Instead he has emphasized the importance of maintaining aggregate demand, sustaining high levels of investment, and preventing great inequalities in the distribution of income and wealth from emerging and becoming entrenched.

The phenomenon of globalization gives rise to new opportunities as well as new threats to the well-being of the poor. Globalization does not simply entail the integration of markets, much as neoliberals may seek to reduce it to this element. It also involves the globalization of governance, including informal governance by civil society as well as the formal rules and regulations of governments. The globalization process today opens possibilities for redefining and reconfiguring rights: rights to food, rights to clean water, rights to environmental quality, rights to natural resources, rights to participate in the political process. All rights, including property rights, are socially constructed. Hence they change over time – if and when people organize to change them. Keith Griffin has played a leading role in showing how economists can contribute to this broader social process.

HETEROGENEITY

A final theme is the importance of heterogeneity. Rather than succumbing to the economist's penchant for elegance through simplification, Griffin has sought to unpack broad categories, like 'the poor', and look at the circumstances of real people in specific times and places. The heterogeneity of the poor implies for example that few policy instruments will have unambiguous impacts on poverty or inequality.

This is a consistent theme in Griffin's work. In *The Transition to Egalitarian Development* (1981), co-authored with Jeffrey James – a book that starts from the bold premise of a government that is committed to the rapid eradication of mass poverty – Griffin analyzes the market disequilibria likely to result from a large-scale redistribution of purchasing power. Foremost among these is excess demand for food, as income shifts to poorer households for whom food constitutes a larger share of family expenditure, resulting in upward pressure on food prices. Griffin emphasizes that 'the poor are highly heterogeneous in terms of their geographical location and, most important, their occupation structure', and that this implies that 'a rapid increase in the price of wage goods is likely to affect the poor in many different ways in their capacity both as producers and as consumers' (p. 20). In this book, a veritable how-to manual for progressive economic policy-making in developing countries, Griffin and James recommend a range of policies to manage both demand and supply.

As this example suggests, heterogeneity has important implications for policy design. In particular it underscores the need for explicit attention to externalities, both positive and negative, a need that again cuts against the grain of the wish for elegance and simplicity. Unlike pure theorists, policy-makers cannot assume away the problems posed by market failures. 'Quite often,' Griffin and Enos wrote in their book *Planning Development* (1970, p. 237), 'the external economies and diseconomies generated by an investment project are more significant than the measured benefits and costs.'

Closely linked to heterogeneity is diversity. In contrast to optimization models that prescribe and predict a single 'first-best' solution – whether in the choice of technology, the design of institutions or economic theories – development economics brings out the value of diversity. Just as crop diversity, as opposed to varietal monoculture, is needed for successful adaptations to changing environmental conditions in the farmers' fields, so too, more generally, diverse technologies and institutions are crucial for long-run economic resilience. Keith Griffin and the contributors to this volume similarly demonstrate in their work the value of intellectual diversity: the fruitfulness of cross-pollination among different theoretical perspectives, and the importance of evolving new ideas under the pressure of changing realities on the ground. Such intellectual diversity, we believe, is crucial to sustain economic analysis as a creative and useful endeavor.

OBSERVING AND PARTICIPATING IN HISTORY

Perhaps uniquely among volumes of this type, our book begins with an essay by Professor Griffin himself, 'A witness of two revolutions'. Professor Griffin originally delivered this chapter as the Distinguished Humanist Achievement Lecturer at the Center for Ideas and Society at the University of California, Riverside in January 2003. Professor Griffin also presented it as the opening paper for our 2004 Festschrift conference. This chapter is an autobiographical introduction to Professor Griffin's work and career, presented with his characteristic eloquence and flair. The first revolution that he considers is the termination of the European imperial system after the Second World War. This led to the corresponding rise of development economics as a tool for advancing effective policy paths for decolonization and beyond. The second revolution is the collapse of Communism in the Soviet Union and Eastern Europe after 1989, and the accompanying transition from centrally planned economies to a more market-oriented economic system. This second political revolution gave rise to the new subfield of economics, the economics of transition. Griffin discusses his involvement in both of these revolutions, in terms of both his academic research and his highly active role as a policy advisor for governments in all parts of the globe.

PERSPECTIVES ON CHINESE DEVELOPMENT

As one major part of his involvement in the second revolution – the movement away from central planning and toward market-guided economies – Professor Griffin has been a highly active researcher on the Chinese economy since the earliest stages of its post-Mao reforms. The three chapters in this section are all by authors who, at various points, have collaborated with Professor Griffin in this work.

In 'The fall in Chinese poverty: issues of measurement, incidence and cause', Carl Riskin discusses problems involved in the measurement of poverty in China. He argues that while it is clear that there has been a decline in rural poverty in China during its period of transition, for various reasons the magnitude of this decline remains a matter of debate. Riskin further argues that though there has been an increase in urban poverty in China in recent years, the reliability of the measures of urban poverty in China is even more problematic than that for rural poverty. Riskin also points out that: (1) estimates of deprivation based on income or expenditure may not give us as dependable a picture of deprivation as that yielded by real indicators such as malnutrition, and illiteracy; and (2) some of the real indicators (for example consumption of calories per day) suggest a much higher level of deprivation in rural areas of China than the official income poverty measure. In general, Riskin's chapter makes clear that many issues need to be resolved before we can have a reliable understanding of the poverty trends in China over the past 20 years and into the future.

In 'The rural–urban divide and the evolution of political economy in China', John Knight, Li Shi and Lina Song also focus on the issue of rising inequality in China. They show that the single greatest source of inequality in China during the the post-Mao reform period is the gap between urban and rural living standards. This gap is a long-standing feature of Chinese society, both during and prior to the Communist era. But the authors show that this gap has been widening since the reform period began in the early 1980s. The authors examine a range of factors behind this gap, including, perhaps most important, the greater political power of the minority of urban workers relative to the majority of rural peasants. This relatively greater power affects a range of government policies, including food subsidies for urban workers, and the superior provision of health and education among urban dwellers. The authors conclude that the Chinese government is more concerned with promoting growth, and alleviating poverty through growth alone, than addressing the sharply rising inequality that has accompanied the growth trajectory since the early 1980s.

In 'Socialist fetters? Land tenure and economic growth in post-Mao rural China', Mark Brenner reviews the evidence concerning the changing distribution of land in rural China since the early 1980s. Brenner's findings are striking

– that in contrast with virtually all other social indicators during the period of post-Mao reform, physical landholdings have become more equal in this period. Brenner attributes this result to China's two-tiered land tenure system, whereby rural households have long-term use rights on their land, while local governments retain ownership of the land. Local governments have used their power of ownership over the land to periodically adjust landholdings on behalf of more egalitarian outcomes. Brenner also makes clear that other forces are acting to counter the egalitarian results of this land tenure system. Thus the value of land is becoming increasingly unequal, reflecting the increasing importance of market forces in establishing land values. In addition, local governments are promoting township and village enterprises, which are focused almost entirely on the coastal region, thereby leading to worsening inter-regional inequality. Given these counter-forces, it is especially significant to recognize the positive role that the land tenure system continues to play in promoting equality in China.

AGRICULTURE AND RURAL POVERTY

The majority of the poor people in developing countries have, over time, lived in rural settings and earned their livelihood through agriculture. It is therefore not surprising that Keith Griffin has focused intensively on issues surrounding agriculture and rural poverty in his research and policy advising. The three chapters in this section reflect these same concerns.

In 'A future for small farms? Biodiversity and sustainable agriculture', James Boyce argues that small farms play a vital role in sustaining the genetic diversity of crops that is essential for long-run food security. In centers of agricultural biodiversity – such as Mesoamerica in the case of maize (corn) and the Andean region in the case of potatoes – small farmers are the 'keystone species' in agricultural ecosystems that underpin human survival. In addition to the policy-induced biases against small farmers to which Keith Griffin has drawn attention – in particular, the ubiquitous subsidies to large farms and capital-intensive technologies – Boyce identifies a further shortcoming of both market signals and present government policies: the failure to value and reward this environmental service. As Boyce explains, although the *ex situ* seed collections in agricultural research institutions are quite valuable, they not an adequate substitute for *in situ* conservation by small farms. He prescribes a range of policies to strengthen both the livelihood security of small farmers and their incentive to continue providing this crucial environmental service: the removal of current policy biases against small farms; the development of markets for 'traditional' varieties of crops and livestock; the provision of local public goods in areas where farmers cultivate diversity; direct payments for on-farm conservation; and support for part-time farming as a component of households' diversified livelihood strategies.

In 'The impact of policy reforms on rural poverty in Brazil', Steven Helfand and Edward Levine seek to explain a very favorable development over the 1990s: a 16 percent decline in the rate of rural poverty in Brazil. Helfand and Levine consider a wide range of factors that may have contributed to the decline in rural poverty, including out-migration from rural areas; the increasing significance of non-agricultural income sources, including government transfer payments; and macroeconomic changes, including the taming of the hyperinflation that had plagued Brazil between 1988 and 1994. Helfand and Levine present a carefully specified data set to examine these alternative possibilities, which enables them to examine, among other things, hetereogeneity in the experiences of different states in Brazil. According to their findings, the single most important factor in reducing rural poverty was the 29 percent increase in per capita income throughout Brazil between 1991 and 2000. This rapid rise in average income compensated for the fact that inequality rose in the rural areas of the country by 7 percent over the 1990s. But Helfand and Levine also conclude that there is no single explanation for the rapid rise in income itself. This suggests that policy measures for reducing poverty will need to pay careful attention to the particular conditions that prevail in different countries and regions afflicted with high rates of poverty.

Albert Berry's chapter asks 'Has Colombia finally found an agrarian reform that works?' To pursue an answer, Berry surveys the history of agrarian reform measures from the 1930s to the present. He shows that, over time, the conditions which led to significant positive agrarian reforms are rare; and as such, that major redistribution of land was never politically feasible over this period of time. The next-best option was therefore to pursue an equitable development of frontier land, before largeholders could make claims on these properties. However the failure of government policy-makers to implement even this more modest approach to land reform has meant a steady decline of favorable policy options. With a rapidly diminishing frontier, Berry argues that the current approach of negotiating land transfers to aspiring smallholders, with the government subsidizing these land purchases, appears to be the only remaining feasible alternative. Berry holds that its success will depend on how much land will actually be available at affordable prices; whether the state will provide effective credit and agricultural support programs for smallholders; and whether the program will be sustainable over several governments. Meanwhile Berry holds that the failure in Colombia to confront rural poverty through land reform has created a major breeding ground for guerilla groups and the illicit drug industry.

DIMENSIONS OF HUMAN DEVELOPMENT

Economists have always known that the promotion of economic development is not simply a matter of accelerating GDP growth. However, too frequently they have lapsed into assuming that GDP growth is a sufficient proxy for capturing the range of factors that comprise development. The pioneering work of Keith Griffin and others has enabled us to attain a much more finely-grained understanding of the factors that comprise human development – that is, an economic growth path that generates broadly-shared improvements in well-being. The three chapters in Part III offer a range of perspectives that help clarify the project of human development.

In 'Death and development', Bob Sutcliffe demonstrates the ways to utilize data relating to mortality for illuminating different aspects of the well-being of societies as well as the well-being of different groups within the same society. The wealth of information gathered and analyzed by Sutcliffe includes, among other things, intertemporal and geographic comparisons of ratios of age-specific mortality; ratios of male and female age-specific death rates in different countries; differences in life expectations of different ethnic groups in the USA, South Africa and Brazil; the age distributions of deaths in different countries; and the age-specific death rates in Africa and the USA due to infectious diseases and causes related to birth and maternity, non-infectious medical conditions, and accidents, suicide and killings. Sutcliffe argues strongly for understanding the causes of death in social, economic and political categories. That is, to know what percentage of deaths and disability in the world now take place due to poverty, to lack of education and knowledge, to inequality and all its causes, to lack of medical facilities or appropriate health policies, to the research and pricing policies of pharmaceutical companies, to the advertising and marketing policies of tobacco companies, to prejudice and denial which prevents adequate education about safe sex, to discrimination and violence based on sex, race or sexuality, or to the multitude of other socially and economically pathological factors which can contribute to premature death. Sutcliffe closes with a striking analogy: that unmasking the social causes of premature deaths can be seen as a counterpart to the political movements which have arisen to confront dictatorship on behalf of those missing through political oppression.

In 'On comparing functioning bundles and capability sets', Prasanta Pattanaik focuses on certain conceptual issues that arise in comparing functioning bundles and capability sets when one seeks to apply the innovative formulation of the notion of living standards introduced by Amartya Sen and Martha Nussbaum. Among other things, Pattanaik discusses: (1) practical limitations of the dominance criterion in comparing functioning bundles; (2) analytical problems involved in using 'local information' about values when comparing functioning bundles; (3) some alternative approaches to the problem of comparing capability sets; and (4) the incompatibility of certain highly plausible properties that one would like to impose on standard-of-living comparisons based on functioning bundles, and a similar incompatibility in the case of standard-of-living comparisons based on capability sets.

In 'Environment, poverty and development', Charles Perrings uses an analytical model to explore certain links between poverty and environmental changes. In his model, the output depends on the stock of produced capital and the amount of extracted natural capital, which is simply the stock of natural capital times the rate of extraction. The decision-maker chooses the fraction of the output to be consumed and the rate of extraction of natural capital to maximize his or her utility. Perrings derives two conclusions from his analysis. Firstly, if there is depensatory growth of natural capital stocks, then there exist at least two distinct equilibria. The first of these involves high levels of environmental stocks and yields and resilience to output shocks, while the second involves low levels of environmental stocks and yields and resilience to output shocks. Secondly, Perrings shows that if initially the decision-maker is in a state of 'subjective poverty', then a shock that adversely affects the output may lead the decision-maker to dissave by drawing down the stock of natural capital through an increase in the extraction rate. This in turn may cause the system to converge on a low-level equilibrium.

GLOBALIZATION AND INEQUALITY

Globalization is a central, overarching fact of contemporary economic life, in both the North and South. Issues surrounding globalization have correspondingly been at the center of Keith Griffin's research and policy advising for more than a decade. The four chapters in Part IV examine a range of questions emanating from the ongoing process of global integration.

In 'Globalization and the transition to egalitarian development', Robert Pollin begins by asserting what he holds to be the single most important fact about the contemporary pattern of global economic integration: that it is being guided by a predominant commitment to neoliberal economic policies throughout the world. Such policies include more openness to trade and foreign direct investment, fewer government regulations of financial markets and institutions and other sectors, and a substantially reduced role for macroeconomic policy management. Pollin then examines what he considers to be three overarching problems that have emerged in this era of neoliberal globalization. The 'Marx problem' refers to the expansion of what Marx termed the 'reserve army of labor', which has resulted from a range of structural changes and policy responses. The 'Keynes problem' is that highly liquid financial markets, such as those that have emerged on a global scale in our current era, are prone to bouts of speculation and instability. Financial instability in turn is frequently transmitted into the real economy, creating severe cyclical volatility in incomes and employment. The 'Polanyi problem' concerns the ability of non-market forces to engender norms of social solidarity that can serve as effective counterweights to the competitive imperatives of a free-market economy. Pollin explores the nature of these problems and proposes policy measures for confronting them, outlining within this context some features of a renewed path toward egalitarian development.

In 'Gender equality, public finance and globalization', Diane Elson analyzes a series of gender-based initiatives (GBIs) in the realm of public finance that have been advanced in both the global North and South. As Elson explains, the GBIs are measures that, from the perspective of gender equity, seek to improve the distribution, adequacy and impact of public expenditures at national, regional and local levels. They also aim to secure greater transparency in the use of public money, as well as greater accountability to women as citizens. The pioneering efforts toward GBIs were taken by so-called 'femocrats' in the government in Australia in the mid-1980s. Elson describes how the Australian example then served as a model for efforts in South Africa and beyond. By 2000, Elson reports that governments throughout the world have come to see gender budget analysis as a potential tool for bringing gender-based concerns into mainstream policy decision-making. But Elson also raises a basic problem confronting this growing movement: that in the era of globalization, governments – especially in the South – have been steadily losing control over their public finance decisions. This is because globalization of trade, investment and finance exert pressure on governments to reduce tax revenues and public expenditures, even as it creates a need for more investment in public goods to counteract inequality and insecurity.

In 'Class transition in the age of globalization: examples from the rural sectors in India and Kenya', Anjan Chakrabarti, Stephen Cullenberg and Mwangi wa Gĩthĩnji develop an insight advanced by Keith Griffin in his 1974 book *The Political Economy of Agrarian Change*: that even in simple rural communities, social and class differences can easily become blurred when landlords and peasants adopt a variety of roles in the economy. The authors synthesize Griffin's perspective with a post-structuralist Marxian class analytic framework to examine the changing class landscapes of rural India and Kenya in the contemporary period of globalization. In both the Indian and Kenyan cases, the authors reach a surprising conclusion: that the impact of globalization has not been leading to a clarification of class-based social identities as in different periods Marx and Engels, and Griffin, had assumed would occur with time. Instead, Chakrabarti, Cullenberg and Gĩthĩnji find that the multiplicity of class sets is continuing in the contemporary period, even while income inequality has sharpened in both countries.

In 'What will become of the welfare state?' Victor Lippit argues that European-style social democracy – that is, its welfare state practices favoring relative equality and the assurance of access to the basic requirements for a decent living standard – is the most humane form of capitalism that the world has managed to produce. But Lippit also argues that welfare-state capitalism has come under increasing challenge. His focus is on the ways in which globalization and technological change are undermining the welfare-state model, because they increasingly force firms throughout the capitalist world to focus on competitiveness and maximizing shareholder value as opposed to focusing on the welfare of their entire community of stakeholders. Lippit also emphasizes that ageing populations and the revolutionary transformation of medicine promise to raise the costs of existing welfare state systems substantially. Lippit discusses the various reforms that have been undertaken by several European countries to handle these challenges faced by the welfare state. His overall conclusion is that welfare-state policies need to be reformed, so that they can operate with increased flexibly in the contemporary era of globalization. In Lippit's view, this is the only way that the welfare state can be preserved until such time as desirable and feasible forms of post-capitalist social organization begin to emerge.

STRATEGIES FOR REDUCING POVERTY AND INEQUALITY

Keith Griffin has always followed in practice the 11th Thesis on Feuerbach by Marx: 'The philosophers have only interpreted the world in various ways. The point, however, is to change it.' It is therefore appropriate that the concluding part of this volume considers, from various perspectives, the question of how to fight effectively poverty and inequality, given the actual world conditions in which we live today.

In 'The structure and distribution of personal income and povery reduction: a case study of Bangladesh during the 1990s', Azizur Khan and Binayak Sen provide a detailed analysis of the sources of the increase in inequality in the distribution of personal income in Bangladesh between 1991–92 and 2000. They distinguish seven different categories of income. For each category, they derive the 'pseudo-Gini ratio' from the 'pseudo-Lorenz curve' for that category. The pseudo-Lorenz curve for the r-th category of income is constructed by plotting cumulative shares of the r-th category of income against the cumulative deciles of population based on the ranking of individuals in terms of their overall income (as distinct from their income from the r-th source). If the pseudo-Gini ratio for the r-th category of income is higher (resp. lower) than the true Gini ratio for the economy, the r-th source is called disequalizing (resp. equalizing). Changes in the Gini ratio arise either from changes in the pseudo-Gini ratios for the different categories of income or from changes in the shares of different categories of income in the total income of the country. Khan and Sen's analysis based on this framework yields much fresh insight into the structure of inequality in Bangladesh and the sources of the change in inequality over the period from 1991–92 to 2000. Khan and Sen also discuss the sources of changes in poverty in Bangladesh over the same period.

In 'Poverty as injustice: refocusing the policy agenda', Rehman Sobhan offers a bold critique of orthodox approaches to poverty reduction and an alternative framework for action. Both his critique and his policy approach are based on his argument that structural injustice remains the source of poverty and exclusion. These structural injustices include insufficient access to productive assets as well as human resources, unequal capacity to participate in markets and undemocratic access to political power. Orthodox approaches to poverty reduction focused on promoting economic growth alone – and here Sobhan includes the so-called Washington Consensus framework and the more recent 'poverty reduction strategy papers' advanced by the World Bank and IMF – do not recognize these structural sources of poverty. They therefore will never be effective as a framework for poverty reduction. Sohban's own policy proposals, such as the creation of mutual funds for the poor, are not radical when considered by themselves. However, taken as a whole, they offer a means of empowering the poor through collective action.

In 'Economic policies and poverty reduction in Asia and the Pacific: alternatives to neoliberalism', Terry McKinley reviews the lessons that emerge from the studies, supported by the United Nations Development Program, of eight countries, namely Bangladesh, Cambodia, China, Indonesia, Mongolia, Nepal, Sri Lanka and Vietnam. McKinley highlights four important policy recommendations in these studies, which differ significantly from what he calls 'the neoliberal policy matrix that has dominated economic prescriptions for the last two decades'. The policy recommendations are as follows. Firstly, governments should use fiscal policies in a proactive fashion to promote pro-poor investment as well as to generate fast growth. Secondly, a relaxed monetary policy should accompany the expansionary fiscal policy. Thirdly, there should be greater mobilization of domestic resources for public investment. Finally, governments should exercise greater control over financial institutions and short-term external capital flows, and they should use state financial institutions to make credit available for poverty reduction and growth. Overall, McKinley is advancing a coherent approach to economic policy that, in the face of the ascendant neoliberal agenda, builds creatively on the decades of research, writings and policy advising by Keith Griffin.

NOTES

1. Marx (1967), p. 429.
2. See Griffin (1970) and Griffin and Enos (1970a).
3. See for example Griffin (1984, 1995, 1998).

SELECT BIBLIOGRAPHY

Griffin, Keith (1965), 'Financing development plans in Pakistan', *Pakistan Development Review*, reprinted in Keith Griffin and Azizur Rahman Khan (eds) (1972), *Growth and Inequality in Pakistan*, London: Macmillan.

Griffin, Keith (1970), 'Foreign capital, domestic savings, and economic development', *Bulletin of the Oxford Institute of Economics and Statistics*, **32**.

Griffin, Keith (1974), *The Political Economy of Agrarian Change*, London: Macmillan, and Cambridge, MA: Harvard University Press.

Griffin, Keith (1978), *International Inequality and National Poverty*, London: Macmillan.

Griffin, Keith (ed.) (1984), *Institutional Reform and Economic Development in the Chinese Countryside*, London: Macmillan.

Griffin, Keith (ed.) (1995), *Poverty and the Transition to a Market Economy in Mongolia*, London: Macmillan, and New York: St Martin's.

Griffin, Keith (ed.) (1998), *Economic Reform in Vietnam*, London: Macmillan, and New York: St Martin's.

Griffin, Keith and John Enos (1970a), 'Foreign assistance: objectives and consequences', *Economic Development and Cultural Change*, **18**, 313–27.

Griffin, Keith and John Enos (1970b), *Planning Development*, London: Addison-Wesley.

Griffin, Keith and Jeffrey James (1981), *The Transition to Egalitarian Development*, London: Macmillan, and New York: St Martin's.

Griffin, Keith and Azizur Rahman Khan (eds) (1977), *Poverty and Landlessness in Rural Asia*, Geneva: International Labour Office.

Marx, Karl (1967), *Capital: Volume I*, New York: International Publishers.

World Bank (1998), *Assessing Aid: What Works, What Doesn't, and Why*, Washington, DC: World Bank.

A witness of two revolutions

Keith B. Griffin[1]

TWO REVOLUTIONS

Economics is sometimes called the 'dismal science', particularly by its critics. It was Thomas Carlyle, the British essayist and historian, who first described economics as 'dismal', and the phrase subsequently was taken out of context and used to call the attention of the general public to one of the principal conclusions of economic doctrine at that time, namely the impossibility of sustained improvement in the standard of living of the majority of humankind.[2] Temporary improvements were possible, for example as a result of technical change, but ultimately the expansion of the population would drive living standards back to a subsistence level and the economy would enter a stationary state.

I have always believed that Carlyle's description was inaccurate and that economics provides us with powerful tools not only to understand the world but also to change it for the better. Indeed I became an economist because I had a passionate interest in issues related to poverty and inequality and thought that economics might help me to do something positive about them. Forty years later, the interest is unabated and the conviction that economics is far from 'dismal' is undiminished.

Economics did not suddenly emerge as a fully formed, independent science (whether dismal or not) around the time Carlyle was writing in the nineteenth century. On the contrary, it grew out of the humanities, and its early association with moral philosophy and political theory was particularly close. Indeed these roots can still be seen in Oxford University, where undergraduates read philosophy, politics and economics (PPE) for a degree. The experience of teaching PPE for more than 20 years no doubt influenced my research interests within economics as well as my view of the world. It also made it easy for me to fit into the department of economics at UC, Riverside, where there is a long tradition of support for political economy.

I have been fortunate to participate in two of the major political and economic transformations of the twentieth century. The first was the termination of the European imperial system after the Second World War and the beginning of the process of decolonization in Asia, Africa and the Caribbean. This political upheaval led to the rise and explosive growth of development economics and the opportunities at that time for young development economists like me were enormous. I rode the coat-tails of history first to Chile, then to Algeria and subsequently to more countries than I can easily count.

The second revolution that I witnessed was the collapse of Communism in the Soviet Union and Central and Eastern Europe after 1989. This political upheaval was accompanied by systemic economic change, namely a transition from a centrally planned economy to a more market-oriented economic system. Systemic change, in turn, gave rise to a new branch of economics called the economics of transition.

China had begun its transition to a market economy in late 1978, long before the disintegration of the Soviet bloc, and as chance would have it, I had been visiting China regularly and conducting research on that country since 1979 and thus I was well positioned to study the transition problems in the low-income, ex-Soviet bloc countries that interested me. In effect I had a ten-year head start on most other economists doing research on transition economies. This created opportunities for me to organize and lead small teams of researchers in Mongolia, Uzbekistan, Kazakhstan, Vietnam and, most recently, Armenia.

GROWTH AND EMPLOYMENT

It is one thing to witness two revolutions; it is another thing to participate in them, even if only marginally. These two revolutions created an enormous amount of intellectual excitement, and to understand this, it is important to have some sense of what the debates were about. Let us start with growth and employment.

The early view in development economics was that growth would suffice to reduce poverty and, ultimately, inequality as well. If average incomes rose, at least some of the benefits of higher output and per capita income would 'trickle down' to the poor; and as industrialization proceeded, along with other structural changes associated with development, the share of lower-income groups in total income would gradually rise and inequality consequently would diminish.

I regarded this view as far too optimistic, indeed as wishful thinking, and did my best to contest it with empirical evidence. In a paper published in Pakistan in 1965, I tried to demonstrate that international trade and investment licensing policies introduced by the military government had promoted industry at the expense of agriculture, and had done so by deliberately increasing inequality in the distribution of income in favor of rich industrialists. Moreover the policy had been carried to such an extreme that the poor, particularly the rural poor, had experienced an absolute decline in their income despite a rise in average incomes in the country as a whole.[3]

The paper created a bit of an uproar. An attempt was made to prevent it from being published, but after it did appear in print it stimulated many other researchers to explore the implications of the government's growth policy on the general well-being of the population. Aziz Khan and I contributed to the debate provoked by my initial paper by editing a book on *Growth and Inequality in Pakistan* that was published in 1972, a year after the east wing of Pakistan became the independent country of Bangladesh.[4]

One of the reasons my paper was so explosive is that it implied that East Pakistan (which was more dependent on agriculture) was being systematically exploited by the government in order to benefit West Pakistan (where investment licenses were issued to promote industrialization). Thus development policy had a pronounced regional bias which eventually destroyed the political cohesion of the country.

The problem of growth accompanied by impoverishment of specific groups was not peculiar to Pakistan. In a series of studies I helped to organize for the International Labour Organization (ILO), we showed that in many parts of Asia the promised 'trickle-down' effects had not occurred and that growth had been accompanied by a fall in the incomes of the poor, particularly landless agricultural workers.[5] When the separate studies were brought together in a book, again edited by Aziz Khan and myself, we ran into an attempt at censorship. This time the problem was that we identified China as the 'great exception': growth had not impoverished the rural population of China, unlike in much of the rest of Asia, and this finding was unacceptable in some quarters during the ideological conflict of the Cold War.

Like it or not, by the late 1970s our research and that of many others had thoroughly discredited the notion of 'trickle-down' and the even more optimistic belief that growth would result automatically in an improvement in the distribution of income. If one were serious about reducing poverty, one could not approach it indirectly by encouraging economic growth; one would have to tackle it head-on.

The ILO argued that this could best be done through a 'basic needs' approach to development policy. I was one of those who worked with the ILO to elaborate the implications of this new approach.[6] The central idea was rather simple, perhaps too simple, namely that priority in development policy should be given not to accelerating growth in general but to satisfying specific 'basic needs' of the population, such as the needs for adequate food, clothing and shelter as well as basic education and primary health care. The new approach represented a shift in thinking from the general (namely, growth) to the specific (basic needs), and from an emphasis on private goods (such as food and clothing) to recognition of the importance of public goods (such as education and health).

Implicit in the basic needs approach was less reliance on the market mechanism to allocate resources and a larger role for intervention by the state, not to promote industrialization behind protectionist tariffs but to satisfy basic needs. Also implicit was the need to redistribute income in favor of the poor, an implication that was spelled out in a short book I wrote with Jeffrey James on *The Transition to Egalitarian Development*.[7] In related research I have argued that a redistribution of productive assets, particularly land, should be a major component of any strategy intended to reduce poverty.[8] This is partly because the distribution of productive assets has a strong direct influence on the distribution of income and partly because control of land gives landowners monopsonistic power in rural labor markets and hence enables them to influence wage rates and the number of days of employment of rural workers. More generally, in a paper with Amy Ickowitz, we have assembled evidence which suggests, contrary to the conventional view, that in some circumstances a redistribution of assets would actually increase the rate of economic growth.[9] That is, there need be no conflict between equity and growth.

One of the ways in which the two objectives of equity and growth can be reconciled is through employment creation. One early strand in the literature on development argued that people in low-income countries were poor in part because they lacked the motivation to work hard, in part because labor supply curves were backward-bending and in part because people failed to possess what some social psychologists called a 'need for achievement'.[10] In short, and rather crudely, people are poor because they are 'lazy slobs'. A second strand argued that because of structural reasons, particularly a high density of labor relative to land, low-income countries are characterized by massive unemployment and 'surplus' labor.

Today we know better. The poor are not lazy and nor are they typically unemployed. On the contrary the poor, especially in the urban informal sector, typically work long hours, often on back-breaking tasks and almost always for very low wages. The poor, in other words, do not lack work, they lack income. In the rural areas however there may be long periods of seasonal idleness, especially where agriculture is dependent on rainfall rather than irrigation.

The problem of the poor then is not to find employment as such, but to create more productive employment. This in turn requires investment in those assets which raise the productivity of the poor. Conventional policies commonly found in rich countries – such as unemployment compensation and minimum wage legislation – are unlikely in poor countries to have much effect on poverty: they are difficult to enforce and, in any case, most of the benefits go to the non-poor. I have argued instead that the state should act as an employer of last resort.[11]

This could be done if the state were to organize labor-intensive public works projects that concentrated on investment in assets from which the poor would benefit directly. Examples include investment in irrigation and drainage, farm-to-market roads, reforestation and soil conservation, orchard planting, construction of reservoirs and fish ponds, and construction of civic buildings such as schools, health clinics and village halls. Anyone seeking employment would be guaranteed a job on one of these investment projects at a wage slightly below the going market wage. The purpose of keeping the wage low is to avoid attracting already employed workers from the private sector, that is, to provide the poor with an incentive to self-select themselves for participation in the employment guarantee scheme.

In some cases employment creation, investment and asset redistribution can be combined by ensuring that upon completion of the public works projects the assets are transferred to a cooperative consisting solely of those who supplied their labor.[12] This would be feasible for example for investments in tube wells, orchards and fish ponds. The purpose of the cooperative would be to manage the assets and charge for their use, for example, through the sale of water, fruit and fish. Part of the income of the cooperative would be distributed to the members to help raise their current consumption and part would be retained by the cooperative to finance future investments. In this way the guaranteed employment scheme would not only provide temporary jobs, it would also strengthen permanently the productive base of the household economy of the poor.

FOREIGN AID

The early literature on development economics was strongly influenced by the notion of 'the vicious circle of poverty': countries are poor because they do not save, and countries do not save because they are poor. As we have seen, I have long been skeptical of the view that poor countries and poor people are unable to help themselves, but many development economists argued that the way to break the vicious circle of poverty was to supply poor countries with lots of foreign aid. Moreover its supporters argued that the need for foreign aid was self-extinguishing, since the higher income that aid financed would result in higher domestic savings and hence a reduced need for aid.

I was skeptical of this line of reasoning and in a series of papers I argued that foreign aid was more likely to reduce domestic savings than to increase it.[13] That is, aid was a substitute for savings and hence large inflows of foreign aid were unlikely to raise the growth rate and might even lower it. The net effect then would be prolonged aid dependency and heavy foreign indebtedness. These arguments stimulated a lively debate and a voluminous literature. At first the debate centered on the negative effect of aid on savings – or the 'Griffin effect' as it was sometimes called – but it soon widened to explore the effects of foreign aid on other macroeconomic categories (investment, consumption, exports), on relative prices (interest rates and exchange rates), on the productivity of investment and on government resource mobilization through taxation. Despite enormous research efforts, the defenders of foreign aid were unable to show that aid in general had beneficial effects on development.

Meanwhile the donor countries had agreed to a United Nations target that foreign aid should be 0.7 per cent of the rich countries' gross national product. In practice however the target was never achieved and in recent years aid ratios have been falling. In 2001 for instance net official development assistance accounted for only 0.22 per cent of donor countries' gross national income.[14] Looking back at the aid debate, it seems to me that never has so much been written about so little.

It is preposterous that the rich countries should ever have imagined that the development of the poor countries depended on foreign aid and the policy advice that inevitably accompanies foreign aid. While it is true that many of the features of underdevelopment have their origin in the 'fatal impact' of Europe on the rest of the world,[15] the solutions to the problems of development are mostly internal. Foreigners can best contribute by doing no harm.

As an alternative to the plethora of existing bilateral and multilateral aid programs, I have suggested that resources should be transferred automatically from rich to poor countries through a global tax-and-grant scheme.[16] Resources would be raised by a progressive tax on the national income of rich countries, and the funds would then be transferred in the form of grants to poor countries, in inverse proportion to their per capita income. Thus the richest donor country would be taxed slightly more heavily than less-rich donor countries, while the poorest recipient country would receive a larger grant per head of its population than less-poor recipient countries.

This scheme can be viewed either as a mechanism to reduce global income inequality or as an extension to the global level of the ideals of solidarity with the poor and rights of citizenship associated with the welfare state in Europe. In contrast to my criticisms of conventional foreign aid programs however, this positive suggestion for a global redistribution of resources has been greeted by a wall of silence.

HUMAN DEVELOPMENT

Meanwhile, thinking about development moved forward quite rapidly on other fronts. T.W. Schultz introduced the concept of 'human capital' to capture the idea that expenditures on such things as education and training, health and nutrition, family planning and child care, agricultural research and extension were similar to investments in physical capital in that they raised the productivity of labor and contributed to economic growth.[17] This simple idea has had an enormous impact on economic theory, empirical research and public policy.

It is now widely understood for example that ill health of a working member of a household can plunge that household into poverty. An episode of illness is likely to result, first of all, in days lost from work and, secondly, in lower productivity while at work, both of which will reduce the income of the household. Thirdly, the cost of medical treatment can be onerous for a poor family and absorb income that otherwise would be available for meeting the household's basic needs. Finally, severe illness may force a household to dispose of productive assets such as land in order to sustain a minimum level of consumption and cover medical expenses, but at the same time asset disposal may impoverish the household permanently. Public expenditure on preventing and eradicating diseases such as malaria, tuberculosis and AIDS can break this vicious spiral and produce high economic returns.[18] Good health is part of a country's stock of human capital.

Amartya Sen took the analysis a step further, arguing that the objective of development should be reconceptualized as the enhancement of human capabilities. Sen substituted a people-centered view of development for the older commodity-centered view. Economic growth, that is, an increase in the production of goods and services, should not be seen as an objective in itself but merely as contributing to the ultimate objectives of enabling people to live a long life, free of avoidable disease, with access to the world's stock of knowledge, and so on. The emphasis then is on giving people the freedom to live the life of their choice. Depending on circumstances, producing more 'stuff', more commodities, might or might not increase human capabilities.

In 1988 a committee of the United Nations brought these two strands of thought together and produced a report in which a human capabilities approach was advocated. I happened to be a member of the committee and was asked to organize the background research for the new approach and to prepare an initial draft of the committee's report.[19] In our report we described human development as 'an approach to overall development which puts the well-being of people first, which regards human beings simultaneously as both the means and the ends of social and economic policy. It is not, of course, a formula that can be applied mechanically, but it does contain ingredients which distinguish it from commodity-centered approaches to development.'[20]

The ideas contained in the report were picked up by the United Nations Development Programme (UNDP) and under the brilliant leadership of Mahbub ul Haq, UNDP promoted human development as an alternative to the conventional approaches offered by the World Bank, the International Monetary Fund and mainstream development agencies. Beginning in 1990, UNDP published an annual *Human Development Report* and a few years later, member countries were encouraged to publish each year a national human development report. Both the international and national reports contain a wealth of statistical information on many dimensions of human development as well as analysis of specific topics. In 2000 the human development approach was further institutionalized by the creation of the *Journal of Human Development.*

It has been my good fortune to be associated with many of these developments. For five years, as a consultant to UNDP, I participated in the drafting of the international *Human Development Report*. I was also involved in writing a regional human development report for the former Soviet bloc countries. With Terry McKinley, one of my former graduate students, I co-authored a book on *Implementing a Human Development Strategy* and, thanks to UNDP, I have been given numerous opportunities to apply these ideas at the country level.[21] Until 2004 I also served on the editorial advisory board of the *Journal of Human Development.*

SYSTEMIC CHANGE

When I was a student a number of us were interested in the transition from capitalism to socialism, for it seemed to us that the currents of history were flowing strongly in that direction. It never occurred to us that the reverse transition – from socialism to capitalism – would become one of the most momentous political and economic transformations of our time. History, it seems, is full of surprises.

The political reaction to the collapse of Communism was exultation and an expectation that the successor states of the Soviet Union would become parliamentary democracies. The reaction among mainstream economists was no less enthusiastic and it was widely expected that the adoption of a market economy would lead to a rapid improvement in the well-being of the people. The conventional view was that systemic change could best be achieved through rapid price liberalization and the transfer to private ownership of state-owned enterprises. If a transition recession occurred, it was expected to be mild and that hardship could be avoided by a small injection of foreign aid.

In the event, the transition to capitalism proved to be much more difficult than most people anticipated.[22] In Russia for instance, prices rose 1353 per cent in 1992, output declined by 42 per cent between 1990 and 1996, the level of investment fell by a half, inequality rose dramatically and the incidence of poverty increased from almost zero before the transition began to 31 per cent of the population in 1994. Alcoholism, drug addiction, suicides and crime rose sharply. Male life expectancy plummeted and by 1995, males in Russia could expect to live only 58 years, as compared to a male life expectancy of 68 years in China, a country with a much lower average standard of living. The birth rate fell and the death rate rose, so that as of 2003, the population of Russia was actually in decline. From an economic and social perspective, the transition in Russia (and most of the other countries of the former Soviet Union) has been a human catastrophe.

What went wrong? Our research on China and subsequent research in several of the former republics of the Soviet Union indicates that the two pillars of the conventional transition strategy could not bear the weight placed upon them.[23] Price liberalization in the absence of high levels of investment resulted in economic contraction. Reform of property rights, and specifically the privatization of state enterprises, did little to create a flourishing private sector. Unless they were accompanied by other measures, liberalization and privatization could lead to disaster.

Everyone agrees that a successful transition to a market economy depends upon profound structural change in the ex-socialist countries. Heavy capital goods and military-related industry must be replaced by consumer goods industries, services and an expansion of the agricultural sector. In short, swords must be converted into ploughshares. The question is how to do this.

The conventional answer is to 'get prices right'. Price liberalization, it is argued, will lead to a change in relative prices and this change in relative prices will provide an incentive for resources to move from the production of 'swords' to the production of textiles, footwear, insurance services, agricultural implements and the like. The problem is that resources are often specific to the industries in which they are located and cannot readily be transferred to another industry. The plant, equipment and even the skilled labor used, say, to produce steel cannot be converted to produce, say, television sets. If the price of steel falls relative to the price of TV sets, production of steel will decline, workers will be dismissed and the steel mills will become idle. The relatively higher price of television sets will not lead to an expansion of the consumer electronics industry, unless there is a substantial investment in that industry. Price liberalization in the absence of investment will simply result in a fall in aggregate output and a rise in unemployment and the incidence of poverty.

Structural change, in other words, requires not only price liberalization but, above all, a high level of investment. Unfortunately investment was allowed to fall sharply in most countries, in part because state expenditure on physical and human capital was reduced and in part because incentives for private investment were weak.

This is where privatization comes into the picture. The transfer of ownership of state enterprises to the private sector was urged partly to weaken the state and make the fall of socialism irreversible and partly to create a capitalist class instantly, without the prior necessity of accumulating private capital. These motives evidently were political. The economic case for giving a high priority to privatization was weak, since the need at the time was not to transfer ownership rights of existing enterprises but to encourage the rapid growth of new private enterprises in those activities where price liberalization indicated substantial gains could be made.

Much valuable time was wasted on privatization and the results in most countries have been disappointing. The struggle to acquire ownership rights sometimes led to the creation of a 'mafia capitalism', almost always led to the creation of great inequalities in the distribution of wealth, and usually led to the creation of a monopolistic structure of industry which thwarts competition and perpetuates an inefficient allocation of resources. Ordinary people gained little if anything from the privatization of large state-owned industrial enterprises and the failure to create 'space' for large numbers of new private enterprises to emerge and grow has made it more difficult for the transition economies to become closely integrated into the global economy, or at least to become integrated in a way that benefits the majority of the population.

GLOBALIZATION

Some might say that integration into the global economy is not necessarily desirable, but I have argued that the problem with globalization is not that it has gone too far but that it has not gone far enough.[24] That is, globalization has been asymmetrical. Trade barriers in general have fallen rapidly, but the process of trade liberalization has occurred much more slowly in products of special interest to poor countries: foodstuffs, textiles, clothing, footwear and leather products. Capital is free to move throughout the world in search of profits, and this clearly is of benefit to international investors, most of whom reside in rich countries. People however are not free to move throughout the world in search of a livelihood, particularly people who possess low skills, most of whom reside in poor countries.

The next step in the struggle for global equity should be to eliminate discrimination against the trade of developing countries, not to retreat from the ideal of free trade. Similarly, international labor markets should be liberalized; we should not retreat from capital mobility by imposing restrictions on international capital markets and in particular on the free movement of long-term capital investments. I believe, too, that we have gone too far in creating 'intellectual property rights'. The World Trade Organization is promoting TRIPS (trade-related intellectual property rights) which force poor countries to protect the 'intellectual property' of rich countries without providing any protection for misappropriation of traditional knowledge of poor countries. TRIPS clearly are asymmetrical in their impact, accentuating global inequality, slowing development and inhibiting the enhancement of human capabilities. Moreover the effort to create a global system of patent rights ignores history and the fact that the now-rich countries copied freely the inventions of other countries during the early stages of their own development.

A case can of course be made for rewarding inventive activity, but patents and copyrights are only one possible type of reward, and it is not obvious that the public interest is best served by bestowing monopoly privileges for extended periods of time on those who discover a new treatment for a disease or a new variety of an edible plant. We ought to be moving in the direction of making knowledge a free good rather than creating more and more property rights in knowledge. Liberalization of the market for ideas, like liberalization of trade and global labor markets, would benefit poor countries and poor people within poor countries.

Lurking behind these specific views on trade, labor mobility and inventive activity is the more general view that cultural exchange and pluralism, globally as well as nationally, are the ultimate sources of economic growth and human development.[25] I first developed this view when I was invited by the United Nations to become a member of the World Commission on Culture and Development in the mid-1990s[26] and have elaborated on it ever since.[27]

The point of departure of the argument is that it is new knowledge, new technology and new institutional arrangements that are the ultimate sources of beneficial change. Cultural contacts have led to a myriad of exchanges and adaptations that in the long run are of benefit to all parties. This does not deny that cultural contacts have also led to conquest, imperialism and exploitation, for these surely have been important historically. That is, asymmetric cultural exchange has profoundly shaped the modern world, but it is cultural exchange rather than asymmetric relationships which in the long sweep of history has had the most lasting effects. Moreover globalization today has made cultural interchange more frequent, deeper and more rapid than in the past. Ideas, information and knowledge are transmitted much more widely and more quickly and this has resulted in greater diversity, not greater homogeneity, as many fear. This increased diversity in turn has led to an acceleration in creativity and innovation, to an explosive growth of knowledge and technology, and consequently to unprecedented rates of economic growth and advances in human development.

The problem we now face is that institutions of global governance lag behind the globalization of market forces.[28] This indeed helps to account for the global asymmetries I have mentioned. Our institutions of global governance are undemocratic, they are underfunded and they are not deeply embedded in a global system of the rule of law. Collective action to 'tame' global market forces and provide global public goods is difficult to organize, and consequently at the global level anarchy prevails or, if you prefer, the rule of 'might makes right'.

Much of the opposition to globalization, I believe, arises from the fact that ordinary people have little control over the global forces that increasingly shape their lives. At the national level, democratic institutions can temper market forces, redress glaring inequalities, maintain social order, supply public goods and bestow legitimacy on the rules that enforce the implicit social contract.

Analogous institutions will have to be created, step by step, at the global level. This in turn implies that states will have to relinquish some of their sovereignty to global institutions. This is beginning to happen in a rather *ad hoc* way. For example active intervention by outside parties, as in Kosovo, part of the sovereign state of Yugoslavia, has established the principle that human rights supersede, or at least qualify, the sovereign rights of states.

Clearly we have a long way to go. Indeed a third revolution beckons us, a revolution that challenges the sovereignty of states and holds out a promise of global democracy and institutions of global governance. I have been lucky to witness two revolutions, and it may be stretching my luck a bit to expect to witness the completion of a third, but I have little doubt that the political forces unleashed by the French revolution and the economic forces unleashed by globalization will transform yet again our world and the people who inhabit it.

NOTES

1. The original version of this chapter was presented as the Humanist Achievement Lecture at the University of California, Riverside in January 2003.
2. See David M. Levy (2001), *How the Dismal Science Got Its Name: Classical Economics and the Ur-Text of Racial Politics*, Ann Arbor, MI: University of Michigan Press.
3. Griffin, Keith (1965), 'Financing development plans in Pakistan', *Pakistan Development Review*, **5** (4), Winter.
4. Griffin, Keith and Azizur Rahman Khan (eds) (1972), *Growth and Inequality in Pakistan*, London: Macmillan.
5. Griffin, Keith and Azizur Rahman Khan (eds) (1977), *Poverty and Landlessness in Rural Asia*, Geneva: International Labour Organization.
6. International Labour Organization (1976), *Employment, Growth and Basic Needs*, Geneva: ILO.
7. Griffin, Keith and Jeffrey James (1981), *The Transition to Egalitarian Development*, London: Macmillan.
8. For a recent statement of the argument see Griffin, Keith, Azizur Rahman Khan and Amy Ickowitz (2002), 'Poverty and the distribution of land', *Journal of Agrarian Change*, **2** (3). For an early statement see Griffin, Keith (1974), *The Political Economy of Agrarian Change*, London: Macmillan.
9. Griffin, Keith and Amy Ickowitz (2001), 'The distribution of wealth and the pace of development', in Terry McKinley (ed.), *Macroeconomic Policy, Growth and Poverty Reduction*, Basingstoke: Palgrave.
10. See McClelland, D. (1967), *The Achieving Society*, New York: Free Press.
11. It is widely accepted that the Central Bank should be a lender of last resort and it is becoming accepted that the central government should be an insurer of last resort (for example against terrorist attacks), but unfortunately it has not become accepted that the government should be an employer of last resort.
12. Griffin, Keith with Ajit Kumar Ghose (1979), 'Growth and impoverishment in the rural areas of Asia', *World Development*, **7** (4/5).
13. Griffin, Keith (1970), 'Foreign capital, domestic savings and economic development', *Bulletin of the Oxford University Institute of Economics and Statistics*, **32** (2). Griffin, Keith and John Enos (1970), 'Foreign assistance: objectives and consequences', *Economic Development and Cultural Change*, **18** (3).
14. The data refer to aid to low-income developing countries and exclude aid to the former Soviet

bloc countries and to more advanced developing countries. If all recipient countries are included, the aid ratio rises to 0.24 per cent of GNI. The United States, incidentally, is the least generous donor country, giving only 0.11 per cent of its GNI to low-income developing countries (see World Bank (2003), *World Development Indicators 2003*, Washington, DC: World Bank, Table 6.9, p. 336).

15. The allusion is to Moorehead, A. (1966), *The Fatal Impact*, London: Hamish Hamilton.
16. Griffin, Keith (1997), 'Globalization and development cooperation: a reformer's agenda', in Roy Culpeper, Albert Berry and Frances Stewart (eds), *Global Development Fifty Years After Bretton Woods*, London: Macmillan.
17. The 'human capital' approach strengthened arguments long made by development economists that relationships of complementarity (for example between education and investment in machines or between health and labor productivity) often were as important as relationships of substitutability. The approach also underlined the importance of 'externalities', another claim long made by development economists.
18. For a detailed analysis of this line of reasoning applied to measles and tuberculosis, see Chan, David (2002), 'Unhealthy and impoverished: modeling the effects of illness on household economic well-being', MSc. thesis, London School of Economics, September. For a general survey of the literature see Deaton, Angus (2003), 'Health, inequality and economic development', *Journal of Economic Literature*, **41** (1), March. Also see Bloom, David and David Canning (2003), 'The health and poverty of nations: from theory to practice', *Journal of Human Development*, **4** (1), March.
19. The background papers were published as Griffin, Keith and John Knight (eds) (1990), *Human Development and the International Development Strategy for the 1990s*, London: Macmillan.
20. United Nations Committee for Development Planning (1988), *Human Resources Development*, New York: United Nations.
21. Griffin, Keith and Terry McKinley (1994), *Implementing a Human Development Strategy*, London: Macmillan.
22. See Griffin, Keith (2000), *Studies in Development Strategy and Systemic Transformation*, London: Macmillan, Chapter 6.
23. See, for example, Griffin, Keith and Azizur Rahman Khan (1995), 'The transition to market guided economies: lessons for Russia and Eastern Europe from the Chinese experience', in Bernd Magnus and Stephen Cullenberg (eds), *Whither Marxism? Global Crises in International Perspective*, New York and London: Routledge; Griffin, Keith (ed.) (2003), *Poverty Reduction in Mongolia*, Canberra: Asia Pacific Press; Griffin, Keith (ed.) (1997), *Social Policy and Economic Transformation in Uzbekistan*, Geneva: ILO; Griffin, Keith (ed.) (2002), *Growth, Inequality and Poverty in Armenia*, Yerevan: UNDP.
24. Griffin, Keith (1996), *Studies in Globalization and Economic Transitions*, London: Macmillan, Chapter 5.
25. Griffin, Keith (2000), *Studies in Development Strategy and Systemic Transformation*, London: Macmillan, Chapter 1.
26. See the report of the World Commission on Culture and Development (1995), *Our Creative Diversity*, Paris: UN and UNESCO.
27. For the most recent statement see Griffin, Keith (2004), 'Globalization and culture', in Stephen Cullenberg and Prasanta Pattanaik (eds), *Globalization, Culture and the Limits of the Market: Essays in Economics and Philosophy*, New Delhi: Oxford University Press.
28. Griffin, Keith (2003), 'Economic globalisation and institutions of global governance', *Development and Change*, **34** (5), November.

PART I

Perspectives on Chinese Development

1. The fall in Chinese poverty: issues of measurement, incidence and cause

Carl Riskin

China's poverty reduction strategy should be brought out of the shadows and become an integral part of overall economic policy.

Keith Griffin, 2000

INTRODUCTION

China's economic record of the past quarter century is commonly seen as a great success in generating high rates of growth and reducing poverty. From a comparative perspective, there is no doubt that this view is accurate.[1] Rejecting the 'market bolshevik' policies of institutional shock therapy pushed on European transition countries by foreign consultants and international financial organizations, which produced an economic and social disaster in Russia, China adopted a pragmatic, step-by-step approach under which both economic growth and social welfare were greatly advanced.[2]

Evaluated critically on its own however, and without the benefit of the contrast with the Russian disaster, China's record displays a number of uncertainties, even about the size and growth of GDP.[3] Poverty too is an area in which there is much uncertainty. That is unfortunate, because when it comes to the global number of poor, the world including China has behaved quite differently than the world excluding it. Table 1.1 tells the story, according to one set of recent estimates.

When China is taken into account, the absolute number of people in the world who are under the World Bank's PPP$1/day consumption poverty line fell markedly (by 26 percent) between 1981 and 2001. But if China is left out of the reckoning, the total number of poor in the rest of the world actually rose by almost 4 percent. China's inclusion causes the headcount index of global poverty (that is, the proportion of population that is poor) to decline by 48 percent, while China's exclusion brings the rate of decline down to 34 percent. In 1981, China's 634 million poor, by the relevant method of estimation, constituted 43 percent of the world's poor people. By 2001, however, China's 211.6 million poor made

Table 1.1 The world's poor

	1981	2001	Change in no. of poor 1981–2001	% change
World: pop. living below $1.08/day	1481.8	1092.7	–389.1	–26.26
China: pop. living below $1.08/day	633.7	211.6	–422.1	–66.61
World excluding China:	848.1	881.1	+ 33.0	+ 3.89
World: Headcount index (%)	40.4	21.1		–47.77
China: Headcount index (%)	63.8	16.6		–73.98
World excluding China (%)	33.8	22.3		–34.02

Notes: Headcount indexes have been roughly estimated using population figures for 1981 and 2001. The poverty threshold of $1.08 per day in 1993 PPP terms is equivalent to the original World Bank $1 per day (1985) standard.

Source: Chen and Ravallion (2004).

up only 19 percent of the world's poor. Thus it is evident that China's success in reducing poverty has greatly improved the global poverty picture. Given its importance in this respect, one would hope that the dimensions of poverty reduction in China were known with certainty, or at least great confidence.

This chapter argues however that such is not the case. Whereas the incidence of rural poverty in China's countryside has by all accounts fallen greatly over the transition period as a whole, there is in fact much uncertainty about the dimensions of this decline, as well as about urban poverty, which has actually risen, and therefore even more uncertainty about the trend in overall poverty.

The following section presents some criticisms of the common measurements of poverty in China. The third section deals with the apparent temporal shape of rural poverty reduction and the reasons for it. Urban poverty and its measurement is taken up next, followed by a summary and conclusion.

MEASUREMENT OF RURAL POVERTY

For many years the world depended upon Chinese government estimates of the poverty rate. These were prepared according to China's very low poverty threshold (equal to about $0.66 in 1985 purchasing power parity – PPP$), and showed rural poverty falling from about one-third of the rural population (some 260 million people) in 1978, to only about 3 percent at the end of 2000 (some 30 million people).[4]

There are various problems with these estimates, suggesting that they substantially overstate the decline in poverty and understate the remaining incidence of it. For one thing, official poverty estimates are for rural poverty only. This may have been justified in the past, when absolute poverty was overwhelmingly a rural phenomenon because urban populations were protected by universal state employment, comprehensive welfare benefits and severely restricted rural–urban mobility. However with the weakening or elimination of all three of these protections in recent decades, urban poverty has grown and is no longer of trivial importance. Yet rural and urban poverty are almost always discussed separately in China and there is no single official measure combining the two.

A number of problems with the statistics on rural poverty, causing them to tend to underestimate its incidence, are highlighted by a recent evaluation:[5]

- The poverty line has not kept pace with inflation over the years, and thus expresses a declining real income. Park and Wang (2001) estimate that this causes the 2000 poverty line to be 13 per cent lower than it should be.
- Before 1998, the food bundle that provided the foundation of the poverty line excluded items that the government regarded as non-essential. Because of this, grain expenditures constituted 88 percent of the bundle, whereas in reality these came to only about 70 percent of the food expenditures of poor households. Since grain is relatively cheap, overweighting it leads to an underestimate of the true cost of purchasing a given amount of calories. This biases the poverty line downward, which of course lowers the measured incidence of poverty.
- After 1998, the non-food share of the consumption bundle was much too low (at 17 percent, compared with actual shares of 27–49 percent in various provinces). This too biases the poverty line and incidence downward.
- The official poverty estimate has been done in terms of income rather than expenditure. A smaller fraction of the population has incomes below a given poverty line than has expenditure below it.

The official rural poverty line (of about 635 yuan/year) comes to about $0.66/day in 1985 PPP dollars. An alternative set of estimates uses the World Bank's international poverty line of $1/day in PPP dollars. This generates much higher poverty rates, especially if the line is interpreted as an expenditure line rather than an income line (Table 1.2).

Although much of the difference between these poverty rates and the official ones is due to the use by Chen and Ravallion of a poverty line that is about one-third higher, even using the PPP equivalent of the official poverty line – but

Table 1.2 World Bank (expenditure-based) estimates of rural poverty in the 1990s

Year	Poverty rate
1990	42.5
1992	40.6
1993	40.6
1994	34.6
1995	30.8
1996	24.1
1997	24.0
1998	24.1
1999	24.9

Note: The poverty threshold used is $1.08 per day in 1993 PPP terms, which is equivalent to the original World Bank $1 per day standard.

Source: Chen and Wang (2001).

as an expenditures line – produces a poverty rate of 12.7 percent for 1999, much higher than the official rate.

The PPP $1/day line has itself been criticized on the grounds that general consumption PPPs are inappropriate for poverty assessment because they include many prices irrelevant to the poor (plane tickets, cars, high-end services and so on).[6] Quite aside from such general criticisms of PPP methodology, it should be recognized that the PPP estimates for China are particularly weakly based.[7] Evaluation of a country's price structure in international comparative context requires an extensive survey of its prices, carried out by the International Comparison Project (ICP). China has never participated in a full ICP price survey; longstanding plans for it to do so have never been realized. The principal existing PPP estimates are based on obsolete price information from secondary sources for a small sample of unrepresentative areas, and for 1986, still an early stage of China's transition to a market economy when both relative prices and expenditure weights were changing markedly. The resulting PPP estimates have been updated using aggregate growth rates based on national accounts rather than on PPP-adjusted sector shares. This procedure exaggerates growth by avoiding the PPP adjustment's effect of reducing the weight of the fastest-growing industrial sectors. It has sometimes been suggested that because China's PPP exchange rates, however flawed, were not changed over time, therefore poverty trend estimates must be more or less accurate. However the opposite argument seems more convincing: Even if initially accurate, fixed PPP rates lose validity if relative prices and expenditure weights change sharply over time.

In fact the period from the mid-1980s to the end of the century was one of rapid and sharp structural change in China's economy. For instance from 1985 to 1999 the primary sector's relative contribution to total GDP fell from 28.4 percent to 17.7 percent, while that of industry and construction rose from 43.1 to 49.3 percent, and that of services rose from 28.5 to 33 percent. The primary sector's share of total employment fell from 62 percent in 1985 to 50 percent in 1999, while that of the tertiary sector rose from 17 percent to 26 percent (*China Statistical Yearbook, 2000* – National Bureau of Statistics of China). Such structural changes were reflected in expenditure patterns, which shifted in response to advancing incomes, the growing availability of new goods and services, and the freeing up of prices as market forces grew stronger. In the late 1980s for instance, controls were lifted for most agricultural goods, farm inputs and for many durable goods. Table 1.3 shows the changing structure of urban and rural spending from 1985 to 1999.

If the initial PPP exchange rate is both inaccurate and also remains unadjusted in the face of changes in relative prices and expenditure weights, there cannot be

Table 1.3 Structure of expenditures, 1985 and 1999 (% of total consumption expenditures)

	1985	1999
Urban		
Food	52	42
Clothing	15	10
Housing	13	18
Health care	2.5	5
Transport	2	7
Recreation, education & culture	8	12
Miscellaneous	7	5
Rural		
Food	58	53
Clothing	10	6
Housing and household articles	23	20
Health care	2	4
Transport, communic.	2	4
Culture, education, recreation	4	11
Other	1	2

Source: calculated from *China Statistical Yearbook* (2000).

a coherent interpretation of the resulting trends. Heston's (2001) recent evaluation is surely still correct: 'The wide range of PPP estimates for China and the large size of their difference from the exchange rate suggest that substantial uncertainty is associated with these numbers … Our earlier hope remains that these PPP estimates for China in PWT 6.0 will soon be superseded by better numbers.'

RURAL POVERTY TRENDS

Whatever the uncertainty about the numbers, all observers agree that rural absolute poverty – however defined and measured – did decline greatly between 1979 and 2000. What is less widely known however is that this decline occurred almost entirely during two relatively brief periods: (1) the first five years of the reform period, that is, 1979–84, and (2) the middle three years of the 1990s. That this is not generally appreciated is probably due to the lack of a single, consistent poverty line for the entire period. The World Bank's analysis of the years before 1990 used a poverty line consistent with the very low official one. But for the more recent period they have switched to their various international poverty lines, especially the much higher $1/day one.

The first period of sharp rural poverty decline – 1978 to 1984 – corresponded to the beginning of the era of reform and transition, when reform focused on the countryside. During this period the incidence of absolute rural poverty declined from about 260 million, or about one-third of the rural population, to 89 million, about 11 percent of the rural population (World Bank, 1992). These were the years when farming was de-collectivized, land was parceled out to households on an essentially egalitarian basis, farmers were encouraged to abandon the previous policy of achieving self-sufficiency in grain, regardless of local conditions, and to diversify production, and farm prices were raised 30 percent. In addition, chemical fertilizer supplies were increasing rapidly.

This combination of restored production incentives and rising supplies of farm inputs brought about a huge growth spurt in both farm production and farmer incomes. Between 1979 and 1984 the gross value of agricultural output grew by two-thirds; per capita net real income of rural households more than doubled. The policy package was thought of at the time as particularly helpful to the poorest rural residents of remote and disadvantaged regions, and in fact it turned out to be remarkably pro-poor.

It is true that much of the increase in output and incomes came from a one-time opportunity for farmers to reallocate resources away from the distorted allocation of the collective period and toward more profitable uses. Nevertheless the record of that period is still a remarkable demonstration of the efficacy of pro-poor policies that promoted rapid growth in farm incomes throughout China and concomitantly greatly lowered poverty.

The second period of sharp decline in rural poverty occurred in the middle three years of the 1990s. In 1990, according to the 1992 World Bank report and based upon a very low poverty line, the rural poverty rate was 11.5 percent, higher than it had been in 1984. However, based on the $1/day expenditure line now used by the Bank, the poverty rate becomes 42 percent of the rural population in 1990 (see Table 1.2). It remained over 40 percent through the first third of the decade, then dropped sharply to about 24 percent by 1996.

The main operative factor in explaining this steep fall is an equally steep rise in farm purchase prices, which doubled in the middle of the decade. Real per capita income of rural Chinese increased by 21 percent in the three years from 1993 to 1996.[8] Thus poverty reduction proved to be highly rural income elastic: a 21 percent increase in rural income was accompanied by a 40 percent decrease in rural poverty.

The years between these two periods of rapid decline in poverty – roughly the decade from the mid-1980s until the mid-1990s – saw no decline in poverty. Indeed the incidence of rural poverty increased from 89 million (about 11 percent of the rural population) in 1984 to 97 million in 1990 (about 11.5 percent) (World Bank, 1992). During these years, farm incomes stagnated, the rural–urban terms of trade deteriorated and the government's investment programs were skewed toward the coastal cities in what was known as the 'coastal development strategy' designed to attract foreign direct investment. Decentralization of the fiscal system badly hurt poorer regions whose central subsidies declined, causing a concomitant fall in public spending on health and education in poor rural regions.[9] A highly regressive fiscal regime burdened the poor, as shown by a 1988 study that found rural income distributed far more unequally than rural taxes (net of subsidies).[10] These years also saw a draconian austerity program to counter rising inflation, but not until the summer of 1988, whereas rural poverty rates had been rising since 1985, despite rapid economic growth: GDP growth averaged around 10 percent per year from 1984 through 1988. And despite the establishment for the first time in 1986 of a coordinated national institutional framework for fighting poverty, the actual record of poverty reduction during this period was disappointing. Macroeconomic trends and policies had disconnected China's strong economic growth from poverty reduction.

Similarly, there was no decline in rural poverty during the last third of the 1990s; in fact, the poverty rate rose slightly (see Table 1.2). During these years the general index of farm prices fell by 23 percent. Prices of wheat and corn dropped by 20–30 percent in 1999 alone.[11] Thus rising farm prices are associated with both periods of poverty decline, and falling farm prices with the years of stagnating or increasing poverty rates.[12] This history points to the importance of general economic policies and trends in affecting poverty. It is these, rather than specific poverty reduction programs, that explains most of what has happened to rural poverty.

In fact the specific poverty program activities actually correlate poorly with the trend of poverty reduction. For instance during the period 1979–85, when the incidence of rural poverty was declining fast, there was no organized national public anti-poverty effort established in China. This happened only in 1986 with the formation of the Leading Group for Economic Development of Poor Areas under the State Council, the Chinese government's highest executive body. Thereafter, for many years, poverty stagnated and even increased, while funding for the poverty reduction effort grew rapidly. By far the fastest growth of anti-poverty funding came at the end of the 1990s, as China rushed to meet the goals of its anti-poverty '8–7' program by the end of the century.[13] Yet that is when rural poverty was in fact increasing again. Helpful as specific poverty reduction interventions may have been in the particular localities that received them, these interventions cannot explain the overall trends in poverty reduction, which were due rather to broader economic and policy trends.

URBAN POVERTY

China's cities and towns have been privileged places of residence since the early years of the PRC. Their populations have been restricted in size by a system of household registration (*hukou*) and food rationing that inhibited population mobility. The state until recently offered employment to nearly all city dwellers; implemented a system of food procurement and supply that guaranteed low-cost access to food in cities; and provided urban residents, as state employees, with free health care and pensions. None of these benefits were available to the rural majority.

The 'Great Wall' between urban and rural China has been eroding, in that the urban population's special protections and guarantees have faded away, food rationing has disappeared, and rural–urban labor mobility has greatly increased. Restructuring the state industries has brought widespread unemployment, and with it burgeoning poverty, to urban residents. Yet the history and residue of urban protection has bequeathed a lower absolute poverty incidence to the cities than the countryside.

There has been no nationally unified official urban poverty definition at all until very recently. And despite some recent progress, it is still unclear whether observers in China accept the same measure. Thus, the All-China Federation of Trade Unions put the urban poverty count at 18.28 million in April 2002, and in January 2003 the Civil Affairs Ministry reported an urban poverty headcount of 19.3 million, or about 6.2 percent of the urban population. This estimate used an urban national income poverty threshold of 152 yuan per month, much higher than the rural poverty threshold (about 53 yuan/month) and amounting to almost \$2/day in 1985 PPP dollars.[14] However given the problems discussed above with PPP estimates for China and the very different price and cost structures facing urban and rural populations, the urban–rural contrast in PPP poverty lines is perhaps not very meaningful.

Especially useful in analyzing urban poverty is a recent Asian Development Bank study[15] which used the urban resident household survey database built by the National Bureau of Statistics to estimate national and provincial poverty lines in 1998. The approach used in this study is generally the same as the one used in defining the rural poverty line, that is, that proposed by M. Ravallion. Thus a basic food bundle yielding 2100 kcal. per day was costed province by province, according to the actual consumption practices of the bottom 20 percent of the urban population, and then an Engel curve was fitted to derive the nonfood share of the poverty line, again by province.

The result is a national average urban poverty line of 2310 yuan in 1998, or 192.5 yuan per month, some 27 percent higher than the Civil Affairs Ministry line for 2002.[16] If this is taken as an expenditure poverty line, the resulting headcount index of urban poverty is 37 million, or about 11.9 percent of the urban population; if it is interpreted as an income poverty line, the poverty incidence is 14.8 million, or 4.7 percent in 1998. The various urban poverty rates are shown in Table 1.4.

The ADB study also made use of a special 1999 survey that included data on migrant residents of 31 cities, to estimate the poverty rate among migrants and among full-status residents of the same cities. It found the (income) poverty rate among migrants, at an average of 15.2 percent, to be 50 percent higher than that among full-status residents in the same sample cities (10.3 percent). The implication is that the inclusion of migrants in the urban population sample would

Table 1.4 Recent estimates of urban poverty

Source	No. of urban poor in 2002 (millions)	Urban poverty rate (%)
Civil Affairs Ministry, 4 Jan 03	19.98	6.2
Athar Hussain (ADB) and Dev. Research Center, for 1998	14.7 (income); 37.1 (expenditure)	4.73 11.87
A. Hussain (ADB) estimate of poverty among migrants in cities, 1999, based on income	–	15.2
ACFTU (April 2002)	18.3	5.9

Sources: Agence France Presse, Beijing 4 January 2003; Hussain (2002); ACFTU: www.chinaonline.com (1 April 2002).

produce a substantially higher urban poverty rate. If we use Hussain's estimate of the base population of migrants in the cities (40.4 million) to integrate his migrant poverty rate with that of the full-status urban population, we would derive an overall urban poverty rate of 5.8 percent in income terms for 1998–99.

SUMMARY AND CONCLUSION

Trends in world poverty since the mid-1980s depend to a peculiar degree on what has happened to poverty in China. This is because of China's great size, the large absolute number of poor there at the start of the reform and transition to a market economy around 1979, and the sharp reduction in this number thereafter. Including China in the world picture greatly enhances the decline in world poverty, whereas excluding China leaves a much more ambiguous and unimpressive global picture. Therefore it is important to assess the poverty measures for China, upon which so much seems to depend.

This chapter has discussed some of the major problems of measuring China's poverty and, consequently, the uncertainties that remain in our understanding of the size of, and trends in, its poverty incidence. Concurrently we have touched on a broad issue of causality, namely what the poverty trends seem to tell us about the forces that give rise to them. The main conclusions are as follows.

There is little doubt that rural poverty has fallen sharply in China during the transition period but by how much is still open to debate. This is because the measurement of poverty in China is in some disarray. The official poverty line is too low, and is biased over time in various ways. The World Bank's $PPP lines for China are not grounded in recent and comprehensive price and expenditure data. Urban and rural poverty are treated entirely separately, except by the Bank when applying the PPP 1$/day line – a problematical measure – to the national population. These problems create considerable uncertainty about the actual incidence of poverty and the true dimensions of the downward trend. Urban poverty has increased in recent years despite rapid economic growth, but the measurement of urban poverty is even less well founded than that of rural, although the recent ADB study has increased our understanding of it.

It is worth pointing out here that even without these problems, the actual deprivations that constitute poverty are not necessarily comprehensively or accurately reflected in income- and expenditure-based measures of poverty. That is why direct measures of deprivation, such as malnutrition, illiteracy, morbidity, short life expectations and so on remain important gauges of the extent of true human poverty. Generally, for China, measures of nutritional deprivation indicate a higher poverty rate than the official income poverty measure but are fairly consistent with measures using the dollar-a-day expenditures line. For instance a study of independent rural survey data for 19 provinces in 1995 found that 28 percent of the rural population had fewer than 2400 kilocalories per day, which was the nutritional basis of the official poverty line.[17] This compares with an official income poverty rate of 7.1 percent for 1995. Surveys carried out by the Ministry of Health found national rates of stunting for rural children under five years of age to be 39.9 percent in 1995 and 22 percent in 1998, again well above the official income poverty measure.[18]

The temporal pattern and causes of the downward trend in rural poverty are less well understood than the fact of the trend itself. Poverty incidence appears to have been governed much more by macroeconomic and general economic policies and patterns than by targeted poverty reduction policies and programs, which in fact correlate poorly with trends in poverty incidence. This is the essential truth captured by the epigraph from Keith Griffin that begins this chapter. Much work remains to be done in understanding Chinese poverty and accurately assessing the numbers of poor, both urban and rural, and their change over time. This would seem to argue for caution in drawing rosy conclusions about world poverty based so heavily on China's experience.

NOTES

1. See D. Ellerman (2002).
2. This is not to say that the European transition economies would have achieved similar high rates of growth had they adopted China's pragmatism. But it is to suggest that they might have avoided much of the economic and social debacle that resulted directly from the Russian approach. See Griffin (2000) and Ellerman (2002).
3. See Rawski (2002).
4. See State Council (2001).
5. Park and Wang (2001).
6. Reddy and Pogge (2003).
7. See Keidel (1994) for a thorough critique of PPP estimates for China. The following sentences are based on Keidel's discussion.
8. *Zhongguo Tongji Zhaiyao* (1998 and 2002), p. 78.
9. A recent study by IFPRI finds that public spending on education had a bigger effect on poverty reduction in China than any other kind of spending. See Fan et al. (2002). This study uses a simultaneous equations model on province-level data for 1970–97 to estimate the effects of different kinds of government spending on rural poverty.
10. This remained true in the 1990s. In 1995 the top 10 percent of rural households appropriated 133 percent of all net subsidies (above taxes and other impositions) received by the rural population, while the two poorest deciles paid nearly half of all net taxes and fees. See Khan and Riskin (2001) for both studies.
11. Prices indexes are available from the China Internet Information Center (Beijing) at www.china.org.cn/e-Internet/JJ/HTM/0-2.htm. See also *Zhongguo Tongji Zhaiyao* (2002), p. 86, and Lardy (2002), p. 25. Farm prices recovered somewhat in 2001.
12. The argument that falling rural poverty in China is associated with periods of rising relative farm prices has recently been supported by a study by John Weiss (2002) at the ADB Institute. Weiss finds that 'The key explanatory variables [re: recent trends in poverty both over time and across regions] appear to be changes in volume of grain production and in procurement prices.'

13. The *baqi* or '8–7' plan was an ambitious program adopted in 1993 to raise the estimated remaining 80 million rural poor above the poverty line within the seven years remaining to the end of the century. Having made this estimable commitment, the government hiked spending in the latter years in an effort to meet the goal, at least on paper. Annual government funding of poverty reduction programs, which had been running at less than 5 billion yuan from 1986 to 1990, rose to between 5 and 10 billion yuan from 1991 to 1995 and to 15, 18 and 26 billion yuan, respectively, in 1997, 1998 and 1999. See Lu (2001).
14. See Khan and Riskin (2001) for a discussion of the case for using different poverty lines for urban and rural populations.
15. Hussain (2002). This study was led by Athar Hussain, working with the Development Research Center under the State Council.
16. This change is unadjusted for price changes between 1998 and 2002. However the urban CPI in fact remained stable over this period, fluctuating very slightly around zero change.
17. Zhu Ling (2001). Zhu found that 17 percent of the rural population consumed less than 2100 kcal. per day, still far above the official income poverty line.
18. Reported in Park and Wang (2001), p. 395.

BIBLIOGRAPHY

Agence France Presse (2003), 'Six percent of China urban residents in extreme poverty: report', 4 January.

Chen, Shaohua and Martin Ravallion (2004), 'How have the world's poorest fared since the early 1980s?', World Bank Policy Research working paper no. 3341, June.

Chen, S. and Y. Wang (2001), 'China's growth and poverty reduction: recent trends between 1990 and 1999', World Bank, July.

Ellerman, David (2002), 'Russia: thoughts on the privatization debates a decade later', World Bank Operations Evaluation Department working paper.

Fan, Shenggan, Linxiu Zhang and Xiaobo Zhang (2002), 'Growth, inequality and poverty in rural China: the role of public investments', IFPRI research report no. 125.

Griffin, Keith (2000), *Studies in Development Strategy and Systemic Transformation*, London: Macmillan.

Heston, Alan (2001), 'Treatment of China in PWT 6', draft, December.

Hussain, Athar (2002), 'Urban Poverty in PRC', TAR-PRC 33448, Asian Development Bank.

Keidel, Albert (1994), 'China: GNP per capita', World Bank, East Asia and Pacific Regional Office, China and Mongolia Division, report no. 13580-CHA.

Khan, A.R. and Carl Riskin (2001), *Inequality and Poverty in China in the Age of Globalization*, New York and Oxford, Oxford University Press.

Lardy, Nicholas (2002), *Integrating China into the Global Economy*, Washington, DC: Brookings Institution.

Lu, Feng (2001), 'Poverty reduction through growth: China's experiences', presentation given at regional conference on national poverty reduction strategies, World Bank and UNDP, Hanoi, 4-6 December, accessed at www.worldbank.org/wbi/attackingpoverty/eap/hanoi_fenglu.pdf.

National Bureau of Statistics of China (2000), *China Statistical Yearbook*, Beijing: China Statistical Press.

Park, Albert and Wang Sangui (2001), 'China's Poverty Statistics', *China Economic Review*, **12**.

Rawski, Thomas G. (2001), 'What's happening to China's GDP statistics?', *China Economic Review*, **12** (4).

Rawski, Thomas G. (2002), 'Measuring China's Recent GDP Growth: Where Do We Stand?', working paper, accessed at http://www.pitt.edu/~tgrawski/papers2002/measuring.pdf.

Reddy, Sanjay and Thomas Pogge (2003), 'How not to count the poor,' accessed at www.socialanalysis.org.

State Council (2001), 'White Paper on rural China's poverty reduction', issued October accessed at http://english.peopledaily.com.cn.

Weiss, John (2002), 'Explaining trends in regional poverty in China', Asian Development Bank Institute working paper, December.

World Bank (1992), *China: Strategies for Reducing Poverty in the 1990s*, Washington, DC: World Bank.

Zhongguo Tongji Zhaiyao (2002), *China Statistical Abstract.*

Zhu, Ling (2001), 'Food security of low-income groups in rural China', in C. Riskin, R. Zhao and S. Li (eds), *China's Retreat from Equality*, New York: M.E. Sharpe.

2. The rural-urban divide and the evolution of political economy in China

John Knight, Li Shi and Lina Song

INTRODUCTION

China is an important economy. It accounts for about 20 per cent of world population and for nearly 20 per cent of the world's poor. Moreover it is becoming more important. During the period of economic reform – roughly the last 25 years – it has achieved a remarkable trend rate of economic growth: over 8 per cent per annum. By comparison with other Communist or ex-Communist countries, it has so far made a smooth transition from a planned economy towards a market economy. The Chinese economy presents fascinating challenges to economists, and Keith Griffin was one of the first Western development economists to accept the challenge (see for instance Griffin and Saith, 1981; Griffin and Griffin, 1983).

As a group we first teamed up with Keith Griffin as members of an international project on income distribution in China, which he led with Zhao Renwei. The project was based on a very detailed and representative national household survey, designed by the team. It was an improvement on official surveys because it permitted empirical analysis at the micro (household and individual) levels, and because it used a broader definition of income, including the various forms of payment in kind that were important in China. The main output of the project was the book edited by Griffin and Zhao (1993). One of the most startling figures to emerge from it was the ratio of urban to rural household income per capita, which had a value of no less than 2.4 to 1. Recognizing that this rural–urban divide deserved further study, we decided to accept the challenge (Knight and Song, 1999a).

There has always been a strong political economy element to Keith Griffin's writings. Our contribution to this Festschrift takes its cue from that. The explanation for the rural–urban divide in China – its creation, its maintenance, its ups and downs – requires a political economy approach, complemented in the reform period by the analysis of market forces.

The chapter has the following structure. In the next section we describe the rural–urban divide in China, and in the third section we attempt to explain it: why and how it came about and has been maintained to this day. We then pose the question: will the rural–urban divide be eroded? To examine this issue we provide a framework of endogenous government responding to various pressures and interests. In particular, we examine three forces now driving economic policies: rural–urban migration, rising income inequality, and state-owned enterprise reform. The rural–urban divide is a common phenomenon, although China represents an extreme case: the fifth section places China in perspective. The sixth section concludes.

DESCRIBING THE RURAL–URBAN DIVIDE

In 1949 almost 90 per cent of the Chinese population was classified as rural. This census definition of rural and urban corresponds closely to the administrative division. In 2002 the rural population accounted for 61 per cent of the total. Despite the urbanization that goes along with economic development, the rural population has grown in absolute terms and the great majority of Chinese people continue to live in rural areas. Almost all of China's arable land was already in

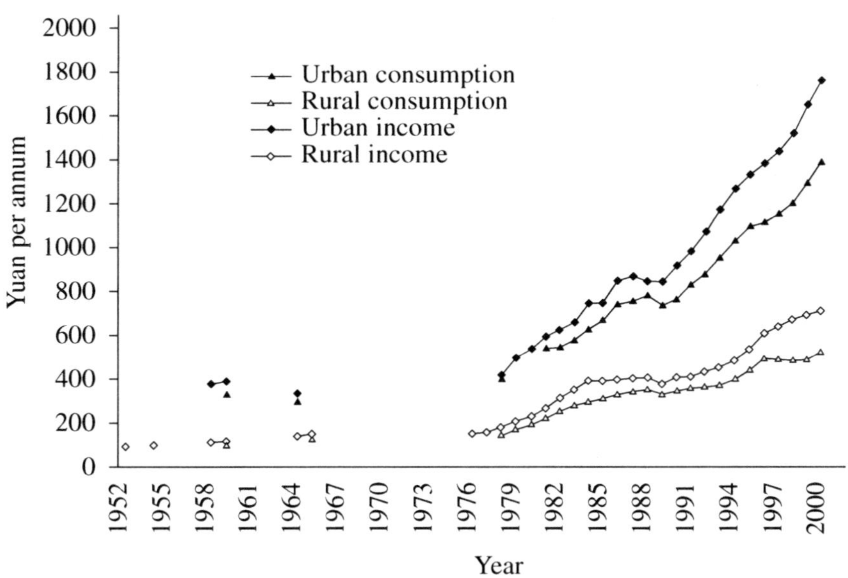

Figure 2.1 Urban and rural real income and consumption per annum at 1985 prices

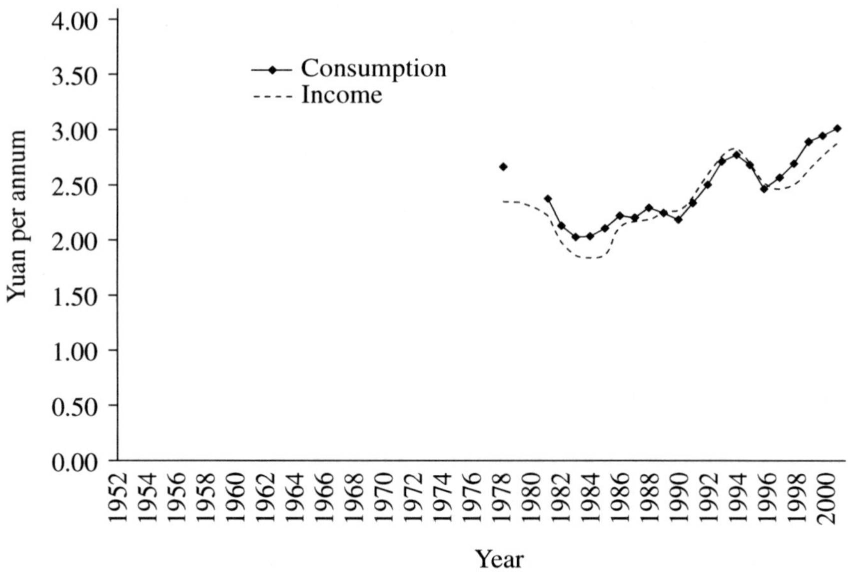

Figure 2.2 Urban/rural income and consumption ratios

use in 1952, and yet over the next 50 years the rural population was to grow by over 350 million. This growing pressure on the land posed a threat to both rural and urban living standards.

Figure 2.1 shows rural and urban income, and also consumption, per capita, expressed in constant prices, from 1952 to 2000, taken from official sources. Both rural and urban income rose very slowly until the process of economic reform began in 1978. Figure 2.2 shows the ratio of urban to rural income, and consumption, per capita over the same period. Throughout the planning era, the ratios exceeded 2 to 1, and they were particularly high (over 3) in the mid-1950s. The ratio narrowed over the years 1978–85, when rural economic reforms – the disbanding of the communes and the restoration of household production – took place. As urban reforms began and accelerated after 1985, urban incomes grew rapidly. The rural–urban divide actually increased, and in the year 2000 the ratios (2.8 for income and 3.0 for consumption) were higher than they had ever been throughout the economic reform era.

The rural–urban divide is not confined to conventionally measured income. It is apparent also in education, health care and housing (Knight and Song, 1999a, Chapters 4, 5 and 6, respectively). The most important factor influencing a person's educational attainment, or enrolment, after his age, is whether he lives in a rural or urban area. The standardized mean difference in educational attainment is no less than 4.6 years in favour of urban-dwellers. Moreover school cost per pupil, public subsidy per pupil, and the average quality of teachers, are all far higher in urban than in rural areas.

There is a considerable gap between urban and rural provision of, and access to, health services. The rural population is at a disadvantage in both quality and quantity of health care. Moreover urban services are much more heavily subsidized, so that rural people have to pay no less than urban people for health care. Yet the difference in mean incomes contributes to the contrast in the underlying healthiness of people in urban and rural areas. Using the extreme measure of unhealthiness – mortality – we find premature mortality rates to be considerably higher in the countryside, especially for infants and children.

There are too many dimensions, with their valuation problems, to decide whether urban- or rural-dwellers are better off in terms of housing. Urban people live in cramped conditions but the quality of their housing is generally higher than that of peasants. Peasants have to build and improve their own houses, and must do so without the help of mortgages, whereas until recently urban-dwellers have paid only minimal rents and have thus enjoyed heavy subsidies of their housing. The recent sale of much urban housing to occupiers at low prices has effectively capitalized the previous rental subsidies.

Even the addition of education, health and housing to income yields too narrow a concept of well-being. There are also the relative degrees of freedom and of security that different people enjoy. Perhaps the greatest difference between rural and urban people is that they have different forms of security. Peasants have secure access to farming and housing land, whereas urban workers have until recently had their 'iron rice bowls', that is, guarantees of secure jobs and pensions. Peasants had more, and earlier, freedom to pursue their economic self-interests locally, but they were in the past prevented from migrating to the cities, and they are still largely prevented from settling in the cities.

EXPLAINING THE RURAL–URBAN DIVIDE

So far we have described the rural–urban divide: now to explain it. Why, and how, did it come about? The Communist Party, when it came to power, proceeded to build an institutional framework in which the state, dominated by the party, divided China into rural and urban compartments, separated in terms of administration, finance and resources. The state either prevented or controlled the flow of funds and resources between the sectors. Rural residents, forming the great majority of the population, were governed by the urban representatives of the state. During the period of economic reform the policies of decentralization and marketization contracted the role of the state and expanded the role of market forces. However the institutional framework remained in place, and the urban–rural income ratio did not decline. The invisible Great Wall which separates rural and urban China remained standing.

Consider the policies of government as they evolved. The first tasks of the Communists, when they came to power, were the elimination of the landlord class, land reform, and the introduction of centralized economic planning. Recall that it was a peasant-backed revolution. Nevertheless the main economic objective was rapid industrialization, and this meant urbanization. The terms of trade between agriculture and industry were an important policy variable to this end. Following the example of the USSR, the government depressed the terms of trade in order to provide cheap food in relation to manufactures, and thereby to secure high industrial profits for reinvestment. This was the so-called 'price scissors' policy (Knight, 1995; Knight and Song, 1999a, Chapter 7). The hand that wielded the price scissors effected a transfer of income and resources from the rural to the urban sector. The relative invisibility of the transfer and the opaqueness of the burden added political attractiveness. The creation of the communes and enforced procurement of food can be seen as the state's need to extract a surplus from agriculture in the absence of price incentives for farmers. In fact it led to rural stagnation up to 1978. The peasants bore most of the sacrifice in consumption, and effectively paid for industrialization.

The real wages of urban workers were set at a level which enabled households to enjoy a higher standard of living than their rural counterparts. Thus part of the investable surplus was diverted to the support of urban workers and their iron rice bowls. It was not only future generations that gained from the price scissors: urban workers also benefited. There is a fine line between the so-called efficiency wage and political pressure explanations of the relatively high urban wage. Worker discontent, low morale and threat to political stability are all aspects of the latent power – latent rather then overt in the Chinese case – which residentially concentrated, interacting workers appear to possess.

The period of decollectivization, 1978–84, was one of rapid growth in peasant incomes. The changes reflect a shift in the concerns of the Chinese leadership from the ideological to the economic. The rural reforms were that rare event, a Pareto improvement with hardly any losers. It is interesting that the reforms, which began at the grassroots level, went further and faster than was intended. A process of atomized peasant behaviour and cumulative causation pulled the leadership along behind.

In the mid-1980s government attention turned from rural to urban reform policies. The once-for-all nature of the gains from decollectivization and the policy reluctance to raise food prices produced agricultural stagnation for some years thereafter. However this was ameliorated by rapid rural industrialization and an increase in temporary migration of rural workers to the cities and towns.

Government policy with regard to procurement, producer prices of grain and other necessities provides a good test of the relative political influence of workers and peasants. Government came to recognize the need to raise producer prices in order to elicit more farm production. However when producer prices rose, government was also concerned to protect the living standards of urban workers. This necessitated a sharp increase in food subsidies. The budgetary expenditure on urban food subsidies actually came to exceed budgetary expenditure on agriculture in the early 1990s. The tardy and tortuous dismantling of the price scissors policy suggests that the urban minority were politically more important to the government than were the rural majority.

Urban real wages rose rapidly over the period of urban reform. This occurred despite the abundant supply of rural labour that was potentially available. It was made possible by the shielding of urban workers from the competition of rural labour, and the decentralization of power to enterprises. Managers appeared willing – possibly for efficiency reasons – to share profits with their employees.

It is of course misleading to speak of *the* urban–rural income ratio. There is considerable inequality within rural and within urban China. Much of the inequality of rural income per capita is spatial in character, reflecting the vast size and diversity of China. Spatial inequality existed even under the egalitarian policies of the pre-reform period, but both spatial and household inequalities increased during the reform period. We have found reasons to expect that processes of cumulative causation are at work, increasing inequality at the province, county, village and household levels (Knight and Song, 1993; Knight and Li, 1997). In some areas rural industrialization has proceeded rapidly, labour shortages have emerged, and rural incomes have risen towards urban incomes. In other areas rural development remains limited, surplus labour is chronic, and the potential economic gain from rural–urban migration is very great.

Spatial variation in urban real wages and incomes is not large across urban China, although it has increased (Knight et al., 2001). Urban incomes have been standardized by the institutional element in pay determination whereas rural incomes reflect regional disparities in natural resources and economic opportunities. This means that the urban–rural gap is greater in poor provinces.

The reason for the superior provision of education in urban areas is to be found mainly in the separate administrative and funding arrangements for rural and urban education. However it also reflects the opportunity costs and the lower perceived economic returns to education for rural households. The educational attainment of a rural area is strongly related to its income per capita, on account of the decentralized funding of rural public expenditures. There is no such urban relationship, owing to the more centralized funding arrangements.

China has a good health record, even in rural areas, by comparison with most poor countries. The emphasis on preventive medicine has borne dividends. It is probably the high quality of health care in urban China that is the real international outlier. The disparity between rural and urban China is the result of the institutional divide in health care arrangements, which in turn stems from the separate administration of rural and urban areas. Urban residents have widespread access to state-supported health care. The rural co-operative health schemes that operated during the commune period collapsed during the reform period. Especially in the poorer villages, which cannot afford collective insurance schemes, rural households face user charges for curative care and medicines. Other than for preventive care such as the vaccination of children, peasants' access to state-subsidized services is limited.

The general stance of the state with regard to education, health care and housing is that the rural sector should be self-reliant. The peasants have had to take care of themselves and not be a burden on the state. There are large differences in urban and rural tax revenue per capita, reflecting the industry-centred tax base, and these differences are not offset by fiscal transfers.

It is arguable that a large urban–rural income gap should not survive the impact of equilibrating market forces. As the Chinese economy became more marketized, why were the returns to factors not equalized across space? Why did the income gap not get competed away? The answer to the question is: the continued control of rural–urban migration. Without this, the income disparity would have served as a magnet to rural people wanting to better themselves, and it would not have survived. The invisible Great Wall has become more permeable during the period of economic reform. However central and local governments have attempted to control the flow of temporary rural–urban migrants. Their objective has been to meet the needs of the growing urban economy while giving preference to urban residents. Moreover it remains very difficult for rural-born people to acquire the right to permanent urban residence.

WILL THE RURAL–URBAN DIVIDE BE ERODED?

Endogenous Government

The policy implications of this analysis can be approached in two ways. One is to assume that government formulates its objectives exogenously, that is, independently of the pressures arising from the economic interests of various groups in society. We might for instance assume that government possesses a given social welfare function which makes no distinction between rural and urban people *per se*, and that the poorer the person, the higher the value placed on additional income. By this criterion, various Chinese government policies are difficult to understand, and must be regarded as errors, attributable to imperfect knowledge or imperfect control. A government with the social welfare function posited above would share our vision for the future elimination of the rural–urban divide. The more complete marketization of the economy would help to achieve this vision, as would the elimination of the administrative and institutional boundaries between rural and urban China.

The second approach is to recognize the endogeneity of government, that is, that government is itself an economic agent, whose objectives are determined by the political economy. The government's social welfare function is in principle predictable from the relevant model, and government – more realistically, different segments and tiers of government – responds in predictable ways to dangers, threats and pressures. Government may be self-interested, in that it is ultimately concerned with staying in power. On this view, the apparent policy errors are in fact chosen correctly in the pursuit of government objectives. For instance there may be good political reasons to favour urban people over rural. The remedy therefore lies in changing those objectives. The issue becomes one of influencing the balance of pressures that mould government policy.

It is necessary to form a view of the factors that shape economic policy in China. In the early years the Communist Party was securely in power, having won over almost all the population. Ideological objectives were therefore a luxury that could be pursued with little hindrance. Later on, particularly after the Cultural Revolution, the state became more sensitive to threats to political stability. The retention of power became an important influence on economic policy.

It is possible to analyse certain policy outcomes by reference to the interests of various institutions and groups in society, and the pressures that they could exert on a government whose primary objective was to stay in power. However these pressures were normally implicit rather than explicit, passive rather than active. Underlying the urban bias often observable in state policies and institutions was state bias, to be explained in terms of the concerns and objectives of the Chinese leadership.

In the early years pressures on government were weak. The process of economic reform gave rise to clearer economic groups and perceptions of group interests. The rural–urban divide has become more apparent because the two sectors now communicate and interact directly, whereas they previously interacted only through the intermediation of the state. Conflicts of interest have come more into the open. A good example is the huge discrepancies that for some years existed between the producer prices, the market prices and the rationed consumer prices of staple goods.

What are the prospects for the erosion of the rural–urban divide, bearing in mind current changes and trends in the economy and society? It has been argued that as South Korea and Taiwan developed, their governments switched from urban bias to rural bias policies (Moore, 1993).The explanation is in terms of the changing structure of the economy, which reduced the need to extract a surplus from the agricultural sector and increased the political treat from rural–urban migration. Similarly, some of the changes taking place in the

Chinese economy may assist the peasants. For instance the price scissors policy has become unimportant for the accumulation of capital. Also the diminishing share of food in urban household budgets makes urban real incomes less sensitive to the price of food. The voice of rural people may be enhanced by the greater awareness of their relative position that better education, greater mobility and improved communications can foster. The increased marketization of the economy may itself reduce the degree of urban bias in government policies insofar as it accords greater weight to market-based allocation of resources and income and less weight to location-based allocation.

The future of the rural–urban divide depends to a great extent on the forces driving economic policies in urban China, in particular those relating to rural discontent, rural–urban migration, rising income inequality, and state-owned enterprise reform. Moreover the evolution of Chinese political economy is well illustrated by these four important phenomena. We consider each in turn.

Rural Discontent

To begin with the rural sector, what is the prospect for the peasant voice to be strengthened, so that peasant interests can acquire a greater weight in government policy objectives? In the 1980s the state's power to govern the countryside was eroded. To cope with the crisis of legitimacy, government decided to rejuvenate grassroots institutions and to encourage peasant participation. It gave legal recognition to village committees and encouraged elections to them, and it encouraged village representative assemblies. This has improved village governance and political consciousness. However it has not given peasants political influence at higher levels of governance, nor has it impacted significantly on the underlying conflict between the peasant and the state on account of its urban bias policies.

The process of economic reform has assisted the development of 'civil society' in rural China, as various social organizations have emerged. These can be seen as intermediaries between government and people and, in principle, can articulate peasant interests. In practice however the influences of rural social organizations are weak, nor are they concerned with the central issue, that is, peasant feelings of relative deprivation and of unfair treatment.

The Evolving Policy on Migration

Before the start of rural economic reform in 1978, rural–urban migration of any sort was tightly restricted and indeed, with only minor exceptions, prohibited. The introduction of the household responsibility system in farming meant that surplus labour, previously disguised by commune work rules, became available for new farm and non-farm activities. In the 1980s peasants began to sell their products in the reopened urban food markets and new grassroots rural industries responded to the demand for consumer goods. The growth of rural industry was the outstanding phenomenon of the 1980s. Township and village enterprise (TVE) employment grew by 13 per cent per annum in the 1980s in response to a market disequilibrium, but by less than 3 per cent per annum in the 1990s as equilibrium was established and competition from the reforming urban economy intensified. Instead, rural–urban migration was the outstanding phenomenon of the 1990s. This redirection of rural labour absorption was assisted by the abolition of urban food rationing, the acceleration of the urban reforms that had commenced in 1985, and – as the one-child family policy took lagged effect – a deceleration of urban labour force growth. The rapid growth of the urban economy compared with the slow growth of the urban-born labour force meant that there was an increasing need for rural workers in the urban economy. Temporary migration expanded to meet that need.

Rural–urban migration should be viewed from three perspectives – those of the migrants themselves, their prospective employers and government – each of which might wish to promote or resist migration (Knight et al., 1999). Consider each in turn. Many rural people have a strong economic incentive to migrate, having few productive opportunities in the village. Some are put off by the transaction costs involved, including lack of information and contacts as well as the costs of movement. Hence the importance of the village itself and of migrant networks in facilitating migration.

Many urban employers have a profit incentive to employ more migrants – essentially because migrants are willing to work for lower pay than are residents, and to accept jobs that urban residents reject. Different parts of government have different objectives. Central government is most concerned to ensure that flows of migrants are orderly and do not threaten social stability. Governments of sending areas – at the province or county level – encourage out-migration and operate recruitment agencies to assist it. As rural–urban migration began to burgeon in the 1990s, city governments, concerned to protect their citizens against the influx of migrants, introduced systems of control over in-migration. Their objectives were to allow temporary migrants into jobs unfilled by urban residents but to protect their residents against undercutting competition.

The late 1990s saw an increase in the number of migrant settlers in the big cities. They were commonly found in distinct migrant communities from a particular sending area, often semi-autonomous and well structured. These migrants continued to be at a blatant disadvantage with respect not only to jobs but also to housing and schools, whereas access to medical care was now a matter of ability to pay. However they – and in particular their children – were becoming urbanized: their reference groups were switching from rural to urban. The late 1990s also witnessed increasing conflict for urban jobs between rural migrants and urban workers. Urban governments responded to the widespread redundancies by restricting the recruitment and re-employment of rural migrants, and urban job centres gave priority to unemployed and laid-off (*xia gang*) urban-registered *hukou* residents. Out-migration from rural China, which had grown rapidly in the early 1990s, was constant in the late 1990s (Du, 2001).

Rising Income Inequality and Social Instability

Except in respect of the rural–urban divide, China was an egalitarian society before economic reform. The Gini coefficient was estimated to be below 0.20 in urban areas and about 0.25 in rural areas in the late 1970s (Adelman and Sunding, 1987). A national household survey for 1988 revealed that a decade after rural reform had commenced, the Gini coefficient (based on micro data) had risen to 0.23 and 0.34 in urban and rural China respectively; the rural–urban divide meant that the national Gini coefficient was higher than either, at 0.38 (Griffin and Zhao, 1993, pp. 41, 45, 48). By 1995, a decade after the start of urban reform, the comparable urban and rural Gini coefficients were 0.28 and 0.42 respectively, and the national figure 0.46 (Gustafsson and Li, 2001, p. 54). An urban household survey for 1999 showed a further sharp rise in the urban Gini coefficient, to 0.40. China was no longer an egalitarian society by international standards.

How important is the income gap between urban and rural areas in the context of overall income inequality in China? A decomposition of the Theil index shows it to have been a major contributor (Gustafsson and Li, 2001, p. 66). In the 1988 household survey, the urban–rural income gap accounted for 43 per cent of overall inequality. This proportion declined to 35 per cent in the corresponding 1995 survey owing to the increase in within-area inequality, but the absolute contribution of the urban–rural income gap to the Theil index actually increased, by over 20 per cent. Thus overall income inequality in China would be reduced considerably if the urban–rural income gap could be eliminated.

How is the sharply rising inequality of incomes to be explained? Here we must look to government objectives in the post-Mao period. Because the Communist Party's grip on power has been firm by international standards, its concern to remain in power can be viewed more as an underlying influence on policy-making than as an over-riding objective. In the reform period the objectives of government have been primarily economic. These can be interpreted as the rapid growth of the economy and of government revenue, the former objective being stressed by central government and the latter by local governments.

The pursuit of growth objectives has generated rising income inequality – among the important mechanisms being the creation of markets, including markets offering initial high profits; the provision of incentives for enterprise and accumulation; and the application of efficiency rather than equity criteria in public decision-taking, including the demise of egalitarian regional policy. A new capitalist class has gradually been emerging. The combination of semimarketized economy, weak legal system and ill-defined or insecure property rights brought greater scope for corruption, cronyism, rent-seeking and appropriation of state assets. That is a further source of income polarization.

Rising inequality may threaten government if it leads to social instability. Moreover social instability may in turn put at risk the continuation of rapid economic growth. Are there signs of growing social instability? If so, does the rural–urban divide play a role in this growth? There is evidence that slow growth of rural incomes – partly due to increases in the taxes and fees charged by local governments – has induced a rise in conflicts between peasants and local officials in recent years (Liu and Fan, 2001) and in peasant refusals to pay local taxes and fees (He, 2001). The appropriation of peasants' land for non-agricultural purposes without adequate compensation has become another source of conflict. The effect of increased rural–urban migration has been to destabilize the cities. Observing their economic disadvantage, migrants may regard themselves as second-class citizens. The weakness of mechanisms of social control among migrants and the relative deprivation that they feel is said to contribute to rising crime in the cities (Liu and Fan, 2001). The number of criminal cases registered in public security organs rose by 127 per cent between 1996 and 2000, with robberies and larceny rising even more rapidly.

The Evolving Policy on State Enterprise Reform

A further source of greater social instability was the policy of reforming the state-owned enterprises, which began in earnest in the mid-1990s. The policy is worth examining in some detail because it appears to be the most serious discrepancy in our explanation of the rural–urban divide.

The remarkable development of rural industry over the economic reform period was a response to extreme market disequilibrium. Supernormal profits were there to be earned by competing against the inefficient, high-price, state-owned enterprises. Township and village cooperatives and private entrepreneurs responded to these opportunities, and the number of workers engaged in rural non-agricultural activities rose remarkably, by 100 million over 20 years. State-owned firms were affected also by private sector development under the urban reforms, and by the tendency for local governments to overinvest. This increased competition for the state-owned sector depressed its profitability severely, and consequently government revenue also suffered. By the mid-1990s the reform of the state-owned enterprises had become a crucial issue which the government could no longer ignore.

One of the problems of the state sector has been overmanning: estimates suggest that about 20 per cent of urban employment has been superfluous (Knight and Song, 1999b). Until recently, government had a political preference for disguised unemployment within enterprises rather than open unemployment on the streets. The reforms involved the withdrawal of subsidies, and state directives to lay off surplus labour. Few young people were recruited, many middle-aged workers were retired early, and many previously protected employees became *xia gang* workers, that is, they continued to be nominally employed by the relinquishing enterprise while receiving a low wage, but they did not have to attend the workplace. Over 24 million redundancies were created in the period 1995–99. For many who continued in their jobs, employment was no longer guaranteed, their iron rice bowls were now made of cardboard, and feelings of insecurity were rife. Even the creation of *xia gang* status for laid-off workers did not protect them from hardship. A survey conducted early in 2000 showed that over half of the workers made redundant since 1992 were still unemployed, that the expected average duration of unemployment was about four years, and that they suffered a considerable loss of income during their period of unemployment (Appleton et al., 2002). There are journalists' reports of social unrest among the unemployed, especially in cities where unemployment in high.[1] When, in a survey conducted in 2000, urban people were asked to rank the most important social problems, unemployment was ranked first, corruption second and increasing income inequality third (Project Team of the Academy of Macroeconomics, 2001).

Does the new determination to reform the state-owned enterprises signify the end of the policy of urban bias? Perhaps the most plausible interpretation runs as follows. The reform was forced on government by the declining profitability and the rising incidence of loss-making in the state-owned sector, with adverse implications for both government revenue and prospects for continued rapid growth. Faced with a threat to the achievement of its main objectives, government was willing to risk a degree of political threat inherent in the erosion of urban-dwellers' privileges.

The risk was worth taking given that there were three safety valves. Firstly, to some extent unemployment could be exported to rural China, through tighter restrictions on the recruitment and renewed employment of migrants in cities. Secondly, as a result of the reform, the state-owned sector should become more efficient, and more difficult therefore for rural industry to compete against. In these ways the burden of the reform could be transferred from urban to rural people. Thirdly, the majority of urban workers continued to be employed, and their real wages continued to rise despite the increase in urban unemployment. Standardized real wage growth averaged 5 per cent per annum over the period 1995–99 (Appleton et al., 2004). The fact that wages were sensitive to profits, and became more so between 1995 and 1999, suggests that managers were willing to share rents with their remaining workers (Knight and Li, 2005). Rent-sharing and efficiency wage explanations are difficult to distinguish, both conceptually and empirically: the wage increases might be viewed as payments for maintaining the morale, goodwill and effort of urban workers. According to the official household surveys, the real income per capita of urban *hukou* residents rose by almost 6 per cent per annum between 1995 and 2000; the ratio of urban to rural income per capita thus actually rose, from 2.71 to 2.79. The new urban hardship was borne unevenly, and by a relatively small minority.

THE CHINESE CASE IN PERSPECTIVE

The Chinese case can be viewed from two perspectives, the empirical and the theoretical. First, we make comparisons with other countries, so as to establish whether the rural–urban divide in China is ordinary or extraordinary.

Empirical Perspective

Table 2.1 presents results for 12 countries on which we could obtain data. Only Zimbabwe and South Africa exceed China in their ratios of urban to rural

Table 2.1 The ratio of urban to rural income, and consumption, per capita, selected countries, recent years

Country	Year	Ratio of urban to rural:	
		Income per capita	Consumption per capita
China	1995	2.72	3.41
Taiwan	1995	1.32	1.43
South Korea	1994		1.03
India	1987/8		1.49
Iran	1991		1.82
Turkey	1994		1.71
Philippines	1991	2.26	2.17
Thailand	1990	2.23	2.66
Sri Lanka	1990/1	1.79	1.33
Egypt	1990/1		1.50
Zimbabwe	1990/1	3.57	
South Africa	1993	3.14	

Notes: In South Korea the ratio is per household, not per capita; in Taiwan, Iran and the Philippines the per capita figure is derived from the household figure and the average number of members per household.

In Taiwan, Thailand, South Africa and Zimbabwe, aggregation into urban and rural categories was necessary, based on population weights.

Source: Knight and Song (1999a), p. 338.

income per capita. These two southern African countries have in the past been subject to powerful class and race bias in government policies, for which rural–urban distinction serves as a proxy. Their rural households, reliant on farming and labour migration, possess very little land and resources, and have been powerless and neglected. China's successful neighbours, Taiwan and South Korea, report extremely low urban–rural ratios; indeed in South Korea there appears to be no difference between urban and rural living standards. The ratios in Sri Lanka, Egypt, Iran and Turkey are all well under 2 to 1. In terms of size, resources, structure and level of development, the economy of India is most similar to that of China. However the Indian ratio of consumption per capita is only half the Chinese. This may be because in India markets operate more freely, factors of production can move unhindered, there is a wealthy landlord class, and there is a more democratic form of government. All but one of our countries has a sizable urban–rural income gap. China is not unique but it is unusual, at least by Asian standards. State institutions and government policies are responsible for China's artificially great rural–urban divide.

Rural–urban inequalities are not only to be found in poor countries of the late twentieth century: they are a more general phenomenon. For instance in *The Wealth of Nations* (1776, Chapter 10), Adam Smith argued that:

> the inhabitants of a town, being collected into one place, can easily combine together … to prevent free competition, whereas … the inhabitants of the country, dispersed in different places, cannot … Throughout Europe, townspeople incorporated themselves, that is they regulated to restrict entry to industries, trades and occupations so as to increase their profits and wages, whereas rural people did not. The effect was to … break down that natural equality which would otherwise take place in the commerce which is carried on between … (town and country). … Stock and labour naturally seek the most advantageous employment. They naturally therefore resort as much as they can to the town, and desert the country.

The forms, mechanisms and degree of rural–urban division may vary from one nation or one era to another, but there are underlying reasons why it is often to be found.

Theoretical Perspective

Consider the relevance to the Chinese case of four possible models of the relationship between the rural and urban sectors of a developing economy. These are the Lewis model, the price scissors model, the urban bias model and the state bias model. Any interpretation of government policy, or of changes in policy, invites the criticism that the beneficiaries of the policy are too readily assumed to have been responsible for it. It is difficult to adduce direct evidence of the influences that govern policy, but all to easy to infer them. We recognize this methodological problem. Nevertheless the four models provide a framework for a plausible and consistent account of policy-making.

We begin with the well-known Lewis model. Recall that this envisages economic development proceeding as a transfer of labour from the rural (identical to agricultural) sector to the urban (identical to industrial) sector. The industrial sector accumulates capital through the reinvestment of profits. In conditions of surplus labour the industrial real wage – being determined by the rural supply price – remains low and constant until rural labour becomes scarce. At first sight, the Lewis model applies well to China, with its abundant labour and its urban industrialization policy, especially during the period of central planning. However it requires qualification.

Economic reform did not simply accelerate the transfer of labour from the rural to the urban sector, in line with the Lewis model. Rather, it led to the growth of the third sector – non-urban, non-state, non-agricultural – the rural industrial sector. The relationship of the new sector to the existing two sectors is mainly complementary in one case and competitive in the other. It was promoted by agricultural development and it in turn promoted agricultural development. Although it diverted resources from agriculture, the opportunity cost of rural labour was low. Rural industry competed with urban industry, particularly for raw materials in the early stages of the reform process, and for markets in the later stages. It contributed to the falling profitability of state enterprises, which occurred as a result of the price reform and the opening up of competition.

The new sector developed in the rural rather than the urban areas largely because of the institutional divide between rural and urban China that the state had created. Only in the rural areas could economic agents respond to the supernormal profits available in light industry. Moreover the policy of rural fiscal self-reliance created a strong incentive for rural authorities to promote the industrialization of their localities. In this sense the institutional divide generated a degree of rural bias, in contradistinction to the more familiar urban bias in state policies. The fact that the most dynamic industrial growth in recent years took place in the rural sector should in itself have reduced the urban–rural income ratio. However as this development was more than offset by other changes, the ratio actually rose after the mid-1980s.

The rural–urban divide has become more porous and less tidy in recent years. The rural–urban distinction is being blurred, and it is no longer equivalent to the agriculture–industry distinction. The main reason for this is rural industrialization – itself a product of the institutional divide – and the socioeconomic changes that it brought about. Although it was trivial at the start of the economic reforms, the overlap between the rural and urban frequency distributions of household income per capita has gradually increased. Some rural people in some parts of China are now better off than most urban people.

The Lewis model of the transfer from agriculture to industry is indeed relevant, but within rural China. The model depicts well the process that operated within the rural sector after 1978. The basic elements of the model are present in rural China: an elastic supply of labour from agriculture to industry, and the rural industrialization which was achieved through the reinvestment of profits within that sector. The Lewis model is a rather less appropriate description of the relationship between the rural and the urban sector. Government set the urban industrial wage at a level which greatly exceeded the supply price of rural labour, and it was necessary for government therefore to restrict and control rural–urban migration. Moreover the funds for industrial investment, although nominally derived from industrial profits, were extracted from agriculture by means of government pricing policy. The relationship between the rural and the urban sector therefore requires a model that incorporates both the price scissors and the urban bias policies.

The theory of price scissors can be readily applied to China. Moreover some government policies such as the formation of the communes, compulsory procurement of food, and urban rationing of food can be seen to flow from the price scissors policy. Government intervention on prices effected a transfer of resources from the rural to the urban sector. These were used for capital accumulation in urban industry, in accordance with the price scissors model of industrialization. However they were also used to raise the consumption of urban workers. Thus the Chinese experience does not correspond precisely to the price scissors model: it also requires a role for the urban bias model.

It is likely that urban bias does exist in China, in two senses. Firstly, government allocates fewer resources to the rural sector than it would if it were concerned only with improving economic efficiency, as determined by shadow prices. Secondly, rural-dwellers receive less priority than they would if the government social welfare function made no distinction between rural and urban residence *per se*, and placed a greater value on additional income, the poorer the person. The urban bias model has perhaps been most forcefully propounded by Lipton (1977). As Lipton put it: 'the rural sector contains most of the poverty, and most of the low-cost sources of potential advance; but the urban sector contains most of the articulateness, organization and power'. Bates (1993) summarized the urban bias displayed by the state in socialist countries in the following terms. Socialist governments create large bureaucracies, forge strong ideological ties with urban labour, and are committed to industrialization and to public ownership; hence their concern to ensure low food prices and high industrial profits. Socialist governments accordingly adopt policies against the interests of their poorest citizens – the peasants. The Chinese case corresponds well to this general account.

Although the policies of the Chinese government can be accurately described as involving urban bias, the underlying reason for the policies is better described as state bias. A primary motivation was the preservation of government by the Chinese Communist Party. The failure to close, or even to diminish, the rural–urban gap in income and welfare stems from the need to stave off potential political threats to the regime. Even during the early years of economic reform, when the rural sector received priority, the motive was to restore political legitimacy with the peasants and to relax the most serious constraint on the growth of the economy. We do not claim that the state entirely understood or controlled economic events. Take for instance the issue of promissory notes instead of money to peasants for their produce in the late 1980s and the early 1990s. This was clearly not a policy objective for central government – indeed it tried in vain to outlaw the practice. However it was the outcome of its other policies, such as that requiring rural local governments largely to raise their own revenue and the set of policies making investment in industry more profitable for local government than investment in agriculture.

The Chinese political process should not yet be viewed as the outcome of conflicting articulated pressures from various organized interest groups. The Communist Party remains too dominant for that. Rather, the urban bias policies reflect the latent political power of urban-dwellers. The government purchases an insurance policy to ensure that urban workers will refrain from political protests which could challenge it, and that they will not threaten production and therefore state revenue. The erosion of the economic security of urban households in the late 1990s – associated with reform of the state-owned enterprises – can be viewed as a risky but necessary response to the financial deterioration of that sector, which posed a threat to the public finances and to continued rapid economic growth.

It is apparent that no single model of rural–urban economic relationships is sufficient to describe the Chinese experience. In fact all four models that we considered are relevant in at least some respect. They were therefore combined to produce an encompassing model "with Chinese characteristics".

CONCLUSION

It appears from the evidence that the Chinese government is more concerned to promote economic growth, and to alleviate poverty through growth, than it is to prevent the sharply rising inequality that is taking place in China. Moreover the government's social welfare function seems to accept two classes of citizenship – one class for urban-dwellers and another, inferior, class for rural-dwellers.

There are two main ways in which the rural–urban divide might be eroded in future, but neither is inevitable. Firstly, rapid economic growth will result in the transfer of rural labour out of farming. This should eventually see rural incomes rise – more generally than at present – as China enters the labour-scarce stage of the Lewis model. Secondly, in an increasingly well-informed society, widening, or even continued, economic disparities – among households, across regions, between city and countryside, and between urban residents and rural migrants – are likely to generate feelings of relative deprivation, expressions of discontent, and outbreaks of social instability. The likely response of party and government to these developments could help to bring inequality issues onto the policy agenda, and also to erode the rural–urban divide.

NOTE

1. See for instance *Newsweek*, 4 March 2002, pp. 24–5.

REFERENCES

Adelman, Irma and David Sunding (1987), 'Economic policy and income distribution in China', *Journal of Comparative Economics*, **11** (3), September, 444–61.

Appleton, Simon, John Knight, Lina Song and Qingji Xia (2002), 'Labor retrenchment in China: determinants and consequences', *China Economic Review*, **13**, 252–75.

Appleton, Simon, John Knight, Lina Song and Qingji Xia (2004), 'Competing paradigms: segmentation and competitiveness in the formation of the Chinese labour market', *Journal of Chinese Economic and Business Studies*, **2** (3), 185–205.

Bates, Robert H. (1993), 'Urban bias: a fresh look', *Journal of Development Studies*, **29** (4), 219–28.

Du, Ying (2001), 'Research on employment issues of out-migrants', Beijing: Ministry of Agriculture of People's Republic of China (in Chinese).

Griffin, Keith and Kimberley Griffin (1983), 'Institutional change and income distribution in the Chinese countryside', *Oxford Bulletin of Economics and Statistics*, **45** (3), 223–48.

Griffin, Keith and Ashwani Saith (1981), *Growth and Equality in Rural China*, Bangkok: Maruzen (for the International Labour Organization).

Griffin, Keith and Zhao Renwei (eds) (1993), *The Distribution of Income in China*, London: Macmillan.

Gustafsson, Bjorn and Li Shi (2001), 'A more unequal China? Aspects of inequality in the distribution of equivalent income', in Carl Riskin, Zhao Renwei and Li Shi (eds), *China's Retreat from Equality: Income Distribution and Economic Transition*, Armonk, NY: M.E. Sharpe.

He, Xuefeng (2001), 'Peasants' burden and rural governance: a survey for Dai village in Hubei', *Management World (China)*, **2**, 156–82.

Knight, John (1995), 'Price scissors and intersectoral resource transfers: who paid for industrialization in China?', *Oxford Economic Papers*, **47** (1), 117–35.

Knight, John and Li Shi (1997), 'Cumulative causation and inequality among villages in China', *Oxford Development Studies*, **25** (2), 149–72.

Knight, John and Li Shi (2005), 'Wages, firm profitability and labor market segmentation in urban China', *China Economic Review*, **16** (3), 229–45.

Knight, John and Lina Song (1993), 'The spatial contribution to income inequality in rural China', *Cambridge Journal of Economics,* **17** (2), 195–213.
Knight, John and Lina Song (1999a), *The Rural–Urban Divide. Economic Disparities and Interactions in China*, Oxford: Oxford University Press.
Knight, John and Lina Song (1999b), 'Employment constraints and sub-optimality in Chinese enterprises', *Oxford Economic Papers*, **51**, 284–98.
Knight, John, Lina Song and Jia Huaibin (1999), 'Chinese rural migrants in urban enterprises: three perspectives', *Journal of Development Studies*, **35** (3), 73–104.
Knight, John, Li Shi and Zhao Renwei (2001), 'A spatial analysis of wages and incomes in urban China: divergent means, convergent inequality', in Carl Riskin, Zhao Renwei and Li Shi (eds), *China's Retreat from Equality. Income Distribution and Economic Transition*, Armonk, NY: M.E. Sharpe.
Lipton, Michael (1977), *Why Poor People Stay Poor. Urban Bias in World Development*, Cambridge, MA: Harvard University Press.
Liu, Renwen and Fan Zaiqin (2001), 'Public security in 2000', in Ru Xin, Lu Xueyi and Shan Tianlun (eds), *Analysis of the Social Situation in China 2001*, Beijing: Social Sciences Documentation Publishing House (in Chinese).
Lu, Xueyi (2001), 'Problems in rural China', in Ru Xin, Lu Xueyi and Shan Tianlun (eds), *Analysis of the Social Situation in China 2001*, Beijing: Social Sciences Documentation Publishing House (in Chinese).
Moore, Mick (1993), 'Economic structure and the politics of sectoral bias: East Asian and other cases', *Journal of Development Studies*, **29** (4), 79–128.
Project Team of the Academy of Macroeconomics, State Commission of Planning and Development (2001), 'Analysis of the impact of income inequality and its acceptability', *Management World (China)*, **5**, 44–57.
Smith, Adam (1776), *The Wealth of Nations*, London: Everyman's Library (1910 edition).

3. Socialist fetters? Land tenure and economic growth in post-Mao rural China

Mark D. Brenner

INTRODUCTION

By most measures, the performance of the Chinese economy over the past generation has been remarkable. In less than a quarter of a century China has evolved from a poor, largely agrarian, society into one of the world's leading industrial producers and among its largest economies. China has seen real GDP per capita increase more than sixfold between 1978 and 2002, and according to official statistics has lifted more than 200 million people out of poverty. Since the onset of reforms in 1978, few have provide more keen or consistent insights into the Chinese development experience than Keith Griffin, whose contributions to development economics we honor in these pages.

Keith was one of the early students of China's transition from central planning to a market-guided economy, and current scholars and policy-makers owe a debt to Keith for his many insights into China's reforms. In addition to providing some of the richest quantitative evidence on income distribution in the late collective era (for example, Griffin and Saith, 1981), Keith and his co-authors correctly predicted many of the dynamics of China's contemporary development. For example, both Griffin and Saith (ibid.) and Griffin (1984) foresaw the rapid growth of rural industry in China after the onset of reforms, along with the accompanying benefits (rapid labor absorption) and costs (sharp increases in rural income inequality). Keith and his early collaborators also recognized the unsustainability of the agricultural pricing policies adopted at the beginning of rural reform, and correctly predicted that the central government could not simultaneously maintain high above-quota prices while subsidizing food supplies for urban residents through artificially low prices.

This early work on China also explored the ways in which Maoist-era institutions struggled to balance egalitarian goals with efficiency considerations. Griffin and Saith (1981), for example, develop a model which demonstrates how egalitarian distribution of productive resources in the commune system will foster faster growth in the relatively poorer brigades or work teams, but how this equalizing tendency may be offset by the faster rate of capital accumulation by richer units. Although Griffin and Saith predicted that collective institutions would, on balance, tend to equalize the distribution of rural incomes, Griffin (1984) was quick to recognize how piecemeal reforms were unraveling the equalizing tendencies of rural institutions, most notably by weakening collective investments in rural infrastructure such as irrigation and by promoting non-farm agricultural employment.

Although this early work was path-breaking in its own right, Keith was unwilling to base his analyses solely on summary statistics provided by the Chinese State Statistical Bureau, or data gathered from individual communes or county governments. Indeed in 1988 he led a team of researchers from within and outside of China in the most ambitious study of poverty and inequality ever conducted by independent scholars. The main findings of this project – too numerous to detail here – were drawn together in Griffin and Zhao (1993a). The importance of this work was succinctly captured by one reviewer when he noted that '[f]or some time to come, efforts to study inequality in China will be measured against the standards established in *The Distribution of Income in China*' (Whyte, 1994). This initial effort led to two subsequent household surveys, in 1995 and 2002, which continue to serve as the best publicly available data on the dynamics of China market transition.

In what follows, I build on Keith's China scholarship, and utilize some of the data he helped produce, to examine the impact of Maoist-era economic and political institutions on the rapid economic growth in rural China during the reform period. This integrated analysis reveals the important ways in which Maoist-era initiatives and institutions set the stage for rapid agricultural growth in the early 1980s. It also demonstrates the crucial role that local government behavior and the local institutions of land tenure played in stemming rising inequality in the Chinese countryside during the transition period. However, as I demonstrate, local governments are struggling to counteract the disequalizing effects of market development in agriculture, let alone address the disequalizing effects that these local governments have themselves induced through their vigorous promotion of township and village enterprises. Unfortunately, without more aggressive measures to address these market-driven inequalities, China now seems poised for a definitive abandonment of its egalitarian legacy.

THE LAND TENURE SYSTEM IN RURAL CHINA

Throughout China's history, land and its distribution have been central to any understanding of the country's complex political economy. Land tenure issues have frequently offered a window into larger national debates over economic policy, political orientation and development strategy. Nowhere is this more true than with the implementation of the Household Responsibility System (HRS) in the early 1980s, which returned farming decisions, and residual claimancy of the agricultural surplus, to rural households. This series of reforms has sparked a vigorous debate amongst policy-makers and scholars regarding the relationship between land tenure and agricultural growth and investment. It has also produced heated disagreements as to what land tenure system is appropriate for rural China in the future, particularly as concerns full-scale land privatization.

At the heart of the controversy is the rapid acceleration of agricultural output in the early 1980s and its stagnation thereafter. The mainstream view attributed much of the increased agricultural growth in the early post-reform period to de-collectivization, which improved incentives for individual effort in the agricultural production process (McMillan et al., 1989; Lin, 1992). These scholars also contended that stagnation after the mid-1980s was due to the particular character of China's land reform, where individuals have long-term use-rights on land but land ownership continues to reside with the local government. This structure, it is argued, raised tenure insecurity and dampened investment incentives. Indeed the purported relationship between agricultural stagnation and China's two-tier land tenure system is what has led many to call for the full privatization of rural China's land markets (Feder et al., 1992; Wen, 1995).

Contrasted with this mainstream account of agricultural growth in the early 1980s, more recent empirical research has reached somewhat different conclusions. First, a range of scholars have reasserted the primacy of initial conditions in shaping reform-era agricultural expansion, particularly the transport and irrigation networks created during the Maoist period. For example Chris Bramall (1995, p. 732) reports on the Sichuan experience, where agricultural growth was spurred in part by reallocation of state investment towards water conservancy and fertilizer production, and rapid growth actually preceded substantial shifts in the land tenure system. Similar evidence is documented by Marc Blecher and Vivienne Shue (1996, p. 175) for Shulu county in Hebei province, where irrigation improvements in the late Maoist period more than doubled grain output, predating any reform in the land tenure system.

Scholars have also underscored the substantial influence that rising procurement prices had on agricultural growth in the early reform period, independent of the tenure system changes. Sicular (1993) for example has noted that the base quota prices rose by roughly 20 percent at the onset of reforms, and that above-quota prices rose by nearly 50 percent. Although supply price responses were clearly amplified by the shift of residual claimancy to the household, the price effects themselves are arguably the most important feature of the early 1980s, witnessed by the slowdown of agricultural growth with the introduction of the 'proportionate' (30:70 quota–non-quota) prices in 1985. This new pricing system reduced the profitability of agricultural production at the margin (at least for those households producing above-quota) and, it has been convincingly argued, led to a serious decline in overall agricultural output (Sicular, 1995).

Finally, in addition to favorable initial conditions and increased procurement prices, scholars have also emphasized the role that weather (Zhang and Carter, 1997) and public research and development (Fan and Pardey, 1997) played in sparking the agricultural growth in the early reform period. Taken together, this new work helps explain recent research on the role of tenure insecurity, which has found that full-scale privatization of agriculture would produce little in the way of efficiency gains (Li et al., 1998, Benjamin and Brandt, 2002) and may be inferior to the current two-tiered system on theoretical grounds as well (Dong, 1996). It also helps to explain the strong support that is displayed by Chinese peasants for the current land tenure system (Kung, 1995; Kung and Liu, 1997). What more recent empirical research does not address however is the link between the evolution of land distribution over the reform period; the role of local government in administering the two-tier system of land tenure; and the effect that this process has had on overall inequality – at least as measured by household per capita income – in the Chinese countryside. I now turn to a treatment of these issues.

THE CHANGING DISTRIBUTION OF LAND IN RURAL CHINA

The recent empirical work on agricultural growth and land tenure in rural China has promoted a renewed interest in understanding the complex and variegated forms of land tenancy found in the Chinese countryside (Liu et al., 1998; Carter and Yao, 1999; Krusekopf, 2002; Benjamin and Brandt, 2002). My own work in this area has focused on the evolution of land distribution since the onset of reforms, attempting to isolate the forces that underlie recent trends (Brenner, 2000, 2004). Using data from two national household income and expenditure surveys from 1988 and 1995, I have documented the changes observed in land distribution, examined the situation of large landholders and the landless, and explored land leasing practices between the two years.[1]

Table 3.1 presents a summary of this research. Before discussing these estimates it is important to highlight briefly the difference between the two measures reported for 1995 in columns three and four. In 1988 land is defined as the 'total cultivated land used by the household at the end of 1988'. In 1995 the survey instrument contains many more questions about landholding, which are used to construct a more disaggregated measure for that year. Defined as the combination of non-irrigated land, irrigated land, land left fallow and land leased out to others, net of land leased in from others, this disaggregated measure is the most

Table 3.1 Average landholdings and distribution of land, 1988 and 1995

Variable	1988	1995 baseline	1995 alternative
Average landholdings (*mu*)	10.2	6.3	7.5
		(11.79)	*(6.93)*
Median landholdings (*mu*)	6.2	5.0	5.7
		–	–
Gini coefficient for unadjusted landholdings	0.499	0.431	0.378
		(3.86)	*(6.92)*
Gini coefficient for irrigation-adjusted landholdings	0.465	0.414	0.365
		(3.47)	*(6.84)*
Gini coefficient for land value	0.323	0.393	–
		(11.64)	–
Gini coefficient for rural per capita income	0.332	0.416	–
		(16.4)	–

Source: Rows 1–5: Brenner (2004), Table 2. Row 6 is based on author's calculations. T-statistics testing 1995 against 1988 are in parentheses below each of the two 1995 estimates.

accurate description of economically productive land controlled by the household. However recognizing that this 'baseline' measure does not correspond exactly to the aggregate landholdings measure used for 1988, we have included an aggregate measure of cultivated landholdings for 1995 for comparison purposes, reported as the 'alternative'.

The first row reports the calculations for the average size of household landholdings.[2] Analyzing the figures for both years, we find that average landholdings are considerably less than a hectare per household, and have decreased quite considerably over the period. In 1988 average landholdings were 10.2 *mu* per household, declining to 6.3 *mu* per household in 1995 using a 'baseline' measure of landholdings, and to 7.5 *mu* per household using an 'alternative' definition of landholdings (15 *mu* equals one hectare). The magnitude of this shift, as I have detailed elsewhere, is due primarily to the presence of households with extremely large landholdings in our 1988 survey (Brenner, 2004). The effects of the upper tail on the 1988 distribution on the mean calculations can be seen immediately, if we compare instead the median household landholdings for the two years, presented in row 2 of Table 3.1. There we see that the median for 1988 was 6.2 *mu* per household, falling to 5.0 *mu* per household in 1995 for our disaggregated measure, and 5.7 *mu* per household for our aggregate measure. Although the trend of declining cultivable land per household remains apparent, its magnitude is greatly attenuated.

Turning to the distribution of land in physical units, we can see from row 3 of Table 3.1 that land has become more equally distributed on a per capita basis over the period. The Gini coefficient falls statistically significantly, from 0.499 in 1988 to 0.431 in 1995. This decline moreover is remarkably robust. If we consider our summary measure of landholdings, the Gini coefficient is even lower, falling to 0.378. This trend is surprising, given the rapid rise in rural income inequality documented for the same period by Khan and Riskin (2001), and summarized in row 6. There we see that the Gini coefficient for per capita income rose from 0.332 in 1988 to 0.416, giving credence to the more general perception that the rapid growth experienced since the early 1980s has led to substantially uneven development across the various regions of the country.[3]

It is also clear that declining land inequality is not an artifact of quality differences. Row 4 presents Gini coefficient estimates for irrigation-adjusted land holdings in both years, falling from 0.465 in 1988 to 0.414 in 1995 for our baseline measure and 0.365 for our alternative.[4] In addition to displaying a virtually identical pattern to unadjusted landholdings, it is also important to note that adjusting for land quality actually lowers measured inequality. Finally, row 5 provides estimates for the distribution of land in value terms.[5] These results serve as an interesting counterpoint to our analysis of land in physical units, since land in value terms has actually become more unequal over the period in question, with the Gini coefficent rising from 0.323 in 1988 to 0.393 in 1995.

How does China's land distribution compare with other countries? Although we have no means by which to compare the distribution of land values, data gathered from the Food and Agriculture Organization (FAO) allows us to make comparisons based on physical holdings. What we find is that even prior to this sharp decline in inequality between 1988 and 1995, land distribution in China was remarkably equal by international standards. For example the Gini coefficient for landholdings in China is lower than in every Latin American country for which data are reported, and these differences are substantial. In the FAO data Gini coefficients range from 0.66 in Honduras, to 0.85 in Brazil, to 0.93 in Paraguay. Even in Asia, land distribution is more skewed than in China, with Gini coefficient estimates of 0.53 for Vietnam, 0.55 for the Philippines and 0.58 for India (FAO, 1997).[6]

LOCAL GOVERNMENTS AND LAND DISTRIBUTION IN RURAL CHINA

What explains this 'double movement' of land distribution? Do our two surveys offer any clues as to their origins or underlying causes? Although our survey data were not designed to answer these questions directly, they do offer some clues. Based on our data, as well as existing research, the first and most likely explanation for rising equality in landholdings is the practice of land reallocation at the village level that has become increasingly widespread in rural China. As discussed above, the process of de-collectivization left China with a land tenure system straddling two eras. 'Topsoil rights' have been controversially privatized, leaving cultivating households as residual claimants in the production process. Villages or other local political units however have retained 'subsoil rights', allowing them to reclaim the land of households who leave farming altogether, or to reallocate land between households when circumstances warrant.

Recent evidence suggests that such reallocation has become increasingly common. For example Kung (1995), in his survey of four counties in rural Sichuan and Hunan, finds that 90 percent of the 400 sample households have experienced land readjustments, with 52 percent having experienced five or more since de-collectivization. Blecher and Shue (1996, p. 193) report a similarly frequent land reallocation system at work in Shulu county. Comparable evidence has been found in more extensive surveys (for example, He, 1995; Benjamin and Brandt, 2002; Krusekopf, 2002) and in more in-depth case study work (for example Judd, 1992). It is important to note that these studies have all concluded that the guiding principle behind these redistributions – much like the initial ones made immediately following de-collectivization – is the egalitarian distribution of the landed wealth of local communities. For example, Kung reports that 85 percent of the readjustments which took place in his four-county sample were made on a per-capita basis, usually to account for changes in household size due to births, deaths or marriages. Judd, in her work, also found that the first readjustments in her case study village were made on per-capita terms, modifying the initial distribution which was based on 'labor power units'. Blecher and Shue (1996) also find both per capita and per agricultural worker allocations in Shulu county, making note of the way in which some villages in the county are explicitly accounting for the fact that an increasing share of households have members working in non-farm economic activity when making their reallocation decisions.

This land reallocation process has led to a host of interpretations among China scholars. One interesting variant is the work of Burgess (1997), who argues that this readjustment process is more complex than merely equalizing per capita or per worker landholdings. He offers evidence for the argument that reallocation is better understood as a means for guaranteeing the food security and nutritional requirements of households at the village level, with the surprising result that not only has this egalitarian redistribution dramatically reduced food poverty, thereby enhancing equity, but it has also been found not to affect productivity negatively. On the basis of his regression analysis he concludes that in the absence of fully developed markets for labor and credit, the land-tenure system in the Chinese countryside allows for the achievement of the twin objectives of equity and efficiency, rather than creating the often-asserted trade-off between them.[7]

Whether or not this more complex allocation rule is at the heart of local land distribution policies, it is apparent that reallocation is likely to have served in the reduction of observed inequality in landholdings. One reason is that reallocation appears to have started only shortly before our 1988 survey.[8] The timing of initial reallocation means that many villages in our 1988 survey were likely to have had mismatches in land-person ratios that were as yet unaddressed by local officials. Such mismatches were much less probable by 1995.[9] It also bears mentioning that the implementation and expansion of land reallocation in rural China has coincided with the period of fiscal decentralization, which has increasingly forced local governments to rely on fees, taxes and levies to sustain local budgets. The fact that these fees are often apportioned based on per-*mu* landholdings only serves to reinforce the argument that extremely large landholders in 1988 were likely to have reduced their allocations by 1995 due to economic – as well as administrative or social – pressure.

If administrative land reallocation accounts for the declines in land inequality in physical units, what accounts for the increased inequality in value terms? As I have detailed elsewhere, the origins of this rise in inequality of land value have their origins in two related phenomena (Brenner, 2004). First is the widening gap between production for market and for self-consumption. Over the period of our two surveys rural households saw agricultural procurement prices increase dramatically, leading to a rise in the commercialization rate of agricultural output. However, many rural households continued to rely heavily on self-provisioning, with more than 45 percent of the gross value of agricultural output being consumed by the producing household in both years. Given the relatively weak incentives to produce for the market in 1988 and much stronger ones in 1995, we have reason to suspect that it is this price response which has increased the dispersion of agricultural output value (and hence land value) between 1988 and 1995. There also appears to be some empirical support for this explanation within our two surveys.[10]

Similarly there is also evidence to support a second explanation, which links off-farm employment to rising land value inequality. As has been frequently documented, returns to non-farm employment continue to outpace the growth of those for agricultural activity.[11] As a result, a greater and greater percentage of the rural labor force is shifting away from agriculture. This is producing an interesting phenomenon, where many rural households continue to retain their land allocations and continue to farm, doing so however with part-time household labor.[12] It is possible that this reduction in household labor inputs for some households has also contributed to increasingly dispersed returns in the gross value of agricultural output. Such an explanation would be consistent with the trends in land value inequality, and is also consistent with the data from our two surveys.[13] While available evidence does not definitively establish that low-value landholders are indeed farming with part-time labor, thereby indirectly increasing measured inequality in land value, it is consistent with such a proposition. Moreover given recent case study evidence, it is becoming an increasingly more reasonable conclusion to draw.[14]

While it is unclear from this discussion what the net effect of this 'double movement' in land distribution will be, it is important to note that ongoing readjustments of landholdings are hardly the only function that the 'local state' has shouldered in the post-Mao period. Indeed as many scholars have demonstrated, local governments have played a central role in the rapid economic growth of the reform era, particularly with regard to the creation and expansion of township and village enterprises (Oi, 1999; Oi and Walder, 1999; Whiting, 2001). Perhaps the most formal theoretical description of this type of official action is 'local state corporatism', a term used by Jean Oi to capture the way in which 'narrow interests within society are organized and integrated so as to achieve higher-order goals – namely stability and economic growth for the state as a whole' (Oi, 1999, p. 12).

Oi argues that local governments emerged as developmental engines due in large part to two reforms: the dismantling of collective agriculture and the reassignment of rights to residual revenue from local industry. Decollectivization deprived local governments of a share of agricultural revenue, at the same time that local officials were being required to undertake a greater proportion of agricultural investment. Had no other changes been implemented this loss of revenue would have created a fiscal crisis for local governments. Fortunately, at least for counties and townships, at the same time as they were being deprived of a revenue stream from agriculture, they were being accorded rights to the residual from local enterprise production. This created the strong incentive for all three levels of local government to develop industrial capacity, leading to the dynamic, albeit unevenly distributed development of rural industry throughout the reform period.

In this context, some scholars have argued that the continued redistribution of land by local governments should be viewed as the major social welfare program managed by the 'local state'. Burgess, for example, notes that guaranteeing households access to the means for satisfying their food needs can be an efficient way of coping with the absence of other social insurance. Such an approach can also be seen as a complement to the development objectives of local governments, as land redistribution is likely to have only minimal effects on non-farm economic opportunities. While further research is necessary to buttress the contention that land redistribution has been an important dimension of local state corporatism, it is possible to evaluate the impact that such redistribution has had on equity, particularly as concerns the distribution of household income. We can also begin to measure the relative importance of rising inequality of land value *vis-à-vis* declining land inequality in physical units as they simultaneously interact with the distribution of income.

THE EQUALIZING AND DISEQUALIZING EFFECTS OF LAND DISTRIBUTION ON INCOME DISTRIBUTION

We earlier established that at the same time as per capita income and the value of land was becoming much more unequally distributed in the Chinese countryside, the distribution of land in physical units was becoming substantially more equal. In this section we want to examine the relationship between these two contradictory movements in land inequality as they relate to income distribution. One analytically appealing approach to this issue is to ask the counterfactual question: 'What would rural income distribution have been if the distribution of land in physical units had remained the same as it was in 1988?' In similar fashion, faced with the rising dispersion of land in value terms, we can ask the related question: 'What would rural income distribution have been if the distribution of land in value terms had remained the same as it was in 1988?' These sorts of counterfactual exercises have long been common in the field of applied econometrics (the Oaxaca wage decomposition is a classic example); however recent advances in nonparametric econometrics coupled with the dramatic expansion of computing power now permit much more intricate counterfactual calculations.

In this section I will employ a counterfactual estimation method similar to the widely cited article by DiNardo et al. (1996) to examine the relationship between land distribution and per capita income inequality. Following Deaton (2003) I expand the DiNardo et al. approach to a fully nonparametric specification. In the simplest terms, the counterfactual estimation method I utilize is as follows.

Let per capita household income be defined as Y_{95}, which a function of landholdings L_{95} and other household attributes, represented by the vector X_{95}. This relationship is represented in equation (3.1):

$$Y_{95} = F(L_{95}, X_{95}) \tag{3.1}$$

If we take $F(\bullet)$ to be the joint cumulative distribution function of land and other household attributes, then we can also represent this relationship as follows in equation (3.2):

$$Y_{95} = F_{95}\,(X \mid L)g_{95}\,(L) \tag{3.2}$$

where $F(\bullet)$ now represents the cumulative density function conditional on landholdings, multiplied times the marginal density function for land $g(\bullet)$. The essence of our counterfactual estimation method can then be illustrated in equation (3.3):

$$Y_{95}^{CF} = F_{95}\,(X \mid L)g_{88}\,(L) \tag{3.3}$$

Table 3.2 Actual and counterfactual distributions of income for rural China

Actual variance for log of per capita income, 1995	0.508
Counterfactual variance for log per capita income in 1995, assuming the 1988 distribution of land	0.517
Percentage increase in inequality of per capita income for 1995, assuming the 1988 distribution of land	1.7
Counterfactual variance for log per capita income in 1995, assuming the 1988 distribution of land value	0.484
Percentage increase in inequality of per capita income for 1995, assuming the 1988 distribution of land value	–4.7

Here we simply substitute the density function for land estimated for 1988 in place of the actual density function for land observed in 1995. Thanks to advances in nonparametric estimation within most mainstream statistical packages, this technique can be readily implemented, using local linear regression techniques to estimate $F(\bullet)$ in equation (3.3) and kernel density estimation methods for $g(\bullet)$. Performing these calculations with data from 1988 and 1995 allows us to produce the statistics reported in Table 3.2.

Following Deaton, we will utilize the variance of logarithm of per capita household income as our measures of inequality. In row 1 of this table we report the actual variance for 1995, a value of 0.508. In row 2 we estimate the counterfactual variance for 1995, assuming that the distribution of land in physical units was unchanged from 1988. Our counterfactual variance of log per capita income is 0.517 in this case. As noted at the beginning of this section, this value represents the income distribution that would have prevailed in 1995 were the distribution of land in physical units the same in 1995 as it was in 1988. We see from row 3 of Table 3.2 that under such a scenario income inequality would be approximately 2 percent higher than it actually was in that year. Given the dramatic reduction in land inequality observed in Table 3.1 (where the Gini coefficients fall from 0.499 to 0.431) this is a somewhat surprising result, unless it is considered in conjunction with the changes in land distribution in value terms.

Given the rise in land value inequality observed over the same period, we must also take account of this movement with a counterfactual variance of log per capita income. We do so in row 4, where our counterfactual measure is equal to 0.484. From row 5, we see that the variance of log per capita income would have actually fallen by 5 percent had the distribution of land in value terms remained unchanged between 1988 and 1995. In this context, any reduction in total income inequality owing to an improved distribution of land in physical units is impressive. However the different magnitudes highlight the quandary facing local governments in the Chinese countryside. The spread of market forces in agriculture has placed greater and greater limits on the ability of the local state to pursue egalitarian goals.

CONCLUSION

In this chapter I have reviewed the evidence concerning the changing distribution of land in rural China in the post-Mao era. What I find is that in contrast with virtually every other dimension of economic life in the countryside, physical landholdings are becoming more equal over the reform period. I argue that this is due in part to the nature of the land tenure system in rural China, where rural households have long-term use rights, but local governments retain ownership of the land itself. This two-tier land tenure system has permitted the local institutions of government to make a practice of periodically adjusting landholdings to account for demographic and other shifts in the rural population. By virtually all accounts this intermittent redistribution continues to be guided by egalitarian considerations. Unfortunately, as I also document, the equalized distribution of landholdings in physical terms has also been undermined by market forces, which have increased, among other things, the dispersion of land value. As I show in the previous section, had the value of landholdings remained unchanged over the period, income inequality would have been reduced by 5 percent. Because of the contradictory movement of land distribution, I calculate that local governments were only able to lower income inequality by 2 percent by attenuating land inequalities over the 1988 to 1995 period. From this result I conclude that although theorists of local state corporatism have said little about the social welfare role of a local developmental state, it seems clear that in the aggregate local governments are promoting equity in modest ways, as well as spurring economic growth.

In closing, it is important to note that this rather sanguine conclusion that local governments have helped offset rapidly rising income inequality must be qualified in at least two additional ways. Firstly, as has been noted by several scholars, the development of local collective enterprises has not been politically neutral. Like all states, local governments in China represent different constellations of interests. Several authors have argued that the development of local enterprise has only strengthened the concentration of power and property in the hands of lower-level government officials, serving neither developmental nor equity objectives (Sargeson and Zhang, 1999; Unger and Chan, 1999). Secondly, it is also clear from available evidence that other local government actions to promote growth have not been 'inequality neutral', and unfortunately have had effects running counter to local government interventions in the land market. Clearly the most important among these contradictory effects are local efforts to develop township and village enterprises, which are after all the focus of most studies of local government behavior (for example Oi, 1999; Whiting, 2001). As most studies of TVE development make clear, their distribution across rural China is highly geographically skewed towards the coastal regions, exacerbating inter-regional inequality. Moreover as Khan and Riskin (2001, p. 30) have made clear, rural wage income (much of it derived from TVEs) has had an overall disequalizing effect during the reforms. By their calculations wage income has risen from 8.73 to 22.38 percent of rural income on average and its contribution to overall inequality has risen from 18.3 percent in 1988 to 39.7 percent by 1995. These facts beg the question of the relative magnitude of the disequalizing effects of TVE wage income on overall household income, something which I must leave to future research. Only then can we get a more complete picture of the disequalizing effects of local government promotion of TVEs *vis-à-vis* its equity-inspired land reallocations.

NOTES

1. The surveys in question were designed and conducted by scholars at the Chinese Academy of Social Sciences' Institute of Economics (CASS), and provide the only publicly available, nationally representative household data from mainland China in the reform era. The 1988 and 1995 data are available through the Inter-University Consortium for Political and Social Research, holding numbers 9836 and 3012, respectively. See Griffin and Zhao (1993b) and Riskin et al. (2000) for more details.
2. These calculations are based on data from the 19 provinces common to both the 1995 and 1988 data.
3. See the discussion in Ke (1996) and Knight and Song (1990).
4. As I have documented elsewhere, we adjust for land quality using a somewhat crude measure, counting 1 *mu* of irrigated land as equivalent to two *mu* of unirrigated land. See Brenner (2004) for details.
5. To the chagrin of many Western scholars and policy-makers, markets for land have been stubbornly slow to emerge in rural China. Moreover rental markets, while enjoying some limited adoption, are still in an embryonic stage. Thus, estimating the 'value' of land, through either its market sale or rental price, is at present an unreliable method for valuation. Therefore we impute the value of land based on the gross value of agricultural output (see Brenner, 2000 for more details).
6. FAO figures are from the 1990 World Census of Agriculture. It is important to note that the Gini calculations reported by the FAO are by and large calculated on the basis of operational holdings. This understates total inequality by both failing to differentiate between owned versus rented land and by ignoring landless households.
7. Dong (1996) also elaborates on the degree to which the present 'two-tiered' land tenure system is optimal, given the pervasiveness of incomplete or missing markets in rural China, particularly for labor and credit.
8. Both Kung and Judd for example find the first reallocation occurring in 1986 for villages in their respective studies.
9. We must re-emphasize however that neither the households, nor villages or counties, sampled in 1995 correspond to those sampled in 1988, thus we have no way of verifying if that is indeed what happened. However if these patterns described above do accurately reflect the experience of many areas in rural China with regard to land reallocation, it is therefore not surprising that we find evidence of such in our 1995 work.

10. Indeed we find evidence to this effect, calculating the Spearman rank correlation coefficient between per capita land value and the commercialization rate of agricultural output, which rises from 0.42 in 1988 to 0.62 in 1995, both significant at the 1 percent level.
11. See for example Khan and Riskin (2001).
12. See for example Croll and Ping (1997) and Wu and Meng (1997).
13. This comes from the fact that in 1988 each decile of the land value distribution reported between 43 and 50 percent of the households having access to non-farm employment, either locally or through rural out-migration. By 1995 that range had widened, with between 44 and 65 percent of the households reporting access to off-farm employment opportunities. More importantly, in both years the decile with the lowest average land value reported the highest average access to non-farm employment, and vice versa. As these figures indicate, between 1988 and 1995 the lowest land value decile witnessed a 30 percent increase in access to off-farm employment, whereas the highest decile experienced a slight decline of 6 percent.
14. Another interesting aspect of the role of part-time farming in raising land value inequality is its potential role in equalizing land distribution in physical terms. Indeed if farming is becoming an increasingly part-time occupation for most household labor, it is possible that this is reinforcing the role of land distribution as a means of ensuring food security and basic welfare discussed at length by Burgess (1997). If so, it is not surprising that village-level allocations are becoming increasingly more equal over time, nor that such egalitarian distributions enjoy overwhelming support from the rural population, as discussed by Dong (1996).

REFERENCES

Benjamin, Dwayne and Loren Brandt (2002), 'Property rights, labour markets, and efficiency in a transition economy: the case of rural China', *Canadian Journal of Economics*, **35** (4), 689–716.

Blecher, Marc and Vivienne Shue (1996), *Tethered Deer: Government and Economy in a Chinese County*, Palo Alto, CA: Stanford University Press.

Bramall, Chris (1995), 'Origins of the agricultural "miracle": some evidence from Sichuan', *China Quarterly*, **143** (September), 731–55.

Bramall, Chris (2000), *Sources of Chinese Economic Growth, 1978–1996*, Oxford: Oxford University Press.

Brenner, Mark D. (2000), 'Reexamining the distribution of wealth in rural China', PhD dissertation, University of California, Riverside.

Brenner, Mark D. (2004), 'The evolution of land distribution in reform-era China', University of Massachusetts Political Economy Research Institute, mimeo.

Burgess, Robin (1997), 'Land, welfare and efficiency in rural China', London School of Economics, mimeo.

Carter, Michael and Yang Yao (1999), 'Market versus administrative reallocation of agricultural land in a period of rapid industrialization', World Bank Policy Research working paper no. 2203, Washington, DC: World Bank.

Croll, Elisabeth and Ping Huang (1997), 'Migration for and against agriculture in eight Chinese villages', *China Quarterly*, **149**, 128–46.

Deaton, Angus (2003), 'Adjusted Indian poverty estimates for 1999–2000', *Economic and Political Weekly*, 25 January.

DiNardo, John, Nicole M. Fortin and Thomas Lemieux (1996), 'Labor market institutions and the distribution of wages, 1973–1992: a semiparametric approach', *Econometrica*, **64** (5), 1001–44.

Dong, Xiao-Yuan (1996), 'Two-tier land tenure system and sustained economic growth in post-1978 rural China', *World Development*, **24** (5), 915–28.

Fan, Shenggen and Philip Pardey (1997), 'Research, productivity, and output growth in Chinese agriculture', *Journal of Development Economics*, **53** (1), 115–37.

Feder, Gershon, Lawrence J. Lau, Justin Y. Lin and Xiaopeng Luo (1992), 'The determinants of farm investment and residential construction in post-reform China', *Economic Development and Cultural Change*, **41** (1), 1–26.

Griffin, Keith (ed.) (1984), *Institutional Reform and Economic Development in the Chinese Countryside*, London: Macmillan and (1987) Hong Kong: Chinese University Press.

Griffin, Keith and Zhao Renwei (eds) (1993a), *The Distribution of Income in China*, London: Macmillan.

Griffin, Keith and Zhao Renwei (1993b), 'Chinese Household Income Project, 1988' (Computer file). New York: Hunter College Academic Computing Services (producer, 1992), Ann Arbor, MI: Inter-university Consortium for Political and Social Research (distributor).

Griffin, Keith and Ashwani Saith (1981), *Growth and Equality in Rural China*, Bangkok: International Labour Organization.

Food and Agriculture Organization of the United Nations (FAO) (1997), *Report on the 1990 World Census of Agriculture: International Comparison and Primary Results by Country (1986-1995)*, statistical development series no. 9, Rome: United Nations.

He, Daofeng (1995), 'Changes in the rural land tenure system at the village level', in *Transition of China's Rural Land System*, University of Wisconsin Land Tenure Center, LTC paper 151, pp. 69–95.

Judd, Ellen (1992), 'Land divided, land united', *China Quarterly*, June (130), 338–56.

Ke, Bingsheng (1996), 'Regional inequality in rural development', in Ross Garnaut, Shutian Guo and Guonan Ma (eds), *The Third Revolution in the Chinese Countryside*, New York: Cambridge University Press, pp. 245–55.

Khan, Azizur R. and Carl Riskin (2001), *Inequality and Poverty in China in the Age of Globalization*, Oxford: Oxford University Press.

Knight, John and Lina Song (1990), 'The determinants of urban income inequality in China', *Oxford Bulletin of Economics and Statistics*, **53** (2), 123–54.

Krusekopf, Charles C. (2002), 'Diversity in land-tenure arrangements under the household responsibility system in China', *China Economic Review*, **13** (2–3), 297–312.

Kung, James Kaisung (1995), 'Equal entitlement versus tenure security under a regime of collective property rights: peasants' preference for institutions in post-reform Chinese agriculture', *Journal of Comparative Economics*, **21**, 82–111.

Kung, James Kaisung and Shouying Liu (1997), 'Farmers' preferences regarding ownership and land tenure in post-Mao China: unexpected evidence from eight counties', *China Journal*, **38**, 33–63.

Li, Guo, Scott Rozelle and Loren Brandt (1998), 'Land rights, and farmer investment incentives in China', *Agricultural Economics*, **19** (1–2), 63–71.

Lin, Justin Yifu (1992), 'Rural reforms and agricultural growth in China', *American Economic Review*, **82** (1), 34–51.

Liu, Shouying, Michael Carter and Yang Yao (1998), 'Dimensions and diversity of property rights in rural China: dilemmas on the road to further reform', *World Development*, **26** (10), 1789–806.

McMillan, J., J. Whalley and Lijing Zhu (1989), 'The impact of China's economic reforms on agricultural productivity growth', *Journal of Political Economy*, **98**, 781–807.

Oi, Jean C. (1995), 'The role of the state in China's transitional economy', *China Quarterly*, December (144), 1132–49.

Oi, Jean C. (1999), *Rural China Takes Off: Institutional Foundations of Economic Reform*, Berkeley, CA: University of California Press.

Oi, Jean C. and Andrew Walder (eds) (1999), *Property Rights and Economic Reform in China*, Palo Alto, CA: Stanford University Press.

Riskin, Carl, Zhao Renwei and Li Shi (2000), 'Chinese Household Income Project, 1995' (computer file), ICPSR version, Amherst, MA: University of Massachusetts Political Economy Research Institute (producer, 2000), Ann Arbor, MI: Inter-university Consortium for Political and Social Research (distributor).

Riskin, Carl, Zhao Renwei and Li Shi (eds) (2001), *China's Retreat from Equality*, Armonk, NY: M.E. Sharpe.

Sargeson, Sally and Jian Zhang (1999), 'Inheritors of the boom: private enterprise and the role of local government in a rural south China township', *China Journal*, July (42), 45–74.

Sicular, Terry (1993), 'China's agricultural policy during the reform period', in Joint Economic Committee of the US Congress, *China's Economic Dilemmas in the 1990's: The Problems of Reforms, Modernization and Independence*, New York: M.E. Sharpe, pp. 340–64.

Sicular, Terry (1995), 'Redefining state, plan and market: China's reforms in agricultural commerce', *China Quarterly*, **154** (December), 1020–46.

Unger, Jonathan and Anita Chan (1999), 'Inheritors of the boom: private enterprise and the role of local government in a rural south China township', *China Journal*, July (42), 45–74.

Wen, G.J. (1995), 'The land tenure system and its saving and investment mechanism: the case of modern China', *Asian Economic Journal*, **9** (31), 233–59.

Whiting, Susan H. (2001), *Power and Wealth in Rural China: The Political Economy of Institutional Change*, New York: Cambridge University Press.

Whyte, M.K. (1994), 'Review of the distribution of income in China', in Keith Griffin and Zhao Renwei (eds), *China Quarterly*, **140**, pp. 1176–9.

Wu, H.X. and X. Weng (1997), 'The direct impact of the reallocation of farm labour grain production in China', *China Economic Review*, **7** (2), 105–22.

Zhang, Bin and Colin A. Carter (1997), 'Reforms, the weather, and productivity growth in China's grain sector', *American Journal of Agricultural Economics*, **79** (4), 1266–77.

PART II

Agriculture and Rural Poverty

4. A future for small farms? Biodiversity and sustainable agriculture

James K. Boyce*

INTRODUCTION

The small farmer is today an endangered species. In the industrialized countries of the global North, the number of farmers has been dwindling for generations. In the United States for example, the total number of farms fell from 6.8 million in 1935 to fewer than 2 million today (Stam and Dixon, 2004). Referring to trends in Europe, where the farming population is now declining by 3 percent annually, a recent *New York Times* editorial derides the idea that 'every village that was inhabited in Charlemagne's day must be sustained', and declares that 'more consolidation, in the form of larger-scale farming and an abandonment of absurdly inefficient production, is inevitable'.[1]

In the developing countries of the global South, governments and international agencies alike appear to be intent on following the same path. Fifty years after the publication of Sir Arthur Lewis's (1954) dual-economy model, in which economic development was identified with the transfer of labor from the 'subsistence' agricultural sector to the 'capitalist' industrial sector, the assumption that small farms are destined for the dustbin of history remains conventional wisdom. 'Those *indios*,' a Guatemalan official told me a few years ago, referring to the country's indigenous majority. 'As long as they grow maize just like their grandparents, they'll be poor just like their grandparents.'[2]

Rather than simply letting nature take its ostensible course, governments often seek to speed it along, promoting agricultural 'modernization' by means of subsidies and other policies that favor large-scale farming, purchases of farm machinery and chemical inputs, and more uniformity in the choice of crops and varieties. In a sense, these policies aim to subsume agriculture itself, and not only its erstwhile labor force, into the industrial economy. Even if the demise of the small farm were not a foregone conclusion, these policies could make it a self-fulfilling prophecy.

In the face of these trends, an intrepid band of economists has rallied to the defense of small farms on grounds of both equity and efficiency. Prominent among them is Keith Griffin, who warned in his classic study, *The Political Economy of Agrarian Change* (1979, p. xxii) against policies that could 'lead to the creation of an inefficient and capital intensive agriculture which is incapable of producing an adequate livelihood for the mass of the rural population'. Over the years, Griffin has held fast to this position. In a recent article co-authored with his colleagues Azizur Rahman Khan and Amy Ickowitz (2002, p. 320), he insists that 'family farms use resources efficiently and can be just as dynamic as large farms'.

Among economists, the arguments in favor of small farms have gained ground in the last few decades. The efficiency advantages of small farms – rooted in their labor intensity – have won increasing recognition, even in bastions of the development establishment such as the World Bank.[3] Yet policies on the ground have been slow to change. As Griffin (1979, p. 84) observed, the policy mix that favors larger farms is primarily attributable not to ignorance, but rather to the political influence of large landowners: 'Governments may claim to rule in the "national interest",' he wrote, 'but in reality they act in behalf of their supporters.' A shift toward pro-small farm policies is unlikely to be brought about by small farmers acting alone.

This chapter offers a further argument on behalf of small farms, based on their role in providing a crucial public good: the conservation of agricultural biodiversity.[4] From the highland maize plots of southern Mexico and Guatemala to the rice paddies of eastern India and Bangladesh, small farmers across the world sustain the crop genetic diversity that underpins humankind's long-term food security. Many of those who provide this public good are desperately poor, and their continued ability and willingness to cultivate diversity can no longer be taken for granted. Policies to reward small farmers for their contributions to global food security would help to ensure both their future and our own.

Of course, this does not mean that all small farms – or, in the *reductio ad absurdum* line of the *New York Times*, 'every village inhabited in Charlemagne's day' – should endure forever. Nor does it mean that we need to create living museums where the agricultural landscape is frozen in time. On the contrary, a hallmark of 'traditional' agriculture is precisely its *dynamism*: in the farmers' fields, the process that Charles Darwin termed 'artificial selection' – natural selection guided by human hands – yields a constant stream of new varieties, adapted to changing needs and changing environmental circumstances.[5] But to say that not all small farms, or all crop varieties, can or should survive is not to say that a world of large, monocultural farms is desirable or feasible as the endpoint of agricultural history. A productive and resilient world agriculture requires a diverse mix of crop varieties, agricultural techniques and farming systems. In this mix, there is a future for small farms.

HUMANS AS A KEYSTONE SPECIES

As early as the 1500s, Spanish settlers began to arrive in the valley of the upper Rio Grande, in what is now the south-western United States. To irrigate the semi-arid lands they found, the settlers constructed *acequias*, earthen channels that divert river water and carry it to valley slopes downstream. These gravity-fed irrigation systems transformed the landscape into a diverse agro-ecosystem that includes wetlands, fields and orchards with unique varieties of beans and fruit trees, riparian corridors for wildlife movement, and fertile soils built by generations of careful land stewardship.

Anthropologist Devon Peña (2003, p. 169) describes humans as the 'keystone species' of this *acequia* landscape mosaic – 'a species so central to the health of the ecosystem that without it many other species could not survive'. The idea that humans can act as a keystone species – playing a role in nature akin to that of beavers in the Canadian forests, or corals in ocean reefs – marks a profound departure from the image, widespread among environmentalists, of human beings as alien intruders whose 'ecological footprint' invariably tramples upon the fragile shoots of the natural world. Instead it evokes a more balanced assessment of the relationship between humans and nature, one in which humans can have positive impacts, as well as negative ones, on the richness and diversity of life.

Another striking illustration of the potential for positive human impacts has come to light in recent years in South America. About 10 per cent of the Amazonian region – with an area roughly the size of France – is covered by deep, dark soil known locally as *terra preta do indio* (dark earth of the Indians) that is prized for its long-lasting fertility. *Terra preta* is a remarkable exception to the general rule that tropical rainforest soils are poor in nutrients, and hence subject to rapid degradation once the forest cover is removed. Soil scientists have concluded that *terra preta* was created by the indigenous people who practiced 'slash-and-char' agroforestry in the region for two millennia.[6] An astonishing feature of *terra preta* is its capacity to regenerate itself: 'In a process reminiscent of dropping microorganism-rich starter into plain dough to create sourdough bread', scientists hypothesize that 'Amazonian peoples inoculated bad soil with a transforming bacterial charge' (Mann, 2002b, p. 52).

More generally, it is not an exaggeration to say that most people today depend for their very survival on the fruits of past human interactions with nature. If we pause to give thanks before we eat a meal, our gratitude should extend to predecessors who first domesticated plants and animals, and over the millennia created the many thousands of varieties of these species that underpin the world's agriculture. Crops such as wheat, rice, maize, potatoes and cotton did not appear on Earth by some happy circumstance. These and the other species on which we rely for our food and fiber arose in a process of 'coevolution' with human cultures. Beginning some 10000 years ago, the inhabitants of Asia Minor domesticated wheat and barley, grains whose seeds have the key property of not 'shattering' and falling to the ground as they ripen. Their counterparts in Asia gave us rice, a versatile plant whose roots can survive in continuously flooded fields. In the Andes, early Americans gave us the potato. In Mesoamerica, perhaps most remarkably of all, the forbearers of today's Mayan *campesinos* evolved maize from its wild relative, teosinte.[7] Were humans to vanish from the planet, these species would vanish in short order, too.

To term these developments 'beneficial' is of course to make a normative judgement. From a 'deep ecology' perspective in which humans are just another species, whose survival is of no greater consequence than that of any other, the judgement that the *acequia* ecosystem, or *terra preta* or food crops can be termed positive achievements might be questioned. If however our value system embraces a concern for the biosphere's capacity to sustain human well-being, then I think these deserve to be called improvements in the state of nature. To be sure, there are plenty of counterexamples where human activities have had negative environmental impacts. But positive impacts are part of our story, too.

SMALL FARMERS: CULTIVATORS OF DIVERSITY

Today, perhaps the single most important examples of humans acting as a keystone species are the agro-ecosystems that maintain the world's crop genetic diversity. Most of the 'keystone' people are small farmers. In part, this is because agricultural biodiversity is concentrated in regions of the world where small farms still predominate. In part too, it is because small farmers have comparative advantages in the cultivation of diversity.

Centers of Agricultural Biodiversity

The centers of origin of the world's crops are concentrated in a few places, known as 'Vavilov centers' after the great Russian botanist of the early 20th century, Nikolai Vavilov. Most of the Vavilov centers are in the developing countries of the global South (see Figure 4.1). Vavilov hypothesized that the ancient centers of crop origin tend to be the modern centers of crop diversity, a suggestion that by and large has stood the test of time. The logic behind this correlation is straightforward: crops evolve as farmers select seed for replanting from individual plants that perform best in the face of local variations in soils, rainfall, altitude, pest populations and so on. Diversity tends to be greatest where this process has had the longest time to unfold. In the Bengal delta for example, where 'a few inches difference in elevation in relation to expected flooding depth

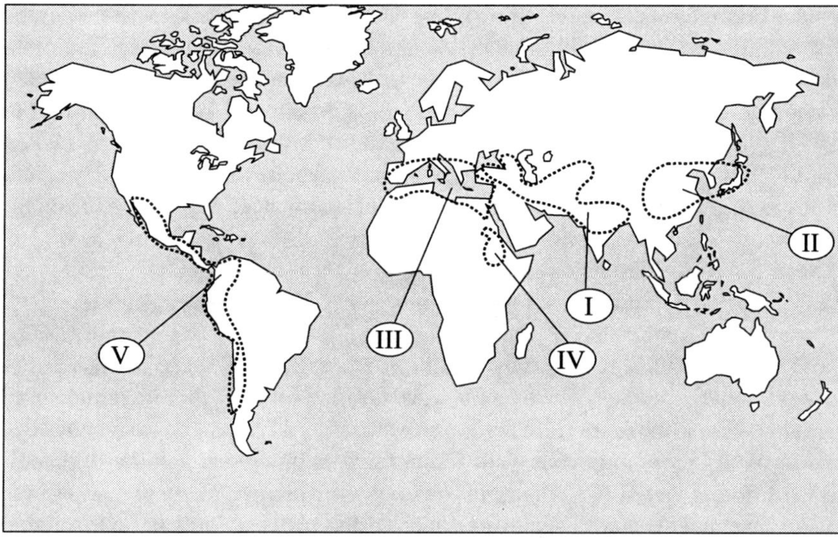

Key: I. Southwestern Asia; II. Eastern Asia; III. the Mediterranean area; IV. Ethiopia and Egypt; V. mountainous areas of Mexico, Central America, and South America.

Source: Vavilov (1992 [1926], p. 127).

Figure 4.1 Centers of origin of crops

and duration can cause farmers to plant different rice varieties', some 10000 different varieties of rice were being grown in the 1970s (Brammer, 1980, p. 25).

Darwin described this process in the opening chapter of *The Origin of Species*: 'The key is man's power of accumulative selection: nature gives successive variations; man adds them up in certain directions useful to him.' One of Darwin's examples was the strawberry, a fruit that was growing in popularity at the time: 'Gardeners picked out individual plants with slightly larger, earlier, or better fruit, and raised seedlings from them, and again picked out the best seedlings and bred from them.' In this way, Darwin explained, 'those many admirable varieties of the strawberry were raised which have appeared during the last half-century' (Darwin, 1859 [1952], pp. 18, 23).

As Vavilov documented, crop genetic diversity is distributed very unevenly across the globe. The available data on this point are remarkably sparse, but a rough indicator is the sources of seed samples that are stored in the world's largest 'gene banks', *ex situ* (off-site) collections maintained for possible future use by scientists and plant breeders. In the case of maize for example, Mexico accounted for 4220 of the maize accessions held at the International Maize and

Wheat Improvement Center (known by its Spanish acronym, CIMMYT) in the mid-1990s, and Guatemala for another 590; by contrast, the United States, with more than three times the maize acreage of Mexico and Guatemala combined, accounted for only 43 samples (Boyce, 1996). Mexican farmers today are believed to grow roughly 5000 different varieties of maize, whereas in the United States – where corn is sown on roughly 70 million acres – more than 70 percent of the acreage is planted with varieties 'based on no more than half a dozen inbred lines' (Goodman, 1995, p. 200).[8]

Comparative Advantages of Small Farmers in Cultivating Diversity

Around the world, it is generally small farms – especially those in the Vavilov centers – that practice high-diversity agriculture. Not only do individual small farmers often choose to cultivate several varieties of the same crop, but also, and probably more importantly, different farmers in a given locality often cultivate different varieties. Large farms, in contrast, are more likely to sow a single variety over a wide area. This inverse relationship between farm size and varietal diversity has several explanations.

Firstly, high-diversity farming is generally more labor-intensive than low-diversity farming. It takes more time and effort to cultivate varieties with different sowing dates, harvest times and other requirements than to practice varietal monoculture. Considerable labor also is needed to maintain the physical infrastructure – such as watercourses and terraces – that often supports high-diversity agriculture. As we know from the many studies of the relationship between farm size and labor use, smaller farms have a comparative advantage in labor-intensive operations. This is because they rely more on family labor, the 'real cost' of which is lower than the wage of hired labor, and because insofar as they do use hired laborers, small farmers have fewer supervision problems (not only is supervision easier on small farms, but also the need for supervision may be less by virtue of the narrower social distance between employer and employee).[9]

Secondly, high-diversity agriculture depends on the farmers' knowledge of different crop varieties and their relationships to microhabitat variations. Small farmers are the repositories of this knowledge. Without them, it would be harder not only to sustain agricultural biodiversity, but also to know the attributes of the varieties that are being sustained. Indigenous cultures are often particularly rich in this knowledge. For example the Mixe language, spoken by maize farmers in southern Oaxaca, Mexico, has words for 'a greater and richer number of stages of plant development (germination, flowering, leaf and whorl development, appearance of black color at base of kernels, etc.) than those existing in conventional scientific literature'.[10]

Thirdly, small farmers often predominate in 'marginal' agricultural environments where the spread of 'modern' varieties has been held in check by unfavorable growing conditions. Hilly terrain, as in the highlands of southern Mexico and Guatemala, is less suitable for monoculture and mechanization; similarly, in deeply flooded parts of the Bengal delta, the short-statured 'high-yielding' (that is, highly fertilizer-responsive) varieties cannot be grown. Such lands are relatively unattractive targets for appropriation and concentration by landowning elites. At the same time, they often have exceptionally high degrees of microenvironmental variation, which favors varietal diversification. In a single village in Oaxaca for example, researchers Raúl and Luis García-Barrios (1990) found that the *campesinos* distinguished among 17 different environments in which they grew 26 distinct varieties of maize. Similarly, Maori weavers in New Zealand recognize more than 80 distinct varieties of flax (Shand, 1997, p. 11, citing Heywood, 1995).

As already noted, 'traditional' agriculture is by no means static. The artificial selection process that created crop genetic diversity continues unabated in farmers' fields, leading botanists to refer to these fields as 'evolutionary gardens'.[11] In this process, the line between 'traditional' and 'modern' agriculture often becomes blurred, as small farmers adopt and adapt new varieties released by professional public-sector and private-sector plant breeders.[12] As Stephen Brush (1995) among others has observed, traditional varieties can coexist with modern varieties. Moreover even after the introduction of new varieties, the processes of cross-pollination, mutation and artificial selection continue to give rise to successive generations adapted to local conditions. In Bangladesh for example, by selecting seed from the tallest plants in fields of short-statured 'green-revolution' rice varieties, farmers developed in the space of a few years new varieties that are suitable for more deeply flooded fields.[13] Given the dynamic character of traditional agriculture, the 'traditional–modern' dichotomy is better described as a contrast between high-diversity and low-diversity agricultural ecosystems.

DIVERSITY AND EFFICIENCY

There is a fundamental tension between the 'efficiency' promoted by markets and a broader notion of efficiency, founded on long-term human well-being, that (1) encompasses externalities, both positive and negative; and (2) puts the welfare of future generations on a par with present-day welfare, rather than discounting it towards zero. The logic of the market puts little value on crop genetic diversity. Instead it dictates that in any given time and place all farmers should grow the same 'optimal' variety, tempered only by local differences in soils, climate and so on. Apart from some variations in response to local differences, the market puts no value on diversity *per se*: less profitable varieties are driven out by more profitable varieties. Yet in the long run, diversity is crucial if agriculture is to be resilient. The farmers who maintain diversity thus provide a positive externality, a social benefit that the market fails to reward.

The Varietal Relay Race

The basic problem with low-diversity agriculture is that time and nature do not stand still. Among the insects and plant pathogens that thrive in the green blanket of corn that covers the midsection of the United States every summer, the Darwinian process of survival of the fittest proceeds, favoring the evolution of new strains of pests that are particularly well adapted to the handful of corn varieties being grown on millions of acres of farmland. State and federal agricultural officials monitor the fields for outbreaks of new insect and plant disease threats. Plant breeders respond by screening their breeding lines for varieties with resistance to these new strains, and incorporating this resistance into the next generation of cultivars (cultivated varieties). The average commercial lifespan of a newly released corn variety in the US is only seven years, after which it is rendered obsolete by the emergence of new strains of insects or plant diseases (Duvick, 1984, p. 164). Surveys of a number of major crops undertaken for the UK Department of the Environment in the mid-1990s found that 'the viability of any given product is only about five years, with pests and disease being the primary factors for the obsolescence' (Swanson and Luxmoore, 1997, p. 98).

The same process occurs wherever agricultural 'modernization' results in a high degree of varietal uniformity. In the case of Asian rice agriculture for example, 'under the intensive cultivation practices, insect pests of short life span and heterogeneous population structure, such as the brown planthopper, can quickly adapt their genetic population structure in response to the resistance gene in the most widely grown cultivar' (Chang, 1995, p. 154). Rice breeders at the International Rice Research Institute (IRRI) in the Philippines and at national agricultural research institutions again must respond by releasing new varieties with resistance to the new threats.

Monocultural optimization not only creates an environment that favors evolution of virulent new pests and diseases. It also creates one in which, if and when such organisms emerge, they can trigger widespread crop failures. This genetic vulnerability – arising from the eggs-in-one-basket syndrome – is the soft underbelly of low-diversity agriculture. To cope with this vulnerability, plant breeders rely on 'diversity through time', breeding and releasing new crop varieties (Duvick, 1984; Duvick et al., 2004). In a sense then, 'low-diversity' agriculture is a misnomer: the viability of modern agriculture rests on the substitution of time-series variation for cross-sectional variation.

The stakes in this 'varietal relay race' are high, as was demonstrated in the United States in 1970, when the southern corn leaf blight destroyed 1 billion bushels of maize, including as much as half the harvest in some southern states.

The epidemic was caused by a new strain of a fungus, *Bipolaris maydis*, which was virulent on plants with a genetic makeup shared by 85 percent of the maize grown in the US at the time. Plant breeders were able to respond in the following year by incorporating genetic resistance that they found in some maize varieties grown in Africa. Scientists were 'shaken by how close the system had come to disaster', Mann (2004, p. 7) reports: 'they had been lucky that the problem was quickly contained, and luckier still that the African maize had not been supplanted by vulnerable modern hybrids'.

As the corn leaf blight example illustrates, the raw material for the varietal relay race ultimately comes from the crop genetic diversity bequeathed to us by previous generations and today sustained by small farmers around the world. In other words, the long-run sustainability of low-diversity agriculture rests on a continuing flow of biological inputs from the high-diversity agriculture. The irony is that by virtue of its superior short-run 'efficiency', modern agriculture is undermining the economic viability of traditional agriculture: the small farmers who cultivate diversity face increasing competition from the 'green revolution' at home, and from cheap agricultural imports from the industrialized countries. In the quest for high productivity, botanist Garrison Wilkes explains, we have 'built our roof with stones from the foundation'.[14]

The Need for *In Situ* Diversity

The seed collections held at public-sector agricultural research institutions around the world are storehouses of crop genetic diversity. When dried and kept under controlled temperature and humidity conditions, the seeds can remain viable for a number of years (often around three decades); if then planted, with care to prevent cross-pollination, the seed can be replicated and stored again. These *ex situ* 'gene banks' – including the wheat and maize collections at CIMMYT in Mexico, the rice collection at IRRI in the Philippines, the potato collection at the International Potato Center in Peru, and the US Department of Agriculture's National Seed Storage Laboratory (NSSL) in Fort Collins, Colorado (now called the National Center for Genetic Resources Preservation) – are public goods of immense value to humankind. They do not represent an adequate substitute for *in situ* (in-the-field) diversity however, for several reasons.

Firstly, the gene banks are not completely secure. Accidents, wars and chronic underfunding all make the survival of the stored seeds precarious. The world's largest *ex situ* collection of crop varieties is – or was – at the Vavilov Institute in what for a time was called Leningrad and now once again is called St. Petersburg. In their book, *Shattering*, Cary Fowler and Pat Mooney recount the drama that unfolded at the Vavilov Institute during the siege of Leningrad in the Second World War. With food supplies cut off by the German army, people ate dogs, cats and even grass in an effort to survive. In the end, more than half a million of the city's residents starved to death. The dead included staff members of the institute, who took extraordinary measures to safeguard seeds that they could have eaten to prolong their own lives. 'When all the world is in the flames of war,' a survivor recalls the staff telling each other, 'we will keep this collection for the future of all people' (Fowler and Mooney, 1990, pp. 221–2).

Today, plant breeders believe that most of the seeds held at the Vavilov Institute are no longer viable – in other words, they are dead. The reason is the inadequate maintenance and replication of the collection in the years before and since the break-up of the Soviet Union. A similar fate may have befallen what was once the world's second largest maize collection (after that of the Vavilov Institute) in Belgrade, the capital of the former Yugoslavia (Plucknett et al., 1987, p. 120). Even in relatively prosperous and stable nations, like the United States, accidents and funding shortages make the *ex situ* collections less than perfectly secure.[15]

A second reason why *ex situ* collections cannot adequately replace *in situ* diversity is that, at best, gene banks conserve only the existing stock of crop genetic diversity. They cannot mimic the ongoing flow of new varieties that happens in the farmer's field under the pressures of natural and artificial selection. 'A main object of *in situ* conservation', Brookfield (2001, p. 248) concludes, 'should be to enhance the processes that create genetic diversity, not to protect any actual body of genetic material.' It would require great hubris to imagine that we can safely terminate the coevolutionary process that small farmers have carried forward for thousands of years, and henceforth delegate all crop breeding to professional scientists mining the existing stock of diversity held in seed collections.

Finally, there is a world of difference between having a seed 'in the bank' and knowing what you have. Many genetic attributes can be observed only by growing plants in the microhabitats from which they come. The fact that a certain maize variety can withstand intermittent drought at four-week intervals for example, or that it is resistant to a particular strain of fungus, is not apparent unless it is grown in circumstances that reveal these qualities. Relying on artificial growth chambers to obtain this information would be very expensive. In effect, knowledge of the attributes of diverse varieties – knowledge that resides in the farmers who grow them – is a vital component of diversity itself. As Garrison Wilkes puts it, 'sun, soil, seeds, and smarts' are the 'four S's of farming'.[16]

None of the foregoing is meant to disparage the importance of *ex situ* collections or minimize their need for adequate financial support. *Ex situ* collections provide a conduit for plant breeders to access diversity, and they provide insurance against losses of diversity in the field. For example Cambodian rice varieties that were lost during the war and the disruption of the Khmer Rouge period were subsequently reintroduced using seeds that had been stored at

IRRI.[17] But the insecurity of *ex situ* collections, the importance of continued evolution in the field, and the need for information about varietal attributes all mean that the world needs *in situ* diversity too. *In situ* and *ex situ* diversity are complements, not substitutes.

SMALL FARMERS AS AN ENDANGERED SPECIES

From the highlands of Mesoamerica to the river deltas of south Asia, the ability of small farmers to sustain agricultural biodiversity is threatened by their lack of livelihood security. For example in Mexico – where there is a striking geographical correlation between maize diversity and the prevalence of infant malnutrition (see Figure 4.2) – outmigration from rural areas is highest 'where corn production is carried out in small plots, with local varieties, and where poverty is pervasive' (Nadal, 2000, p. 8).[18] In the last few years, rural outmigration has been limited by Mexico's economic crisis and the lack of urban employment opportunities, but this could change quickly if the economy improves (Ackerman et al., 2003). Poverty cannot provide a durable basis for conserving *in situ* diversity.

Outmigration of farmers is propelled by 'pull' factors and 'push' factors. On the 'pull' side are the lures of urban employment, the 'bright lights' of the city, and better access to education and health services. Yet the fate of displaced small farmers in urban areas is often grim: the work that awaits them is often low-paid, insecure and hazardous; their housing is precarious and inadequate; and they no longer have access to land for subsistence production. To understand what makes these urban options seem attractive in comparison to farming, we must look at the 'push' side of the migration equation. Two factors that help to explain why small farmers find it increasingly difficult to earn a living on the land are agricultural 'modernization' and international agricultural trade. On a level playing field, neither of these necessarily would be inimical to the small farmer. All too often however, both are played out on a terrain that is tilted against small farmers.

Agricultural 'Modernization'

Agricultural 'modernization' is often spearheaded by the introduction and diffusion of highly fertilizer-responsive crop varieties, a process epitomized by the 'green revolution' in rice and wheat agriculture that was launched in Asia and Latin America in the 1960s. In principle, this technology was divisible and labor-intensive, and thus well suited to small farms. In practice, as Keith Griffin documented in *The Political Economy of Agrarian Change*, large landowners often reaped the lion's share of the benefits. Small farmers lost out not only in

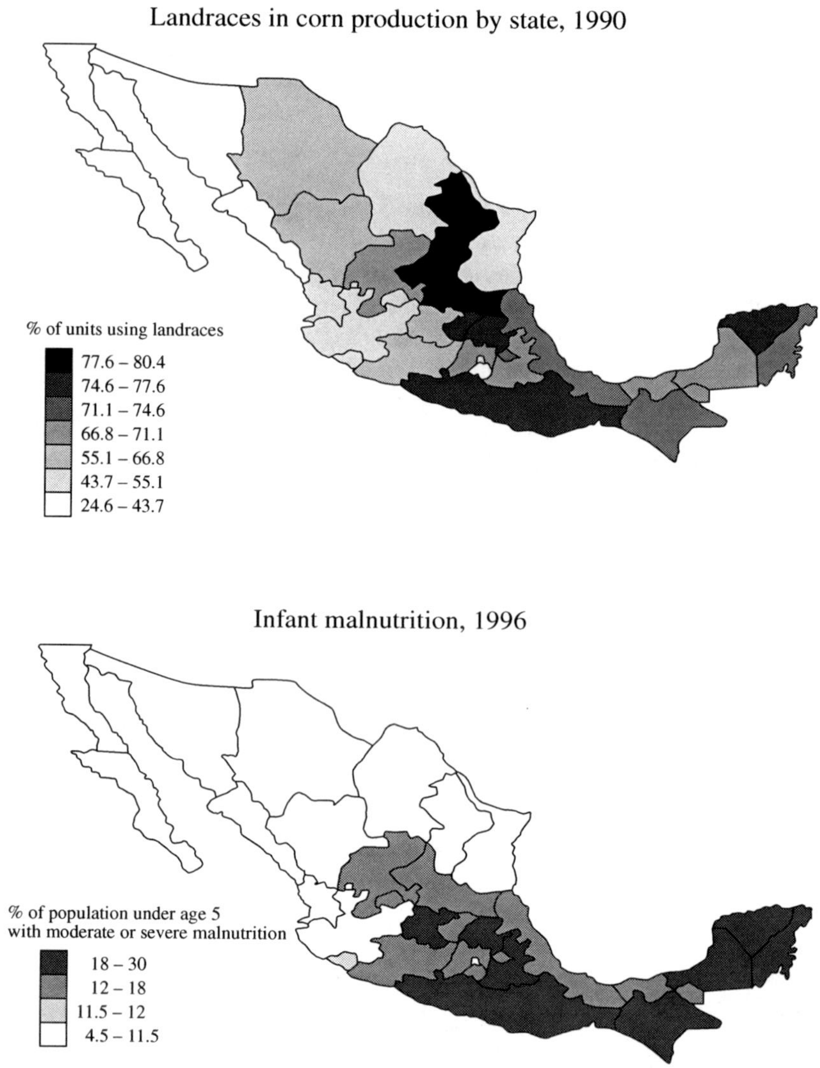

Source: Nadal (2000, pp. 50, 90).

Figure 4.2 Maize diversity and infant malnutrition in Mexico

relative terms, but also absolutely insofar as large farmers were able to expand operations at their expense.

This polarization occurred for several reasons. Firstly, the new varieties were best suited to regions well endowed with water-control infrastructure, such as the states of Punjab and Haryana in India, leaving producers in poorer regions to face adverse effects from falling output prices and/or rising input prices. Secondly, within regions, large farmers had preferential access to irrigation hardware and subsidized credit, positioning them to reap windfall gains as 'early adopters' of the new technology. Thirdly, large farmers used their political power, bolstered by these income gains, to extract further state support, including subsidies for farm machinery that helped to offset the labor-cost advantages of small farmers. Fourthly, in settings where land often changes hands through transactions that involve some degree of 'extra-economic' coercion, the green revolution enhanced both the incentive for large landowners to wrest control of lands from smaller farmers, and their power to do so.[19]

Insofar as agricultural modernization triggers displacement of small farmers, it undermines the social basis for agricultural biodiversity. To be sure, new technologies can lead to genetic erosion on small farms, independently of changes in the agrarian structure, if small farmers themselves decide to replace numerous local varieties with fewer new ones.[20] As noted above however, it is possible for traditional crop varieties and farming practices to coexist with new ones. Indeed one can imagine situations where the introduction of new varieties enhances diversity rather than diminishing it.[21] The impact of 'modernization' on agricultural biodiversity hinges, in no small measure, on how it affects the livelihood security of small farmers. As the small farmer goes, so goes diversity.

International Agricultural Trade

A second 'push' factor arises from the growth of international agricultural trade. Small farmers in the developing countries of the global South now face intensifying competition from cheap grain imported from the industrialized countries of the global North. A striking example is Mexico's imports of maize from the United States: since the North American Free Trade Agreement (NAFTA) went into effect in 1994, imports have risen from 1 million metric tonnes/year to more than 6 million, a volume equivalent to roughly one-quarter of Mexico's annual consumption (Audley et al., 2004, p. 22). These imports, coupled with the Mexican government's withdrawal of price supports for maize farmers, have caused real producer prices to plummet by 70 percent (OXFAM, 2003, p. 2).

The competitive edge that permits US corn to capture Mexican markets has several sources. Genuine comparative advantage is part of the story: the regular rainfall, fertile soils and harsh winters that suppress pest populations help to make the midwestern US 'corn belt' a good place to grow maize. The broad array of agricultural support policies and subsidies in the US also make a contribution.[22] The failure of market prices to internalize environmental costs ('negative externalities') confers a further advantage to US agriculture; the supply price of

US maize does not include for example the social costs of widespread contamination of groundwater and surface waters by the herbicide atrazine.[23] Last, but not least, the failure of market prices to internalize the environmental benefits of *in situ* conservation of crop genetic diversity (a 'positive externality') hobbles the competitive position of small-scale Mexican farmers.

International trade thus allows low-diversity agriculture in the North to displace high-diversity agriculture in the South. Trade reform efforts – for example efforts to curtail US and European Union policies that foster overproduction and the dumping of agricultural products on world markets – would help to level the playing field for small farmers. But as long as externalities are left out of the picture, systematic biases against small farmers will persist. For small farmers in the global South, and above all in the centers of diversity, policies to reward the environmental service of *in situ* conservation are of key importance. In effect, these small farmers subsidize modern agriculture and food consumers worldwide. The way to end this subsidy is not to eliminate the environmental service by driving small farmers off the land, but instead to reward their contributions to world food security.

WHAT IS TO BE DONE?

A wide range of policies can be envisioned that would reward small farmers for sustaining agricultural biodiversity. Such policies would both strengthen rural livelihood security and provide incentives for continued *in situ* conservation. In other words, rather than posing a trade-off between poverty reduction and environmental protection, these are policies that would advance both goals simultaneously:[24]

1. *Removal of anti-small farmer policy distortions.* As noted above, the competitive advantage of large farmers and low-diversity agriculture rests in part on government policies that favor capital-intensive agricultural technologies and promote the dumping of surplus agricultural products on world markets. While the removal of these distortions would not eliminate other biases that arise from neglect of externalities, this would be a step in the right direction.
2. *Social recognition.* Another important step would be to promote 'non-economic' rewards for the conservation of agricultural biodiversity. At the annual *feria del elote* (corn fair) in Jala, Mexico for example, farmers get prizes for producing the finest examples of the valley's traditional landrace maize. Such recognition not only makes farmers feel good; it also helps to create public awareness of the need for policies to provide economic rewards.

3. *Market development.* 'A rose is a rose is a rose', wrote the poet Gertrude Stein. However that may be (and rose lovers no doubt would have something to say about this), one ear of corn is not the same as any other. Traditional varieties of grains, vegetables and fruits not only have different genetic attributes than modern varieties; they also look different, and most importantly, taste different. In part for this reason – and in part, by virtue of commitments to environmental values – there is scope for development of domestic and international markets in which traditional varieties command a price premium. Labeling systems, like the denominations of origin established for French wines in 1935, can assist in creating such markets (Mann, 2004). Again this could not only provide direct rewards to growers, but also help to raise public consciousness of the importance of diversity and the need for public policies to sustain it.[25]
4. *Provision of local public goods.* Out-migration of small farmers is propelled in part by lack of local public goods, such as schools and health clinics. To encourage small farmers to remain on the land, and to provide tangible evidence of the value society places on the environmental services they provide, governments and international agencies could invest in local public goods. Even in the absence of concerns over the erosion of agricultural biodiversity, there are compelling equity and efficiency arguments for such investments. The need to conserve diversity merely adds to the case.
5. *Payments for environmental services.* A further possibility that warrants serious exploration is payments to farmers who provide the environmental service of *in situ* conservation. For such payments to become a part of the policy mix, two main questions would need to be resolved: how to structure the payments, and how to finance them. Payments could take the form of a 'bonus' per unit output, (as suggested by Nadal, 2000, p. 104), or a payment per unit area under the crop, which would have the advantage of removing biases against varieties with low yields per unit area. In determining which individuals or communities should receive payments, there may be trade-offs between precision and inclusivity, and a good case can be made for the latter. 'When money falls from heaven into a poor community,' Peter Rosset comments, 'it often ends up accentuating the power and wealth differences in the community,' and can 'even lead to violence.'[26] Structuring payments so as to strengthen rural communities will be a key challenge.[27] With regard to sources of finance, the fact that the benefits of agricultural biodiversity are truly global means that local and national governments should not have to bear the entire cost of sustaining it. There is a need to mobilize international resources, perhaps under the aegis of the Global Environment Facility.[28]
6. *Policies to encourage part-time farming.* Finally, we should recognize that farming need not be an all-or-nothing occupational choice. In Japan for

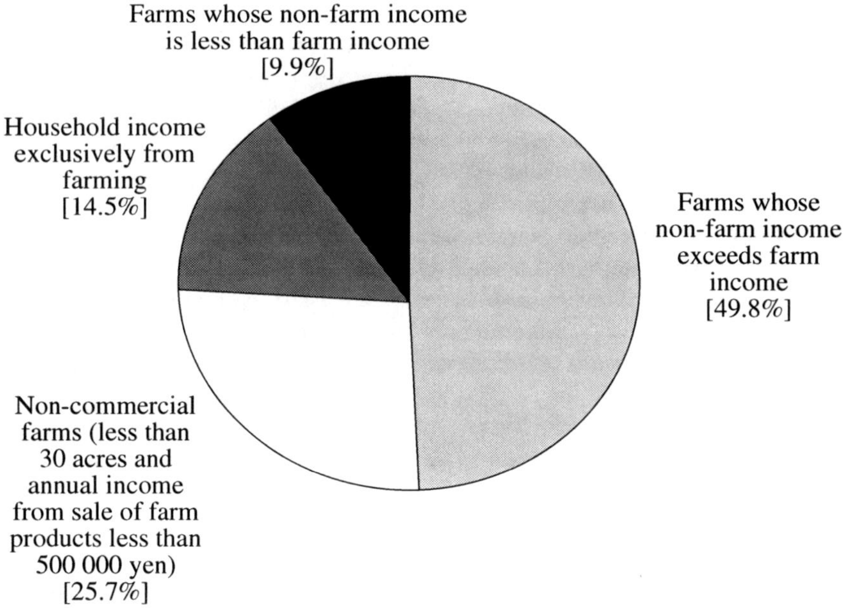

Source: Government of Japan (2003, p. 57).

Figure 4.3 Distribution of farm households in Japan, 2002

example only 15 percent of the country's 3 million farm households (a number that is down from 6 million in 1960) earn their livelihoods entirely from farming; three-quarters derive most of their income from non-farm sources (see Figure 4.3). Just as the adoption of 'modern' crop varieties does not necessarily eliminate 'traditional' varieties, so the expansion of non-farm employment does not necessarily eliminate farming. Policies that help to generate part-time, off-farm employment opportunities in rural areas can help to sustain small farms. So can policies that promote agriculture-friendly tourism, thereby internalizing another positive externality often generated by small-farm landscapes: scenic beauty.[29] In supporting small farms, such policies could help to sustain agricultural biodiversity, especially if accompanied by other policies that recognize and reward the social value of *in situ* conservation.

These policies are not mutually exclusive, nor is any one policy alone likely to be sufficient. Taken together however these policies could do a great deal to support small farms and stewardship of agricultural biodiversity.

CONCLUSION

There is a future for small farms. Or, to be more precise, there can be and should be a future for them. Given the dependence of 'modern' low-diversity agriculture on 'traditional' high-diversity agriculture, the long-term food security of humankind will depend on small farms and their continued provision of the environmental service of *in situ* conservation of crop genetic diversity. Policies to support small farms can be advocated therefore not merely as a matter of sympathy, or nostalgia, or equity. Such policies are also a matter of human survival.

The diversity that underpins the sustainability of world agriculture did not fall from the sky. It was bequeathed to us by the 400 generations of farmers who have carried on the process of artificial selection since plants were first domesticated. Until recently, we took this diversity for granted. The ancient reservoirs of crop genetic diversity, plant geneticist Jack Harlan (1975, p. 619) wrote three decades ago, 'seemed to most people as inexhaustible as oil in Arabia'. Yet, Harlan warned, 'the speed which enormous crop diversity can be essentially wiped out is astonishing'.

The central thesis of this chapter is that efforts to conserve *in situ* diversity must go hand in hand with efforts to support the small farmers around the world who sustain this diversity. Economists and environmentalists alike by and large have neglected this issue. In thrall to a myopic notion of efficiency, many economists fail to appreciate that diversity is the *sine qua non* of resilience and sustainability. In thrall to a romantic notion of 'wilderness', many environmentalists fail to appreciate that agricultural biodiversity is just as valuable – indeed arguably more valuable from the standpoint of human well-being – as the diversity found in tropical rainforests or the spotted owls found in the ancient forests of the north-western United States.

Today a formidable nexus of market forces and political forces threatens both small farmers and the agricultural biodiversity they sustain. Several countervailing public policies have been suggested here: removal of policy biases against small farmers; social recognition of the contribution of *in situ* conservation to human well-being; development of markets for 'traditional' varieties; provision of local public goods in areas where farmers cultivate diversity; payments for the environmental service of on-farm conservation; and policies to support part-time farming as a component of household livelihood strategies.

Only an awakened and mobilized public opinion can bring such policies into being. Small farmers cannot do it alone: they need allies. A process of 'artificial selection' is needed in the policy arena to yield outcomes that will not come about from 'natural selection' by market forces and the political influence of the powerful. No less than farming itself, ensuring a sustainable future requires human intelligence and human agency. In the present era of globalization, all of us share responsibility for the cultivation of agricultural biodiversity.

NOTES

* I am grateful to Liz Stanton and Sue Holmberg for research assistance, and to Garrison Wilkes for comments on an earlier draft of this chapter.

1. 'A French roadblock to free trade', *New York Times*, 3 August 2003.
2. Personal interview, Guatemala City, December 1997.
3. For the incorporation of this recognition into recent thinking at the World Bank, see Deininger (2003).
4. The term 'agricultural biodiversity' is often used to refer not only to crop genetic diversity, but also other related forms of biodiversity, including pathogens, insects and soil microorganisms (see for example Wood and Lenné, 1999). Here my focus is crop genetic diversity, and I will use the terms interchangeably; much of the discussion could be generalized however to other forms of agricultural biodiversity.
5. Wilkes (1995, p. 207) suggests that we call this process 'anthro-selection', in recognition of the human-centered nature of the process.
6. See Mann (2002a). See also Brookfield (2001, pp. 96–7) for discussion of this and other examples of 'manufactured soils'.
7. For discussions of the origins of these and other crop plants, see MacNeish (1992), Harlan (1995), Smartt and Simmonds (1995) and Smith (1995).
8. For further discussion of the contrasts between Mexican and US maize agriculture, see Boyce (1996).
9. For discussion of differences in the 'real cost' of family labor versus hired labor, see Sen (1975). For discussion farm size and labor supervision, see Boyce (1987, pp. 39–40, 213).
10. Nadal (2000, p. 122), citing Ortega Paczka (1997). Women often play a particularly important role in agricultural biodiversity conservation; for example, surveys in indigenous communities in the Guatemalan highlands have found that women often select the seed for the next production cycle, doing so on the basis of culinary requirements and Mayan cosmology as well as agronomic characteristics (FAO/IPGRI, 2002, pp. 22, 39–40).
11. The term 'evolutionary gardens' is used by Wilkes (1992, pp. 24–6) to describe the hilly, rain-fed *milpa* plots cultivated by the *campesinos* of Mesoamerica.
12. Most plant breeding is still performed in the public sector, notwithstanding the growing importance of private-sector breeders and the publicity that has accompanied this trend.
13. See Brammer (1980) and Biggs (1980). See also Bellon et al. (1997).
14. Quoted by Fowler and Mooney (1990, p. xii).
15. In the late 1960s, for example, CIMMYT sent 'back-up copies' of about 5000 varieties of Latin American maize to the NSSL in Fort Collins. When CIMMYT asked for some of these back, having lost some of its own samples in a period of budgetary shortfalls, it turned out that most of the seeds sent to the NSSL had been inadvertently discarded (Raeburn, 1995, pp. 62–3). See also Brookfield (2001, p. 247), who concludes that 'a high proportion of the world's seed storage has substandard conditions, and there is concern about the viability of many collections'.
16. Personal communication, May 2004.
17. Personal interview with Joel Charny, who retrieved the seed samples from IRRI while working for OXFAM-America in the 1980s.
18. For examples of genetic erosion associated with this outmigration, see Nadal (2000, pp. 90–91).
19. For further discussion, see also Griffin (1979; 1999, Chapter 6) and Boyce (1993, Chapters 3–5).
20. For examples in the case of potato cultivation in the Andes, see Ochoa (1975).

21. For discussion, see Qualset et al. (1997), Wood and Lenné (1997), Edwards et al. (1999) and Jana (1999).
22. For discussion, see Wise (2004).
23. See Boyce (1996) and Ackerman (2002).
24. The policies sketched here are examples of the 'internalization' route to building natural assets in the hands of the poor (Boyce, 2003). For further discussion, see 'Crop genetic diversity and rural livelihoods', the minutes of a June 2001 meeting organized by the Political Economy Research Institute in San Cristóbal de las Casas, Chiapas (available at http://www.umass.edu/peri/pdfs/CGDMinutes.pdf). See also Thrupp (1998) and Brush (2000).
25. For examples from Switzerland, see Bardsley and Thomas (2004). For discussion, see also Smale et al. (2004, pp. 130–31).
26. Quoted by Mann (2004, p. 23).
27. In Guatemala's western highlands for example, small farmers who cultivate traditional maize varieties also invest in labor-intensive land improvements such as terracing and the cultivation of live barriers to control soil erosion, despite lack of formal land titles. Elizabeth Katz (2000, p. 124) attributes their willingness to undertake these investments to 'informal social recognition of property rights – a manifestation of social capital – at the community level, which effectively replaces formal legal title'. If payments for environmental services were to erode this social capital, the net effect paradoxically could be to undermine such investments. See also Rosa et al. (2006).
28. The Global Environment Facility (GEF) has begun to contemplate work in this area; see GEF (2000).
29. In some cases, agricultural biodiversity itself has tourism value. For example, in Cusco, Peru, tour groups can visit a potato museum, demonstration plots, and restaurants featuring traditional produce (Cromwell et al., 1999, p. 35).

REFERENCES

Ackerman, Frank (2002), 'Is the United States a pollution haven?' Silver City, NM: Interhemispheric Resource Center, accessed at www.fpif.org/americas/commentary/2002/0203corn.html.

Ackerman, Frank, Timothy A. Wise, Kevin Gallagher, Luke Ney and Regina Flores (2003), 'Free trade, corn, and the environment: environmental impacts of US–Mexico corn trade under NAFTA', Medford, MA: Tufts University, Global Development and Environment Institute, working paper no. 03-06, accessed at http://ase.tufts.edu/gdae/Pubs/wp/03-06-NAFTACorn.PDF.

Audley, John J. et al. (2004), *NAFTA's Promise and Reality: Lessons from Mexico for the Hemisphere*, Washington, DC: Carnegie Endowment for International Peace.

Bardsley D. and I. Thomas (2004), 'In situ agrobiodiversity conservation in the Swiss inner alpine zone', *GeoJournal* **60** (2), 99–109.

Bellon, M.R., J.-L. Pham and M.T. Jackson (1997), 'Genetic conservation: a role for rice farmers', in N. Maxted, B. Ford-Lloyd and J.G. Hawkes (eds), *Plant Genetic Conservation: The In Situ Approach*, London: Chapman & Hall, pp. 263–89.

Biggs, Stephen D. (1980), 'Informal R&D', *Ceres*, Rome: Food and Agriculture Organization, **13** (4), 23–6.

Boyce, James K. (1987), *Agrarian Impasse in Bengal: Institutional Constraints to Technological Change*, Oxford: Oxford University Press.

Boyce, James K. (1993), *The Philippines: The Political Economy of Growth and Impoverishment in the Marcos Era*, London: Macmillan.

Boyce, James K. (1996), 'Ecological distribution, agricultural trade liberalization, and *in situ* genetic diversity', *Journal of Income Distribution* **6** (2), 263–84.

Boyce, James K. (2003), 'From natural resources to natural assets', in James K. Boyce and Barry G. Shelley (eds), *Natural Assets: Democratizing Environmental Ownership*, Washington, DC: Island Press, pp. 7–28.

Brammer, Hugh (1980), 'Some innovations don't wait for experts', *Ceres*, Rome: Food and Agriculture Organization, **13** (2), 24–8.

Brookfield, Harold (2001), *Exploring Agrodiversity*, New York: Columbia University Press.

Brush, Stephen B. (1995), '*In situ* conservation of landraces in centers of crop diversity', *Crop Science*, **35**, 346–54.

Brush, Stephen B. (ed.) (2000), *Genes in the Field: On-Farm Conservation of Crop Diversity*, Rome: International Plant Genetic Resources Institute.

Chang, T.T. (1995), 'Rice', in J. Smartt and N.W. Simmonds (eds), *Evolution of Crop Plants*, 2nd edn, Harlow: Longman Scientific and Technical, pp. 147–55.

Cromwell, Elizabeth, David Cooper and Patrick Mulvany (1999), 'Agriculture, biodiversity and livelihoods: issues and entry points for development agencies', London: Overseas Development Institute, accessed at: www.ukabc.org/odi_agbiod.pdf.

Darwin, Charles (1859), *The Origin of Species by Means of Natural Selection*, reprinted 1952, Chicago: Encyclopaedia Britannica.

Deininger, Klaus (2003), *Land Policies for Growth and Poverty Reduction*, Oxford: Oxford University Press.

Duvick, Daniel N. (1984), 'Genetic diversity in major farm crops on the farm and in reserve', *Economic Botany*, **38** (2), 161–78.

Duvick, D.N., J.S.C. Smith and M. Cooper (2004), 'Changes in performance, parentage, and genetic diversity of successful corn hybrids, from 1930 to 2000', in C.W. Smith, J. Betrán and E.C.A. Runge (eds), *Corn: Origin, History, Technology, and Production*, New York: John Wiley & Sons.

Edwards, P.J., J. Kollmann and D. Wood (1999), 'Determinants of agrobiodiversity in the agricultural landscape', in D. Wood and J.M. Lenné (eds), *Agrobiodiversity Characterization, Utilization and Management*, Wallingford: CABI Publishing, pp. 183–210.

Food and Agriculture Organization of the United Nations (FAO) and International Plant Genetic Resources Institute (IPGRI) (2002), *The Role of Women in the Conservation of the Genetic Resources of Maize*, Rome: FAO/IPGRI.

Fowler, Cary and Pat Mooney (1990), *Shattering: Food, Politics, and the Loss of Genetic Diversity*, Tucson, AZ: University of Arizona Press.

García-Barrios, Raúl and Luis (1990), 'Environmental and technological degradation in peasant agriculture: a consequence of development in Mexico', *World Development*, **18** (11), 1569–85.

Global Environment Facility (GEF) (2000), 'Elements of a GEF operational program on conservation and sustainable use of biological diversity important to agriculture', 12 April, accessed at: www.gefweb.org/COUNCIL/GEF_C15/GEF_C15_7.pdf.

Goodman, Major M. (1995), 'Maize', in J. Smartt and N.W. Simmonds (eds), *Evolution of Crop Plants*, 2nd edn, Harlow: Longman Scientific and Technical, pp. 193–202.

Government of Japan (2003), *Statistical Handbook of Japan, 2003*, Tokyo: Ministry of Public Management, Home Affairs, Post and Telecommunications, Statistics Bureau.

Griffin, Keith (1979), *The Political Economy of Agrarian Change*, 2nd edn, London: Macmillan.

Griffin, Keith (1999), *Alternative Strategies for Economic Development*, 2nd edn, London: Macmillan.

Griffin, Keith, Azizur Rahman Khan and Amy Ickowitz (2002), 'Poverty and the distribution of land', *Journal of Agrarian Change*, **2** (3), 279–330.
Harlan, Jack R. (1975), 'Our vanishing genetic resources', *Science*, **188** (9 May), 618–21.
Harlan, Jack R. (1995), *The Living Fields: Our Agricultural Heritage*, Cambridge: Cambridge University Press.
Heywood, V.H. (1995), *Global Biodiversity Assessment*, Cambridge: Cambridge University Press.
Jana, S. (1999), 'Some recent issues on the conservation of crop genetic resources in developing countries', *Genome*, **42**, 562–9.
Katz, Elizabeth (2000), 'Social capital and natural capital: a comparative analysis of land tenure and natural resource management in Guatemala', *Land Economics*, **76** (1), 114–32.
Lewis, W. Arthur (1954), 'Economic development with unlimited supplies of labor', *Manchester School of Economic and Social Studies*, **22**, 139–91.
MacNeish, Richard S. (1992), *The Origins of Agriculture and Settled Life*, Norman, OK: University of Oklahoma Press.
Mann, Charles (2002a), 'The real dirt on rainforest fertility', *Science*, **297**, 920–23.
Mann, Charles (2002b), '1491', *Atlantic Monthly*, March, 41–53.
Mann, Charles (2004), *Diversity on the Farm*, New York: Ford Foundation and Amherst, MA: Political Economy Research Institute.
Nadal, Alejandro (2000), 'The environmental and social impacts of economic liberalization on corn production in Mexico', Oxford: OXFAM and Gland: WWF International, accessed at www.oxfam.org.uk/what_we_do/issues/livelihoods/corn_mexico.htm.
Ochoa, Carlos (1975), 'Potato collecting expeditions in Chile, Bolivia and Peru, and the genetic erosion of indigenous cultivars', in O.H. Frankel and J.G. Hawkes (eds), *Crop Genetic Resources for Today and Tomorrow*, Cambridge: Cambridge University Press.
Ortega Paczka, Rafael A. (1997), 'Maíz en el Tratado de Libre Comercio: Implicaciones para el medio ambiente. Recursos genéticos', consultant's report to the Commission on Environmental Cooperation.
OXFAM (2003), 'Dumping without borders: how US agricultural policies are destroying the livelihoods of Mexican corn farmers', Oxford: OXFAM briefing paper no. 50, August, accessed at www.oxfam.org/eng/pdfs/pp030827_corn_dumping.pdf.
Peña, Devon (2003), 'The watershed commonwealth of the Upper Rio Grande', in James K. Boyce and Barry G. Shelley (eds), *Natural Assets: Democratizing Environmental Ownership*, Washington, DC: Island Press.
Plucknett, D.L. et al. (1987), *Gene Banks and the World's Food*, Princeton, NJ: Princeton University Press.
Qualset, C.O., A.B. Damania, A.C.A. Zanatta and S.B. Brush (1997), 'Locally based crop plant conservation', in N. Maxted, B. Ford-Lloyd and J.G. Hawkes (eds), *Plant Genetic Conservation: The In Situ Approach*, London: Chapman & Hall, pp. 160–75.
Raeburn, Paul (1995), *The Last Harvest*, New York: Simon & Schuster.
Rosa, Herman, Deborah Barry, Susan Kandel and Leopoldo Dimas (2005), 'Compensation for environmental services and rural communities: lessons from the Americas', in James K. Boyce, Sunita Narain and Elizabeth A. Stanton (eds), *Environmental Justice and Ecological Restoration*, London: Anthem Press.
Sen, Amartya (1975), *Employment, Technology, and Development*, Oxford: Oxford University Press.
Shand, Hope (1997) *Human Nature: Agricultural Biodiversity and Farm-based Food*

Security, Ottawa: Rural Advancement Foundation International, accessed at www.etcgroup.org/documents/other_human.pdf.

Smale, Melinda, Mauricio R. Bellon, Devra Jarvis and Bhuwon Sthapit (2004), 'Economic concepts for designing policies to conserve crop genetic resources on farms', *Genetic Resources and Crop Evolution*, **51**, 121–35.

Smartt, J. and N.W. Simmonds (eds) (1995), *Evolution of Crop Plants*, 2nd edn, Harlow: Longman Scientific & Technical.

Smith, Bruce D. (1995), *The Emergence of Agriculture*, New York: Scientific American Library.

Stam, Jerome M. and Bruce L. Dixon (2004), 'Farmer bankruptcies and farm exits in the United States, 1899–2002', US Department of Agriculture Economic Research Service, agriculture information bulletin no. 788, Washington, DC: accessed at www.ers.usda.gov/publications/aib788/aib788.pdf.

Swanson, T.M. and R.A. Luxmoore (1997), 'Industrial reliance on biodiversity', World Conservation Monitoring Centre biodiversity series no. 7, Cambridge, accessed at www.eldis.org/static/DOC6611.htm.

Thrupp, Lori Ann (1998), *Cultivating Diversity: Agrobiodiversity and Food Security*, Washington, DC: World Resources Institute.

Vavilov, Nikolai I. (1992 [1926]), *Origin and Geography of Cultivated Plants*, Cambridge: Cambridge University Press.

Wilkes, Garrison (1992), *Strategies for Sustaining Crop Germplasm Preservation, Enhancement, and Use*, Washington DC: Consultative Group on International Agricultural Research.

Wilkes, Garrison (1995), 'The ethnobotany of artificial selection in seed plant domestication', in Richard E. Schultes and Siri von Reis (eds), *Ethnobotany: Evolution of a Discipline*, Portland, OR: Dioscorides Press, pp. 203–8.

Wise, Timothy A. (2004), 'The paradox of agricultural subsidies: measurement issues, agricultural dumping, and policy reform', Medford, MA: Tufts University Global Development and Environment Institute, working paper no. 04-02, accessed at http://ase.tufts.edu/gdae/Pubs/wp/04-02AgSubsidies.pdf.

Wood, David and Jillian M. Lenné (1997), 'The conservation of agrobiodiversity on-farm: questioning the emerging paradigm', *Biodiversity and Conservation*, **6**, 109–29.

Wood, David and Jillian M. Lenné (1999), *Agrobiodiversity: Characterization, Utilization and Management*, Wallingford: CABI Publishing.

5. The impact of policy reforms on rural poverty in Brazil: evidence from three states in the 1990s

Steven M. Helfand and Edward S. Levine

INTRODUCTION

This chapter analyzes the puzzle of what happened to rural poverty in Brazil in the 1990s and why. The 1990s were a period of considerable policy reform and economic change. In response to the debt crisis and the exhaustion of the import substitution model, beginning in 1988 the Brazilian government rapidly liberalized trade. Throughout the 1990s the state reduced the extent and scope of its interventions and deregulated many markets. Simultaneously, the Brazilian economy struggled with hyperinflation, and the government adopted numerous stabilization plans between 1986 and 1994, when the Real Plan finally succeeded in taming inflation. Interestingly, the agricultural sector outperformed the manufacturing sector in the context of the debt crisis of the 1980s, and outperformed both manufacturing and services in the neoliberal environment of the 1990s. The positive performance of agriculture as a whole is one factor that might have led us to expect a decline in rural poverty in the 1990s.

There were a number of forces however that suggested an increase in rural poverty or at least a more nuanced assessment. Firstly, agricultural growth was extremely heterogeneous across regions, crops and farm sizes (Helfand and Rezende, 2004). The Center-West for example, where extremely large farms produce many exportables, was a booming region in the 1990s. Increased demand for labor in this region might have contributed to reducing rural poverty. The South, in contrast, experienced substantial problems of competitiveness. This is a region where small and medium-sized farms produce many importables. Thus whatever the net effect on rural poverty for Brazil as a whole, it is unlikely that there is a single story that can adequately describe the multiple experiences of growth, adjustment and poverty the 1990s.

Secondly, in part due to the appreciation of the real exchange rate, real agricultural prices fell by over 50 per cent between the mid-1980s and the late 1990s.[1] Trade liberalization and exchange rate appreciation also contributed to lowering input prices by a similar magnitude. There is evidence that large farms were able to take advantage of falling input prices to a greater extent than small farms, and that they achieved much more rapid productivity gains in the 1990s than did small farms (Helfand, 2004). There is also evidence that only on large farms was output able to grow fast enough to compensate for falling prices and to keep revenue from declining. Thus, on average, income from agricultural production appears to have fallen for small farms in the 1990s and this is likely to have increased poverty in rural areas.

Finally, there was a substantial decline in the rural population and in the labor force employed in agriculture in the 1990s. According to the demographic censuses of 1991 and 2000, the rural population fell by 11 percent, and according to the national household surveys (PNAD), agricultural employment (including the self-employed and their unpaid family members) fell by 14 percent between 1992–93 and 2001–02. The decline in employment in agriculture was driven by both the crisis of competitiveness of small farms and the adoption of labor-saving technologies on large farms. An exodus of this proportion suggests that employment growth did not keep up with population growth, and it could easily have been a reflection of an increase in rural poverty. Paradoxically, rapid migration out of rural areas could also contribute to reducing rural poverty if the poor leave disproportionately, or if out-migration occurs randomly, but at a faster rate than the decline in income received by the poor.

Two recent papers in Brazil shed some light on the evidence regarding poverty. They both conclude that poverty in agriculture fell substantially in the 1990s. Corrêa (forthcoming), using family income per capita of those people employed in agriculture, reports a decline in the headcount ratio of 9.5 percentage points between 1992 and 1998. Using a similar measure, Barros et al. (2004) estimate a decline of 7.6 percentage points between 1992 and 2001. For rural – rather than agricultural – families, these authors estimate an even larger reduction in poverty (9.8 percentage points).

In this chapter we seek to understand this rather surprising decline in rural poverty. In the next section we discuss a number of explanations of why poverty declined in the 1990s. In contrast to the analysis of Barros et al. (2004), we suspect that migration out of rural areas is likely to have played an important role in reducing rural poverty in this period. We also believe that because of the heterogeneity of regional experiences in the 1990s it is essential to study the determinants of changes in rural poverty at not only a national, but especially a sub-national level. The third section presents evidence on income, poverty and inequality in rural areas of Brazil in the 1990s. Using micro data from the demographic censuses of 1991 and 2000, and a county level unit of analysis, in the next section we present several tests of the hypotheses discussed earlier for three states in Brazil. The final section provides conclusions and thoughts for future research.

ALTERNATIVE EXPLANATIONS OF CHANGES IN RURAL POVERTY IN THE 1990s

There are three groups of explanations of the decline in rural poverty that we would like to investigate in this chapter. They relate to out-migration from rural areas, the importance of different sources of household income (such as government transfers or non-agricultural earned income), and macroeconomic forces. Although we believe that macroeconomic events were important, for reasons discussed below we are not able to address them satisfactorily with the data that we are using here. We emphasize that the explanations are not mutually exclusive. Thus, we seek to quantify their relative importance.

Although out-migration is likely a reflection of high or rising rates of rural poverty, if it happens fast enough it can also contribute to a reduction in poverty. Because out-migration took place on such a large scale in the 1990s, a key hypothesis that we wish to test is that migration out of rural areas contributed to a decline in rural poverty. There are a number of mechanisms through which this could have occurred. Firstly, it could be that migration occurs disproportionately from the bottom end of the income distribution. Thus if poor families leave rural areas at a faster rate than non-poor families, the poverty rate could fall and average income could rise without a single household experiencing income growth. Secondly, and this is what Barros et al. (2004) focus on in relation to migration, the demographic characteristics of the families that remain in rural areas could change in such a way that contributes to reducing poverty. For example there could be an increase in the share of working-age adults in poor households.[2] Thirdly, if the initial situation involved low-productivity 'surplus' labor within small farms, migration of family members could have come at little or no cost in terms of output. As a result, household income per capita would rise. Fourthly, migration could lead to an inward shift of the labor supply curve and, consequently, an increase in wages paid in rural areas. Finally, to the extent that some family members migrate from rural areas while others stay behind, it is likely that remittances will flow to the remaining rural family members at some point in the future and thus contribute to reducing poverty. In such cases, it may be that both those who leave and those who remain behind experience lower rates of poverty. In the empirical section of this chapter we simply test for a significant effect of migration. If we find that it contributes to reducing poverty, future research should seek to identify the relative importance of the mechanisms discussed above.

The second set of explanations for the decline in rural poverty relates to differential growth of alternative sources of income. Graziano da Silva and Del Grossi (2001) and Ferreira and Lanjouw (2001) for example argue that the growth of non-agricultural sources of earned income in rural areas has been a fundamental force contributing to lowering poverty rates. Delgado and Cardoso

Jr. (2000), Beltrão et al. (2002) and others have emphasized the importance of increased social security benefits for reducing rural poverty in the 1990s. Social security benefits grew considerably in rural areas in the early 1990s as a result of changes in the 1988 Constitution. Finally, in regions such as the Center-West where agriculture has been especially dynamic, it is likely to have had a positive effect on rural poverty through its impact on the demand for agricultural labor. Thus we seek to quantify the relative importance of these income sources and to explore whether they have played different roles in different regions of the country.

The third explanation of a decline in rural poverty relates to macroeconomic factors. The Real Plan succeeded in bringing inflation (as measured by the CPI) down from an average of over 1000 percent per year between 1988 and 1994 to around 20 percent in 1995 and under 10 percent in 1996. To the extent that hyperinflation disproportionately harmed the poor, stabilization should have contributed to reducing poverty in rural and urban areas. In addition to lower inflation, five years of respectable rates of growth between 1993 and 1998, and a 15 percent increase in the real minimum wage in 1995–99 relative to 1990–94, should have helped to raise the incomes of the poor. Urban and rural poverty rates did in fact fall markedly in 1995 relative to 1993 (www.ipeadata.gov.br; Barros et al., 2004). While we would like to explore the relative importance for poverty reduction of the individual factors discussed here, and of the macro factors as a group in relation to the determinants discussed above (migration, government transfers and so on), the census data we use are drawn from only two points in time: 1991 and 2000. Time-series or panel data would be necessary to identify the importance of macroeconomic factors in the 1990s. For this purpose the annual household surveys would be a more appropriate source. The household surveys however are only representative at a state level. Because we have chosen to focus on migration, the demographic censuses have the advantage of being representative at a county level. Thus for now we implicitly adopt the assumption that macroeconomic factors had a similar impact across counties in the 1990s. If so, the discrete decline in poverty that occurred between 1993 and 1995 will be absorbed in the intercepts of our county level regression models.

EVIDENCE ON RURAL INCOME, POVERTY, AND INEQUALITY IN THE 1990s

In this section of the chapter we provide an overview of trends in poverty and related variables in the 1990s at a national level and for three states. The states – Alagoas, Santa Catarina and Mato Grosso – had very different experiences with rural poverty reduction in the 1990s and are located in different regions of the country. Thus we chose them to capture some of the heterogeneity in performance in this period. We do not however claim that these states are statistically representative of the national experience. In future research we intend to extend the analysis to the rest of the country. We begin this section with a brief discussion of the data and the methodology used to construct the variables. We then analyze the evolution of income, poverty and inequality in the 1990s.

Data and Methodology

The data used to construct the measures of income, poverty and inequality come from the long form of the demographic censuses of 1991 and 2000. Approximately 10 percent of the Brazilian population answered this questionnaire in both years. Income is measured as domicile income per capita. As is common in studies of poverty in Brazil, we exclude (1) collective domiciles (such as prisons and hospitals); (2) domestic employees and their family members (to avoid double counting their income); and (3) people who pay rent to the domicile head to live in the domicile. Income includes earnings from all sources, government transfers and other forms of unearned income. One of the most important limitations of the definition of income in the demographic censuses is that it does not include non-marketed production for own consumption. For small farmers who consume a significant portion of what they produce, this is likely to lead to a significant underestimation of their true incomes. If own consumption is relatively constant over time, then it should not have a large impact on the measured change in income between 1991 and 2000.[3]

Poverty and extreme poverty are measured in relation to uniform national poverty lines. While it would be preferable to use poverty lines that take account of differences in the cost of living across regions and rural–urban areas, existing poverty lines that incorporate these differences are based on outdated data from the 1980s (and in some cases the 1970s). Thus we have adopted the same poverty lines as the recently released *Atlas of Human Development* (UNDP et al., 2003). The poverty and extreme poverty lines were set at one-half and one-quarter of an August 2000 minimum wage per person. With a minimum wage of 151 reals, this translated into a poverty line of approximately US$1.33 per person per day in that month. While a uniform national poverty line is likely to overstate poverty in some areas, such as in the rural North-East, the changes in poverty between 1991 and 2000 are much less sensitive to this problem.

The Gini coefficient is estimated from a piecewise linear Lorenz curve. The Gini is a measure of inequality that lies between zero and one, with larger numbers indicating greater inequality. The Gini measures inequality of total domicile income per capita, that is, income from all sources. In order to identify the contribution of specific income sources to overall inequality – such as agricultural or wage income – we also calculate the concentration ratio for each source of income. The concentration ratio shows the degree of inequality in the distribution of a particular source of income. It is calculated from a 'pseudo-Lorenz' curve. The standard Lorenz curve has the cumulative percentage of household income per capita on the vertical axis, and the cumulative percentage of the population ranked by household income per capita on the horizontal axis. The pseudo-Lorenz curve uses the same ranking as the Lorenz curve (rather than the ranking that corresponds to the source of income in question). Thus it measures the cumulative percentage of income from the source in question on the vertical axis, and the cumulative percentage of the population ranked by household income per capita on the horizontal axis.[4] A concentration ratio for a particular source of income – say social security – that is smaller than the Gini is considered to be an equalizing force, because if this source were to grow relative to other sources (and the concentration ratio were to remain unchanged) the Gini would fall. A concentration ratio for a particular source of income – say non-agricultural income – that is larger than the Gini is considered to be a disequalizing force, becasuse if this source were to grow relative to other sources (but holding the concentration ratio constant) the Gini would rise. The Gini can be decomposed into a weighted sum of concentration ratios, where the weights are the shares of each source of income in total income.

Income, Poverty and Inequality

The first row of Table 5.1 shows that – without disaggregating rural from urban areas in Brazil – poverty and extreme poverty both fell substantially in the 1990s. The poverty headcount ratio fell by 21 percent, from 0.40 down to 0.32. Extreme poverty fell by a similar proportion. Table 5.1 also shows that the Gini ratio of inequality rose slightly in this period from 0.63 to 0.65. Thus it appears that the 29 percent increase in household income per capita explains the entire decline in poverty in the 1990s. It is important to note that poverty rose in Brazil as a result of the debt crisis of the 1980s. It was only in the post-stabilization period since 1994 that Brazil finally achieved poverty rates below those that were observed in the late 1970s.[5]

The second row of Table 5.1 shows that the evolution of poverty and extreme poverty in rural Brazil was similar to that of the national level.[6] Poverty fell by 16 percent and extreme poverty fell by 19 percent. In contrast to the national average, rural income grew by more (32 percent versus 29 percent), yet inequality rose by more (7 percent versus 2 percent). Because inequality rose, we must look to the income growth of 32 percent to provide the likely explanation for the decline in poverty. Also the decline of 11 percentage points in the rural population may have contributed to the high income growth and may have prevented inequality from rising even further. In a similar fashion to what happened

Table 5.1 Descriptive statistics, 1991–2000

	Population			Income			Inequality			Poverty (1/2 MW pc)			Extreme poverty (1/4 MW pc)		
	1991	2000	change	1991	2000	change	1991	2000	change	1991	2000	change	1991	2000	change
	(Millions)			(R$ of 1/2002)			(Gini)			(Headcount)			(Headcount)		
Brazil[1]															
Total	147	170	16	255	330	29	0.63	0.65	2	0.40	0.32	–21	0.20	0.15	–23
Rural	36	32	–11	90	119	32	0.58	0.62	7	0.72	0.61	–16	0.45	0.36	–19
Urban	111	138	24	308	379	23	0.61	0.63	3	0.30	0.25	–17	0.12	0.11	–14
Alagoas															
Rural	1.03	0.91	–12	57	59	4	0.48	0.59	24	0.84	0.82	–3	0.55	0.57	3
Urban	1.48	1.92	29	166	201	21	0.63	0.67	7	0.55	0.50	–9	0.27	0.26	–4
Santa Catarina															
Rural	1.33	1.14	–14	141	231	64	0.52	0.53	1	0.48	0.27	–43	0.22	0.11	–50
Urban	3.21	4.22	31	305	430	41	0.53	0.56	6	0.19	0.12	–34	0.06	0.04	–27
Mato Grosso															
Rural	0.54	0.52	–4	136	186	37	0.59	0.63	7	0.58	0.45	–23	0.29	0.22	–22
Urban	1.49	1.99	34	261	356	36	0.58	0.62	6	0.30	0.22	–27	0.10	0.08	–23

Note: 1. We excluded the Northern state Roraima from national level estimates of income, inequality, and poverty due to significant errors in the 1991 data files.

Source: Authors' calculations based on the micro data from the demographic censuses.

with national level poverty in the 1980s and 1990s, Corrêa (forthcoming) reports that poverty among the families of people working in agriculture rose between 1981 and the early 1990s. It then fell markedly in the 1990s. Thus it is likely that the achievements in rural poverty reduction in the 1990s were mostly just eliminating the setbacks of the 1980s.

The remainder of Table 5.1 shows what happened to poverty and related indicators in the three states that we have chosen to analyze in detail. Income per capita in rural Alagoas, a poor state in the North-East of Brazil, was about two-thirds of the national rural average in 1991. As a result, poverty in Alagoas was considerably higher than the national average. Alagoas was also the worst-performing state of the three that we have chosen. Rural poverty barely fell in the 1990s, registering a decline from 0.84 to 0.82, and extreme poverty in rural areas actually rose slightly from 0.55 to 0.57. The reason for the lack of progress in reducing poverty relates to the fact that household income per capita only rose by 4 percent in this decade, and income growth was distributed very unequally. The Gini for rural Alagoas rose by 24 percent. It is possible that without the observed 12 percent decline in the rural population, average income would have grown less or inequality would have grown more, so that poverty would have risen rather than remained roughly constant.

In contrast to Alagoas, the Southern state of Santa Catarina made dramatic gains in poverty reduction in the 1990s. The 43 percent decline in rural poverty in the 1990s was caused by rapid growth in income (64 percent) and virtually no change in inequality (1 percent). It is possible that the 14 percent decline in the rural population contributed to the rapid rate of average income growth, and prevented inequality from rising substantially, therefore facilitating the lowering of the rate of rural poverty.

Mato Grosso, a state in the Center-West of Brazil, represents an intermediate case. Mato Grosso grew in the 1990s, but not by as much as Santa Catarina. Mato Grosso also followed a disequalizing growth path. Rural household income per capita rose by 37 percent, but this was accompanied by a 7 percent increase in the Gini. For both reasons, poverty fell by less than in Santa Catarina, dropping by 23 percent in the period. Unlike in the other two states, the decline in the rural population was only 4 percent. Thus it is unlikely that out-migration had much of an effect on poverty in Mato Grosso.

Given the importance of changes in inequality for explaining the different state level trajectories of poverty reduction in the 1990s, it would be useful to know how the relative importance of different components of income changed over time. Table 5.2 provides this information. For each source of income, the table shows its share in total rural household income, its concentration ratio and its contribution to the Gini index of total rural household income per capita. Table 5.2 shows that the share of agricultural earned income in total rural household income declined in all three states. In 2000 it continued to account for more

Table 5.2 Components of rural household income per capita: concentration ratios and shares

	Alagoas			Santa Catarina			Mato Grosso		
	1991	2000	change	1991	2000	change	1991	2000	change
Gini	0.48	0.59	24%	0.52	0.53	1%	0.59	0.63	7%
Agricultural earned income[1]									
Share	0.57	0.37	–35%	0.51	0.45	–12%	0.62	0.57	–8%
Concentration ratio	0.36	0.45	26%	0.46	0.54	18%	0.51	0.60	18%
Contribution to Gini (%)	43%	28%	–34%	46%	47%	3%	53%	54%	1%
Non-agricultural earned income[1]									
Share	0.29	0.32	9%	0.38	0.36	–5%	0.32	0.30	–7%
Concentration ratio	0.68	0.72	5%	0.61	0.55	–10%	0.72	0.71	–2%
Contribution to Gini (%)	41%	38%	–7%	44%	37%	–16%	39%	34%	–15%
Income from secondary occupations									
Share	0.02	0.02	–7%	0.02	0.02	–1%	0.02	0.01	–63%
Concentration ratio	0.74	0.91	24%	0.67	0.73	8%	0.87	0.80	–8%
Contribution to Gini (%)	3%	3%	–7%	3%	3%	6%	4%	1%	–68%
Income from social security or pensions									
Share	0.10	0.23	124%	0.06	0.13	122%	0.02	0.07	169%
Concentration ratio	0.49	0.64	31%	0.32	0.38	19%	0.43	0.46	6%
Contribution to Gini (%)	11%	25%	137%	4%	10%	161%	2%	5%	166%
Other Income									
Share	0.01	0.06	316%	0.03	0.03	10%	0.01	0.05	298%
Concentration ratio	0.68	0.55	–20%	0.72	0.53	–26%	0.78	0.69	–12%
Contribution to Gini (%)	2%	5%	168%	4%	3%	–20%	2%	6%	227%

Note: 1. Income from principal occupation only.

Source: Authors' calculations based on the micro data from the demographic censuses.

than 50 percent of household income only in Mato Grosso. The concentration ratios for agricultural income were lower than the Gini ratios in each of the three states in 1991, implying that agricultural income played an equalizing role at the beginning of the decade. In the 1990s however agricultural income became a less equalizing force in all states, and in Santa Catarina it even became slightly more concentrated than overall household income. The fourth row of the table shows that in 2000 the contribution of agricultural income to overall income inequality was in the neighborhood of 50 percent in Santa Catarina and Mato Grosso. In these two states, the drop in agriculture's share of rural income approximately balanced out increases in the agricultural concentration ratios, so that the agricultural contribution to overall inequality changed by less than 3 percent in each case. In Alagoas, in contrast, the contribution of agricultural earnings to overall inequality declined markedly in the 1990s – due to the sharp drop in agriculture's share in overall rural income – and only accounted for 28 percent by the end of the decade.

Non-agricultural earned income accounted for around a third of household income in all three states in both periods. It was a highly disequalizing force in Alagoas and Mato Grosso. Income from secondary occupations was the most disequalizing source of all, with concentration ratios between 0.73 and 0.91 in 2000. It is not surprising that income from secondary occupations should be distributed very unequally, given how rare a phenomenon it is. However, in no state did this source of income account for more than 2 percent of total income. Thus its contribution to the overall Gini was less than 3 percent in all states in 2000.

Social security payments to rural residents grew rapidly in the 1990s, and some authors believe that this provides an important part of the explanation for the decline in poverty. Table 5.2 shows that the share of rural income from social security and pensions more than doubled in all three states. In Alagoas it came to represent 23 percent of rural household income in 2000. Unfortunately social security benefits were distributed more unequally than income as a whole in this state. In the other two states, in contrast, social security benefits were a strongly equalizing force. In both cases the concentration ratios were at least 15 percentage points lower than their respective Ginis.

In order to shed light on how income sources differ for the poor and the rich, Table 5.3 reports income shares by source for the bottom and top halves of the rural income distribution. Several important conclusions can be drawn from this table. Firstly, income grew by the same proportion for the bottom and top halves of the income distribution in Santa Catarina, but by much more for the top half of the distribution in Alagoas and Mato Grosso. In Alagoas, income per capita actually fell for the bottom 50 percent. This confirms the pattern of changes observed in the Gini ratios in Table 5.1. Secondly, in the lower half of the income distribution, the share of income coming from agricultural earnings fell by more

Table 5.3 Components of rural household income per capita: bottom and top halves of the income distribution

	Alagoas			Santa Catarina			Mato Grosso		
	1991	2000	change	1991	2000	change	1991	2000	change
Bottom 50%									
Household income per capita[1]	22	14	–34%	47	77	65%	38	44	17%
Earned income in principal occupation	0.90	0.77	–14%	0.88	0.80	–9%	0.95	0.85	–11%
Agricultural	0.77	0.60	–21%	0.66	0.48	–28%	0.82	0.64	–22%
Non-agricultural	0.13	0.16	26%	0.21	0.31	49%	0.14	0.20	44%
Earned income in secondary occupation	0.01	0.00	–76%	0.01	0.01	–24%	0.01	0.00	–49%
Income from social security or pensions	0.09	0.14	57%	0.10	0.16	61%	0.04	0.11	202%
Other income	0.01	0.09	1097%	0.01	0.03	167%	0.00	0.05	872%
Top 50%									
Household income per capita[1]	92	104	13%	235	384	64%	234	327	40%
Earned income in principal occupation	0.85	0.68	–20%	0.89	0.82	–8%	0.94	0.88	–6%
Agricultural	0.52	0.34	–35%	0.48	0.45	–7%	0.58	0.56	–5%
Non-agricultural	0.33	0.34	3%	0.41	0.36	–11%	0.35	0.31	–11%
Earned income in secondary occupation	0.02	0.02	–9%	0.03	0.03	1%	0.03	0.01	–64%
Income from social security or pensions	0.11	0.25	129%	0.05	0.13	145%	0.02	0.06	165%
Other income	0.02	0.05	246%	0.03	0.03	–2%	0.01	0.05	267%

Note: 1. Income in constant R$ of 1/2002.

Source: Authors' calculations based on the micro data from the demographic censuses.

than 20 percent and the share coming from non-agricultural earnings rose by 25 to 50 percent in all three states. Thus in 2000 the poorest half of the rural population in these states received between 36 and 52 percent of their income from sources outside of agriculture. Thirdly, real social security benefits and the share of household income coming from this source grew for the bottom half of the distribution in all three states. Thus although social security became a less equalizing force in the 1990s, considerable benefits flowed to the poor as a result of the expansion of this program.

In addition to the heterogeneity in experiences across states that we have been discussing thus far, it is important to point out that there was substantial variability within states. Two examples should suffice. Although income per capita only rose by 4 percent in rural Alagoas as a whole, in a third of the counties it rose by more than 22 percent. In another third it contracted. Similarly, although the rural population in Alagoas declined by 12 percent, it grew in 40 percent of the counties. It is these differences in county level experiences that we seek to explain in the regression analysis of the next section.

REGRESSION RESULTS

We can test the hypotheses discussed above using a regression framework and county-level data derived from the demographic census micro data for 1991 and 2000. All measures refer only to the rural population in each county.[7]

We first examine the direct relationship between changes in poverty and changes in per capita income, inequality and population. We note that the incidence of poverty is determined by the average level of income and the distribution of income. Thus we explore the relationship between each of these and poverty. Table 5.4 presents the results of regressions of the change in the headcount poverty ratio on a set of independent variables. In models 1–3, we estimate individually the relationship between changes in poverty and changes in each of: (1) average income, (2) the Gini ratio, and (3) population.[8] Model 4 includes the changes in all three variables, and model 5 controls additionally for their initial levels.

In the first regression, the coefficient on per capita income growth is negative, as we would expect, and statistically significant. On average, counties with higher average income growth experienced greater poverty reduction. On the other hand, the second regression shows no statistically significant relationship between changes in poverty and changes in the county-level Gini ratio. This could be for a combination of two reasons. First, the correlation between changes in the Gini and changes in the level of income is positive, 0.38. Without controlling for average income growth, the estimated coefficient on the Gini in regression 2 picks up the combined effect of a larger increase in inequality and the associated higher per capita income growth. By contrast in regressions 4

Table 5.4 Regression results for change in headcount poverty rate, 1991–2000

	(1)	(2)	(3)	(4)	(5)
Changes in the variables[1]					
Income per capita	–0.08			–0.14	–0.12
	(–6.00)**			(–8.39)**	(–8.99)**
Gini		0.05		0.59	0.63
		(0.77)		(8.07)**	(10.25)**
Population			0.01	–0.01	–0.02
			(0.50)	(–0.32)	(–1.54)
Initial levels of the variables[2]					
Poverty					–0.36
					(–11.84)**
Gini					0.24
					(4.95)**
Population					–0.01
					(–1.71)
State dummies					
Alagoas	–0.02	–0.04	–0.04	–0.09	0.18
	(–2.84)**	(–3.66)**	(–4.26)**	(–7.57)**	(3.24)**
Sta. Catarina	–0.14	–0.20	–0.20	–0.10	0.00
	(–12.21)**	(–25.05)**	(–25.03)**	(–9.04)**	(0.09)
Mato Grosso	–0.08	–0.12	–0.12	–0.08	0.05
	(–5.52)**	(–8.47)**	(–9.05)**	(–6.37)**	(0.86)
Observations	372	372	372	372	372
Adjusted R-squared	0.76	0.68	0.68	0.83	0.89

Notes:
1. The changes in income and population are measured as proportional changes, i.e., 0.2 = 20% growth. The change in the Gini is measured as the change in the Gini ratio, which has a range from zero to one.
2. The level of poverty is measured by the headcount ratio. It has a range from zero to one. The natural log of initial population is the measure of initial population level.
   Robust t statistics in parentheses; * significant at 5%; ** significant at 1%.

and 5, the estimated coefficients on both per capita income growth and inequality change have the expected signs and are statistically significant. Thus, controlling for growth in average income and other factors, regressions 4 and 5 suggest that an additional standard deviation (0.11) in the decline in the Gini was associated with an additional 6.6 to 7.2 percentage point decline in poverty. Similarly, an additional standard deviation (0.69) in the rate of per capita income growth was associated with an additional poverty decline of 8.1 to 9.6 percentage points over the nine-year period.

A second possible explanation for the coefficient in regression 2 is that the Gini, a scalar summary statistic, imperfectly captures the changes in the income distribution that matter for poverty. Thus changes in the income distribution in favor of those who are either far above or far below the poverty line are unlikely to affect the incidence of poverty. Poverty will likely only fall when the distribution of income changes in favor of people who previously had incomes close to the poverty line. The state level evidence from Alagoas, where inequality rose substantially but poverty remained largely unchanged, is suggestive of this type of effect.

Regression 3 relates the change in poverty to the rate of population growth, without other controls. We emphasize that we are estimating a reduced-form equation that reflects a potentially simultaneous relationship. In future research, we would like to identify these two relationships separately. For now, we simply estimate the net statistical relationship between poverty change and population growth. Regression 3 shows no statistically significant relationship between the two. Regressions 4 and 5 show a negative relationship, but in neither case is the coefficient statistically significant at the 10 percent level. Thus, either we could treat the coefficient as zero, or we could conclude that it provides weak evidence for a negative impact of population change on poverty (after controlling for the effect of levels and changes in the Gini and average income). A weak negative effect runs contrary to our hypothesis that population decline contributed to poverty reduction. It implies that greater population decreases were associated with a slightly lower poverty reduction. We tentatively call this the 'direct effect' of population change on poverty. It may be however that there exists an indirect relationship between population change and a reduction in poverty via average income growth and/or change in the Gini. An important question then is to determine which of these two effects dominates. We now address this question.[9]

Table 5.5 presents the results of regressions of: (1) per capita income growth, and (2) change in the Gini, on population growth and a set of controls.[10] The statistically significant coefficients on population growth in both equations, each with the expected sign, provide evidence that population decline is significantly associated with both faster per capita income growth and greater decline in inequality. Thus the estimated coefficients suggest that one additional standard deviation (0.32) of population decline is associated with an additional 1.3 percentage point decline in the Gini index, and an additional 5.1 percentage points of average income growth. Both forces should contribute to accelerating the decline in poverty.

Combining the results of Table 5.5 with those in equation 5 of Table 5.4, we can calculate that an additional standard deviation of population decline is associated with improvements in average income and the Gini that together account for an additional 1.4 percentage point reduction in poverty. On the other

Table 5.5 Regression results for changes in Gini and per capita income, 1991–2000

	Change in Gini (1)	Growth of income per capita (2)
Changes in the variables[1]		
Population	0.04	–0.16
	(3.34)**	(2.15)*
Income per capita	0.08	
	(12.03)**	
Gini		4.08
		(7.02)**
Initial levels of the variables[2]		
Population	0.009	–0.092
	(1.62)	(2.73)**
Income per capita	–0.011	–0.375
	(0.90)	(4.73)**
Gini	–0.523	1.687
	(10.80)**	(4.71)**
State dummies		
Alagoas	0.31	1.20
	(4.11)**	(2.65)**
Sta. Catarina	0.18	2.50
	(2.19)*	(5.33)**
Mato Grosso	0.27	2.00
	(3.38)**	(4.16)**
Observations	372	372
Adjusted R-squared	0.69	0.70

Notes:

1. The changes in income and population are measured as proportional changes, i.e., 0.2 = 20% growth. The change in the Gini is measured as the change in the Gini ratio, which has a range from zero to one.
2. The level of poverty is measured by the headcount ratio. It has a range from zero to one. The natural log of initial population is the measure of initial population level.

   Robust t statistics in parentheses; *significant at 5%; **significant at 1%.

hand, if we admit that the coefficient on population change in equation 5 is not zero, the additional standard deviation of population decline also has a direct effect on poverty that leads to an additional 0.6 percentage point increase in poverty. The net impact of the direct and indirect effects is an additional 0.8 percentage point decline in poverty. These findings are consistent with our hypothesis that out-migration contributed to poverty reduction. We are not able to conclude however if it is simply due to removing poorer individuals from the rural population or by improving the living standards of rural residents who were previously classified as poor.

Finally, we turn to the relationship between changes in income and inequality and the composition of income by source. Table 5.6 reports the results of regressions of per capita income growth and change in the Gini on initial shares of total income from various sources and changes in those shares. The omitted categories are the share and change in share of income from social security and pensions. None of the initial shares is statistically significant in either equation, but all of the changes are statistically significant in the income growth equation (1), and all but the change in the share of income from agriculture is significant in the Gini change equation (2). However the statistical significance of the change in a given share depends on the choice of omitted category. The more interesting question is whether two share changes are statistically significantly different from each other. The coefficients on the share changes are all positive and jointly significant in each regression, relative to the omitted category – the change in the share from social security and pensions. Thus in counties where the share of income from social security increased more, both average income and inequality grew less. Given the dramatic and generalized increase of social security coverage in rural areas over this period, it is likely that the share of income from social security grew faster simply where the denominator – total income – grew slower. However the coefficients in the equation for inequality change are consistent with the concentration ratios reported in Table 5.2, which show that in two out of the three states studied social security income is equalizing, and more equalizing than income earned from the primary occupation.[11]

The changes in shares of income from agricultural and non-agricultural employment are statistically different from each other in the Gini change equation, but not in the per capita income growth equation. In both cases the agricultural coefficient is smaller than the non-agricultural one. Thus counties where the importance of non-agricultural employment income grew relative to that of agricultural employment income experienced a larger increase in inequality. This is consistent with the fact, seen in Table 5.2, that non-agricultural employment income is disequalizing in both census years in every state, and always more disequalizing than agricultural employment income. On the other hand, though not statistically significantly different, the relative size of the two corresponding coefficients in the income growth equation would tend to suggest that greater decline in the agricultural share of employment income, in favor of non-agricultural employment, is associated with greater average income growth. To interpret the coefficients, an additional standard deviation (0.17) decline in the agricultural employment income share, all in favor of non-agricultural employment income, is associated with an additional 8.6 percentage points in per capita income growth and an additional 3.5 point increase in the Gini index over the

Table 5.6 Regression results for effects of income sources on changes in income and inequality, 1991–2000

	Growth of income per capita (1)	Change in Gini (2)
Shares		
Agricultural employment[1]	0.49	–0.12
	(0.40)	(0.63)
Non-agricultural employment[1]	–0.01	–0.12
	(0.01)	(0.55)
Secondary occupations	2.31	0.04
	(1.16)	(0.11)
Other sources	–0.33	0.08
	(0.16)	(0.27)
Changes in shares		
Agricultural employment[1]	3.34	0.17
	(5.30)**	(1.63)
Non-agricultural employment[1]	3.84	0.37
	(5.31)**	(3.29)**
Secondary occupations	5.43	0.38
	(4.19)**	(1.47)
Other sources	4.52	0.55
	(3.12)**	(3.26)**
State dummies		
Alagoas	0.18	0.22
	(0.16)	(1.20)
Sta. Catarina	0.72	0.13
	(0.61)	(0.69)
Mato Grosso	0.27	0.16
	(0.22)	(0.79)
Observations	372	372
Adjusted R-squared	0.57	0.38

Notes:
1. Agricultural and non-agricultural employment refer to income in primary occupation only.
Robust t statistics in parentheses; *significant at 5%; **significant at 1%.

nine-year period. According to the coefficients in Table 5.4, these changes are offsetting, so that if anything, poverty would have a slightly greater tendency to increase.

These results do not support the proposition that the shift to non-agricultural sources of earned income is significantly responsible for a reduction in poverty.

Future research could further test this relationship by focusing more specifically on the composition of income of those who are poor or relatively near the poverty line.

CONCLUSIONS

In this chapter we analyzed the decline in rural poverty in the 1990s. For Brazil as a whole, rural poverty fell by 16 percent in this period. The decline was largely explained by a 32 percent increase in household income per capita. The Gini index of inequality rose by 7 percent and thus partially offset the improvements from income growth. At the state level, the record was much more varied. In one state that we examined, poverty declined by more than twice the national average, due to rapid per capita income growth (64 percent) and virtually no change in inequality. In another state, poverty declined by only 3 percent due to weak income growth and a 24 percent increase in the Gini. Finally, using county-level data from three states, we also found that income growth was the most important factor that contributed to the decline in poverty. Median household income per capita grew by 43 percent at the county level in this period, while the median Gini actually rose by 9 percent.

Brazil also experienced a significant decline in the rural population and in the workforce in agriculture in the 1990s. We found that where the rural population declined at a faster rate, inequality rose less and household income per capita grew more. On the other hand we found that, controlling for population decline's 'indirect' relationship to poverty changes via changes in income level and the Gini, greater population decline was also weakly associated with a greater increase in rural poverty. This 'direct' relationship was likely due to the fact that the Gini imperfectly summarizes the entire income distribution in a single number. The indirect effect dominated however, and on balance population decline was associated with greater poverty reduction. In future research we would like to identify whether this finding was due to poor people migrating disproportionately, or to real improvements in the standard of living of the poor in rural areas of Brazil. In order to overcome problems of endogeneity and have greater confidence in our statistical results, in future research we would also like to move to a simultaneous equations framework that could capture the multiple ways in which changes in poverty, population, income, and inequality mutually determine each other.

There has been considerable debate in Brazil recently about the importance of non-agricultural sources of earned income for the rural poor, and about the potentially beneficial effects of the expansion of the rural social security program in the 1990s. In light of the evidence that agricultural earned income became much more concentrated in the 1990s, both non-agricultural earned income and social security could have played important roles in poverty reduction. With regard to the distribution of income at a state level however, non-agricultural sources of earned income were a strongly disequalizing force in two of the three states that we analyzed. At a county level, our results suggest that where non-agricultural income increased faster than income from either agriculture or social security, inequality grew at a faster rate. Growth of non-agricultural relative to agricultural earned income was also weakly associated with faster growth. The net effect of an increase in the share of non-agricultural earned income was a slight increase in the rate of growth of poverty.

Income from social security, in contrast, was a strongly equalizing force in two of the three states, but it became less equalizing in all states in this period. For the bottom half of the income distribution, social security benefits grew in real terms in all three states and were likely to have played an important role in reducing poverty. At a county level, the growth in the share of income derived from social security was also associated with slower growth in inequality.

In conclusion, this study of three Brazilian states has important implications for the debate about the causes of the decline in Brazilian rural poverty in the 1990s. Firstly, it is clear that income growth was the driving force behind poverty reduction in this period. The sources of income growth however varied considerably across states, suggesting that there is no single path to rural poverty reduction in Brazil. Secondly, although we found that migration was associated with a decline in the rural poverty rate, the magnitude of the effect was not as large as we had expected. Finally, the expansion of social security benefits in rural areas in the 1990s played a very important role in contributing to poverty reduction. However the concentration of income from this source rose in all three states. Thus although the social security program had a positive impact on poverty, it is likely that a targeted anti-poverty program could have achieved the same reduction at a lower fiscal cost.

NOTES

We would like to thank Keith Griffin for the endless inspiration, insight, and guidance he has offered to us over the years. We also thank the following individuals for helpful comments: Aziz Khan, Eustáquio Reis, Gervásio Castro de Resende, and the participants at the conference Egalitarian Development in the Era of Globalization: A Conference in Honor of Keith Griffin, held at University of Massachusetts, Amherst, 22–24 April 2004. This material is based upon work supported by a grant from the United States Agency for International Development, and a subcontract from BASIS/CRSP/University of Wisconsin at Madison. The views expressed in this paper are solely those of the authors.

1. The decline of agricultural prices was reversed with the floating of the currency in January 1999 and the upward trend in many international commodity prices in the subsequent few years.
2. Barros et al. (2004) do not find a particularly large effect due to demographic changes of this type. They show that although these changes contributed to raising household income, they

also increased inequality. As a result, the impact on poverty is overshadowed by other variables in their study.

3. Additional research is necessary to investigate the magnitude of own-consumption, its stability over time, and to develop an approach for estimating total income in rural Brazil. There is no doubt that the exclusion of own consumption biases estimates of poverty upward. In terms of the distribution of income however there are offsetting forces and the net impact is unclear. Hoffman (1999) for example cites the under-reporting of incomes at the upper end of the income distribution as an important limitation of the census and the household survey (PNAD) data.
4. See Khan and Riskin (2003) for a more detailed discussion of concentration ratios.
5. A time series on national level poverty in Brazil is available at www.ipeadata.gov.br.
6. There are limitations to analyzing 'rural' vs 'urban' Brazil that stem from how these areas are defined by the Brazilian Institute of Geography and Statistics (IBGE), and from the fact that what might have been classified as rural in 1991 was sometimes reclassified as urban in 2000. Nevertheless the analysis conducted in Barros et al. (2004) shows that the levels, trends, and explanations regarding poverty in the 1990s are similar for households in 'rural' Brazil and households of people who work in agriculture.
7. Because of changes in county boundaries between the two census years, it was necessary to aggregate counties into 'smallest comparable areas' (AMCs in Portuguese) in order to obtain consistent geographic units across the two years. For the three states under study, there were 520 counties in 2000, 409 in 1991, and we aggregated these into 372 AMCs following the guidelines provided to us by the Institute of Applied Economic Research (IPEA) in Rio de Janeiro, Brazil. We thank Marcia Pimentel at IPEA for valuable assistance in this process. For simplicity, in the following discussion we refer to them as 'counties'.
8. All regressions include state dummies to control for the heterogeneity across states that we observed in Table 5.1.
9. The existence of a weak direct relationship between population change and poverty change might be explained by the fact that the Gini imperfectly captures changes in the income distribution as they relate to poverty. Thus, due to the nature of the Gini as a scalar summary of an entire income distribution, it is possible for population change to have a 'direct effect' on poverty rather than only an indirect effect via income and the Gini.
10. Of course, as the table makes clear, the two dependent variables are correlated, and it may be that causation goes in both directions. Although we would ideally find adequate exogenous instruments for each one in order to properly identify and estimate the whole system, our focus here is on the partial correlation between each of these and population growth.
11. Of course, a difference between Tables 5.2 and 5.6 is that the state-level concentration ratios for social security income reported in Table 5.2 reflect both within-county and between-county concentrations.

REFERENCES

Barros, Ricardo Paes de, Mirela de Carvalho and Samuel Franco (2004), 'Pobreza Rural e Trabalho Agrícola no Brasil ao Longo da Década de Noventa', mimeo, Rio de Janeiro, January.

Beltrão, Kaizô Iwakami, Sonoe S. Pinheiro and Francisco E.B. de Oliveira (2002), 'Population and social security in Brazil: an analysis with emphasis on constitutional changes', IPEA, discussion paper no. 862, Rio de Janeiro, March.

Corrêa, Angela M.C.J. (forthcoming), 'Evolução do Rendimento Médio, Desigualdade e Pobreza entre as Pessoas Ocupadas na Agricultura Brasileira: Uma Análise Regional do Período 1981–1998', in Mauricio F. Blanco (ed.), *Estrutura Agrária, Mercado de Trabalho e Pobreza Rural no Brasil*, IPEA.

Delgado, Guilherme and José Celso Cardoso Jr. (2000), 'Principais Resultados da

Pesquisa Domciliar Sobre a Previdência Rural na Região Sul do Brasil (Projeto Avaliação Socioecômica da Previdência Social Rural)', IPEA discussion paper no. 734, Rio de Janeiro, June.

Ferreira, Francisco H.G. and Peter Lanjouw (2001), 'Rural nonfarm activities and poverty in the Brazilian northeast', *World Development*, **29** (3), 509–28.

Graziano da Silva, José and Mauro E. Del Grossi (2001), 'Rural nonfarm employment and incomes in Brazil: patterns and evolution', *World Development*, **29** (3), 443–53.

Hanson, Gordon H. and Christopher Wodruff (2003), 'Emigration and educational attainment in Mexico', University of California, Riverside mimeo, April.

Helfand, Steven M. (2004), 'What can be learned from the agricultural censuses about rural poverty in Brazil?', paper prepared for presentation at the conference of the Sociedade Brasileira de Economia e Sociologia Rural (SOBER), Cuiabá, Mato Grosso, Brazil, 25–28 July.

Helfand, Steven M. and Gervásio Castro de Rezende (2004), 'The impact of sector-specific and economy-wide policy reforms on the agricultural sector in Brazil: 1980–98', *Contemporary Economic Policy*, **22** (2), 194–212.

Hoffmann, Rodolfo (2000), 'Mensuração da Desigualdade e da Pobreza no Brasil', in Ricardo Henriques (ed.), *Desigualdade e Pobreza no Brasil,* Rio de Janeiro: IPEA.

Hoffman, Rodolfo (2001), 'Desigualdade no Brasil: A Contribuição das Aposentadorias', UNICAMP, Instituto de Economia, mimeo.

IBGE (2000 and 1999), *Censo Demográfico*, Rio de Janeiro, IBGE.

Khan, Aziz R. and Carl Riskin (2003), 'Growth and distribution of household income in China between 1995 and 2002', mimeo, December.

United Nations Development Program, IPEA, and Fundação João Pinheiro (2003), *Atlas of Human Development in Brazil*, Rio de Janeiro: UNDP.

6. Has Colombia finally found an agrarian reform that works?

Albert Berry

INTRODUCTION

Like most Latin American countries, Colombia has been characterized by extreme inequality in the distribution of access to agricultural land (CIDA, 1966) and very serious ambiguities around property rights; these related problems have contributed to many other social and economic ills, including most notably the waves of violence which swept the country periodically during the twentieth century and part of the nineteenth.[1] There has been periodic recognition of these land issues as serious problems by independent observers, political parties and governments and, on occasion, attempts have been made to 'reform' the agrarian structure. Had any of these attempts been successful either in improving the size distribution of landownership or in clarifying land rights in a positive way, Colombia's currently very unhappy state might be quite different. Several at least half-hearted attempts have been made and one initiative – undertaken in the 1930s – appears to have had the potential for a serious positive impact.

Effective land reforms, where achieved, have taken a variety of paths, depending on the nature of the agrarian structure, administrative issues and politics. In cases where there is no feasible way to provide land to those who need it except to expropriate it from current owners (or holders), a serious political confrontation is probable. Most of the effective reforms undertaken under such conditions have been carried out quickly, in spite of possibly high administrative costs,[2] some injustice (for example horizontal inequality among former owners) and some inefficiency, as where the redistribution does not get the right land into the right hands. The latter problem is often alleviated by the fact that the current tillers are the obvious recipients of the land they are currently tilling. Another feature of the most successful reforms is the establishment of a land ceiling (or ceilings),[3] which discourages reconcentration of land and helps to keep market prices for land down by reducing the channelling of savings into that asset. Where, instead, the pressure for land is satisfied on a 'frontier', the main challenge is not how to get land away from the current largeholders but rather how to prevent the creation of new largeholdings on the frontier, and thereby assure that all the families in need of land will in fact get it. Countries with successful homesteading experiences (like the US in the West) had laws which sufficiently limited the size of the newly created farms and achieved reasonably well-functioning property rights; they also provided adequate support via investments in infrastructure (roads, markets, communications and so on). Colombia has never been land scarce in the way of many Asian nations, and a healthy evolution of land structure on the frontier could have very positive effects.

Four features of the unfolding pattern of control over land and its use from the time of independence of Gran Colombia – spanning present-day Colombia, Venezuela, Ecuador and Panama – are particularly worthy of note:

1. Ambiguity as to who had rights to land has often been as striking a problem as inequality in the distribution of that land *per se*. The ambiguity has been the combined result of situations where ownership is not yet defined juridically, of conflicting interpretations of what is correct or legal, and of inconsistency between law and practice.
2. The state has been an important actor or potential actor, most obviously because most of the currently exploited agricultural land was once in the public domain,[4] so much depended on how that land was alienated. How the land laws were implemented depended on governmental administrative capacity. At times the government acted as referee between disputing parties on land and related issues.
3. The state was not one consistent actor, partly because different parties and factions had different views on land questions, but more importantly because local governments systematically favoured the largeholders (or aspirants to that status) while the national governments took a wider range of stances, depending on party, timing and interpretation of the impact of agrarian structure.
4. Control of land was part of the bigger issue of control of the factors of agricultural production, the other principal factor being labour. Many of the tensions over the years can be seen as tugs-of-war between largeholders and smallholders (or aspirants to those two statuses) but they can also be seen as disputes between labour and land or capital, where those who controlled the bulk of the land also needed access to labour – hence the discussion of vagrancy laws and labour coercion, while the workers who supplied labour wanted better conditions under which to apply it, the best being ownership of land.

The national government was the most able of these actors to take a broad perspective of the welfare of all parties, including society's need for an adequate food supply. Accordingly, from early on administrations attempted something of a balancing act among interests. But many of the results of such involvement were unplanned or inadvertent. A number of its early policies had the effect of concentrating land, including the division of the *resguardos* (reserves for the indigenous populations), which took place mainly between 1830 and 1860 (Safford, 1995, p. 120). More important in this process of concentration was the wholesale alienation of public land during the nineteenth century in return for depreciated government bonds, in order to shore up the finances and the credit of the national government. Public lands were also ceded in large tracts to induce foreign immigrants to take them over. Much of the alienated land was not developed however, and when laws were passed making continued ownership contingent on exploitation, much of it was abandoned. From the time that actual appropriations of such alienated lands began to occur on some scale (in the 1870s with a temporary boom in chinchona bark) these 'exploitation laws' were laid down with the intent of protecting squatters who might be on land claimed by largeholders (Safford, 1995, p. 121). Such laws however had limited effect, with the powerful usually getting their way.

THE TRAGIC FAILURE OF THE 1930s ATTEMPT

The unfolding scenario of the 1920s and 1930s precipitated the first and most serious approach to a significant agrarian reform in Colombia, and the one whose success could clearly have had the greatest impact on the subsequent evolution of the economy and society.[5] Events conspired to bring Colombia closer to a real reform than any other country of the region at the time, but then conspired to induce the central government to pull back at the critical moment.[6] The push for reform was the result of a combination of chronic inequalities and injustices; the added tensions associated with the fast growth of coffee production and the overall economic buoyancy of the 1920s; and the new pressures associated with the reversal of those upward trends when the Great Depression made itself felt in Colombia in the 1930s.

History shows that the conditions which lead to significantly positive agrarian reforms are rare. Sometimes foreign involvement is important; in its absence a special combination of internal factors must create the opening. In Colombia the combination as of the early 1930s included a serious level of rural unrest which was of direct concern to political leaders because of its destabilizing impact and which also worried those who saw it as a major impediment to agricultural production,[7] especially of food crops, at a time when the supply of these appeared insecure. At the same time, important figures in the Liberal Party saw the dissatisfied squatters (*colonos*) and smallholders as a political resource on which they might draw.

Several factors contributed to the rural unrest. The inequality *cum* insecurity or ambiguity of land distribution constituted a dangerous backdrop, a frequent source of conflict and tension[8] especially when complemented by a conscious sense of grievance by those with little or no land that the largeholders were on properties which rightfully belonged to them. Inter-party tension was high, a legacy of the history of periodic rural violence.[9] Stagnating or declining incomes due to the world depression and to heightening population pressure on the land were conjunctural elements of the Colombian brew in the 1930.[10] Towards the end of the period 1880–1930 during which coffee became Colombia's dominant export, land had become increasingly valuable and an increase in government revenues, together with an inflow of foreign resources, had permitted a burst of public investment in infrastructure, further raising land values and the demand for labour. The improved transportation network and the growing demand for coffee led to a great increase in the encroachments on squatter-occupied land between 1918 and 1931. A combination of the pressure from these encroachments and increasing confidence that action might now bear fruit (Legrand, 1986, p. 93)[11] led to a peasant counter-offensive after 1928, during which many of the great estates formed earlier were invaded; at this point the public land issue became a national political problem, inducing the government to intervene in order to clarify the legal definition of private property (Legrand, 1986, p. xvii).

The national authorities' concern with agricultural production was related in part to the impact of the conflicts on overall agricultural output,[12] but also to the longer-run issue of land structure and food production. As the government focused more on the needs of the industrialization process, it became increasingly concerned with agricultural production for the domestic market – most of which came from the small farm sector – and less with exports; spurring such production might require a reform of land policy. Most observers identified the monopoly of land by the great *latifundia* (large agricultural estate administered by wealthy landowners) as the root of agricultural backwardness (Lopez, 1927; Uribe, 1936). Support for small cultivators included the country's first planned colonization programme and a 1926 landmark decision of the supreme court which made it more difficult for largeholders to claim ownership of land. The advent of the Great Depression ended an economic boom in Colombia and provided added impetus for colonization; the government now provided free rail tickets to get the unemployed back to rural areas. Haciendas, afflicted by falling profits, tried to reimpose the low wages and arduous work conditions of the pre-boom years (Palacios, 1980; Jimenez, 1986). Many people now struck out to find their own plots and independence.[13] An increasing share, instead of going to the hinterland, tried for better-located public land or unused portions of large estates.

Once the *colono* movements got under way, the squatters became mobilizable political capital, in particular for the Liberal Party which had just returned to power. All of the standard arguments in favour of helping and defending the small settlers were aired at this time and various approaches were taken to deal with the two problems perceived by policy-makers – the conflict and violence associated with competing claims to land and the (related) problem of inadequate agricultural production. A judicial approach through application of the 1926 Supreme Court ruling would have deprived the landlords of much territory and was hence too radical to have a chance of success.[14] Purchase and parcelization of large properties was widely viewed as both amicable and logical. The purchase of three haciendas in areas of most serious conflict and the provision of free title to *colonos* who had occupied them in the late 1920s and early 1930s did calm social unrest, but the fiscal cost was high and the government decided that thenceforth the peasants should pay full market value. The programme then failed, as peasants refused to pay for land which they believed to be public and hence legally available to them (Legrand, 1986, p. 139). By the time the legislative response finally came in the form of Law 200 of 1936, the balance of power had shifted back to the landlords. The *colono* movement had lost some political influence due to co-optation of leaders and to internal dissention around the parcelization programme. Land struggles continued unabated but the leftist threat they posed gradually receded as the *colonos*' representatives sought accommodation with the Liberal Party. President Lopez was now in the process of building a power base among urban labour. Meanwhile the largeholders mounted a sophisticated campaign against his regime by focusing elite hostility against any state intervention on the land issue, claiming that the government was trying to destroy private property, and warning of the threat of revolution. Lopez became convinced that he could regain political control only by resolving the land issue in favour of the landlords.[15] The government continued to assert the objective of expanding independent peasant properties, and it revoked unused land grants and supported colonization and parcelization projects. But Land Law 200, commonly thought to favour the settlers (see for example Hirschman, 1965), in fact reinforced the position of the large estate owners: by making it easier for them to claim land as theirs, it detracted from the argument that such land was still in the public domain. At the same time it put a premium on large aspirants to ownership to evict small squatters in order to avoid a conflict over claims. It was also accompanied by a vagrancy law which facilitated the removal of expelled *colonos* (Safford, 1995, p. 141). All of these factors no doubt contributed to the escalation of the rural violence which broke out a decade later. In short, Law 200 did little or nothing to slow the continuing large-scale appropriation of public lands in the frontier regions, nor to deal with the underlying tensions between settlers and large entrepreneurs over public lands that were to remain a root cause of social conflict in the Colombian countryside. Failure to resolve the land issue when there appears to have been a chance contributed significantly to 'La Violencia', the worst wave of violence to afflict Colombia. Although the earlier and still fairly standard interpretations of that violence have tended to treat it as a product of the Liberal–Conservative hatreds, and hence give little weight to its social and economic roots, there seems no doubt that these factors were very important. Rather than improving the situation of aspiring smallholders, Law 200 appears to have backfired by promoting both privatization by largeholders and expulsion of *colonos*.[16] The rate of privatization of public land rose precipitously during La Violencia from an average of 60000 hectares per year over 1931–45 to 150000 hectares over 1946–54 and to 375000 hectares over 1955–59 (Legrand, 1989, p. 13, citing Diot, 1976), so based on the historical experience one would assume that the incidence of expulsion also increased at this time.[17]

In the event this attempt at reform had a very limited effect on Colombia's agrarian history; it may never be clear whether it really came close to having a large one. Motivation was present from various sources: a desire to help the *colonos* in their struggle, probably partly out of a sense of fairness but certainly in the expectation that this would help to avoid a food crisis; a recognition or belief that the large estates were unproductive and a basic source of production stagnation; a fear of escalating violence; and the positive political incentive of using the *colonos* as a political support group. Might this have been enough? What sort of reform might have been politically possible? Despite some recognition that large estates were a source of inefficiency (the research on this point was of course much less definitive than it is today), the idea of a fully equalizing reform which would have done away with large farms (as occurred in Japan, Korea and Taiwan) would have been too radical. The only way to equalize the distribution would have been to expropriate at low prices, and this would have created too much resistance, as can be seen from the reaction which occurred within a few years of the landlords perceiving a serious threat to themselves. Two related questions stand out. Could enough have been done in defense of small farmers' rights to affect the overall agrarian structure over the course of time? And were policy-makers likely to take the right steps to achieve that goal? A program which went as far as implementing the *colonos*' interpretation of the homestead laws of 1874 and 1892 would have done the trick, but it would have created much resistance from the largeholders who had taken over lands claimed by the *colonos*. Rectifying much of the past injustice, as defined by the *colonos*, would thus have been a tall order. A more realistic goal politically would have been to implement *de facto* the homestead provisions to lands in the process of being settled and developed, thus focusing the effort on future colonization rather than what had already taken place – in other words following a course similar to that of the United States. As of the 1930s, a large amount of colonization was still to take place in Colombia. Widespread social tension, violence, and injustice accompanied this process. Such outcomes were unavoidable, but a few ameliorative measures might have reduced their severity. The best hopes for amelioration were through modest contributions from redistribution of purchased estates and expropriation of selected haciendas. A determined implementation of homestead laws would have established tough groups of homesteaders who would themselves have been a powerful force in defense of their interests and rights. Had it been possible to implement something of this sort even in, say, half of the newly settled agricultural zones from the 1930s onward, the contemporary agrarian structure would be significantly different.

Might policy-makers have come up with this solution and been able to implement it? I am unaware of anything close to this 'vision' having been mooted at the time. Such long-run planning is unusual; most policies respond to shorter-term pressures. And even with the vision, implementation of laws in frontier areas is hard, so Colombia's central government would have had to greatly improve its presence in the hinterlands. A fully successful strategy of this sort would also have required a reasonable level of public sector support to the new frontier smallholders so that, unlike their neglected *ejidatario* counterparts in Mexico but like the small farmers in the East Asian countries, their productivity would rise over time, creating a prosperous smallholder society. In retrospect Colombia has off and on provided some support of this sort, especially in the case of coffee, though in that case substantially executed through the offices of the more private than public Coffee Growers' Federation. Given a starting point at which the government saw a production crisis looming, it had the incentive to move in this direction. The experience of many countries has shown that when a large and reasonably secure and prosperous smallholder sector exists it can put some pressure on governments to provide the research, extension, credit and other types of support which it needs.[18]

Whatever the possibilities of a productive reform in the 1930s, history took a different course, and the next decades saw the ferocious 'Violencia' for which the country became notorious.

AGRARIAN REFORM 1960s-STYLE: LAW 135 OF 1961 AND THE *USUARIOS*

Since the 1930s experience just described, Colombian governments have addressed problems of agrarian structure several times and in different ways, always against a backdrop of high levels of rural conflict and violence.

The next period of activity occurred in the 1960s. By that time Colombia had entered a period of relatively fast but very dualistic growth in agriculture (3.5 percent per year over 1950–90). A rapid expansion of commercial agriculture was due partly to incentives to mechanize and to intensify the use of modern inputs and partly to the pattern of protection from imports (Jaramillo, 1998, p. 29). The growing power of modern commercial farmers represented an important contrast with the 1930s and helped to limit agrarian reform efforts (de Janvry and Sadoulet, 1993). Traditional (*campesino*) agriculture, without comparable incentives and support, was generally stagnant. Under this dualistic pattern of growth, labour demand grew slowly, at only 0.6 percent per year over 1950–87; the exclusionary pattern of growth fed social tensions and violence in the rural areas.[19] Fajardo (1986, p. 93) and others refer to massive expulsions of *campesinos* during this period, some through the displacement of former workers and tenants on the traditional haciendas as they converted to modern agriculture, and some due to the way the 'Violencia' played itself out.

As in the early 1930s, there was some recognition of deep injustices in Colombia's agrarian structure.[20] Carlos Lleras Restrepo, later president, agreed that fending off the sort of rural-based revolution exemplified by China was not solely a military matter but required improving the living conditions of the rural poor (Lleras Restrepo as quoted by Perry, 1985, pp. 104–5). Of more immediate concern to most politicians was the fact that, despite its impressive growth, modern commercial agriculture produced little of the chief traditional foods (except for rice); the price of basic items rose at an average of 40 percent per year over 1955–59. Population growth was now reaching its peak rate of 3 percent or a bit higher. But the pressures against significant reform were, as usual, very strong and the supporters of the status quo were articulate and persuasive. The Sociedad Colombiana de Agricultores (SAC) pushed for colonization as the way to provide new smallholdings, and even worried that a redistribution of land could flood the markets for agricultural goods (Fajardo, 1986, p. 105).

Law 135 of 1961 which founded the Instituto Colombiano para la Reforma Agraria – (INCORA) had the backing of the Alliance for Progress with its reformist rhetoric, but both the law itself and its implementation reflected its compromise character. The easy way out was to opt for the colonization route (which appeared to hurt no one), while promising to touch private property only in special cases. Tellingly, the prominent Conservative leader Alvaro Gomez Hurtado agreed that Law 135 was indispensable.[21]

More than half of INCORA's projects and 75 percent of the titling during the 1960s took place in the 'red areas' of intense *campesino* conflict, guerrilla influence and strict military control; its activities were coordinated with those of the armed forces (Perry, 1985, pp. 105–6). Over 1962–70 the main expenditure categories were land improvement and subsidized credit (both over a quarter) with land purchase accounting for only 8.3 percent; this reflected the fact that the law was basically designed to undertake directed colonization, with the state supplying the infrastructure, both economic and social.[22]

As well as being too small to make a major difference to agrarian structure, the INCORA reform was badly designed and executed. Though on its first projects there was in principal a ceiling of 50 hectares per newly established farm, none of INCORA's projects stuck to it and in some cases land concentration was in fact very high and treatment unequal among beneficiaries.[23] The lack of any general landownership ceiling meant that by the late 1980s, of 3.3

million hectares titled over the years by INCORA, 60 percent was in the hands of larger ranchers (Legrand, 1989, p. 27), reflecting both INCORA's focus on titling and the tendency for small settlers to clear the land, then pass it on to ranchers. The cost of the investments in land improvement, financed in part with World Bank credit, was very high (INCORA, 1970, p. 20). Obligatory supervised credit and a high level of intervention by INCORA in the selection of crops and use of inputs were questionable features of the INCORA model of agrarian reform. In any case, this one did not achieve much positive result.[24]

It is clear that the programme was too small to have had any lasting impact on the inequality of land ownership. By 1972 only 13 367 families had been granted land apart from that in colonization zones with an average of 18.8 hectares (Perry, 1985, p. 111, citing IICA-CIRA, 1970), when perhaps a half million families were looking for it. The reform had virtually no effect on largeholdings or the best lands in the country.

President Carlos Lleras Restrepo (1966–70) took the agrarian issue more seriously than the other National Front presidents. Law 1 of 1968 provided more funding to INCORA, and established a period of ten years by the end of which land was to be passed on to sharecroppers or tenants who had applied for it and who satisfied certain (in fact difficult) conditions (Fajardo, 1986, p. 111). But like most such presumably well-meaning legislation on landlord–tenant relationships, this one backfired by providing an incentive for landlords to accelerate the process of tenant displacement. Of the 545 000 tenants inscribed, by June 1974 only 2.3 percent had become owners, with some of this occurring at the expense of small or medium owners, according to Mejia Vallejo (1974, pp. 302, 312).

The most important potentially positive step taken by this administration was the promotion of a *campesino* organization (the Asociación Nacional de Usuarios Campesinos – ANUC), designed as a sort of pseudo pressure group for the recipients of government services in rural areas, while still essentially under the control of the government.[25] Lleras saw the need for *campesino* involvement to assure that agrarian reform would in fact help them, and realized they would not organize unless its potential was clear to them (Fajardo, 1986, p. 111). Although for its first couple of years ANUC's ideological directions were those of the founders, its heterogeneity (members ranging from small and medium-sized capitalist farms to landless workers) made it vulnerable to division, and its internal differences were deftly exploited by the opponents of reform, especially under the new Conservative administration of Misael Pastrana (1970–74). Controlling ANUC required a high level of repression, which helped to radicalize the group and heighten the internal conflict between the moderates and the radicals. With many of the majority hardline group persuaded that invasions were the only way to get access to land (Fajardo, 1986, p. 125), these now became common. What began as a plausible way to involve the *campesinos* as pressure group and participant in a process of reform wound up leading to their repression and setting the stage for the next, quite different, approach to the '*campesino* problem', mainly during the government of Alfonso Lopez.

THE 'COMMUNAL FARMS' (*EMPRESAS COMUNITARIAS*): A FOOTNOTE IN THE HISTORY OF AGRARIAN POLICY IN COLOMBIA

The final attempt to finesse the dilemma of keeping peasant unrest under control (by the early 1970s conflict was particularly acute on the north coast), without either taking land from the largeholders or spending seriously on creating potentially productive small farms, took the form of the *empresas comunitarias.* IICA-CIRA supported and provided advice on this initiative, having reached the conclusion that there was not enough land on the agricultural frontier for the needs of land aspirants, whereas the already existing *empresas comunitarias* were characterized by a high density of families, indicating a greater capacity to provide livelihood per unit of land (IICA-CIRA, 1970, p. 15). Former Minister of Agriculture and functionary of IICA-CIRA, Armando Samper Gnecco reported positively on the first efforts along these lines (Samper Gnecco, 1971), and the 'Acuerdo de Chicoral' agreement reached by a bipartisan commission (with heavy representation of the traditional largeholding families) defined this as the replacement for the model of individual allocation of land to smallholders (Perry, 1985, p. 117). It was enshrined in Law 4 of 1973. The collective element was attractive to many left-leaning observers (Perry, 1985, p. 117) and soon-to-be President Lopez was also a fan. INCORA's control over these *empresas* was virtually complete, from the choice of members (beneficiaries) to a close monitoring of their activities. By 1974, 1177 such *empresas* had been created with 11 832 members; most of them collapsed fairly soon thereafter (Perry, 1985, p. 119). The reasons for failure were recognized in a 1977 study by the institutions which had promoted them (IICA-OEA e INCORA, 1977), including inadequate amounts of land, low-quality land (reflected in the fact that 60 percent of the land was used for cattle production), uncertainty of tenure and lack of or untimeliness of credit.

INTEGRATED RURAL DEVELOPMENT

The early 1970s also saw the next serious phase of Colombia's *campesino* policy, a rejection of agrarian reform as commonly understood in favour of an attempt to raise the productivity of existing small farms. Such a policy has obvious merits, not least of them the political advantage that it does not directly challenge the largeholder sector. Like the other attempts however, it probably failed when judged against the criterion of major and lasting impacts on the earnings of poorer members of the agricultural sector.[26]

The situation confronting the incoming Pastrana government at the beginning of the 1970s was difficult. Among *campesinos*, productivity was stagnant and their frustration was accentuated by the scuttled hopes of agrarian reform. From the government's perspective, ANUC was out of control, producing over 800 invasions in 21 departments by 1972 (Escobar Sierra, 1972). In short, the land wars were accelerating again. Though it was viewed by some as inconsistent with the basic logic of the Pastrana government's Four Strategies Plan (Departamento Nacional de Planeación, 1972), in which small-scale agriculture did not play a role, it could be seen as an interim step while the core strategies came to fruition; it had international support based on demonstrations (in Mexico and elsewhere) that Green Revolution varieties could pay off on small farms provided they were appropriately complemented with credit and a knowledge of small farmers' needs; and it could be seen as a substitute for agrarian reform – a more palatable way of raising the incomes of small farmers.

In the Plan National de Alimentación y Nutrición (PAN) strategy of the incoming Lopez Michelson administration, this policy was given prominence. The importance of an adequate supply of food for all, now buttressed by studies highlighting the nutritional problems of Colombian children, became a focal point in the discussions with the international banks. Meanwhile a Planeación report (DNP-Dirección DRI, 1979, p. 58) indicated that the small farmer was losing his hold generally as well as in the DRI districts.[27] The programme offered the hope of dealing with both problems. It was structured to focus on food production, relying heavily on increased use of fertilizers together with the better strains, but not on mechanization or (of course) land expansion.

The first five-year phase was slowed by administrative inefficiencies; the limited decentralization of the national agencies posed a problem for effective execution (Fajardo, 1986, p. 137). By the end of 1981 about 71 000 families had been benefitted directly. Problems notwithstanding, the relatively generous level of resources; better and more opportune availability of credit to permit the reasonably intensive exploitation of the farms; a greater supply by government of basic services like education and health, clean water and electricity; and improvement in the access to markets, raised incomes and improved living conditions (DRI, as quoted by Fajardo, 1986, p. 139). Under subsequent administrations DRI remained a significant element of overall agricultural–rural policy, with some fluctuations in emphasis between the production and poverty-alleviation functions and with some ups and downs on the funding front.[28]

DRI is the hardest of Colombia's *campesino*-oriented programs to evaluate due to lack of adequate data and the problem of distinguishing its effects from the other important currents affecting small agriculture. Accordingly, credible judgements vary greatly. A most favourable assessment would conclude that it was based on a valid interpretation of the needs of the *campesino* sector, grew 'from a small, pilot scale operation run by a group of young and dedicated local professionals to a virtually nationwide program' (Lacroix, 1985, p. 33), with periodic support from international agencies, and had a significant positive impact on food output and *campesino* incomes, along with a damping effect on food prices and rural inequality. Enough direct local production gains[29] have been observed and enough evidence on rising *campesino* yields accumulated to make this view somewhat plausible.

An intermediate view would see this as a promising approach which needed more time, resources, and effort (for example to improve the institutional performance) in order to have a large positive impact in the country. Apart for the bureaucratic impediments noted above,[30] the decision to focus on food crops diminished the potential benefits to the farmers themselves. The inadequate attention to marketing also limited the benefits; economies of scale might have been more fully reaped, for example through producers' associations contracting collectively for transportation services (Arango et al., 1987, p. 22). Even if these limitations had been largely overcome, the potential impact on the *campesino* general population might have been curtailed if many *campesino* families could not develop into effective small farmers.[31] Perhaps spillover effects would have benefited quite a few other small farmers, but a really large aggregate impact might have required improvement in land access (amount of land and/or security of tenure). At the other end of the spectrum, some have viewed DRI as nothing more than a general plan to favor large capital, by keeping food cheap, wages down and unrest limited.[32]

Unfortunately the lack of adequate data makes it impossible to get a good reading on the productivity changes of the *campesino* sector due to the DRI programme. The Mision Agropecuario (Ministerio de Agricultural y Departamento Nacional de Planeación, 1990) concluded that the sector did achieve yield gains over the next decade or so,[33] but the benefits from this were curtailed by a fall in the real prices of its main crops (Jaramillo, 1998, p. 33). What increase in the income of campesino households did occur came mainly from off-farm activities, including those of females. And there were gains in many dimensions of rural living standards during the 1970s and early 1980s (Berry, 1978; Lopez and Valdes, 1998).[34] Perhaps they would have been enough to allay tensions in the absence of the disturbing effects of the drug industry, soon to appear on the scene.

MARKET-BASED REFORM OF LAND STRUCTURE (IN THE CONTEXT OF OTHER MARKET-FRIENDLY REFORMS)

By the early 1990s rural violence was again very high, fuelled by a deadly mix of strong guerrilla groups, the drug industry and the paramilitary. The *apertura* (opening) of the economy to international markets carried out by the Gaviria administration (1990–94)[35] had inherently unpredictable effects on agriculture and in particular on poorer farm families, partly because the country's agrarian structure and agricultural sector were inadequately understood,[36] and partly because the economy was now more vulnerable to international price movements, many of which were near historic lows. The setting was further complicated by the industrial world's recession and a local drought. The large mechanized farm sector lacked the flexibility to adjust quickly to the elimination of protection and credit subsidies and responded with a vigorous lobbying campaign (Deininger, 1999, p. 655). Although the liberal trade policy regime was gradually modified by numerous crop-specific support measures, overall farm output continued to stagnate between 1992 and 1997, and the relationship between the government and most farming groups became embittered.

This difficult setting provides the context for the late 1990s 'market-oriented' effort at land reform in Colombia, an approach reflecting the current popularity of market mechanisms in supporting IFIs like the World Bank. INCORA's loss of its earmarked source of finance (a share of duties on agricultural imports – eliminated with agricultural trade liberalization) helped to undercut its traditional approach to agrarian reform, as did the clear failure after 35 years to bring about a significant improvement in agrarian structure;[37] too much of INCORA's average annual budget, US$140 million as of the late 1980s, was spent on a large bureaucracy (Deininger, 1999, p. 655). The immediate goal of the new programme of 'negotiated' land transfer to aspiring smallholders was to subsidize (by up to 70 percent of the negotiated price of the land) the purchase of 1 million hectares to benefit 70 000 families between 1995 and 1998 (Jaramillo, 1998, p. 93).

It is too early to reach a final judgement on this most recent effort to deal with land problems in Colombia, given the current prevalence of instability and violence, the fact that the programme shows (at least in the experiments in five selected municipalities) a level of design competence well above that of the previous approach, and the interesting refinements that have been made or tested since its launching. What is clear though is that it has to date fallen far short of its goals – over 1995–98 INCORA reports only 17 372 beneficiary families, of whom 10 536 fell under the new 'market-assisted' rubric (Deere and Leon, 2001, p. 197). The fiscal constraints of the next few years have put the programme on the back burner.

Under more favourable circumstances, might this approach make a major contribution to Colombia's healthy development? It must first be recognized that it is now too late to get such enormous benefits from an agrarian restructuring as are frequently attributed to the major success stories of Asia, or which could have followed a significant reform in Colombia in the 1930s. Conversely there is the advantage that later in the development process the previous owners can be bought out with a smaller share of GDP than would have been the case earlier. Colombia's current condition is critical enough so that any step which could significantly reduce rural poverty, tension and violence would be worthwhile.

Will the reforms fulfill hopes and make a significant difference? This depends on four questions. First, how much land will be available for purchase at what for the programme are affordable prices. Second, will the process of connecting aspiring groups of beneficiaries to available land and the overall administration of the programme work well?[38] Third, will the state be able to do its part by providing complementary services? And fourth, even if everything else looks good about the programme, will be it be politically sustainable over several governments, given that by its nature it cannot effect a significant land redistribution quickly? Such sustainability requires both political dedication and adequate finance from domestic or international sources.

Because its success in a given locale depends on a set of conditions which are neither automatically nor easily met – including effective local administration, serious farm planning and availability of technical assistance and credit – the speed with which it could respond to the needs of aspirants across Colombia is much less than in the East Asian style of reform. Starting with those municipalities which meet the conditions and then proceeding to others, gaining experience en route, is a promising tack. If, to take a very round number, it were hoped to improve land access to 400 000 families (60 per cent more that the number of units titled by INCORA over 1960–88; Misión Agropecuario, 1990, p. 114) and the costs were say US$10 000[39] per unit, then total cost would be $4 billion. This corresponds to over 25 years of INCORA spending at the rate of the late 1980s, and to a small share of the current cost of dealing with the insecurity which has plagued the country. Overall administrative costs of US$1800 per family during the first years were less than a third of what INCORA was previously spending and quite reasonable in absolute terms. Prices paid for land may have been much as 40 percent less than what INCORA was paying for comparable land under the previous regime (Deininger, 1999, p. 660).

Negotiated land reform, like spontaneous settlement, requires considerable initiative on the part of the beneficiaries: group formation, selection of viable farm plans, analysis of the productive potential of various farms, negotiation and arrangement for credit. Most aspirants need help with at least some of these steps. In the five pilot municipalities, a quarter of those pre-selected were illiterate, 70 percent had agricultural experience and many were in a great rush to get land (Deininger, 1999, p. 660). Many came in pre-formed groups but the groups had little evident capacity to solve problems, resolve conflicts and so on. In the pilot experience it turned out that nearly all of these pre-formed groups disbanded and were replaced by others with more commonality of interest. So an in-depth training program for those pre-selected (about twice the ultimate beneficiaries) was developed, including some general ideas on developing cooperative behaviour and on economic analysis.

Predictably, practical difficulties have arisen in the negotiations between poor beneficiaries and powerful landowners. Some corruption scandals around the acquisition process have again come to light (Jaramillo, 1998, p. 96). Subsidies for land purchase have met with strong institutional and political resistance as the new approach clashes with decades of patron–client management, dominated by local politicians (Jaramillo, 1998, p. 95; Hollinger, 1998). Some design problems were inherited from the previous approach.

A number of positive refinements have been made or tested, including:[40] creation of a mechanism to facilitate use of grant funds to finance non-land investments, rather than just the purchase of land (as in the law itself); reduction of the target agricultural income of beneficiaries by a third, based on plans allowing for non-agricultural income;[41] a decentralization of responsibility for approval of land reform grants from INCORA headquarters to regional offices; insistence on a transparent public process of project approval, with monitoring, in order to avoid beneficiaries being picked in a arbitrary and *ad hoc* way; attempts to lay the groundwork for an effective land market; and much greater attention to meeting the conditions for economic success by the beneficiaries.

Provision of irrigation (where relevant) and agricultural extension services have posed a large problem. The institution responsible for irrigation, INAT, has not been effective, due to a combination of external and internal sources of inefficiency (a pattern of project selection through patron–client ties,[42] and a strong union respectively) and the common design weakness of a too-high level of subsidization to beneficiaries.[43] Implementation of the new agricultural research policies proposed under the Gaviria administration has moved very slowly. A new institution, CORPOICA, was designed to get the private sector seriously involved in these processes, but this has led to conflicts.

The evidence reviewed in the literature on market-based agrarian reform confirms a need to temper one's optimism. When complemented by traditional confiscatory reform, the new approach may have more promise, partly through the 'threat effect' which can make landlords more flexible in the face of expropriation and lower land prices. Credit schemes may need ceilings to become operative. Removal of subsidies favouring large farmers or their crops can be a valuable supportive device for credit or land laws to help the poor, and can be nudged along both by fiscal stringency and by dedication to making reform work. Lower subsidies help to discourage the rich from subverting reforms since the reforms are less costly to them in the absence of those subsidies.[44] The liberalization policies of the early 1990s did cut the implicit subsidies to one set of large farms in Colombia. Unfortunately much land is now in the hands of agents who cannot be expected to respond to the same economic incentives as traditional largeholders.

LESSONS FROM THE COLOMBIAN EXPERIENCE

If one accepts that a major redistribution of land could never have occurred in Colombia, then the best alternative would probably have been a reasonably equitable development on the frontier as it was gradually brought under cultivation; essentially a preventive step rather than a curative one.[45] This option should in principle have been easier than redistribution of land already claimed or controlled by largeholders, since the future largeholders who got land on the frontier did not yet constitute a pressure group. But success with this alternative required much foresight to recognize the extent to which new land would be brought into production and how its allocation would gradually affect the overall agrarian structure; a recognition that the level of support (including infrastructure development) to new small farmers would need to be fairly high; and enough political power and administrative capacity at all times to prevent the predictable incursions of aspiring largeholders into the frontier.

As of 2004, with much less frontier remaining than was the case 40 years ago, the 'negotiated' reform now being tested may well be the best option available. It too appears to have interesting potential in some regions if implemented in a professional way. But with many regions scourged by rural insecurity and violence, with much land apparently appropriated by paramilitaries and drug barons, it would be unrealistic to expect more than a marginal impact on overall agrarian structure.

General support for existing small farmers can achieve much if carried out in an effective way, and probably has made a significantly positive contribution in Colombia through DRI and more generally. But to achieve its potential this approach requires a substantial flow of resources, a good understanding of what is needed, and a high level of continuity. Given that the initial understanding of what will work best is usually not very good, a capacity to learn, modify and refine becomes very important.

The lessons of a more political nature from Colombia's experience, apart from the obvious fact that there will always be powerful status quo opposition to proposals for major reform, and the important corollary that the conditions which might permit a serious reform which faces strong opposition will usually be transitory, include:

1. The fact that, even within a generally elite-dominated polity, the differences in agrarian policy between political parties and administrations have been substantial. The steps taken or contemplated by the Lopez Pumarejo administration in the 1930s would not have occurred under a Conservative administration. The fostering of ANUC by the Lleras Restrepo administration would not have been considered by the previous or the succeeding Conservative governments. Given such differences, the chance for reform is often fleeting.
2. Though *ex post* events have had little chance to demonstrate it in Colombia, it is probably true, as Lleras Restrepo believed, that some form of empowerment of the rural poor is ultimately essential to the consolidation of a healthy agrarian structure if not to its establishment.[46] How this may best be brought about is however a very complicated matter.
3. Also hard to assess quantitatively, but very persuasive in general, is the hypothesis that the failure to successfully confront rural poverty and dissatisfaction through astute agrarian policy has provided a base of strength for the guerrilla groups (Fajardo, 1986, p. 90) and fertile ground for the illicit drug industry (Barragán, 1999), a *raison d'être* for the paramilitary forces and ultimately the single main explanatory factor of Colombia's current social, political and economic crisis.
4. Economic policy in all its dimensions has now taken on an international dimension less in evidence during the first half of the twentieth century. Undoubtedly the biggest failure of the international agencies from the early 1980s to the present, during which they have directed considerable attention to poverty, has been their unwillingness to get involved in agrarian reform processes until the World Bank's very recent (but still marginal) support for market-based reforms.
5. How agrarian issues are understood by the key actors matters. Many mistaken or partially misguided views widely held in Colombia and elsewhere appear to have had an impact on outcomes. These include the always widespread impression that small farmers are less efficient economically than large ones; a faulty understanding of the economic logic of such landlord–tenant arrangements as sharecropping, whose discouragement through legislation led landlords to displace tenants; the tantalizing idea that cooperative farming had a lot to be said for it. When information on agrarian reality is quite limited, the general tendency to lean on simplistic models thereof is accentuated. Rigid Marxist views have guided some interpretations of the *campesino* world in Colombia while rigid conservative (status quo) and neoliberal views have guided others. All have probably been distant from the truth.

NOTES

1. For a recent, brief commentary, see Tirado Mejia (1998). More extensive reviews are presented by Sánchez (1985) and Ortiz Sarmiento (1994).
2. Prosterman and Riedinger (1987, pp. 183–4) cite the case of Taiwan, where 'an independent cadre of administrators who had fled the mainland after the communist victory created a comprehensive land-records system, which was then meticulously finalized in a plot-by-plot and household-by-household rechecking process and implementation of retention claims was again closely monitored by beneficiary-dominated local committees'.
3. Or more generally a tendency to allocate land in relatively small parcels.
4. As late as 1850, Agustín Codazzi estimated this share at 75 percent (Legrand, 1989, p. 6).
5. For more details, see Berry (1999).
6. Most agrarian reforms in Latin America have fallen far short of producing the 'growth with equity' outcome of a Taiwan. Mexico and Bolivia exemplify the case of partial reform leading to modest benefits but not to a thoroughgoing transformation of the economy and the society. Ironically, perhaps the strongest support for the peasant was that provided by Trujillo's government in the Dominican Republic, beginning in the 1930s (Turits, 1997); but, to put it mildly, the process was not participatory. Each of these experiences had its own special history and limiting conditions, so the resulting outcomes do not imply that there was no hope under Colombia's different circumstances.
7. The idea that the large *latifundista* was inefficient and/or inflexible, giving rise to food price increases as development proceeds, was one element in the thinking of Latin America's structuralist school (Kafka, 1961). Many observers of Colombia commented on the paradox of large farms using good land extensively while smaller ones tried to eke out a subsistence through intensive cultivation of poorer land, perhaps most famously by Lauchlin Currie, who led the World Bank's mission to Colombia in the late 1940s (International Bank for Reconstruction and Development, 1950).
8. Lack of clarity to land title is especially characteristic of new frontier areas; conflict arises easily, both because the land is being contested currently and because the state is not strong enough to settle the dispute on its preferred terms. Much Latin American experience over long periods of time fits this category as settlement has moved into previously thinly populated lowlands and jungle areas. Some of the expansion has involved production for the domestic market, but mostly it has been directed at exports. In either case peasant settlers come into conflict with land entrepreneurs.
9. The antagonism between the two political parties has historically provided a major source of hostility which, together with the often fairly equal strength of these two groups, helps to explain Colombia's high rate of death through political violence over more than a hundred years, in contrast to those countries where a strong military, oppressive as it might be, controlled power so completely that no other forces could do battle with it (Maingot, 1968). Colombia's present wave of violence does not appear to owe much to this factor, however.
10. Brown (1971, pp. 194–5) concludes that 'there is probably enough despair, anger, perceived relative deprivation and "consciousness" to start an uprising in most any traditional rural community in Latin America on any given day ... Thus whenever the local landed elite begins to lose its grip, usually because of larger economic or political circumstances, peasant activism springs up rather quickly, often with little or no initial debt to outside agitation.'
11. Over the period 1870–1920 conflicts had centred on the resistance of peasant settlers to the encroachment of land entrepreneurs. Prior to 1874 the independent *colonos* (settlers) were not in a position to fight, and the process of creation of the great estates appears to have been mainly a peaceful one. After this date the *colonos* resisted that trend with greater frequency. The decisive factor that tipped them in this direction, according to Legrand (1986, p. 64), was the passage of national legislation supportive of settlers' rights – the *colonos* often referred to the laws of 1874 and 1882, which clarified their right to homestead on national domain and implied that the land was legally theirs. Though the laws themselves were generally ineffectual they did influence the settlers' perception of their situation, and provided the incentive to take cases to court collectively – though usually unsuccessfully, as the landlords connived with the local authorities.

12. Landlords responded to the squatters' initiatives by expelling them, but were wary of bringing lawsuits for fear of losing. The *colonos*, while doing better than before, could not force the landlords to give up their claims and the result was chronic conflict. The landlords were of course increasingly disaffected, fears of class conflict were expressed, and the disturbances appeared to be undermining efforts to raise agricultural production.
13. Colombia's population growth was accelerating through the first half of the century and was by this time approaching 2 per cent per year.
14. Madrid (1944, cited by Legrand, 1986, p. 145) estimated that three-quarters of privately held property would have reverted to the nation had a 1933 proposal (defeated in Congress) been implemented. Its implications were probably not too different from those of the 1926 Supreme Court ruling.
15. The motivation of Lopez has been the subject of some debate. Some authors (for example Cronshaw, 1986) credit him with positive intent to help the aspiring smallholders, but lack of execution. Sánchez (1977) and Legrand (1986) are more negative, asserting that Lopez and associates planned the effect to be conservative. While Law 200 proclaimed the social function of property, the fact that its Article 1 made it easier for both the large and the small to claim public lands if they put them to use ultimately worked mainly in favour of the former. Legrand (1986, p. 141) emphasizes the fact that Lopez promised large holders that the law would help them to validate their titles.
16. The (presumably) unintended effect of encouraging expulsions through the fear of largeholders that it was dangerous to have *colonos* on the land they claimed. Law 100 of 1944, another effort to bring order to rural society, has often been described as the law to re-establish service tenancy, by calling for clearer specification of the terms established between landowner and tenant through written contracts. This law can also be thought of as designed to mitigate the unintended disasters wrought by Law 200 (Safford, 1995, p. 141). It did not achieve the objective of reintroducing service tenancy.

    The misjudgement of failing to predict the 'indirect' effects of legislation was more or less repeated in the 1960s when land rental, especially sharecropping, was discouraged, leading to another wave of evictions and another shift in the agrarian structure (see below).
17. The once common view that Law 200 resolved the agrarian conflict of the 1930s until pre-electoral infighting sparked violence in 1946 appears simplistic and wrong. Continuing tensions with tenant labour led large owners to try to buy them out, or failing that to evict and replace them with wage labour; some even shifted cultivated land into grazing to cut down on the number of workers required, thereby making it even more difficult for the peasants to earn a living. Frictions among peasants were common. 'La Violencia' of the two decades 1948–65, which left 200 000 dead and 800 000 homeless (Oquist, 1980) was neither simply a political conflict nor simply a peasant war, but a complicated phenomenon with many roots and many mechanisms (Zamosc, 1986; Legrand, 1986; Gilhodes, 1974; Cronshaw, 1986).

    Bergquist (1986) argues that the poverty and insecurity of very small coffee producers made them principal victims and actors in La Violencia of circa 1948–65. The violence brought the collapse of state authority and under the resulting anarchy, many forms of warfare broke out. In the frontier zones a lot had to do with the fight for land, probably with little regard for political affiliation. Political violence often forced the small to sell at despair prices, with some others who started small but had good connections being able to accumulate (Safford, 1995, p. 143).
18. Hayami and Ruttan (1985) make this point in a famous comparison between the focus of public support for agriculture in the USA and in Japan.
19. Some studies show an association between low rates of employment and/or output growth and intensity or rural violence (World Bank, 1996; Bejarano, 1988), possibly reflecting a vicious circle from violence to low investment to low employment opportunities to violence. Violence may have reduced agricultural GDP in the 1980s by as much as 16 per cent, according to the Colombian Planning Commission (Departamento Nacional de Planeación, 1990). Regional evidence points to an impact of violence on private investment in irrigation.
20. Hernán Toro Agudelo, writing in *La Calle*, anticipated the evidence on this point thrown up by the 1960 agricultural census (Toro Agudelo, 1985, Chapter 1). Though in fact the *campesino* sector accounted for a smaller share of food output than in the 1930s, the overall cost of an

unproductive agricultural sector and the associated curtailment of the rural market for the output of Colombian industry were decried.

21. Arango et al. (1987, p. 14) see the 1961 episode as a fight between Currie's *gran-burgues* approach and Lleras' small farm approach. Though the latter won the battle, Mariano Ospina Perez (head of the Conservative Party) succeeded in so restricting INCORA's range of action that its activities boiled down to just the reversion of unused land to the state (as earlier decreed in Law 200 of 1936), the titling of public lands, investment in irrigation and other infrastructure and a few purchases in zones of acute conflict.
22. By the early 1970s the evidence from Latin America in general was indicating that directed colonization usually failed to achieve its objectives while spontaneous colonization was typically more successful (Nelson, 1973).
23. Frequently, whereas small beneficiaries had to satisfy the letter of the law in paying for the improvements received, on the lands of well-connected largeholders such debts would be cancelled (Perry, 1985, p. 108, citing the somewhat veiled comments in Departamento Nacional de Planeación, 1977, vol. 1, p. 14).
24. Perry (1985, p. 109) reports that by 1966 a third of the settlers in the Tolima projects had abandoned their farms because of poor soil or other negative conditions. He argues that the forced receipt of credit was one of the problems. Arango et al. (1987, p. 19) report that in the DRI projects they studied the ratio of credit to assets was very small, reflecting in part the risk aversion of the producers.
25. ANUC was formed in 1967 under the Ministry of Agriculture. Its first Congress in 1970 fixed its objectives and limited its activities to the execution of official programmes (Fals Borda, 1982, p. 146). For detailed histories of ANUC, see Zamosc (1986) and Rivera Cusicanqui (1987).
26. As noted below, opinions on the pay-offs from DRI vary.
27. As noted earlier, there was a major difference between the Planeación estimate that in 1975 the *campesino* (under 20 hectares) share of food production was 55 percent and the contrasting figure of Siabato of just 28 percent (Arango et al., 1987, pp. 20–21). In light of his estimate, Siabato (1986) argued that it would make more sense to focus the development programmes and the *campesino* effort where it would be most profitable, that is, non-mechanizable lands and labor-intensive products, including some exportables, luxury products and so on.
28. Lacroix (1985, p. 30) describes the evolution of objectives a little differently from Arango et al., suggesting that the programme was initially conceived with emphasis on raising living standards in the rural areas, albeit mainly through raising production, but gradually moved towards a focus on food production and marketable surplus, with poverty alleviation 'a welcome but not necessary, secondary benefit'. He notes that by the mid-1980s project areas were being chosen only for their production potential.
29. Lacroix (1985, p. 32) notes that production increases of some crops were large enough to create marketing problems, confirming the view that possibly too little effort went into planning for such contingencies.
30. Lacroix (1985, pp. 30–33) concurs that coordination among the various sectoral institutions involved remained a problem as of the mid-1980s. He also notes that the considerable support the programme has attained among the rural population has been a mixed blessing, in inducing politicians to try to use it to advance other than project-related interests. Jaramillo (1998, p. 97) notes that political influence has crept increasingly into DRI operations since Colombia's adoption of a new Constitution in 1991, which banned the previous practice of funding political projects of members of Congress who supported the administration.
31. Fajardo (1986, p. 148) puts the figure as low as 10 percent of all *campesino* families (that is, about 120 000).
32. Thus Moncayo (1986) interprets it as designed to consolidate the essential function of the small-scale sector – to produce cheap foodstuffs in order to facilitate global accumulation by preventing either the breakdown of *campesino* agriculture or its conversion into small capitalist units. Horowitz (1993) models reform as a strategy by the rich to give a little and backtrack whenever possible.
33. As did Balcazar (1998), who estimates an implausibly big increase in small farm yields over 1973–76 to 1988 of 82 percent while judging that those on large farms stagnated. In a later

study (Balcazar, 2001) he concludes that for all but the top decile of rural families real incomes fell over 1978–91, more the lower the income level, whereas over 1991–95 it was the reverse – the top decile lost and all the others gained. These conclusions are highly sensitive to the comparability of the income survey data at the three points of time, and should thus be considered very tentative.

34. The ideal information with which to judge the net impact of the various forces impinging on rural life in Colombia over these years would have included an agricultural census to throw light on the changing distribution of land and income surveys to clarify patterns of income distribution. No really useful agricultural census has been taken since 1960, and no demonstrably comparable income surveys in the rural areas are available prior to the 1990s, if then. One of the confusing bits of information for the 1990s is a dramatic reported drop in income inequality over 1991–95, the Gini coefficient falling from 0.57 to 0.44 (Ocampo et al., 1998). This decline is so rapid as to defy credibility; although it would be almost impossible that such a sharp reduction really happen over such a short span, there is the possibility that, though exaggerated, the data do suggest a decline of smaller proportions.
35. The dramatic nature of this change is reflected in the fact that the import to GDP ratio jumped from 15.5 percent in 1990 to 46.9 percent in 1997 (Jaramillo, 1998, p. 124).
36. The last few decades saw a rapid expansion of the land frontier, major involvement of the drug lords in rural property holding and significant technological change; as noted above, the information with which to describe the trends in agrarian structure fell behind, to put it mildly.
37. The Gini coefficient of the distribution of parcels added to the cadastral registry between 1960 and 1988 was 0.773 compared to one of 0.868 in 1960; INCORA's titling and other programmes accounted for much of the increase in land area and the distribution of that new land when initially allocated (Misión Agropecurio, 1990, p. 118). But there appears to have been some reconcentration after the original allocation such that the net decrease in the Gini coefficient was small.
38. Successful reform is harder in such systems than it was in countries like Japan, Korea and Taiwan, where the new owners were former tenants already cultivating the land and where no major change in the operational side of agriculture was called for. This feature made it easier for the reforms to be effected quickly, thereby avoiding the danger of lack of follow-through.
39. Deininger (1999, pp. 660, 668) reports that average administrative cost in the five pilot municipalities has been running at US$1800, or less than a third of that in the previous approach where such costs mounted to about half of the total land reform budget of US$15 000 per beneficiary in the early 1990s. If the cost of land were to continue at about $8000, the total would be $10 000. It depends, of course, on the amount of land provided.
40. This section is based mainly on Deininger (1999).
41. Like many reforms, the 1994 one specified a high target income assuming full-time involvement in agriculture, which implied an average plot size of about 15 hectares. The resulting concentration of the benefits on a relatively few has such political advantages as silencing the criticism that the programme is not generous enough and yet getting to the 10–15 per cent of the peasantry which is well organized and collaborates with INCORA (Deininger, 1999, p. 660). But it is not socially or economically defensible.
42. The general weakening of the executive under President Samper gave regional power bosses more influence in the selection of projects and beneficiaries.
43. The internal resistance was eventually defeated with the dismantling of unions and reduction of employment from 2500 to 1000. Getting foreign loans was harder than expected, partly due to INAT's poor implementation record in the 1980s with small irrigation projects funded by the World Bank (Jaramillo, 1998, p. 96).
44. This was the experience in North-East Brazil (Lipton, 1993).
45. The importance of preventing land concentration in the first place is particulary pertinent to future events in Sub-Saharan Africa. Although the recent agrarian history of Colombia is less parallel to that of SSA than are those of some other regions of Latin America (for example much of Central America where communal land systems were extinguished by the intruding Iberians) the current threat in SSA is certainly that as communal systems give way to Western-

ized property rights a Latin American-style concentration will take place, with ultimately similar results. The details of the process of concentration are eerily similar. There is a legitimate debate on the relative merits on grounds of efficiency of traditional land rights systems in various parts of SSA and of the extent to which they could be maintained even if this were desirable. But there can be no debate on the looming threat of land concentration through a combination of unhealthy political and economic processes. What is quite clear is the need, there too, for a system of land ceilings which would remove the threat of such concentration, provide greater security to smallholders and, not inconsequentially, face governments with the fact that their task is to interface with and support the smallholder. In many countries this will be done with dedication only when there is no apparent alternative.

46. In the context of Japan's successful post-war land reform, this was the firm belief of General MacArthur based on the advice of the famous expert Wolf Ladejinsky (1977).

REFERENCES

Arango, Mariano, Alonso Cardona, Conrado Duque, Efrain Estrada, Luz Elena Lopez and Saul Mesa (1987), *Economica Campesina y Politicias Agrarias en Colombia: Una Evaluación del Program DRI*, Medellin: Centro de Investigaciones Economicas, Universidad de Antioquia.

Balcazar, Alvaro (1990), 'Tamaño de finca, dinamica tecnologica y rendimientos agricolas', *Coyuntura Agropecuaria*, **7** (3).

Balcazar, Alvaro (1998), 'Las transformaciones agrícolas en la decada de los noventa', Bogota, Colombia, Centro de Estudios Ganaderos y Agrícolas, CEGA.

Barragán, Jackeline (1999), 'Quienes Ganan y Quienes Pierden Con la Industria de las Drogas Ilicitas en Colombia', mimeo.

Bejarano, J.A. (1988), 'Efectos de la violencia en la producción agropecuaria', *Coyuntura Económica*, **18** (3), Bogotá, FEDESARROLLO.

Bergquist, Charles (1986), *Labor in Latin America: Comparative Essays on Chile, Argentina, Venezuela and Colombia*, Stanford, CA: Stanford University Press.

Berry, R. Albert (1978), 'Rural poverty in twentieth-century Colombia', *Journal of Inter-American Studies and World Affairs*, **20** (4).

Berry, Albert (1999), 'Could agrarian reform have avoided Colombia's crisis?', mimeo.

Brown, Marion (1971), 'Peasant organizations as vehicles of reform', in Peter Dorner (ed.), *Land Reform in Latin America*, published by *Land Economics*, University of Wisconsin-Madison.

Comité Interamericano de Desenvolvimiento Agrícola – CIDA (1966), *Tenencia de la tierra y desarrollo socio-económico del sector agrícola*, vol 1, Washington, DC.

Comité Estadounidense para Refugiados (1998), *La Crisis Silenciosa de Colombia*, Washington, DC.

Cronshaw, Francine (1986), 'Landowners and politics in Colombia, 1923–1948', PhD dissertation, University of New Mexico.

Deere, Carmen Diana and Magdalena Leon (2001), *Empowering Women: Land and Property Rights in Latin America*, Pittsburgh, PA: University of Pittsburgh Press.

Deininger, Klaus (1999), 'Making negotiated land reform work: experience from Colombia, Brazil and South Africa', *World Development*, **27** (4).

de Janvry, Alain and Elisabeth Sadoulet (1993), 'Path-dependent policy reforms: from land reform to rural development in Colombia', in Karla Hoff, Avishay Braverman and Joseph E. Stiglitz, *The Economics of Rural Organization: Theory, Practice and Policy*, New York: Oxford University Press.

Departamento Nacional de Planeación (1972), *Guias para una Nueva Estrategia*, Bogotá: DNP.
Departamento Nacional de Planeación (1977), *Estudio de evaluación de proyectos de adecuacion de tierras PAT)*, Planeación, Unidad de Estudios Agrarios, Bogotá.
Departamento Nacional de Planeación-Dirección DRI (1979), *El subsector de la pequeña producción y el Programa DRI*, Bogotá: DNP.
Departamento Nacional de Planeación/Unidad de Estudios Agrarios (1982a), *Diagnostico del subsector campesino o tradicional*, Bogotá: DNP.
Departamento Nacional de Planeación (1982b), *Experiencias obtendias en la fase 1 y recommendaciones para la fase 11*, Bogotá: DNP, División de Evaluación DRI. Mecanografiado.
Departamento Nacional de Planeación (DNP) (1990), *El Desarrollo Agropecuraio en Colombia*, Bogota: Editorial Presencia.
Diot, Joelle (1976), 'Estadísticas históricas: baldíos, 1931–1973, legislación y adjudicaciones', *Boletín Mensual de Estadística*, Departamento Administrativo Nacional de Estadística (DANE), No. 296, March.
Escobar Sierra, Hugo (1972), *Las Invasiones en Colombia*, Bogotá: Ediciones Tercer Mundo.
Fajardo, Darío (1986), *Haciendas, Campesinos y Politicas Agrarias en Colombia, 1920–1980*, Universidad Nacional de Colombia, Centro de Investigaciones Para el Desarrollo.
Fals Borda, Orlando (1982), *Historia de la Cuestion Agraria en Colombia*, Bogotá: Carlos Valencia Editores.
Gilhodes, Pierre (1974), *La Question Agraire en Colombie, 1958-71*, Paris: Armand Colin Cahiers de la Fondation Nat des Sciences.
Hayami, Yujiro and Vernon Ruttan (1985), *Agricultural Development: An International Perspective*, revised and expanded edition, Baltimore, MD: Johns Hopkins University Press.
Hirschman, Albert O. (1965), 'Land use and land reform in Colombia', in Albert O. Hirschman, *Journeys Towards Progress*, Garden City, NY: Doubleday.
Hollinger, Frank (1998), 'Reforma Agraria a traves del Mercado: Lecciones de Colombia', occasional paper, Centro de Estudios Ganaderos y Agricolas (CEGA), Bogota.
Horowitz, A.W. (1993), 'Time paths of land reform: a theoretical model of reform dynamics', *American Economic Review*, **83** (4).
IICA-CIRA (1970), *Anotaciones preliminares para el análisis del estado de la Reforma Agraria en Colombia. Informe para la FAO*, Bogotá.
IICA-OEA e INCORA (1977), *Análisis de las Empresas Comunitarias Campesinas en Colombia*, Bogotá: INCORA.
INCORA (1970), *La realidad rural y la reforma agraria como factor de cambio*, Bogotá: INCORA.
International Bank for Reconstruction and Development (1950), 'The basis of a development program for Colombia', report of a mission headed by Lauchlin Currie, Baltimore, MD.
Jaramillo, Carlos Felipe (1998), *Liberalization, Crisis and Change in Colombian Agriculture*, Boulder, CO: Westview Press.
Jimenez, Michael Francis (1986), 'The limits of export captialism: economic structure, class, and politics in a Colombian coffee municipality, 1900–1930', PhD dissertation, Harvard University.
Kafka, Alexandre (1961), 'The theoretical interpretation of Latin American economic

development', in Howard S. Ellis and Henry C. Wallich (eds) *Economic Development for Latin America*, London: Macmillan & Co.

Lacroix, Richard L.J. (1985), 'Integrated rural development in Latin America', World Bank staff working paper no. 716, Washington, DC.

Ladejinsky, Wolf (1977), *Agrarian Reform as Unfinished Business; The Selected Papers of Wolf Ladejinsky*, New York: Oxford University Press for the World Bank.

Legrand, Catherine (1986), *Frontier Expansion and Peasant Protest in Colombia, 1850–1936*, Albuquerque, NM: University of New Mexico Press.

Legrand, Catherine (1989), 'Colonization and violence in Colombia', *Canadian Journal of Latin American and Caribbean Studies*, **14** (28).

Lipton, Michael (1993), 'Land reform as unfinished business: the evidence against stopping', *World Development*, **21** (4).

López, Alejandro (1927), *Problemas Colombianos*, Paris: Editorial Paris America.

Lopez, Ramon and Alberto Valdes (1998), 'Determinants of rural poverty in Colombia', in Ramon Lopez and Alberto Valdes (eds), *Rural Poverty in Latin America*, Baltimore, MD: Johns Hopkins University Press.

Machado, Absalón (ed.) (1986), *Problemas agrarios colombianos*, Bogotá: Siglio Veintiuno Editores-CEGA.

Madrid Malo, Nestor (1944), 'Genesís e ineficácia de la reforma sobre tierras', *Revista Trimestral de Cultura Moderna*, Universidad Nacional de Colombia.

Maingot, Anthony (1968), 'Colombia: civil–military relations in a political culture of conflict', unpublished PhD dissertation, University of Florida, Department of History.

Mejía Vallejo, Hernán (1974), *Anales del Congreso, Martes 20 de Agosto de 1974, Año XVII*, no. 19.

Ministerio de Agricultura y Departamento Nacional de Planeación (1990), *El Desarrollo Agropecurio en Colombia: Informe Final*, Bogota.

Ministerio de Agricultura, Departmento Nacional de Planeación (1990), *El Desarrollo Agropecuario en Colombia, Tomo 1, Mision de Estudios Del Sector Agropecurio*, Bogota: Ministerio de Agricultura, Departamento Nacional de Planeación.

Moncayo, Victor Manuel (ed.) (1986), 'Política Agraria y Desarrollo Capitalista', in Absalón Machado *Problemas agrarios colombianos*, Bogotá: Siglio Veintiuno Editores-CEGA.

Nelson, Michael (1973), *The Development of Tropical Lands: Policy Issues in Latin America*, Baltimore, MD: Johns Hopkins University Press, for Resources for the Future.

Ocampo, J.A., M.J. Pérez, C. Tovar and F.S. Lasso (1998), 'Macroeconomía, Ajuste Estructural y Equidad en Colombia: 1978–1996', Archivos de Macroeconomía, Departamento Nacional de Planeación.

Oquist, Paul (1980), *Conflict and Politics in Colombia*, New York: Academic Press.

Ortiz Sarmiento, C.M. (1994), 'Historiografía de la violencia', in Universidad Nacional, *La historia al final del milenio. Ensayos de historiografía colombiana y latinoamericana*, Bogotá: Universidad Nacional.

Palacios, Marco (1980), *Coffee in Colombia (1850–1970): An Economic, Social and Political History*, Cambridge: Cambridge University Press.

Perry, Santiago (1985), *La Crisis Agraria en Colombia: 1950–1980*, 2nd edn, Bogotá: El Ancora Editores.

Prosterman, Roy, and Jeffrey M. Riedinger (1987), *Land Reform and Democratic Development*, Baltimore, MD and London: Johns Hopkins University Press.

Rivera Cusicanqui, Silvia (1987), *The Politics and Ideology of the Colombian Peasant*

Movement: The Case of ANUC (National Association of Peasant Smallholders), Geneva: United Nations Research Institute for Social Development (UNRISD), in collaboration with Centro de Investigación y Educación Popular (CINEP).

Safford, Frank (1995), 'Agrarian systems and the state: the case of Colombia', in Evelyne Huber and Frank Safford (eds) *Agrarian Structure and Political Power: Landlord and Peasant in the Making of the State*, Pittsburgh, PA and London: University of Pittsburgh Press.

Samper Gnecco, Armando (1971), 'La reforma agraria en la encrucijada', *El Espectador*, 10 November.

Sánchez, Gonzalo (1977), *Las ligas campesinas en Colombia*, Bogotá: Ediciones Tiempo Presente.

Sánchez, G. (1985), 'La Violencia in Colombia: new research, new questions', *Hispanic American Historical Review*, **65** (4).

Siabato, Tarsicio (ed.) (1986), 'Perspectivas de la economía campesina', in Absalón Machado *Problemas agrarios colombianos*, Bogotá: Siglio Veintiuno Editores-CEGA.

Tirado Mejia, Alvaro (1998), 'Violence and the state in Colombia', in Eduardo Posada-Carbó *Colombia: the Politics of Reforming the State*, London: Palgrave Macmillan Press, in association with the Institute of Latin American Studies, University of London.

Turits, Richard L. (1997), 'The foundations of despotism: peasants, property, and the Trujillo regime (1930–61)', unpublished PhD dissertation, University of Chicago, Department of History.

Uribe Echeverrí, Carlos (1936), *Nuestro problema, producir*, Madrid.

World Bank (1994), *Colombia: Poverty Assessment Report*, Washington, DC: World Bank.

World Bank (1996), *Review of Colombia's Agricultural and Rural Development Strategy*, Washington, DC: World Bank.

Zamosc, Leon (1986), *The Agrarian Question and the Peasant Movement in Colombia: Struggles of the National Peasant Association 1967–1981*, Cambridge: Cambridge University Press.

Zandstra, Hubert, Kenneth Swanberg, Carlos Zulberti and Barry Nestel (1979), *Caqueza: Living Rural Development*, Ottawa: International Development Research Centre.

PART III

Dimensions of Human Development

7. Death and development*

Bob Sutcliffe

TRAGEDY AND STATISTICS

A noted twentieth-century tyrant once allegedly remarked that 'a single death is a tragedy, a million deaths is a statistic'. As far as is known, the author of this remark never killed anyone with his own hands; he was however responsible for many statistics. This chapter is a synthetic description and discussion, from the point of view of those who study development, of death – both as a statistic and as a tragedy. My aims are to summarize and assess important recent data about mortality and life expectancy, to discuss the ways in which it is and can be used as an indicator of egalitarian development, to comment on two contemporary crises of mortality and to make some general suggestions about some future tasks for social scientists on these questions. There can be few things which have more effect on the quality of people's lives than the time and the way in which they and other members of their society die. What we know about death reveals a great deal about not only the quantity but also the quality of life. If, unlike Joseph Stalin, we can discern the tragedies behind the statistics then perhaps we can contribute something to the pursuit of human development.

During 1999 the number of human beings crossed the 6000 million mark. This has been tentatively 'guesstimated' as being about 6 per cent of the members of our species who have ever been alive (Haub, 1995). About 1 percent of them, about 60 million people, die each year. The pattern of these deaths is not haphazard; it is written, a reflection both of the biology of mortals and of every material inequality and social injustice which exists. We already know many of the characteristics of the 60 million human beings who will die in the next year. Most of these deaths will be premature or unnecessary, in the sense that they occur before they would if the people concerned had been able to live materially and socially better lives, lives which have already in places shown themselves to be attainable. Poets have turned resentment and cynicism towards worldly wealth and power into the cliché that death is the great equalizer; in the words of John Donne, 'death comes equally to us all and makes us all equal when it comes'. Biologically this makes some sense: unless we are lucky (or unlucky) enough to be frozen or embalmed we will all in no time at all be ashes, rotting flesh or a vulture's lunch, and then bones, dust and greenhouse gas. But humans do not come equally to their deaths: they vary hugely in the age at which they die, in the degree of unnecessary suffering which they endure, in the support which they have from their fellows, and in the dignity with which they are permitted to die. The timing and nature of most human deaths is influenced by unnecessary deprivation and inequality. In this sense, to extend an idea of Amartya Sen, human history is characterized by perhaps 100 billion people who have died before their biological time and by hundreds of millions of currently missing persons who would be alive today if they had not died in some sense prematurely (Sen, 1990). Not only are human beings a race of mortals; most of us have been and are more mortal than we need to be.

AGE, SEX, CLASS AND RACE IN THE STATISTICS OF MORTALITY

Most people are surprised when they learn that the death rate in OECD countries is higher than that of Latin America (9 per 1000 population as opposed to 6.2) (World Bank, 2004). Explaining this apparent anomaly will explain something about mortality patterns. The quoted figures are crude mortality rates. As with virtually all demographic puzzles the surprise is explained by looking at differences in the age structures of the populations. In these two, and indeed all other groups of countries the age pattern of mortality is as follows: mortality among children of 0–4 years (child mortality) is higher than for children of 5–9 years. Between 10 and 14 years mortality is at its minimum; from there it climbs, slowly at first, to approach 100 per cent for the oldest age group, producing, as seen in such graphs as Figures 7.1a and b, a tick- or spoon-shaped curve (the difference being caused by the larger number of age-groups in Figure 7.1b). In every age group the mortality rate in Latin America is higher than in the developed capitalist countries. But the overall mortality rate is lower because the younger age groups, with lower mortality, are a much higher percentage of the population. A common way round the misinformation produced by crude death rates is to compare areas or countries by applying their age-specific mortality rates to a population with a standardized age structure to produce the 'adjusted or standardized mortality rate'. But it is more illuminating to look directly at the age-specific mortality rates themselves.

Part of this spoon-shaped pattern of age-specific mortality is natural, common to all human populations, and indeed to most other living species. But between human populations the level of the spoon-curve and its slope at various ages are very different and these differences are socially determined. In Figure 7.1a the lines for seven world regions have similar shapes but different levels. There is a striking parallel between the age mortality curves of the OECD countries and

a Between seven world regions, 2002

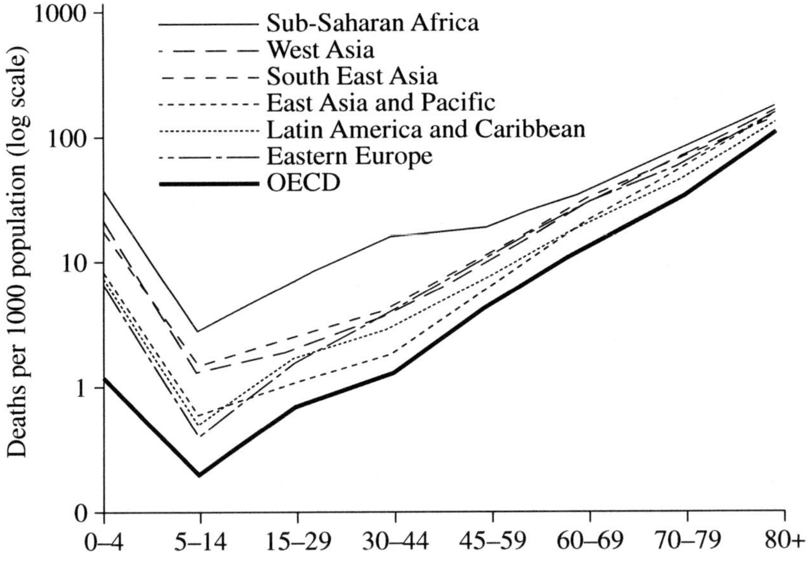

Source: WHO (2002).

b In England and Wales, 1838–2002

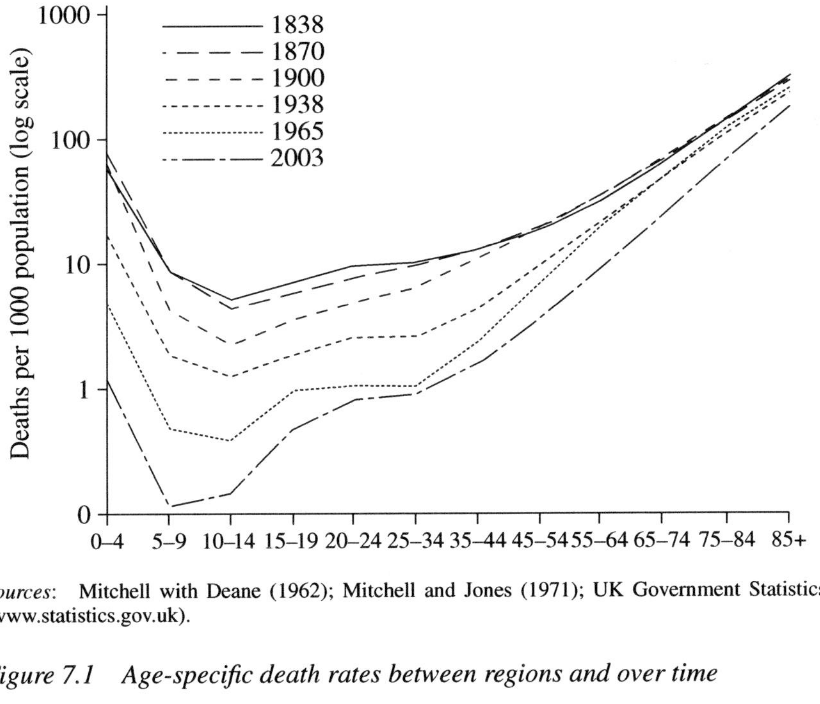

Sources: Mitchell with Deane (1962); Mitchell and Jones (1971); UK Government Statistics (www.statistics.gov.uk).

Figure 7.1 Age-specific death rates between regions and over time

Sub-Saharan Africa in 1990 in Figure 7.1a, and those of England and Wales in 1838 and 2002. Cross-section comparisons closely parallel recent changes over time in the countries normally considered most developed, although mortality in England and Wales in 1838 was considerably worse than in Africa today. From both graphs it appears that if the medical, social and economic conditions are right, nature will permit the reduction of the child mortality rate to not much more than 1 per 1000 and delay the onset of mortality rates above 100 per 1000 until beyond 70 years of age (the present situation in the OECD countries). Today it is the infant and child mortality rates which account for most of the difference between the overall standardized mortality between different countries and so for differences in their life expectancies, and this also parallels historic changes in England and Wales as can be seen in Figure 7.2. And it is rapid reductions in child and maternal mortality, due usually to basic public health measures, especially perinatal services and child innoculation, which have been the major causes of the important extension of human lives in many regions characteristic of the second part of the last century.

Hidden in these patterns of mortality are differences of sex, race and class; but each one of these factors has a profound influence on the number of deaths

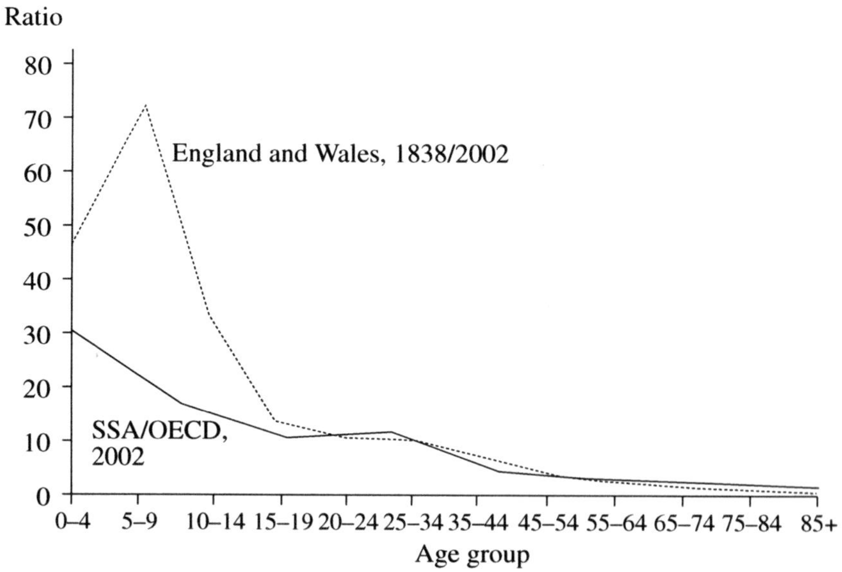

Sources: See Figure 7.1.

Figure 7.2 Comparison of ratios of age-specific mortality over time and across space

and their nature. Naturally, more boys than girls are born and then male mortality rates are higher than female rates in all age groups. That is what we observe in nearly all areas of the world and nearly all countries, leaving almost everywhere a majority of women in older age groups. What is interesting therefore are the exceptions: either places and ages where female mortality is higher than male, or exceptional differences in the ratio of male to female mortality. In Figure 7.3a we see the ratios of male to female mortality by age, as calculated in the 2002 *World Health Report* (WHO, 2002) (being an update of the data first presented for 1990 in the monumental study *The Global Burden of Disease* (GBD) (Murray and Lopez 1996a, 1996b, 1997)). Of the seven regional groups shown in Figure 7.3a there are exceptions to the rule that male mortality is higher than female. In the group labelled South and South-East Asia (dominated by India) girls and young women up to nearly 30 years of age are more mortal than males of the same ages, another way of observing the phenomenon of missing women already well known from the work of Sen and others (Sen, 1990). And in Sub-Saharan Africa young women in the age groups 5–29 are more at risk of dying than men of the same age. In India, this difference may be caused by discrimination of many kinds: in the diet (Harriss White, 1990), in access to medical treatment in the case of illness (Filmer et al., 1998) and in physical cruelty, including murder. In Sub-Saharan Africa this phenomenon is new (it did not appear in the figures for 1990) and is a consequence of AIDS (see below). And in both cases maternal mortality is likely to have considerable influence.

If these exceptional cases go so clearly against what is a biologically natural pattern of mortality, the other startling thing shown by Figure 7.3a is the ages and places where the difference between sexes becomes exaggeratedly large. Young men in developed (OECD) countries, former socialist countries and in Latin America have much higher mortality rates than young women. The difference reaches its peak at ages of 15 to 29 when male mortality is as much as three times as great as female (even more in some individual countries). The phenomenon is not seen so much in other parts of the world; nor is it visible in the historical statistics of England and Wales up to the Second World War (Figure 7.3b). The 1838 ratios in fact show a similar pattern to that of India today. By 1965 however, two peaks in relative male mortality, in youth and later middle age, have clearly appeared. By 2002 the second of these had been considerably attenuated but the first was more acute than ever. A feature of actually existing capitalist development and formerly existing socialism, it appears, is an extraordinary, and recent, difference in the degree of risk in the life experience of young men and women. A first surmise might be be that this is due to a fatal conflation of modern machismo with alcohol, drug consumption, firearms and motor vehicles. Later however we shall see that the analysis of deaths by cause shows that that reason why this peak appears only in more developed regions and in

a Seven world regions

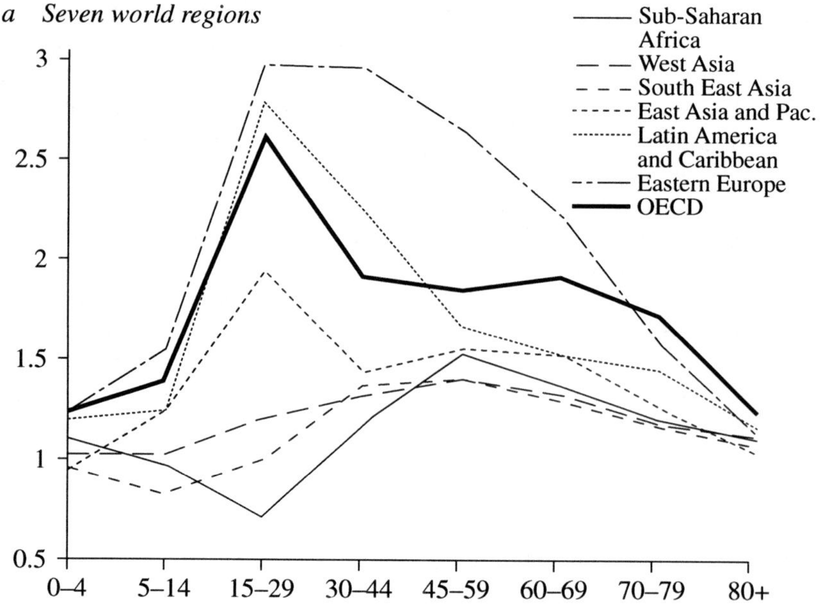

Source: See Figure 7.1a.

b In England and Wales, 1838–2002

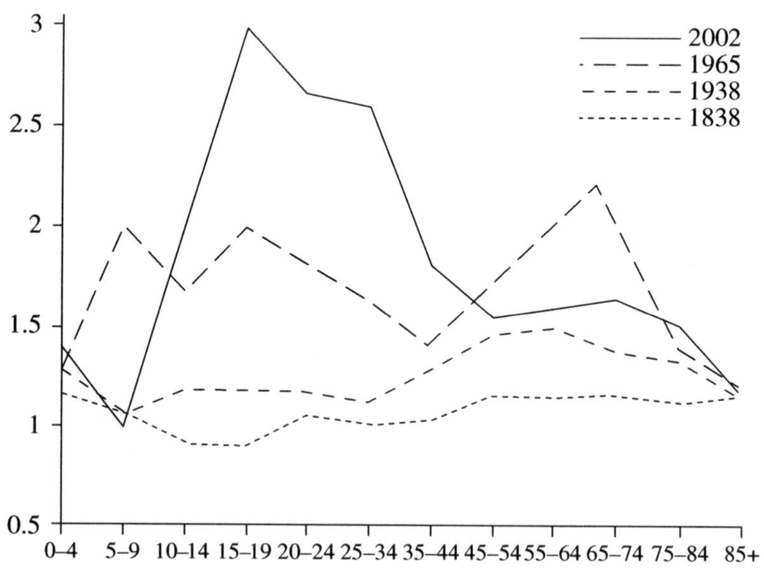

Sources: See Figure 7.1b.

Figure 7.3 Ratios of male to female age-specific death rates across space and over time

more recent times is not so much the peak of male mortality due to particular causes (which is general), but whether or not there is a balancing peak in female mortality among the same age groups due to other causes. The other smaller peak in the male mortality ratio visible in the OECD countries (Figure 7.3a), and since the second World War in England and Wales (Figure 7.3b), around the ages of 45 to 59, is associated with the 'developed' disease patterns to be mentioned below.

Ethnic difference and inequality are other fundamental determinants of mortality differences. They are often invisible in the social sciences because in many countries statistics for separate ethnic groups are not published. But the importance of this factor is seen in the variation in life expectancy at birth in three countries where figures are available by ethnic group. In South Africa, the USA and Brazil whites live between 7 and 20 years longer than blacks or non-whites (Table 7.1).

Figure 7.4 shows the ratio of age-specific mortality rates for males and for females (ratios of black to white) as well as the male to female ratios for blacks

Table 7.1 Ethnic difference and life expectancy: South Africa, USA and Brazil

Country and ethnic group	Life expectancy at birth		
	Total	Men	Women
South Africa 1997			
White	73	69.5	76.6
Black	53	52	55
All*	*54.7*	*51.5*	*58.1*
USA 1996			
White	77	74	80
Black	70	66	74
All	76.1	73.2	79.2
Brazil 1997			
White	70	69	71
Non-white	64	62	66
All	67.4	63.5	71.4

Sources: South Africa: South African Institute of Race Relations 1998; USA: US Census Bureau (1999), UNDP (1998); Brazil: NHSS (National Household Sample Survey) quoted in Sant'Anna (2001). Data elaborated by Juarez Oliveira (DEISO/IBGE) quoted in Sant'Anna, (2001); World Bank (2004) (for the row labelled South Africa 'All' which is not wholly consistent with the previous rows).

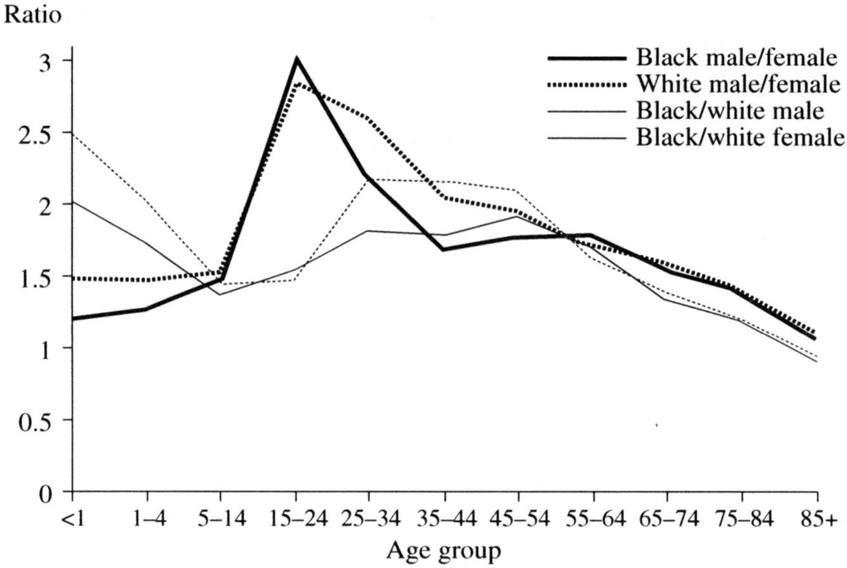

Source: United States Census Bureau (1999, 2003).

Figure 7.4 Ratios of male to female and black to white age-specific mortality, USA 1996

and whites in the USA. The male–female differences are similar to those we have already seen. The extraordinary peak in male mortality in the 15–24 age group is common to both groups, though considerably more pronounced for blacks. The ratios at the other ages are similar as between whites and blacks. For all age groups (except curiously the over-85s) the black mortality rate is higher than the white. The greatest differences are to be seen in child mortality (both sexes), where the gap has been rising since 1950 (Cutler and Meara, 2001), and then in the age groups from 25 to 55, where the difference is especially marked for women. Since there is a smaller gap in pay but a larger gap in mortality between black and white women than between men at these ages, the income-adjusted mortality rates may be relatively even more unfavourable to black women than the quoted figures imply. A sample-based study found that the black–white gap between standardized income-adjusted overall mortality rates is greater for women (2.2 to 1) than for men (1.2 to 1) (Otten et al., 1990).

The fact that these differences are even greater without the income adjustment implies of course that mortality varies also with economic level or social class. Numerous studies, carried out especially in the developed countries, have confirmed that the rich and materially and socially privileged live longer lives than the poor. Health and mortality rates are closely associated with deprivation and so with the relative level of income. A study carried out in 1994 among 300000 white US men shows a very high negative correlation level between income and mortality. The highest of 12 income groups had an overall mortality rate one-half of that of the lowest income group (Wilkinson, 1994; also see Acheson et al., 1998). There is considerable debate however about whether these results are due entirely to absolute deprivation among part of the population or whether relative deprivation (income distribution) plays an independent explanatory role. This is connected with an important ongoing debate about whether poverty or inequality should be the priority target of social and economic policy. Much remains to be shown about exactly what combination of detailed factors account for the undisputed existence of inequality in health and mortality outcomes (Deaton, 2001; 2003).

LIFE EXPECTANCY AS AN INDEX OF DEVELOPMENT

The age distribution of mortality is what lies behind the now extremely widely used indicator, life expectancy at birth. Of the three indicators which compose the Human Development Index (HDI) it is the one which has undergone the fewest changes during the 10 years in which the HDI has been calculated. The difference between male and female life expectancy is also an important component of the Index of Development related to Gender, where the contribution to the index is calculated using different limits for men (22.5 to 82.5 years) and women (27.5 to 87.5 years). This will mean that a country is penalized in this index compared with the HDI if women's life expectancy in fact is less than about 6 percent superior to men's. And in compiling some national *Human Development Reports* the UNDP has calculated regional and provincial life expectancies, which in India in 1992–96 for example varied between 73.1 years in Kerala and under 57 in three states (Government of India Planning Commission, 2001), in Bangladesh provinces at a similar time ranged between 69 and 42 years (Haq, 1997) and in districts of Nepal in 2000 varied between 71 in urban areas and 58.7 in rural areas, being barely more than 40 years in the far western mountain region (UNDP Nepal, 2001).

Life expectancy seems an easy indicator to understand, it is available for virtually all parts of the world, and clearly says something about the quality of human life and human capacity. For that reason it has become extremely widely used, sometimes as a simple substitute for human development as a whole. In a recent article, Amartya Sen rather convincingly dismissed four alleged limitations of life expectancy as a development indicator: that other objectives may be more important than the lengthening of life, that it might be better to look at the economic variables which determine longevity, that morbidity is more important than length of life and that it is a sluggish indicator of change (Sen, 1998).

There are other issues related to life expectancy however, more specific to its role as one of the three key variables which make up the HDI. One of the main problems with the present HDI, as its compilers have always been well aware, is that it does not explicitly take inequality into account. A rise in income, whatever the level of income per head, may be produced by nothing more than a rise in the income of the rich. The question of distribution has not even been an explicit question of concern in relation to the other components of the HDI. To some extent this is because these other indicators, including life expectancy, are partly different; they contain an implicit distribution factor which income per head does not. Since life expectancy, at least at any given time, has a biological maximum, and the education variables have a logical maximum (100 per cent), which income does not have, this means that no country can obtain values close to the maximum with a relatively equal distribution of the variable among the population. Once again the conclusion seems to be that life expectancy is a 'better' variable than income per head and so ought to have more and not less influence on the index. This argument however depends on the assumption that years of life and literacy are homogeneous variables, a point to be returned to in the next section on disability.

In any event, there remain even in highly developed countries important elements of inequality in life expectancy within countries based on race, class and gender. Especially at lower levels of the non-income indicators it is therefore important to look for ways of adjusting them to take inequality into account. One way of dealing with the problems of the maldistribution of all the indicators would be to abandon, or at least to give less importance to, the production of indices of national averages and instead produce indices relating to the underprivileged sections of the community, including not income per head but the income per head of, say, the poorest fifth of the population, not overall life expectancy but the mortality or education rate, say, of women between 15 and 30 years of age in those states or provinces or classes or ethnic groups with lowest life expectancy. Each country would be represented by its worst-off part, something which would surely make the index approximate better to the concept of human development and perhaps also have a more explosive political effect.

LONGEVITY AND DISABILITY

Years of life are not of course homogeneous and so life expectancy alone is not an ideal measure of health or physical welfare. But we could measure welfare better if we also had indicators of morbidity or disability. One of Sen's defences of the use of life expectancy as a development indicator is that, as a practical question, the relevant information about morbidity is to a great extent absent or, because of its low quality, misleading (Sen 1998). True as this will no doubt be for some time to come, one of the original contributions of the GBD study has been to produce the first usable worldwide inventory of disability, combining it with their mortality estimates in order to produce a global measure of the burden of disease. For 14 somewhat peversely defined world regions the WHO now regularly updates some of the data in the annual *World Health Report* (for example World Health Organization, 2004a) and these estimates of disability can be used by development specialists to point a way beyond life expectancy to more discriminating indicators of human development, though they are still highly speculative.

The GBD study takes a standardized full lifespan of women and men (82.5 and 80 years respectively) as a benchmark to be applied to all countries. On the basis of actual estimated life expectancies it calculates the potential years of life which are lost because people die before those ages. In addition it calculates the relative loss of welfare produced by different disabilities and diseases (that is, one year of life lived with disability X produces $(1 - \alpha_x)$ disability adjusted life years where α is the percentage loss of welfare experienced by a person suffering from X. It then sums for regions, sexes, age groups and medical causes the equivalent of years of life lost both through premature death and through disease and disability. The sum is the loss of disability adjusted life years (DALYs). This estimate is used to adjust country life expectancy estimates for the disability component of DALYs to produce an estimate of healthy life expectancy (HALE).

As a calculus of the burden of disease and premature death this still embryonic method differs markedly from previously popular cost–benefit approaches which evaluate loss from death or illness by their effect on some economic variable, usually GDP. On that basis an average death in a rich country implied greater loss than an average death in a poor country; the DALY methodology implies that the loss would be the same in both countries since it is counted in undifferentiated years and not in dollars (see Murray and Lopez, 1996a, 1997; Michaud 1999). The WHO does however also provide DALY-based calculations which weight DALYs by age-group – a controversial and unconvincing procedure which there is no space to discuss here.

The DALY method of calculating welfare losses leads to some important novel conclusions. Life expectancy, as usually calculated, ranges between countries from 85.3 to 35.7 years for women (from 78.4 to 32.4 for men); but the range of healthy (disability adjusted) life expectancy is proportionally wider – between 77.7 and 29.9 years for women (72.3 to 28.6 for men). This possibly more 'real' figure for life expectancy implies greater inter-country inequality than the figures normally quoted. The DALY methodology was devised partly to form the basis of a more rational prioritization of health spending in the world. On that question the figures confirm that there is a dramatic maladjustment in the world between the distribution of the burden of disease and that of health expenditure: 85 percent of the world's deaths and 92 percent of lost DALYs occur in non-OECD countries but only 30 percent of health spending (25 percent of government health spending) takes place in those regions (WHO, 2003, spending figures in purchasing power parity). Another source has shown that an even greater imbalance also applies to health research (Global Forum for Health Research, 2004).

THE CAUSES OF DEATH

Less than 30 percent of deaths which take place in the world are registered with a cause given. A further major aim of *The Global Burden of Disease* has been to produce for the very first time an internally consistent (though still to some extent speculative) estimate of the relative importance of all causes of death in the world. The authors of the study remark that adding up previously produced estimates of deaths from individual causes tends to produce totals which are greater than the deaths which in fact take place. Even the WHO has a long way to go before it produces consistent statistics in this sense: in 2004 it produced almost simultaneously its *World Health Report* and a special report on diabetes (WHO and World Diabetes Federation, 2004); the annual total of deaths attributed in each of these publications to this cause was 1 and 3.2 million respectively.

The GBD study and its updates sets out the causes of death from two viewpoints. The first is the medical cause. For the regions used in the study the proportion of deaths by cause is estimated and the causes are divided into three types: type I – infectious diseases and causes connected with birth and maternity; type II – non-infectious medical conditions, most notably cancers and heart disease; type III – accidents, killing and suicide. The resulting distribution (as estimated in the 2002 update of the GDB, WHO, 2002) is summarized in Figure 7.5, for which I have disaggregated the regions more than in previous graphs. The two rectangles represent the annual total of world deaths and the shading shows their division by cause and age.

The study confirms that there is a strong relationship between level of development and the pattern of causes of death. In the poorest regions the majority of deaths have type I causes. In the most developed regions these causes have been virtually eliminated and the enormous majority of deaths have type II causes. Type III causes produce a relatively small percentage of deaths, varying between regions but without any apparent relationship to the level of development. The difference highlighted by the study can be seen most clearly by

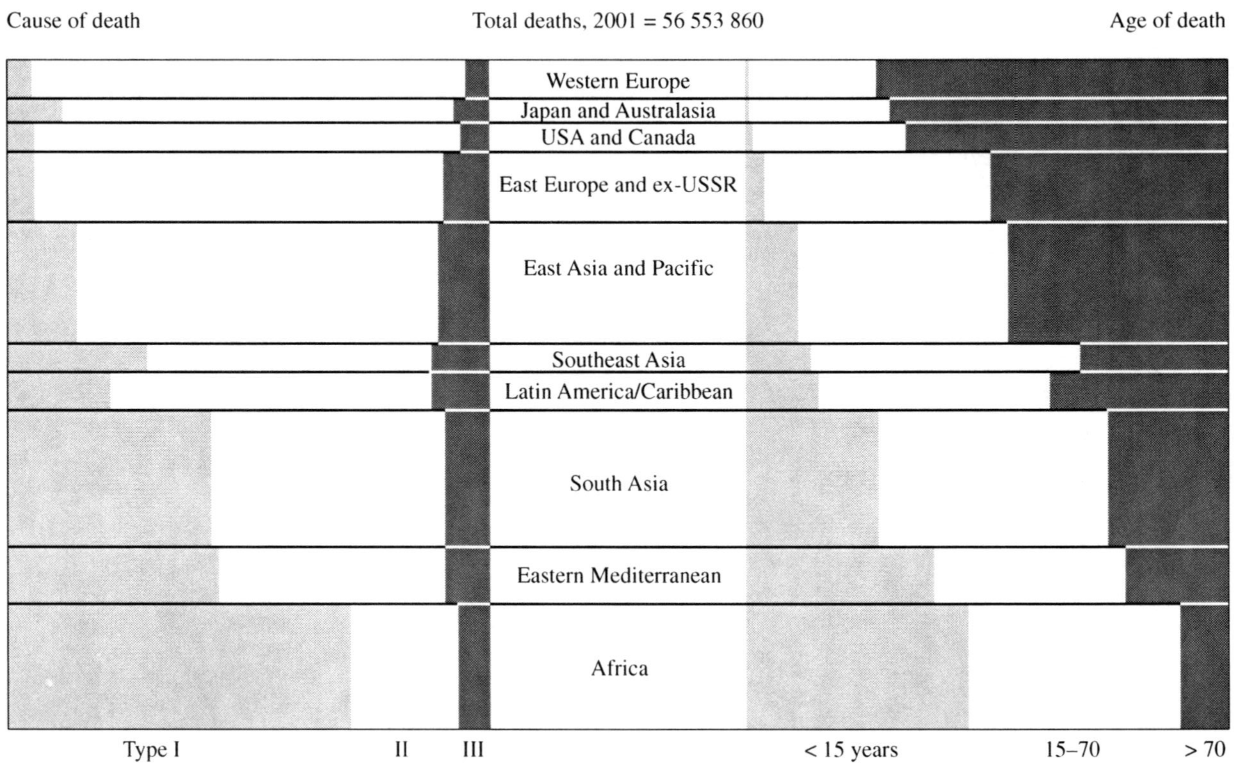

Source: WHO (2002).

Figure 7.5 Causes and age of death in ten world regions

comparing Sub-Saharan Africa where 71 per cent of deaths have type I causes, with Western European countries where only less than 6 per cent have type I causes. It is assumed that, as before, this spatial difference also parallels the historical pattern of change in developed countries, and this is confirmed by other data (Frank and Fraser Mustard, 1994; Sen, 1993; Wilkinson, 1994).

This change is known as the epidemiological transition, an important concept to set alongside other concepts of transition which make up a large part of conventional thinking about what development is. Among those is the demographic transition (from a high birth and death rate equilibrium to a low birth and death rate equilibrium) and the not so often named but equally commonly postulated structural economic transition (the decline in the proportion of labour and output in agriculture, the primary sector, to a rise in the importance of industry and modern services, the secondary and tertiary sectors).

The GBD study disposes of some common misconceptions about the epidemiological transition. When infant and maternal mortality are reduced as a result of a reduction of type I causes of death, then type II causes assume more importance, not so much because, as is often argued, these are 'diseases of development' as because more of the population survive infancy and childbirth

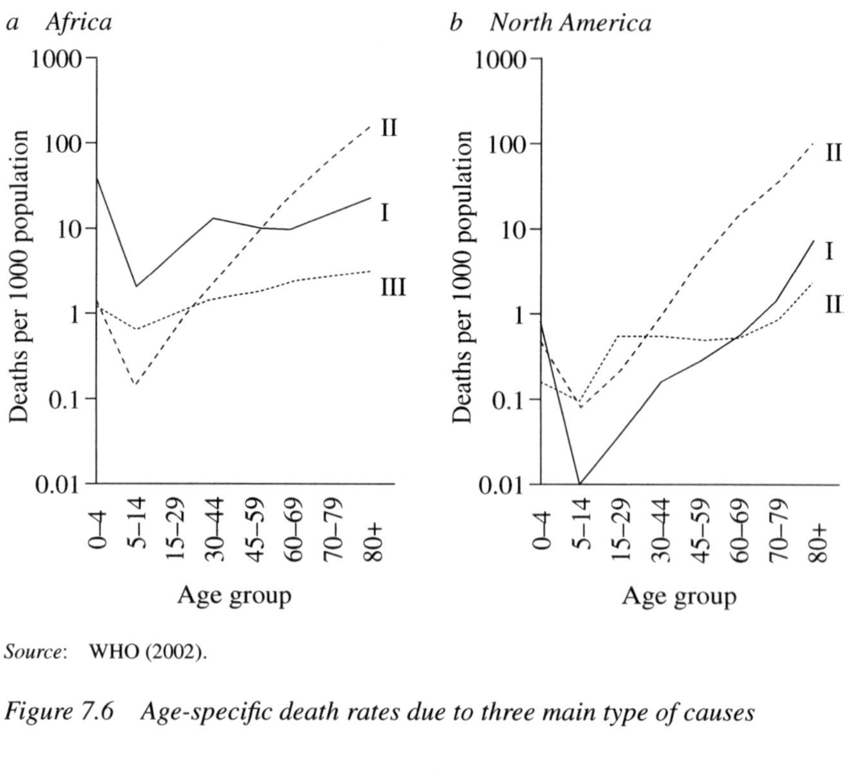

Source: WHO (2002).

Figure 7.6 Age-specific death rates due to three main type of causes

and thus die of adult diseases. But, as the GBD shows, the risk of dying from non-communicable (type II) causes in general is greater for an adult in Sub-Saharan Africa than for an adult in OECD countries (Murray and Lopez, 1997). While some of these diseases may be affected by diets and other aspects of lifestyles in developed countries, they (above all cancers and coronary diseases) are more important as causes of death and disability in developed countries but they are not in the usually understood sense 'diseases of development'.

A more detailed vision of the results can be seen by comparing two regions – Africa, the least developed region by most criteria and North America, one of the most developed. Figures 7.6a and 7.b show mortality rates due to the three major groups of causes by age group for these two regions. The most striking difference between the two is the placement of line I. At all ages type I disorders cause very much more mortality in Africa than in North America. And those are of course the causes of death which have been most dramatically reduced in developed countries during the past 100 years. The type II and III mortality is also greater at most ages in Africa, but by a much smaller factor than deaths due to Type I causes.

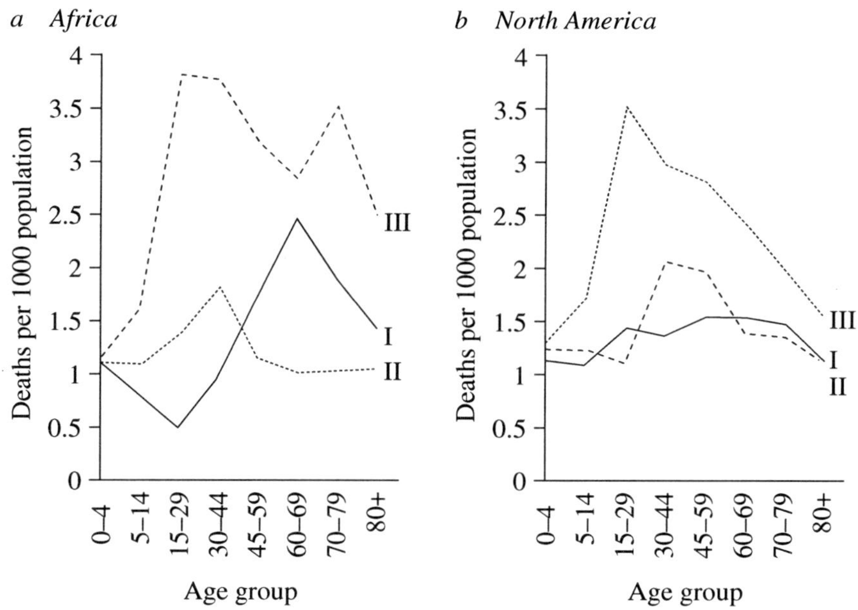

Source: WHO (2002).

Figure 7.7 Sex ratios of age-specific death rates due to three main type of causes

Figures 7.7a and 7.7b show for the same two regions the sex ratio of mortality from the three types of causes. Again it is in relation to type I causes of death that the greatest differences are apparent. In North America male mortality is higher than female for all types of cause and for all age groups. But in Africa female mortality is higher than male in the age groups from 5 to 30. The two most important reasons for this are AIDS (see next section) and maternal mortality. The relative peak in male type I mortality between 45 and 79 is due to multiple causes, among the main ones being a higher level of tuberculosis and of lower respiratory system infections among men. The enormous excess of male over female type III mortality (accidents, violence and wars) is seen over a much wider age range than in North America. A recent detailed WHO report on road traffic accidents confirms that they are one of the main causes of this (WHO, 2004b). The WHO estimates that 72 per cent of those killed in traffic accidents worldwide are men. That figures varies very little between different areas of the world. It is highest in the richer countries of the Eastern Mediterranean region, connected no doubt with Saudi Arabia's prohibition of women drivers; and they are lowest in North America where a greater proportion of women drive road vehicles. In the previous section of the chapter and Figures 7.3 and 7.4 above, the peak in overall male mortality in late youth and early adulthood was drawn attention to; it appeared in developed countries but not in Africa or other poorer regions. Dividing the causes of death according to sex however shows that the cause of that phenomenon was not an increase in male mortality for those age groups since the enormous predominance of male deaths with type III causes is as characteristic of Africa, or more so, as it is of developed regions. What exists in Africa but does not exist in North America is the large predominance of female type I mortality in the same age groups. This is largely due to maternal mortality and more recently also to the biased incidence of AIDS (see next section).

It is for type II causes that the patterns of mortality by sex between North America and Africa are most similar. Figure 7.6 shows that the incidence of this kind of mortality is greater in Africa than in North America for virtually all age groups but not by a very large margin. The epidemiological transition reduces type I mortality more than mortality from other causes and the two major elements of this are a reduction in the death rates of children and of young adult women.

Accelerating the epidemiological transition will benefit women disproportionately. Or, to put it in another way, women suffer disproportionately from the absence of the measures necessary to reduce the number of type I causes of death; and similarly the young suffer more than the old. The reduction in mortality in developed countries during the last century has been most marked among the youngest age groups (Cutler and Meara, 2001).

The concept of development as transition is an obvious and omnipresent one. But it is not without its dangers. It suggests perhaps too strongly that development is an irreversible metamorphosis, as if from the pupa to the butterfly, to a permanently different state of equilibrium, when in reality the conditions of maintaining the post-transition state can be difficult and reversal is always possible. Ideas of transition can thus exaggerate a tendency to see the world in terms of two qualitatively distinct pre- and post-transition states rather than as a more complex and changing continuum. And this 'before' and 'after' technique tends to obscure the negative aspects of the 'after' state. There may be an excessive suggestion in ideas of transition that the movement to the post-transition state is in some way natural and necessarily desirable. Moreover virtually all concepts of transition define the post-transition state as actually existing developed capitalism. The tendency to see the post-Communist states as 'countries in transition' is a clear reflection of this. Ecologically or socially critical views of modern developed capitalism present a much less teleological view of these various transitions.

The epidemiological transition of course encapsulates the obviously desirable objective of reducing to a very low level deaths from infectious and birth-related factors. But even the most complete transition in this sense is no guarantee against future reversion. The elimination of fatal infections is a permanent social battle. And new ones always threaten. The development of resistant strains arouse fears that the epidemiological transition may be much more temporary than it has seemed. The enemy was not killed but is simply, as in the conventions of monster movies, biding its time. That neither the epidemiological transition nor the long-term extension of life expectancy are permanent and guaranteed has been demonstrated from the mid-1990s to the present by the eruption of new crises of disease and mortality.

MORTALITY CRISES: THE FORMER SOVIET UNION AND CENTRAL AND SOUTHERN AFRICA

Ironically, what has seemed to some observers the most violent century of human history has also been the one in which population has grown most rapidly (presumably with the exception of the very first few human generations). This is hardly at all due to the fact that humans have had more children; it is because there are progressively relatively fewer premature deaths, fewer missing persons. The long-term figures for longevity and income in five Latin American countries for instance, shown in Figure 7.8a, indicate only one decade in one country (Haiti from 1990 to 2002) in which overall life expectancy has fallen. In Nicaragua during 50 years when real income was no higher at the end than at the beginning, life expectancy had risen from 23 to 69 years.

Such encouraging signs of the resilience of the demographic and epidemiological changes however are not unqualified. In two major areas of the world, the former Soviet Union and many countries of Central and Southern

Africa, life expectancy has recently fallen precipitously for partially different sets of causes.

The mortality crisis in the Soviet Union was already visible before the end of the socialist regime. The Soviet area did not share at all in the expansion of life expectancy which affected practically the whole of the rest of the world from 1960 to 1990. Between those years life expectancy in the USSR increased by two years while it rose 8–10 years in Southern European countries starting from a similar base and rose by 13–14 years in the world as a whole. Then, between 1990 and 1994 in Russia (and many other East European states) there was a sudden sharp rise in mortality and consequent fall in life expectancy (from 74 to 71.5 years for women and from 65 to 57.5 years for men) (Bennett et al., 1998). This is an increase in mortality comparable to that caused by the worst wars, famines, epidemics and natural disasters. The trajectory of income per head and life expectancy from 1980 to 2002 is shown in Figure 7.8b.

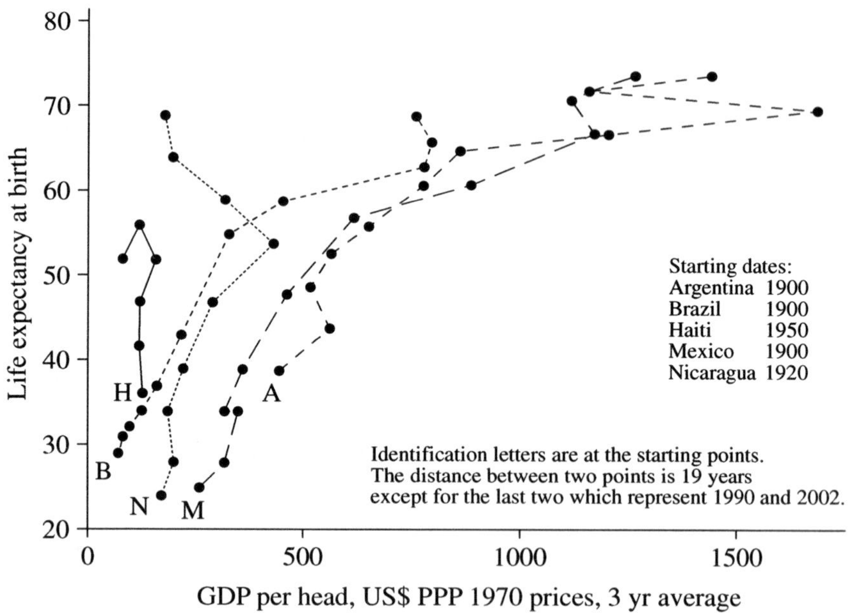

Source: Astorga and Fitzgerald (1998), 'Statistical Appendix' in Thorp (1998); World Bank (2004).

Figure 7.8a The trajectory of GDP per head and life expectancy, five Latin American countries, 1900–2002

This post-Communist mortality crisis has been very concentrated: it affects men considerably more than women or children, and disproportionately affects the 30 to 50-age group, single men, poorer people, those living in the more remote rural regions of Russia and less-educated people (Becker and Bloom, 1998; Shkolnikov et al., 1998).

In spite of the decline in public health spending in the region, not much blame is put by analysts on this factor. There has not for instance been a significant increase in infant mortality and male 5–9 years mortality has unaccountably improved during the crisis (Becker and Bloom, 1998; Bennett et al., 1998). While real per capita incomes have fallen very fast during the transition crisis the inter-regional evidence does not suggest that this has been the immediate direct influence on mortality.

It was not an epidemic which produced this mortality crisis; the rising number of deaths were due to causes of all three types (Zohoori et al., 1998). But most close observers seem to have drawn the conclusion that behind all the specific statistics is a kind of causation which is difficult to quantify but is related to the sudden change from the extremely conservative and protective society which

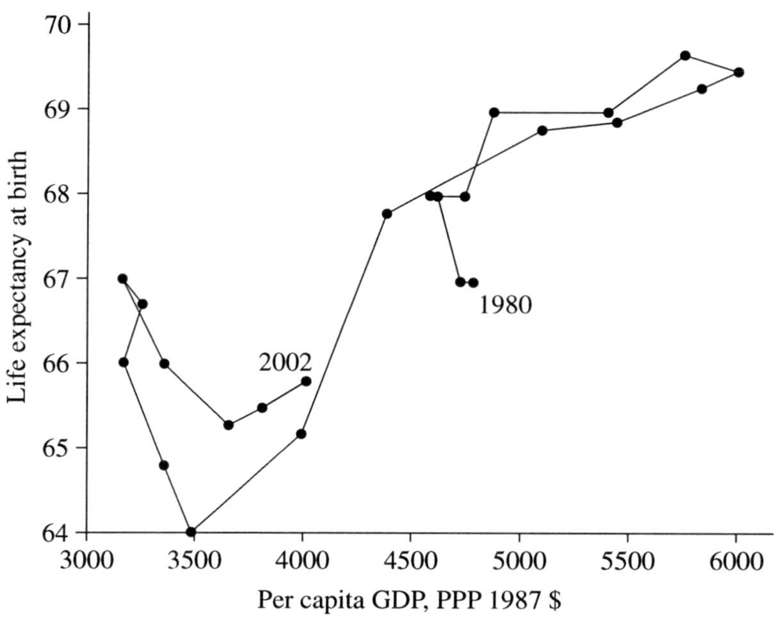

Source: World Bank (2004).

Figure 7.8b The trajectory of GDP per head and life expectancy, Russian Federation 1980–2002

Soviet Russia became, to a society in the course of massive, unpredictable change beset by violence, greatly increased male alcohol consumption, confusion, uncertainty, unemployment, growing equality and the need to resolve the problem of survival anew every day. That may well be so, although it seems worth pointing out that Nicaragua, for example, where since the early 1980s that need to survive from day to day has been part of the life of a great part of the population, has experienced a steady rise in life expectancy to a level higher than that in Russia and most ex-Communist countries in Europe, previously thought of as developed. Perhaps Nicaraguans are more experienced in coping with instability, and the (still erratic and incomplete) improvement in Russian mortality figures after 1995 attest to the Nicaraguanization of Russian society. Or perhaps, as some analysts speculate, the key question is 'social cohesion': being part of groups which know how to survive collectively and which produce mutual support (Kennedy et al., 1998).

And in a sense that may mean groups which prevent despair. The apparent importance of alcohol consumption in the Russian demographic crisis, in particular the prevalence of binge drinking, suggests that what is really happening for many people is not far from being a form of suicide. One wonders therefore if its causes have anything in common with other situations in recent years in which rates of suicide have risen steeply (young men in their twenties and thirties in France, young rural men in Ireland, teenagers in the USA (Cutler and Meara, 2001), or young rural women in China (Rosenthal, 1999)).

It is an immense task to investigate what there might be in common between these increases in suicide. It is true that all of them take place in communities affected by very rapid social and economic change, in all cases in the direction of a 'transition' to a more competitive market economy. But if there is a cause in common, what could it be? The social change itself, its speed, the lack of social protection against its worst effects, the difference in its impact on genders? The possibilities are wide-ranging. But they all point to the fact that mortality is one of the social variables which is affected by virtually any social change. As social scientists we are always recommending change. Usually we presumably want our recommended changes to prolong life. But it is as well to be aware that some of them, for reasons which we do not remotely understand, may shorten lives.

Scarcely had the precipitate decline in Russian life expectancy begun to abate in the mid-1990s when UNAIDS, the international agency charged with monitoring AIDS worldwide, began to single out Russia and other ex-Communist states as those where the number of new HIV infections was growing most rapidly. The agency's 2003 update estimates that HIV cases per million population rose from about 100 in 1998 to close to 2000 in 2002. In Russia, if the epidemic is still relatively new, it is growing in the words of UNAIDS 'at a fearsome rate', especially among people under 30 years of age; and it seems extremely doubtful that either the social solidarity, the openness of public discussion, the state enlightenment or the resources exist to decisively reduce infections and mortality in the short term (UNAIDS/WHO, 2003).

The calamitous effects that inadequately managed AIDS epidemics can have on mortality is shown in the second area of the world to experience in the last decade of the twentieth century a mortality crisis: Central and Southern Africa. UNAIDS estimated that at the end of 2003, 7 per cent of adults in Sub-Saharan Africa were HIV-positive. The figure is much higher in the worst-affected countries in Southern Africa, reaching 39 per cent in Botswana and Swaziland. It is estimated that in eight countries (Botswana, Kenya, Lesotho, Namibia, South Africa, Swaziland, Zambia, Zimbabwe) life expectancy fell by more than ten years during the 12 years from 1990 to 2002. In Africa a very high proportion of the extra deaths are caused by AIDS. Figure 7.9a shows the increase in mortality in Sub-Saharan Africa in the young adult age groups between 1990 and 2001. And Figure 7.9b shows both how AIDS directly hits these age groups, and the other salient feature of this epidemic which is that it is killing more women than men. More than 60 percent of the deaths of women in the 30–44 age group in Sub-Saharan Africa are, according to the WHO's estimates, caused by AIDS. These terrible reversals, as well as that of Russia, and the comparison with regions and countries with difference recent experiences are

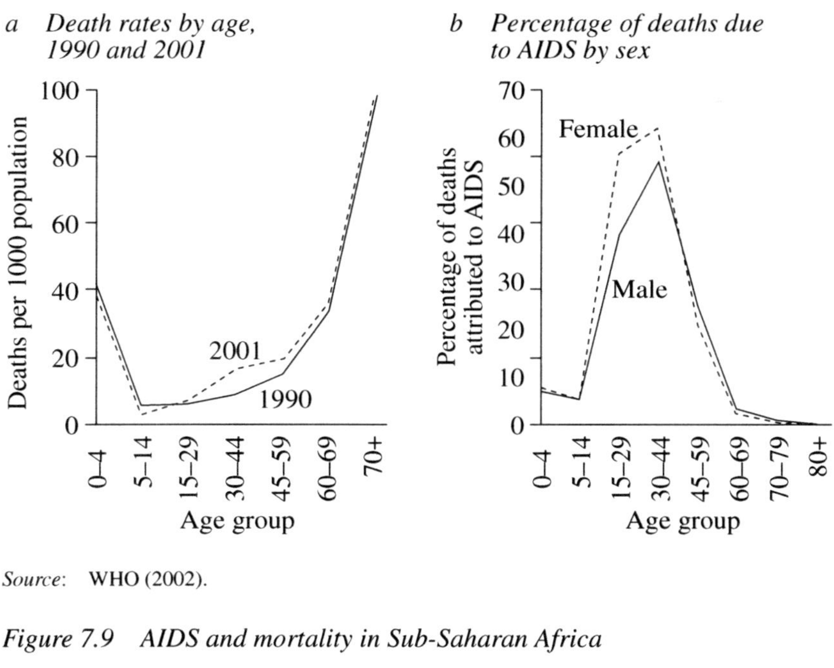

Source: WHO (2002).

Figure 7.9 AIDS and mortality in Sub-Saharan Africa

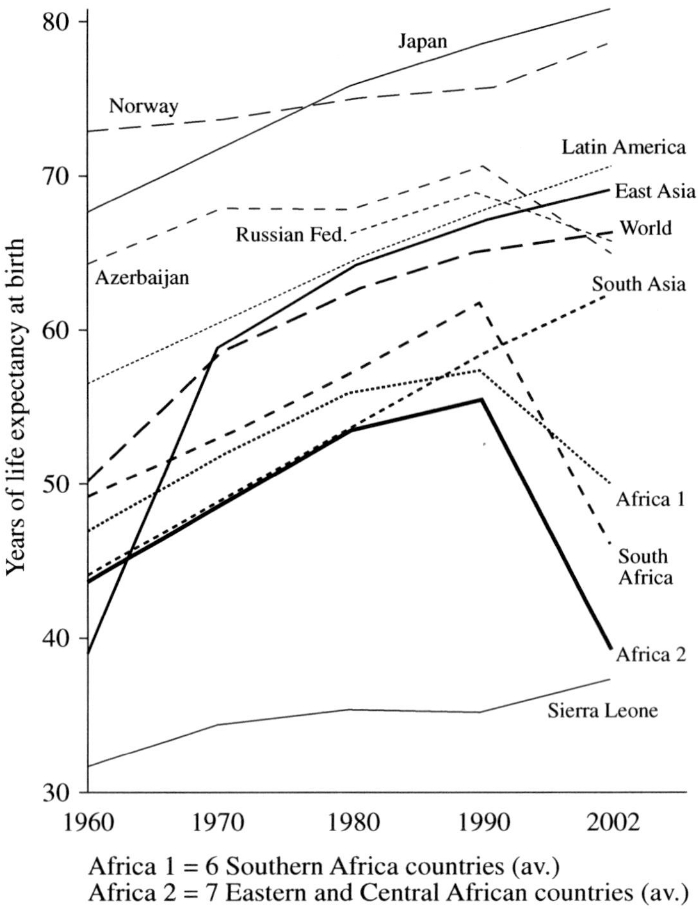

Source: World Bank (2004).

Figure 7.10 Life expectancy, 1960 to 2002

clearly visible in Figure 7.10 showing the evolution of life expectancies from 1960–2002.

A crisis such as the AIDS epidemic is not only one of the individuals, families and villages but of society in a more general sense. Like illness in general its impact displays many of the social inequalities already mentioned: it affects women more than men and the working class and poor more than the rich (Sutcliffe, 2004). Such a massive and sudden increase in deaths is difficult for communities to absorb, both emotionally and economically. Observers have reported from African villages how the traditional form and function of funerals have had to be abandoned. In nearly all societies funerals both mark tragedies and aid social continuity. They are (often expensive) social occasions which help to purge the death emotionally; they enable families and friends periodically to renew their links and friendship (or hostility). When deaths come so fast none of this remains possible. But the most affected communities are really, to repeat Oscar Wilde's macabre jest, 'dying beyond their means' in all possible senses.

FROM MORTALITY TO DEATH

At the beginning of his memoir on his period of banishment by Mussolini to a remote southern Italian village (*Christ Stopped at Eboli*) Carlo Levi returns in his imagination 'to that other world, hedged in by custom and sorrow, cut off from History and the State, eternally patient, to that land without comfort or solace, where the peasant lives out his motionless civilization on barren ground in remote poverty, and in the presence of death' (Levi [1947] 1982). Death here is not a statistic but a chronic tragedy.

Most studies of mortality look at mortality rates and life expectancies, but not so much at death itself. But different patterns of mortality change the phenomenon of death. The j-shaped distribution of mortality by age, common to all countries, surely underestimates the social and cultural dimension of death in different communities. Those curves suggest that although some countries have tragically high infant mortality, death is still basically what happens to people who have grown old. If however we look not at mortality rates but at the deaths which actually take place, a different picture emerges. In a country with high infant mortality rates and a high proportion of children in the population, death is not predominantly something suffered by old people, but by children. Though many of the poorest countries lack the appropriate figures, some startling examples exist: in Mali almost 60 per cent of the people who die are under five years old; in Pakistan 40 per cent of those who die are under 1 and 50 per cent under 5. In the UK by contrast three-quarters of those who die are over 70 years old and half are over 80. Figure 7.11a shows the cumulative distribution of death by age for seven world regions and 7.11b shows similar information by country. The overall picture conveys the enormous difference which the phenomenon of death assumes in different countries. In Britain, like other rich countries, it is exceptional for a young person to die. In many parts of Africa the death of an old person is the exceptional event. When, as a matter of course, children die before their parents, the presence of death must be especially oppressive.

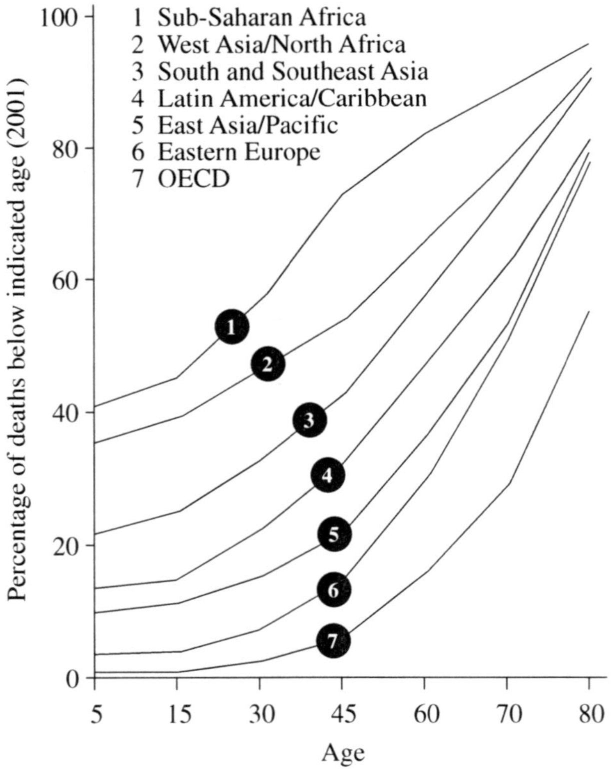

Source: WHO (2002).

Figure 7.11a The age distribution of deaths, seven world regions and groups

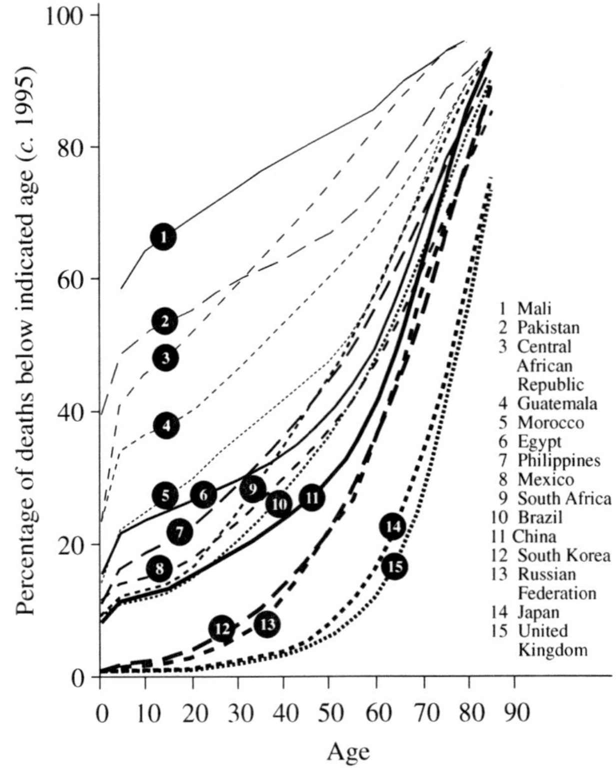

Source: United Nations (1999).

Figure 7.11b The age distribution of deaths, 15 countries

FROM MEDICINE TO POLITICAL ECONOMY

In developed countries it is illegal to die of old age; one must be certified to have died of a recognized fatal condition. Death certificates must carry a medically authenticated cause of death. And when a person dies naturally but is not known to be suffering from a life-threatening illness an autopsy is performed until a doctor is satisfied as to the cause of death. Such a measure may be necessary as a protection against murder, though in many cases it results in bureaucratic torment for bereaved people. It is only the absence of death registration in poorer countries which stops all deaths in the world being given a medical cause. And the primary thing which the authors of the GBD have done is to fill in those blanks in a plausible way.

But theirs is not the only way of looking at the cause of death, nor is it necessarily the most important. The GBD methodology analyses the deaths which take place according to various criteria: age and sex, proximate medical cause and 'risk factor'. The first ten medical causes of death in the world in 2002 were found to be: ischaemic heart disease, cerebrovascular disease, lower respiratory infections, HIV-AIDS, perinatal conditions, diarrhoeal diseases, tuberculosis, trachea, bronchus and lung cancers and malaria. Together these ten cause 53 per cent of deaths. The study remaps this data in various ways. One of them is to take disability-adjusted life years (DALYs) lost instead of deaths and another is to calculate (both for deaths and for DALYs) the importance of the ten most significant causal 'risk factors' (a hybrid category which includes medical, social and environmental conditions). The percentages of the world's lost DALYs accounted for by each risk factor were found to be childhood and maternal malnutrition (28 per cent), other diet-related risks and physical inactivity (23 per cent), sexual and reproductive health risks (12 per cent), tobacco, alcohol and drugs (16 per cent), environmental risks (15 per cent), occupational risks (3 per cent) (WHO, 2002).

But the cause of death or disability has many dimensions. It is not only a question of medical science but also of common sense. We all understand what it is to die of old age; it seems not to matter all that much whether a very old person dies of heart disease or cancer; we feel that they were bound to die of something. And surely the poets, doctors notwithstanding, have convinced us that is possible to die of unrequited love, or neglect, or rage, or despair. Social scientists could also usefully join in this activity of divining the causes of death and disability. The majority of deaths, as the GBD shows, are in some sense biologically premature. A task of social science in relation to development could in a sense be seen as that of explaining the social and economic causes which underlie that biological prematurity. The explanation of why not everyone can die in, if not of, old age is more than anything else a task for us. We need to try to remap these deaths not just according to disease, or risk factor, but in social, economic and political categories. To know what percentage of deaths and disability in the world now take place due to poverty, to lack of education and knowledge, to inequality and all its causes, to lack of medical facilities or appropriate health policies, to the research and pricing policies of pharmaceutical companies, the advertising and marketing policies of tobacco companies, to the absence of sufficient international economic aid, to prejudice and denial which prevents adequate education about safe sex, to discrimination and violence based on sex, race or sexuality, or to the multitude of other socially and economically pathological factors which can contribute to premature death. The recent advances which, thanks to demographers and epidemiologists, have been made in our knowledge about death and deaths in the world make this important task more feasible than ever before.

Unmasking the social causes of premature deaths can be seen as a counterpart to the powerful political movements which have arisen to confront dictatorship on behalf of those missing through political oppression. It is part of an effort to reveal the fate of the world's hundreds of millions of missing persons, and so a contribution to preventing others from sharing their fate in the future – in other words to egalitarian development.

NOTE

* For help in writing this chapter and comments on a draft I am grateful to Nancy Folbre, Nino de Leo and Arthur MacEwan.

REFERENCES

Acheson, Donald et al. (1998), *Independent Inquiry into Inequalities in Health, Report*, (The Acheson Report), London: Stationery Office.

Astorga, Pablo and Valpy Fitzgerald (1998), 'Statistical Appendix' in Rosemary Thorp, *Progress, Poverty and Exclusion: An Economic History of Latin America in the 20th Century*, Baltimore, MD: Johns Hopkins University Press.

Becker, C.M. and D.E. Bloom (1998), 'Demographic change in Russia during the transition period', *World Development*, **26** (11).

Bennett, N.G., D.E. Bloom and S.F. Ivanov (1998), 'Demographic implications of the Russian mortality crisis', *World Development*, **26** (11).

Brainerd, E. (1998), 'Market reform and mortality in transition economies', *World Development*, **26** (11).

Cutler, David M. and Ellen Meara (2001), 'Changes in the age distribution of mortality over the 20th century', NBER working paper, no 8556 accessed at www.nber.org/papers/w8556.

Deaton, Angus (2001), 'Health, inequality and economic development', WHO Commission on Macroeconomics and Health working paper series, WG1 3.

Deaton, Angus (2003), 'Health, inequality and economic development', *Journal of Economic Literature*, **41** (March) 113–58.
Filmer, Deon, Elizabeth M. King and Lant Pritchett (1998), 'Gender disparity in South Asia: comparisons between and within countries', World Bank policy research working paper 1867, Washington, DC.
Frank, John W. and J. Fraser Mustard (1994), 'The determinants of health from a historical perspective', *Daedalus*, **123** (4) (special issue on health and wealth).
Global Forum for Health Research (2004), *10/90 Report on Health Research 2003–2004*, Geneva: Global Forum for Health Research.
Government of India Planning Commission (2001), *National Human Development Report 2001*, accessed at http://planningcommission.nic.in/reports/genrep/nhdrep/nhdreportf.htm
Haq, Mahbub Ul (1997), *Human Development in South Asia 1997*, Oxford: Oxford University Press.
Harriss White, Barbara (1990), 'The intrafamily distribution of hunger in South Asia', in Jean Drèze and Amartya Sen, *The Political Economy of Hunger*, Oxford: Clarendon Press.
Haub, Carl (1995), 'How many people have ever lived on earth?', *Population Today*, February.
Kennedy, B.P., I. Kawachi and E. Brainerd (1998), 'The role of social capital in the Russian mortality crisis', *World Development*, **26** (11).
Levi, Carlo (1947 [1982]), *Christ Stopped at Eboli*, Harmondsworth: Penguin.
McNeil, Donald G. Jr (1998), 'Aids stalks Africa's struggling economies', *New York Times*, 15 November.
Michaud, Catherine (1999), 'The global burden of disease and injuries in 1990', *International Social Science Journal*, **161** (September).
Mitchell, B.R. with Phyllis Deane (1962), *Abstract of British Historical Statistics*, Cambridge: Cambridge University Press.
Mitchell, B.R. and H.G. Jones (1971), *Second Abstract of British Historical Statistics*, Cambridge: Cambridge University Press.
Murray, Christopher J.L. and Alan D. Lopez (eds) (1996a), *The Global Burden of Disease: A Comprehensive Assessment of Mortality and Disability from Diseases, Injuries, and Risk Factors in 1990 and Projected to 2020*, Cambridge, MA: World Health Organization, World Bank, Harvard School of Public Health.
Murray, Christopher J.L. and Alan D. Lopez (eds) (1996b), *Global Health Statistics: A Compendium of Incidence, Prevalence and Mortality Estimates for over 200 Conditions*, Cambridge, MA: World Health Organization, World Bank, Harvard School of Public Health.
Murray, Christopher J.L. and Alan D. Lopez (1997), 'Global burden of disease study', four articles, *The Lancet*, **349**, 3 May, 10 May, 17 May, 24 May.
Otten, Mac W., Steven M. Teutsch, David F. Williamson and James S. Marks (1990), 'The effects of known risk factors on the excess mortality of black adults in the United States', *Journal of the American Medical Association*, **263** (6).
Rosenthal, Elisabeth (1999), 'Suicides reveal the bitter roots of China's rural life', *New York Times*, 24 January.
Sant'anna, Wania (2001), 'Racial and gender inequalities in Brazil: possible revelations of the HDI and the GDI', *Jornal da Rede Deminista de Saude*, 23 August.
Sen, Amartya (1990), 'More than one hundred million women are missing', *New York Review of Books*, **37** (20), 61–6.
Sen, Amartya (1993), 'The economics of life and death', *Scientific American*, May.

Sen, Amartya (1998), 'Mortality as an indicator of economic success and failure', *Economic Journal*, **108** (January).
Shkolnikov, V.M., G.A. Cornia, D.A. Leon and F. Meslé (1998), 'Causes of the Russian mortality crisis: evidence and interpretations', *World Development*, **26** (11), 1995–2011.
South African Institute of Race Relations (1998), *South Africa Survey 1997–98*, Johannesburg: Institute of Race Relations.
Srinivasan, K., Abusaleh Shariff, Wasim A. Zaman and Christina Bierring (1997), *India: Towards Population and Development Goals*, Delhi: United Nations Population Fund/Oxford University Press.
Sutcliffe, Bob (2004), 'The economics of AIDS; long term damage to the world's economies', *Index on Censorship*, **1**.
Thorp, Rosemary (1998), *Progress, Poverty and Exclusion: An Economic History of Latin America in the 20th Century*, Washington, DC: Inter-American Development Bank/Johns Hopkins University Press (also published in Spanish).
UNAIDS/WHO (2003), *AIDS Epidemic Update: December 2003*, accessed at www.unaids.org/html/pub/publications/irc-pub06/jc943-epiupdate2003_en_pdf.pdf
UNDP (1998), *Human Development Indicators*, (computer database).
UNDP Nepal (2001), *Nepal Human Development Report 2001; Poverty Reduction and Governance*, accessed at www.undp.org.np/publications/nhdr2001/.
United Nations (1999), *Demographic Yearbook 1998*, New York: United Nations.
United States Census Bureau (1999 and 2003), *Statistical Abstract of the United States*, accessed at www.census.gov/statab/www/.
Wilkinson, Richard G. (1994), 'The epidemiological transition: from material scarcity to social disadvantage', *Daedalus*, **123** (4), (special issue on health and wealth).
World Bank (2004), *World Development Indicators 2004*, accessed on CD-Rom, Washington, DC: World Bank.
World Development (1998), 'The demographic crisis in the former Soviet Union', special issue of *World Development*, **26** (11).
World Health Organization (1999), *The World Health Report 1999*, Geneva: WHO.
World Health Organization (2002), *The World Health Report 2002*, Geneva: WHO.
World Health Organization (2004a), *The World Health Report 2004*, Geneva: WHO
World Health Organization (2004b), *World Report on Road Traffic Injury Prevention*, Geneva: WHO.
World Health Organization and World Diabetes Federation (2004), *Diabetes Action Now*, Geneva: WHO.
Zohoori, N., T.A. Mroz, B. Popkin, E. Glinskaya, M. Lokshin, D. Mancini, P. Kozyreva, M. Kosolapov and M. Swafford (1998), 'Monitoring the economic transition in the Russian Federation and its implications of the demographic crisis – the Russian Longitudinal Monitoring Survey', *World Development*, **26** (11), 1977–93.

8. On comparing functioning bundles and capability sets*

Prasanta K. Pattanaik

INTRODUCTION

The measurement of the standard of living in terms of functionings or capability sets or both constitutes one of the most important recent developments in welfare economics.[1] The purpose of this chapter is to review two specific conceptual issues that arise in this context. Firstly, how do we compare functioning bundles of the same individual in different situations or the functioning bundles of different individuals? Secondly, how do we compare different capability sets (that is, different sets of available functioning bundles) for the same individual or the capability sets of different individuals? Comparisons of functioning bundles and capability sets are not the only important issues that arise in the functioning-based conception of the standard of living, and these may not even be the most important issues that arise here. However, the problem of comparison is of considerable importance in many practical applications of this approach to the measurement of the standard of living.

One can compare living standards at different levels. Thus one may be interested in comparing the living standards of a given person in different situations or the living standards of different persons. Alternatively, one may be interested in comparing the living standards of different groups of individuals. In this chapter, I do not discuss the problem of comparing the living standards of groups of individuals, though that is usually the problem that confronts policy-makers. Instead, I focus on the conceptually more primitive problem of standard-of-living comparisons at the level of single individuals.

The plan of the chapter is as follows. In the next section, I introduce a few basic notations and concepts. I then consider some aspects of the problem of comparing the functioning bundles. Next, I consider the problem of comparing capability sets. I conclude in the final section.

THE NOTATION AND SOME BASIC CONCEPTS

Let the set of all individuals under consideration be denoted by $N = \{1, 2,\ldots, n\}$. Depending on the context, the individuals in N may belong to the same social group or society, or they may come from different social groups or societies. I assume that there is general agreement about what constitute the relevant functionings, that is, 'the various things that a person may value doing (or being)' (Sen, 1997, p. 199). Let $F = \{f_1,\ldots,f_m\}$ denote the set of functionings. I shall sidestep the problem of measuring the functionings. It is an important problem but I want to focus on other issues. I shall assume that all functionings can be measured on a ratio scale, the quantity of a functioning being a non-negative real number. It is a strong assumption: for many functionings, such as being able to 'lead a life without shame' (see Sen, 1987, p. 18), which have been discussed in the literature, it is difficult to think of a ratio scale. For all $i \in N$, let $x_i = (x_{i1},\ldots,x_{im})$ denote a functioning bundle of individual i, where, for all $k \in \{1,2,\ldots,n\}$ and all $l \in \{1,\ldots,m\}$, x_{kl} denotes k's achievement in terms of functioning l. Alternative functioning bundles of individual i will be denoted by x_i, y_i and so on.

The capability set of individual i is defined to be the set of all mutually exclusive functioning bundles available to individual i. Intuitively, the capability set of an individual reflects the opportunities that the individual enjoys. Alternative capability sets of individual i will be denoted by A_i, B_i, and so on. When I need to talk about capability sets in general, without referring to specific individuals, I shall use the notation A, B and so on. Since the term 'capability' has been used in different senses by different writers,[2] I avoid using the term altogether and use instead the term 'capability set' used by Sen (1997).

COMPARING FUNCTIONING BUNDLES

In the framework of functionings and capability sets, one can think of several alternative conceptions of an individual's standard of living. One can assume that the individual's standard of living depends exclusively on the functioning bundle actually achieved by the individual. Alternatively, one can assume that the individual's standard of living depends exclusively on the individual's capability set. Finally, one can have a more inclusive formulation where an individual's well-being depends both on their achieved functioning bundle and their capability set. In this chapter, I do not choose one of these alternative formulations. Instead, I discuss the problem of comparing functioning bundles if one wants to follow the first approach and, similarly, the problem of comparing capability sets if one decides to take the second approach.

Suppose one takes the standard of living of an individual as being determined exclusively by her achieved functioning bundle. Then, how does one compare the standards of living of the same individual with two alternative functioning bundles or the standards of living of two individuals? First, consider the domination principle, which by invoking a minimal evaluative judgement avoids much of the problem involved here (however, see the next section for a discussion of conflicts between the domination principle and certain other important value judgements).

The Domination Criterion

If one believes that the assessment of the standard of living of an individual should be based on the achieved functioning bundle alone, then it would seem compelling to accept that, if $x_i > x_i'$ (that is, if x_i contains more of some functioning and no less of any functioning as compared to x_i'), then x_i offers i a higher standard of living than x_i'. It seems almost equally compelling to accept that, if $x_i > x_j$, then i's standard of living with x_i is greater than j's standard of living with x_j. In a framework where the achieved functioning bundle is the determinant of a person's standard of living, the comparison of the standards of living seems straightforward if one is able to apply the dominance principle. The problem lies in the incompleteness of the dominance ranking. Many pairs of functioning bundles may not be comparable under the dominance principle. The important question would seem to be how frequently such violation of completeness occurs in real life. As far as I know, Chakraborty (1995, pp. 42–4) was the first writer to investigate this issue. Taking the functioning bundles for different countries, as reported in the *Human Development Report* (UNDP, 1993), Chakraborty (1995) demonstrated that the domination relation over functioning bundles failed to yield any ranking over a large number of pairs of countries. In what follows, I undertake an exercise similar to Chakraborty's. I consider three distinct sets of countries with different levels of human development, and I use the *Human Development Report* for a more recent year, namely 2003 (UNDP, 2003). Though comparisons of living standards of individuals constitute my main concern, the inter-country comparisons are of some interest insofar as they give us some idea about the extent of non-comparability under the dominance criterion.

In Table 8.1, I have randomly chosen six countries from each of the three different categories of high human development (HHD), medium human development (MHD) and low human development (LHD).

As can be seen from the table, the dominance relation can successfully rank many pairs of countries belonging to different categories. For example, except in the comparison between Tajikistan and Pakistan, every MHD country dominates every LHD country, though the corresponding pattern is less prominent in inter-category comparisons of HHD and MHD countries. As can be expected, the real failure of the domination principle arises in intra-category comparisons. There are 15 possible pairwise comparisons within each category. Out of these,

Table 8.1 Human development

Country	Life expectancy index	Education index	GDP index	HDI rank	GDP rank
		High human development			
Germany	0.88	0.96	0.92	18	13
Portugal	0.85	0.97	0.87	23	30
Slovakia	0.80	0.90	0.80	39	44
Qatar	0.78	0.82	0.88	44	25
Lithuania	0.79	0.94	0.74	45	57
Belarus	0.74	0.95	0.72	53	62
		Medium human development			
Russian Federation	0.69	0.93	0.71	63	66
Belize	0.78	0.88	0.67	67	83
Jamaica	0.84	0.83	0.60	78	105
Turkmenistan	0.69	0.92	0.63	87	100
Armenia	0.78	0.86	0.55	100	119
Tajikistan	0.72	0.90	0.41	113	154
		Low human development			
Pakistan	0.59	0.41	0.49	144	137
Yemen	0.57	0.49	0.34	148	169
Djibouti	0.35	0.51	0.53	153	125
Côte d'Ivoire	0.28	0.46	0.45	161	149
Angola	0.25	0.38	0.50	164	132
Burundi	0.26	0.43	0.32	171	171

Note: All the indices are normalized values between 0 and 1 of the actual achievement in each of the different dimensions.

Source: UNDP (2003).

the dominance principle fails to give a ranking for eight comparisons within the HHD category, 13 comparisons within the MHD category and ten comparisons within the LHD category.

'Local' Information about Values

If neither $x_i > x_j$ nor $x_j > x_i$, then it is not possible to compare the two bundles without bringing in trade-offs between functionings. All such trade-offs will clearly depend on value judgements. Suppose we have a unique set of such value judgements, which are universally acceptable. Further, suppose that these value judgements are embodied in an evaluation function V, which for every conceivable functioning bundle z specifies a real number indicating the standard of living corresponding to that functioning bundle.[3] Later I shall discuss possible sources of the evaluation function V and its uniqueness. For the moment however we assume that there is a valuation function shared by everybody concerned, namely, the individuals in N and the economist evaluating the standards of living of these individuals. For the sake of simplicity, we assume that there are only two functioning (so that $m = 2$).

We assume that the evaluation function V satisfies 'strict monotonicity' (other things remaining the same, an increase in the amount of a functioning improves the standard of living) and is quasi-concave, so that the 'indifference curves' corresponding to the evaluation function have the usual properties of being downward sloping and convex to the origin. While we may know these general characteristics of the indifference map, it is perhaps too demanding to require that we know the entire indifference map, that is, we know the shape of the evaluation function everywhere in the relevant space of functionings. Can we then use some relatively limited information for the purpose of our comparisons? In the traditional income-based approach, when one compares a competitive consumer's standards of living in different situations by computing the values of the alternative consumption bundles at a fixed vector of prices, P, one uses a very limited amount of (implicit) information about the consumer's indifference map, namely, the marginal rates of substitutions at the consumption bundle that the consumer buys at the price vector P. The popular practice of using a fixed set of weights for the functionings to compare different functioning bundles would seem to be a counterpart of the use of a fixed price vector to compare consumption bundles in the income approach, and it suffers from some of the problems that arise in the conventional income approach.[4]

Consider the implications of using a fixed weighting vector $w = (w_1, w_2)$ to determine the ranking of alternative functioning bundles in terms of living standards, that is, the implications of saying that for all pairs of functioning bundles, x_i and x_i', under consideration, x_i offers i at least as high a standard of living as x_i' if and only if $w.x_i \geq w.x_i'$. Note the following facts.

Firstly, given that the indifference curves generated by the evaluation function are convex to the origin, if w_1/w_2 is not equal to the marginal rate of substitution of f_1 for f_2 at x_i, then $(w.x_i > w.x_i')$ does not ensure that x_i offers i a higher standard of living than x_i' (see Figure 8.1).

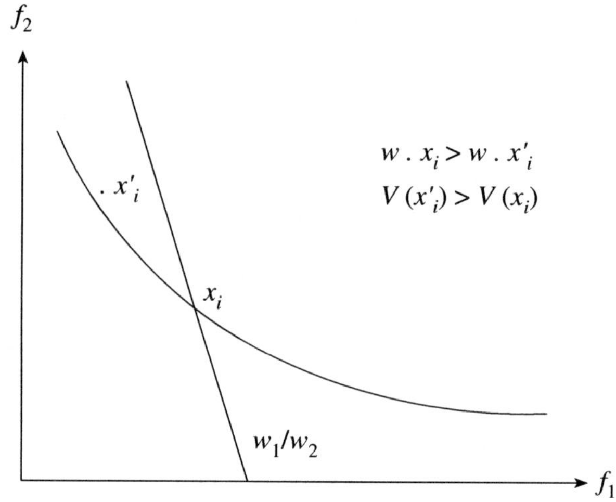

Figure 8.1

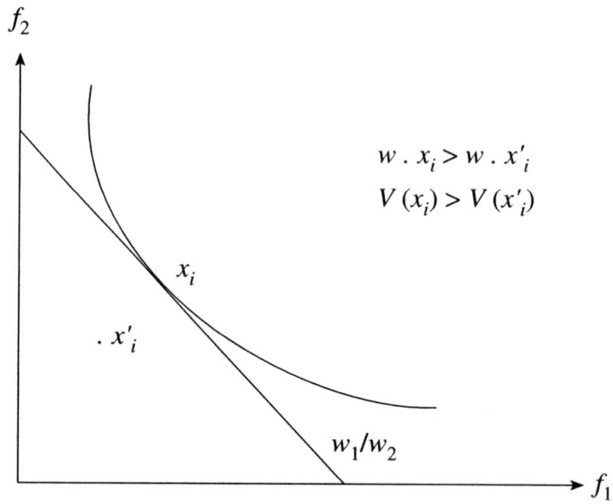

Figure 8.2

Secondly, given that the indifference curves generated by the evaluation function are convex to the origin, if w_1/w_2 is equal to the marginal rate of substitution of f_1 for f_2 at x_i, then $(w.x_i > w.x_i')$ implies that x_i must offer *i* a higher standard of living than x_i' (see Figure 8.2), and $(w.x_i = w.x_i')$ implies that the standard of living offered by x_i must be at least as great as the standard of living offered by x_i'.

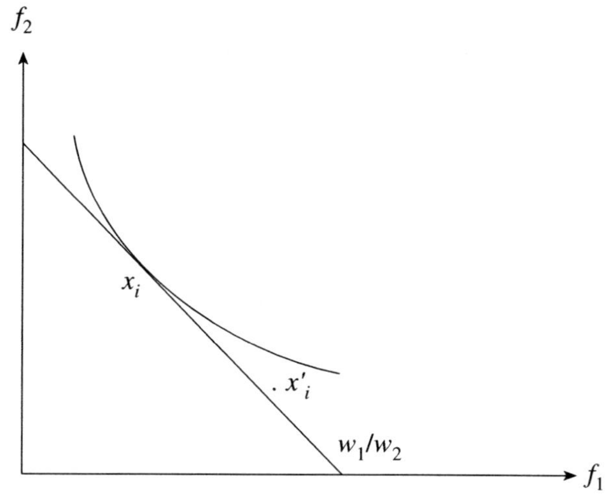

Figure 8.3

Thirdly, if any of the indifference curves generated by the (quasi-concave) evaluation function has a non-linear stretch, then one can find two functioning bundles x_i and x_i' such that [w_1/w_2 is equal to the marginal rate of substitution of f_1 for f_2 at x_i, and $w.x_i < w.x_i'$], and yet x_i offers a higher standard of living than x_i' (see Figure 8.3).

Thus, given a quasi-concave evaluation function V and a fixed weighting vector $w = (w_1, w_2)$, the only case in which, for all x_i and x_i', ($w.x_i > w.x_i'$) necessarily implies that x_i offers a higher standard of living to i than x_i' is the highly counter-intuitive case where the indifference curves are all parallel straight lines with the slope $-w_1/w_2$.

Of course one is not often faced with the problem of ranking all possible functioning bundles. However if our fixed weighting vector is $w = (w_1, w_2)$, and we have, say, ten functioning bundles, $z^1, \ldots z^{10}$, such that [$w.z^1 > w.z^2 > \ldots > w.z^{10}$], then the only circumstances under which we can be sure that this ranking coincides with the ranking of the bundles yielded by the function V is where w_1/w_2 is equal to the marginal rate of substitution of f_1 for f_2 at each of the bundles $z^1, z^2, \ldots,$ and z^9. This is a rather restrictive condition.

Global Information about Values

We have seen that local value information, that is, information about the marginal rate of substitution between functionings at any particular point, may not be very helpful in comparing two functioning bundles. Therefore we need an explicit evaluation function that will trace out the entire map of indifference curves over our two-dimensional space. At least, we need enough information about the evaluation function V so as to know the ranking under V of all the functioning bundles we are interested in.

So far I have assumed that there is a single agreed evaluation function. The question arises as to the interpretation of this evaluation function and whether it is reasonable to assume that there is a unique evaluation function that should be used to compare living standards. One can think of several interpretations of the evaluation function(s). Firstly, we can interpret the evaluation function as reflecting the evaluation that the individual, whose standard of living is under consideration, arrives at after careful reflection (see Sen, 1987, p. 32). If we adopt this interpretation, then the problem of non-uniqueness of the evaluation function would not arise when comparing the living standards of the same person corresponding to alternative functioning bundles (assuming that her evaluation function does not change with a change in her functioning bundle). However, it does not solve the problem of non-uniqueness when comparing the living standards of individuals with different evaluation functions. If one uses i's evaluation function, the functioning bundle x_j may offer a higher living standard than the functioning bundle x_i, while the ranking may be just the opposite if we use j's evaluation function. While there is no inherent contradiction if this happens to be the case, in taking policy decisions a politician or an economic planner may still need to know whether i with the functioning bundle x_i 'really' has a higher standard of living than j with the functioning bundle x_j, or vice versa.

Under a second interpretation, an evaluation function reflects the norms prevalent in a society. One does not have to deny the existence of social norms to argue that even in a given society, there may be divergent norms in different subgroups. In that case, we are back to the problem of multiple evaluation functions. The possibility of divergent norms is even greater when we are interested in comparing living standards across societies with very different cultures.

A third interpretation may be that an evaluation function represents the values that a 'reasonable person' may have. Insofar as reasonable people can evaluate different functioning bundles differently, this interpretation would allow for different evaluation functions even for a given society. There is also the further issue of whether the notion of a reasonable person may be culture-specific.

One can plausibly argue that the set of functionings that people value is essentially the same for all individuals, irrespective of the society they come from. The appeal to similarity however is much less convincing when the issue is not what functionings people value, but how people value the different functioning bundles in relation to each other. A group of people may agree about the relevant space of functionings, but their relative evaluations of different points in this space may be very different. Nor are such differences necessarily due to transient impulses and likely to disappear after the individuals have had a chance for careful reflection on the problem of evaluation. Even after the individuals have had adequate time to reflect on the matter, their evaluation functions may be significantly different, especially if they come from different societies with different norms and standards. For example it is not obvious that, in general, the Americans and the Europeans have similar attitudes towards leisure *vis-à-vis* other functionings; nor is it clear that people in an industrial society value interaction with extended families as much as people in tribal societies.

In the face of such differences, one possibility is to take a route that Sen (1987, pp. 30–31) has suggested. Sen writes:

> the ... approach of using contemporary standards can, of course, be used to *rank* the overall living standards of different persons and groups. The essential feature of this general approach is the reliance on some uniformity of judgements (when such uniformity exists) on the respective importance of different objects of value. (p. 31)

The suggestion that one can rely on the uniformity of judgements, when such uniformity exists, involves the priciple that a person with a functioning bundle x has a higher standard of living than a person with functioning bundle y if, in terms of all the relevant evaluation functions, x ranks higher than y (depending on one's approach, the relevant evaluation functions may be the evaluation functions of all individuals in a given society, the evaluation functions of all people in all contemporary societies, the evaluation functions that a reasonable person may have, and so on). How far can the unanimity rule take us? In the absence of extensive empirical studies, it is difficult to answer this question with much confidence. It is possible that the unanimity rule will enable one to compare living standards in a large number of cases. However, so far we do not have any convincing empirical evidence for that.

'Agent-invariance' in Standard of Living Comparisons

The possible multiplicity of evaluation functions raises another important issue, which has been recently discussed in some detail in Pattanaik and Xu (2004). Though it is not possible to discuss here their formal results, it may be worthwhile outlining briefly one of their intuitive concerns.

Let x and y be any two functioning bundles. Consider the problem of ranking x and y in terms of the standard of living of a given person (note that this problem does not involve any interpersonal comparison of living standards). Should this ranking of x and y be invariant with respect to the person whose living standards are under consideration? Such invariance (for convenience, I shall call it 'agent-invariance') would imply that if for some individual i, x offers a higher standard of living than y, then for every other person j, x must also offer a higher standard of living than y. If the individuals under consideration have similar evaluations of functioning bundles and if they belong to social groups or societies with similar attitude towards functionings, then agent-invariance would not be a restrictive property irrespective of whether we go by the individual's evaluation of his own living standards or by the norms prevailing in the society to which the individual belongs. However if the individuals have significantly different attitudes towards functionings even after careful reflection and if the social groups they come from also differ in their standards, then the requirement of person-invariance in standard-of-living comparisons would seem to be a highly unreasonable demand.

The basic message that emerges from Pattanaik and Xu (2004) is that if we relax agent-invariance in any way to accommodate differences in evaluations of functioning bundles either between individuals or between communities, and if our standard of living comparisons satisfy a very plausible property of continuity, then we would end up by violating the dominance criterion[5] ('a person with a bigger functioning bundle has a higher standard of living than a person with a smaller functioning bundle'). Thus given the property of continuity of standard-of-living comparisons, the dominance criterion, which has been widely accepted in the literature, forces us to subscribe to agent-invariance, which seems to be an undesirable property in the presence of significant differences in evaluations of functioning bundles.

COMPARISONS OF CAPABILITY SETS

The notion of capability sets occupies a central place in Sen's theory of the standard of living. If this important notion is to be used in practice, we need to find a way, however imperfect, of comparing capability sets.

Some Alternative Approaches to the Problem of Comparing Capability Sets

Let A and B be two capability sets. If $A \subset B$, then it is clear that B offers more opportunity, or at least as much opportunity, as A. But if neither of the two sets is a subset of the other, then it is not obvious how to rank them. The existing literature has explored various approaches here.[6] First, when A and B are finite sets, we have the approach that ranks A and B on the basis their cardinalities, a set with a larger number of functioning bundles being ranked higher in terms of opportunity than a set with a smaller number of functioning bundles (see Steiner, 1983 and Pattanaik and Xu, 1990 among others). An alternative approach introduces a reference set of orderings defined over the universal set of alternatives (see for example Foster, 1990) and makes use of the orderings in this reference set to rank capability sets. The orderings in the reference set may be interpreted differently as: (1) the set of preference orderings (or, if one likes, evaluations) that the individual whose freedom is under consideration may have in the future (see Arrow, 1995); (2) the set of preference orderings or evaluations that the individuals in a given society actually have; and (3) the set of preference orderings or evaluations that a reasonable person may have (see for example Jones and Sugden, 1982; Sugden, 1998; Pattanaik and Xu, 1998).

While studies of the cardinality-based ranking of capability sets in the literature have provided some useful insights, there now seems to be a consensus that the assessment of opportunities or freedom requires evaluation of the options involved. Therefore, I concentrate on the approach based on a reference set of orderings over the universal set of functioning bundles. For the sake of simplicity, let us consider the case where, for every admissible capability set A and every ordering R in the reference set, Ω, of orderings over functioning bundles, there exists a best alternative in A, defined in terms of R. Then the following criterion for ranking capability sets seems to be fairly plausible: for all capability sets A and B, if for every ordering $R \in \Omega$, the R-greatest alternatives in A are all strictly preferred to the R-greatest alternatives in B, then A offers more freedom than B.

What happens if, for some ordering R in the reference set, the R-greatest elements in A are strictly preferred (in terms of R) to the R-greatest elements in B, and, for some other ordering R' in the reference set, the R'-greatest elements in B are strictly preferred (in terms of R') to the R'-greatest elements in A? As far as I know, the literature does not have any very compelling answer to this question. It is however of interest to consider two interesting suggestions that have been made by Muellbauer (1987) for ranking capability sets.

Muellbauer (1987) suggests two alternative methods for ranking capability sets. For the sake of convenience, assume that there are only two functionings. Consider a given capability set A. In the first method for ranking capability sets suggested by Muellbauer, we start with a probability distribution p over a fixed finite set of rays through the origin. For simplicity, suppose that this set contains only two rays through the origin – og_1 and og_2, which intersect the frontier of the capability set A at h_1 and h_2, respectively, and which have the probabilities $p(og_1)$ and $p(og_2)$, respectively (see Figure 8.4).[7]

Muellbauer suggests $[p(og_1).oh_1 + p(og_2).oh_2]$ as a possible index of the opportunity or freedom offered by the capability set A. Given the finite set of rays through the origin and the probability distribution p over this set, such an index can be computed for every capability set. The capability sets can then be ranked on the bases of these indices, a capability set with a higher value of the index being ranked higher than a capability set with a lower value of the index. The second index suggested by Muellbauer relies on slopes. Suppose we have a probability distribution q over the slopes of a fixed finite set of downward sloping straight lines. Suppose there only two such straight lines, a_1b_1 and a_2b_2, in the set (see Figure 8.5).

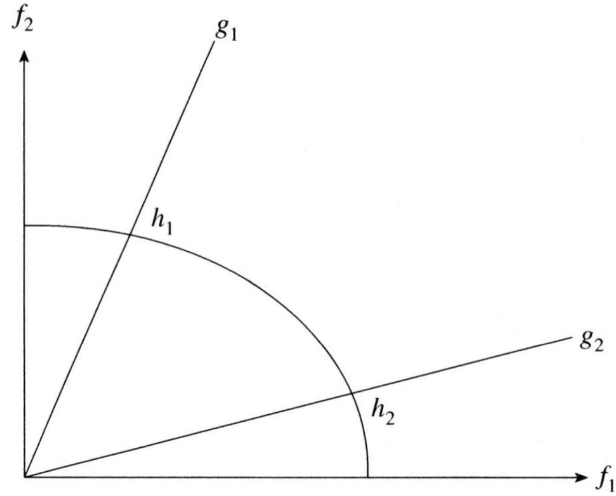

Figure 8.4

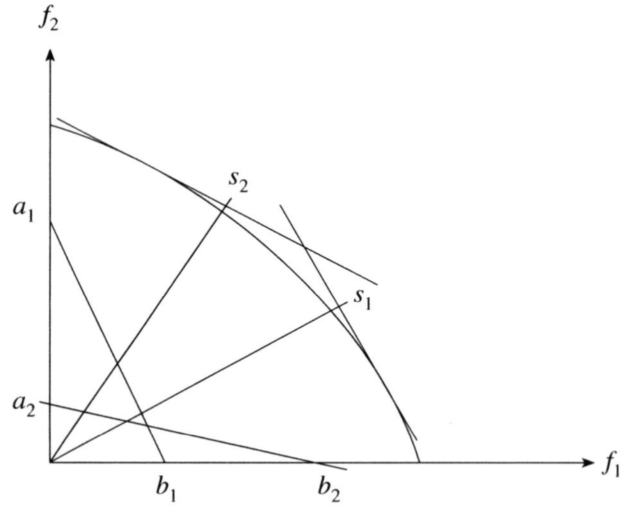

Figure 8.5

Let the slopes of a_1b_1 and a_2b_2 be α_1 and α_2, respectively. Muellbauer suggests $[q(\alpha_1).os_1 + q(\alpha_2).os_2]$ as another possible index for the opportunity offered by the capability set A where os_1 is the distance of the origin from the straight line which is parallel to a_1b_1 and tangent to the frontier of A, and os_2 is the distance of the origin from the straight line which is parallel to a_2b_2 and tangent to the frontier of A.

What exactly is the meaning of these indices suggested by Muellbauer? A possible interpretation for each index can be given by using the notion of a reference set of orderings when the orderings are assumed to be of a particular type. Consider the first index of Muellbauer. Suppose Ω has only two orderings, R_1 and R_2. First, assume that the 'indifference curves' corresponding to each ordering in Ω are 'rectangular', the 'corners' of all the rectangular indifference curves generated by R_1 being located on og_1 and the corners of the rectangular indifference curves generated by R_2 being all located on og_2 in Figure 8.4. Then og_1 can be considered to be a measure of how 'high' one can go up in the indifference map corresponding to R_1 while remaining in the capability set A, and og_2 can be interpreted in a similar fashion. So far as the probabilities $p(og_1)$ and $p(og_2)$ are concerned, the interpretation of these probabilities will depend on the interpretation of Ω. If Ω is interpreted as the set of all orderings that the individual under consideration may have in the future, then it will be plausible to interpret $p(og_1)$ and $p(og_2)$ as the probabilities of the individual's having orderings R_1 and R_2, respectively. If Ω is interpreted as the set of orderings that the individuals in the society have, then we can interpret $p(og_1)$ as the fraction of the people in the society who have the ordering R_1 and $p(og_2)$ as the fraction of people with the ordering R_2. Finally, if Ω is interpreted as the set of all orderings that a reasonable person may have, then it seems plausible to assume that $p(og_1) = p(og_2) = ½$ (on the ground that every ordering that a reasonable person may have carries the same weight). Given the assumption of rectangular indifference curves, and given the chosen interpretation of Ω and the corresponding interpretation of the probabilities, Muellbauer's first index seems to have considerable intuitive appeal. However in the absence of rectangular indifference curves, it is not clear what – if any – intuitive meaning can be attached to the fixed set of rays through the origin. So far as the interpretation of Muellbauer's second index is concerned, assume that the indifference curves generated by each ordering in Ω are parallel straight lines. The slope of a_1b_1 in Figure 8.5 is then the common slope of all the indifference curves generated by R_1 and the slope of a_2b_2 in Figure 8.5 is the common slope of all the indifference curves generated by R_2. In that case, os_1 can be considered to be a measure of how high the agent can move up the indifference map corresponding to R_1 while remaining in the capability set A, and similarly for os_2. As before, interpreting Ω in a suitable fashion and using a corresponding interpretation of Muellbauer's probabilities, the second index of Muellbauer can be seen to be intuitively plausible. However if the indifference curves generated by each ordering in Ω are not parallel straight lines, it becomes difficult to see what intuitive significance one can attach to Muellbauer's second index.

Agent-invariance and Comparisons of Capability Sets

The issue of agent-invariance that arises in comparing functioning bundles has its counterpart in comparisons of capability sets. If evaluations of functioning bundles are to be used in ranking opportunity sets, then given the differences in such evaluations as between individuals and communities, it would seem plausible to allow the ranking of opportunity sets for a given individual to depend on the values of that individual or the standards of the community to which the individual belongs. However as Pattanaik and Xu (2004) show, given a mild assumption of continuity of the ranking of capability sets, such 'relativism' conflicts sharply with a very appealing property that requires that, if a capability set B is a proper subset of another capability set A, and if for every functioning bundle b on the 'frontier' of B, there exists another point a on the frontier of A such that a dominates b, then any person with the capability set A has a higher standard of living than any person with the capability set B (the frontier of a capability set D is the set of all functioning bundles d in D such that d is not dominated by any other functioning bundle in D).[8]

Strategic Interdependence and the Notion of Capability Sets

So far I have assumed that the notion of opportunities available to an individual is adequately captured by the concept of a capability set. Now I would like to raise some questions regarding the adequacy of the concept of a capability set for this purpose. Recall that a capability set is a set of (mutually exclusive) functioning bundles. The interpretation of the set is that it represents the set of all functioning bundles available to the agent in some actual or hypothetical situation, so that in that situation, the agent can have at will any functioning bundle in the capability set. One can think of many circumstances where this is a reasonable conception of an individual's opportunities. Consider the classical case of a perfectly competitive economy where each agent is a very small part of the market for any commodity and is therefore a price taker. Suppose the functioning bundle of a consumer depends exclusively on their consumption of marketed commodities, and suppose for each consumer the achieved functioning bundle is determined exclusively by the consumption bundle of marketed commodities (this assumption can be relaxed without substantially affecting the argument). Then it is clear that given the competitive equilibrium prices, which an individual consumer cannot affect no matter which bundle she decides to consume, there will be a set of feasible functioning bundles from which she can choose any bundle that she may decide to have. However the real world offers plenty of examples of situations where the agent is not in a position to choose a functioning bundle from a given set of feasible functioning bundles. Let me give an example to illustrate my point. Consider a society where sexual harassment of women often takes place, despite laws against it. Faced with such harassment, a female employee of a firm can of course go to the court, but the outcome of such a decision will depend on a number of factors such as whether her fellow employees will be willing to come forth to give evidence, whether the employer will find some excuse to dismiss her, whether her decision to go to the court will lead other employers in her town to blacklist her, and so on. The basic point is this. The woman has the option of taking alternative actions. However her action, by itself, does not determine what bundle of the two functionings – being able to live without shame and being able to live without hunger – she will have. Her functioning bundle depends on the actions of many other agents as well as her own action. Similarly, an 'untouchable' in an Indian village may have the legal right to get his drinking water from the village well, used by people of upper castes, rather than drinking water from the polluted village pond. However there may be some possibility that by exercising his legal right, the untouchable person may lose the livelihood that he earns by working as an agricultural worker in the farms of the upper-caste people in the village. Whether he will lose his employment as an agricultural worker may depend crucially on whether the other untouchables in the village will join him in getting drinking water from the village well or whether he is the only person to challenge tradition.

Thus it seems to me that in a wide range of situations we are not really free to pick up at will a functioning bundle from a given set of feasible functioning bundles. Our freedom often comes not directly in the form of the freedom to choose a functioning bundle, but in the form of freedom to choose alternative actions which, together with other people's actions, determine our achievements in terms of functionings. While the formulation of opportunities in terms of capability sets can be very useful in many situations, there is a case for going beyond it when strategic interactions are important in determining an individual's functioning bundle.

When strategic interactions are important in determining an individual's functioning bundle, it is natural to think of formulating the notion of his opportunities in the framework of game forms and games. For simplicity, consider a two-person society. Let the interactive process through which the functioning bundle of each individual is determined be represented by a game form G where $\{s_1,s_1',s_1''\}$ is the set of strategies available to 1; $\{s_2,s_2',s_2''\}$is the set of strategies available to 2; and a,b,c and so on are the 'outcomes' or 'states of affairs' that result as consequences of the individuals' choices of strategies.

The orderings of the two individuals over the set of all outcomes in the game form G (Table 8.2) are denoted by $\tilde{R}_1$ and $\tilde{R}_2$. Then $(G, \tilde{R}_1, \tilde{R}_2)$ constitutes a game. For every outcome o, let $v_1(o)$ and $v_2(o)$ denote, respectively, the functioning bundles that 1 and 2 achieve in outcome o.

How should we specify the opportunities that i (i = 1, 2) enjoys when he or she plays the above game? This is an issue of considerable conceptual and techni-

Table 8.2

		2		
		s_2	s_2'	s_2''
	s_1	a	b	b
1	s_1'	b	a	c
	s_1''	d	a	b

cal complexity, and I do not propose to discuss it here in detail. However I give just one example of the various approaches that one may take. Note that it is open to 1 to choose strategy s_1, and, if he or she does so, then depending on what 2 does, 1 will get some functioning bundle in the set $\{v_1(a),v_1(b)\}$. Suppose $v_1(a) \neq v_1(b)$. Then, from the point of view of the individual's achievements in terms of functionings, $\{v_1(a),v_1(b)\}$ represents an uncertain prospect where the individual may achieve either the functioning bundle $v_1(a)$ or the functioning bundle $v_1(b)$.[9] Similarly, s_1' is associated with an uncertain prospect $\{v_1(a),v_1(b),v_1(c)\}$ and s_1'' is associated with an uncertain prospect $\{v_1(a),v_1(b),v_1(d)\}$. One can then identify the capability set of 1 with the class $\{\{v_1(a),v_1(b)\}, \{v_1(a),v_1(b),v_1(c)\}, \{v_1(a),v_1(b),v_1(d)\}\}$, where each element of the class is to be interpreted as an uncertain prospect. 2's capability set can be specified in an analogous fashion. As I indicated, there are other ways of identifying the capability sets of the two players in this game. The analytical features and intuitive implications of alternative specifications of capability sets in the framework of game forms and games have not yet been studied and the problem needs detailed and independent investigation.

CONCLUDING REMARKS

In this chapter, I have reviewed several problems that arise when we try to compare functioning bundles or capability sets. Some of these problems, such as the difficulties of using local information about values, are exact counterparts of problems that one encounters in the literature on real income comparisons. Other problems, such as the difficulties that arise when one seeks to relax the unacceptably rigid assumption of 'agent invariance', and the difficulties of capturing the notion of freedom as an aspect of the standard of living, relate to the specific framework of the approach based on functionings and capability sets. Many of the problems are conceptually difficult and we do not yet know satisfactory ways of handling them. This of course does not constitute any foundational shortcoming of the functioning approach to the assessment of living standards. The approach is still relatively new and it is not surprising that there are many unresolved basic issues. It is however important to continue revisiting and exploring these issues because not only is the functioning approach one of the most significant conceptual innovations in welfare economics in recent times, but it also has far-reaching practical implications.

NOTES

* I am indebted to Indranil Dutta for preparing for me Table 8.1 in this paper, and to Stephen Marglin and Amartya Sen for stimulating conversations. The chapter was first presented in a conference in honour of Keith Griffin in April 2004, and, as a keynote lecture, in the Fourth International Conference on the Capability Approach in September 2004. For helpful comments, I am grateful to several participants in these two conferences.

1. There is now a substantial and rapidly growing literature on the subject. However, the path-breaking contributions of Sen (1985, 1987) constitute some the clearest exposition of the fundamental ideas. See also Nussbaum (1988), Nussbaum and Sen (1993), Nussbaum and Glover (1995), Sen (1997) and Nussbaum (2000), among others.
2. In fact, sometimes the term 'capability' has been used in the sense in which Sen (1985, 1987) uses the term 'functioning'. In a scholarly discourse, one is of course free to use a term in any sense one likes so long as one gives a clear definition. However there is some advantage in using a uniform terminology, at least for the most basic concepts, in a given area of research.
3. I assume that the evaluation function is ordinal. Actually, the assumption of an ordering over the set of all functioning bundles, which is weaker than the assumption of an evaluation function, is adequate for much of my discussion.
4. Classic investigations of some of the problems that arise in the income approach to the standard of living are to be found in Hicks (1940) and Little (1957, Chapter 3).
5. See above.
6. Strictly speaking, much of the existing literature on opportunity or freedom studies the problem in a general framework where the options in the universal set are not necessarily interpreted as functioning bundles. However, in referring to this literature, I shall ignore this aspect.
7. In depicting the capability set in Figures 8.4 and 8.5, I have assumed certain properties for the set, such as compactness and convexity.
8. Pattanaik and Xu (2004) assume that the class of all 'admissible' capability sets is the class of all non-empty, compact, convex, and comprehensive subsets of $\Re^m_+$.
9. A certain prospect may be considered to be a special case of an uncertain prospect, where the set of functioning bundles constituting the uncertain prospect is a singleton.

REFERENCES

Arrow, K.J. (1995), 'A note on freedom and flexibility', in K. Basu, P.K. Pattanaik and K. Suzumura (eds), *Choice, Welfare, and Development: A Festschrift in Honour of Amartya K. Sen*, Oxford: Clarendon Press, pp. 7–16.

Chakraborty, A. (1995), 'The concept and the measurement of the standard of living', PhD dissertation, University of California, Riverside.

Foster, J. (1992), 'Notes on effective freedom', mimeo.

Hicks, J. (1940), 'Valuation of social income', *Economica*, **7**, 105–24.

Jones, P. and R. Sugden (1982), 'Evaluating choice', *International Review of Law and Economics*, **2**, 47–69.

Little, I.M.D. (1957), *A Critique of Welfare Economics*, 2nd edn, Oxford: Oxford University Press.
Muellbauer, J. (1987), 'Professor Sen on the standard of living', in Geoffrey Hawthorn (ed.), *The Standard of Living*, Cambridge: Cambridge University Press.
Nussbaum, M. (1988), 'Nature, function, and capability: Aristotle on political distribution', *Oxford Studies in Ancient Philosophy*, supplementary volume, New York: Oxford University Press.
Nussbaum, M. (2000), *Women and Human Development: The Capabilities Approach*, New Delhi: Kali for Women.
Nussbaum, M. and J. Glover (1995), *Women, Culture and Development: A Study of Human Capabilities*, Oxford: Clarendon Press.
Nussbaum, M. and A.K. Sen (eds) (1993), *The Quality of Life*, Oxford: Clarendon Press.
Pattanaik, P.K. and Y. Xu (1990), 'On ranking opportunity sets in terms of freedom of choice', *Recherches Economiques de Louvain*, **56**, 383–90.
Pattanaik, P.K. and Y. Xu (1998), 'On preference and freedom', *Theory and Decision*, **44**, 173–98.
Pattanaik, P.K. and Y. Xu (2004), 'Relativism, dominance, and the functioning approach to the measurement of living standards', mimeograph.
Sen, A.K. (1985), *Commodities and Capabilities*, Amsterdam: North-Holland.
Sen, A.K (1987), 'The standard of living', in Geoffrey Hawthorn (ed.) *The Standard of Living*, Cambridge: Cambridge University Press.
Sen, A.K. (1997), *Economic Inequality*, expanded edition, Oxford: Clarendon Press.
Steiner, H. (1983), 'How free: computing personal freedom', in A. Philips-Griffiths (ed.), *Of Liberty*, Cambridge: Cambridge University Press, pp. 73–89.
Sugden, R. (1998), 'The metric of opportunity', *Economics and Philosophy*, **14**, 307–37.
United Nations Development Program (UNDP) (1993), *Human Development Report*, New York: United Nations Development Program.
United Nations Development Program (UNDP) (2003), *Human Development Report*, New York: United Nations Development Program.

9. Environment, poverty and development*

Charles Perrings

THE PROBLEM

The Brundtland Report supported the notion that there are close causal links between environmental change and poverty, both within and between generations. This reflected existing evidence of a correlation between poverty and accelerating environmental degradation in many countries, especially in Sub-Saharan Africa. Since that time, considerable effort has been committed to uncovering the microeconomic connections between poverty, resource degradation and population growth. In two seminal studies, Dasgupta (1993, 2001) has explored the connection between poverty, fertility decisions and environmental change. Others have focused on the connection between poverty and discount rates (Perrings, 1989; Holden et al., 1998), poverty and savings or investment rates (Bartolini and Bonatti, 2002), or poverty and institutional conditions (Lopez, 1992; Heath and Binswanger, 1996). The empirical evidence is however ambiguous. While poverty appears to be positively correlated with environmental degradation in some cases, it does not in others (Ekborn and Bojo, 1999; Duraiappah, 1996; Markandya, 2000, 2002).

This chapter reconsiders the relation between poverty and environmental resources, noting that the stock of assets includes not only produced capital, but also natural or environmental capital. Most existing measures of capital neglect the latter. The most inclusive of all System of Natural Accents (SNA) measures, net national product (NNP), still excludes depreciation of both human and natural capital along with transboundary environmental flows. One attempt to capture at least the first of these is the genuine savings index (GSI) due to Hamilton and Clemens (1999) and Hamilton (2000). Dasgupta (2001) has developed the same idea, calling it genuine investment. It is a measure of the change in a country's wealth. If wealth at a moment in time, t, is defined as V_t, a sufficient condition for wealth to be non-declining at that moment is that $\mathrm{d}V_t/\mathrm{d}t = \sum_i p_{it}\mathrm{d}K_{it}/\mathrm{d}t \geq 0$, K_{it} being the ith type of capital (produced, human or natural) at time t, and p_{it} being the social opportunity cost of that type of capital.

In principle, NNP is simply the sum of consumption and genuine investment. That is $NNP_t = C_t + dV_t/dt$, where C_t is consumption at time t. It follows immediately that a test of the sustainability of consumption is whether it is less than or equal to NNP. Dasgupta (2001) showed that countries that recorded strongly positive average annual percentage rates of change in per capita GNP from the 1960s onwards showed strongly negative rates of change in per capita wealth over the same period. Consistent with this, Hamilton (2000) found that the majority of countries with less than the median world income have been declining in terms of per capita wealth.

In fact the poor fit between measures of performance based on income (GNP per capita) and wealth (genuine investment) causes concern not just because it masks the sustainability of economic development, but also because it misleads us as to the nature of the linkages between poverty and environmental change. The genuine investment data show that many people in Africa and South Asia are dissaving to maintain consumption. Few are drawing down savings accounts or converting financial assets to do so. Most are dissaving by converting real assets, usually environmental assets held in common rather than private property. While this comes at the cost of lower productive potential in the future, it is largely ignored by institutions concerned with both poverty and development. Indeed it is regarded as an environmental problem of little or no relevance to the development process. In reality, by changing the portfolio of assets available to the poor, it has important implications for their development prospects.

This chapter considers the potential for changes of state that involve a reduction in both the size and productivity of the environmental resource base. What it reports is a way of thinking about the problem, rather than a complete set of results. A full analysis of the problem is being developed elsewhere. The approach is however thought to be sufficiently interesting that it is worth describing at this stage.

ENVIRONMENTAL ASSETS IN THE DECISION PROCESS

Wealth – the value of the assets over which people have rights or entitlements – comprises both marketed private assets whose prices will reflect the discounted stream of incomes they yield, and non-marketed public assets to which people have rights of access though not ownership. The private value of these assets reflects the discounted stream of private benefits they yield. Their social value includes the impact on private benefit streams of the interactions between users of those assets.

Environmental assets comprise the resources of the biosphere that support the provision of environmental goods and services. Environmental goods and services are typically necessary both for life support and for the production of marketed goods and services, but are not themselves marketed. Environmental services include the regulation of atmospheric chemical composition; the regulation of global temperature, precipitation and other biologically mediated climatic processes; the regulation of hydrological flows; the storage and retention of water; soil retention and soil formation; the cycling, processing and acquisition of nutrients; the movement of floral gametes; the trophic-dynamic regulation of populations and the provision of habitat (Daily, 1997).

To model the use of environmental assets, I assume that society has two sorts of capital available. Produced capital comprises durable manufactured assets. Natural capital comprises non-marketed environmental assets. These are usually subject to common property, but this is not crucial to what follows. The representative decision-maker's problem is assumed to take the following form:

$$\text{Max}_{c_t z_t} \int_0^\infty e^{-\delta t} u(c_t f(K_t, z_t R_t))dt \qquad (9.1)$$

subject to:

$$\dot{K} = f(K_t, z_t R_t)(1 - c_t) \qquad (9.2)$$

$$\dot{R} = g(R_t) - z_t R_t \qquad (9.3)$$

where:
K_t is the stock of produced capital
R_t is the stock of environmental assets
$f(K_t, z_t R_t)$ is output
z_t is the share of natural capital extracted
c_t is the share of output consumed
δ is the discount rate.
$u(.)$ is assumed to be continuous, twice differentiable and to satisfy $u_c > 0$ and $u_{cc} < 0$.

There are two choice or control variables available to the representative decision-maker: c_t, the consumption rate or share of output consumed, and z_t, the extraction rate or share of environmental resources used.

The equation of motion for K_t describes the net growth of the produced capital stock as a function of investment. The equation of motion for R_t describes the net growth of environmental assets in terms of a density-dependent growth or regeneration function.

From the current value Hamiltonian:

$$\tilde{H} = u(c_t f(K_t, z_t R_t)) + \lambda(f(K_t, z_t R_t)(1 - c_t)) + \mu(g(R_t) - z_t R_t) \qquad (9.4)$$

the first order conditions include:

$$\tilde{H}_c = u_c f'(\cdot) - \lambda f'(\cdot) = 0 \tag{9.5}$$

$$\tilde{H}_z = u_c c_t f'(\cdot) + \lambda f'(\cdot)(1 - c_t) - \mu = 0 \tag{9.6}$$

$$-\tilde{H}_K = \dot{\lambda} - \delta\lambda = -u_c c_t f'(\cdot) - \lambda f'(\cdot)(1 - c_t) - \tag{9.7}$$

$$-\tilde{H}_R = \dot{\mu} - \delta\mu = u_c c_t f'(\cdot) z_t + \lambda f'(\cdot)(1 - c_t) z_t + \mu(g'(\cdot) - z) \tag{9.8}$$

$$\tilde{H}_\lambda = \dot{k} = f(K_t, z_t R_t)(1 - c_t) \tag{9.9}$$

$$\tilde{H}_\mu = \dot{r} = g(R_t) - z_t R_t \tag{9.10}$$

and the appropriate transversality conditions. Taking the time derivatives of equations (9.5) and (9.6), and substituting into (9.8) and (9.9), the conditions on the evolution of the shadow prices of produced and natural capital, we have the following condition on the rate of change in consumption:

$$\dot{c} = \frac{u_c}{u_{cc}}(\delta - g'(\cdot)) = \frac{u_c}{u_{cc}}(\delta - f'(\cdot)) \tag{9.11}$$

That is, in the steady state the opportunity cost of capital should equal the marginal rate of regeneration of natural capital and the marginal productivity of produced capital.

Whether this generates one or more equilibria depends on the form of the growth function for the two types of capital stock. Since my primary concern is with environmental assets, let us consider the growth function for natural capital and take two cases – compensatory and depensatory growth. If there is compensatory growth then condition (9.11) implies a unique equilibrium value for natural capital that is stable from both the right and the left – a saddlepoint (Figure 9.1). If there is depensatory growth, condition (9.11) implies two equilibria. One of these is stable from both the right and the left. The other is stable from the right only (Figure 9.2). The first implies a high level of environmental stocks and yields. The second implies a low level of environmental stocks and yields. The first is associated with a high level of resilience with respect to shocks to natural capital (ecological sustainability). The second is associated with a low level of resilience to such shocks, and is vulnerable to collapse if natural capital stocks fall below the equilibrium value (since it is unstable from the left) (Brock and Malliaris, 1989).

If growth is depensatory there accordingly exists a critical value for natural capital stocks, above which it is optimal to converge on the high-yielding equi-

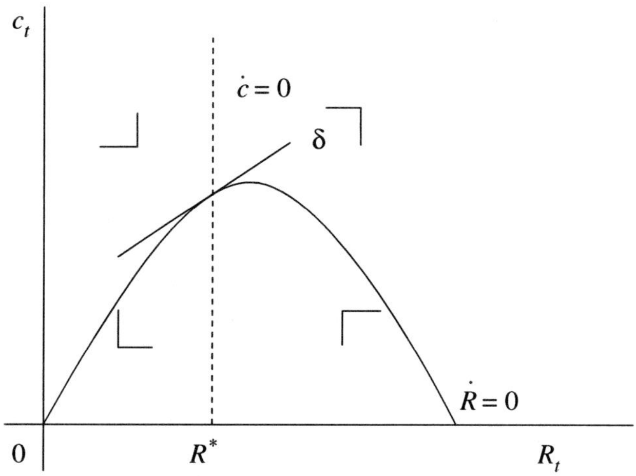

Figure 9.1 *The optimal stock of natural capital: compensatory growth*

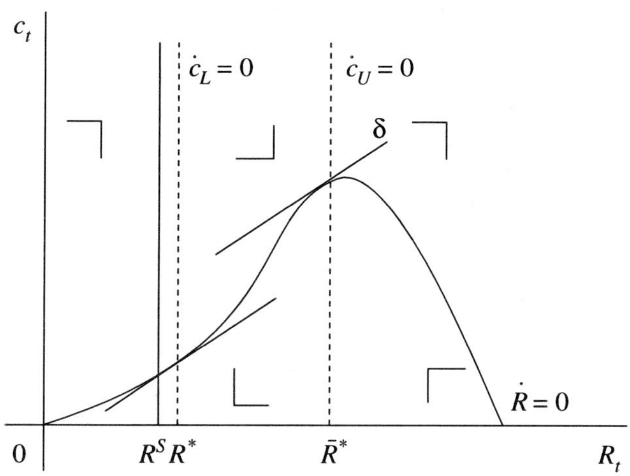

Figure 9.2 *The optimal stock of natural capital: depensatory growth*

librium, and below which it is optimal to converge on the low-level equilibrium. This is the Skiba point. If initial natural capital stocks lie to the right (left) of this point, the optimal trajectory will converge on the upper (lower) equilibrium.

POVERTY, SAVINGS AND ENVIRONMENTAL ASSETS

To connect poverty, the environment and development we need to consider how changes in income may induce a change in the stock of natural assets, and how this may shift the system from one state (equilibrium) to another. Since compensatory growth is associated with an optimum stock of natural capital that is unique for any given discount rate, this implies that we are interested in the case where the growth of natural capital stocks are depensatory (or critically depensatory).

The notion of poverty applied here is 'subjective poverty' (borrowed from Drewnowski, 1977). It is defined by the decision-maker's perception of the minimum acceptable level of consumption. Such perceptions vary both from individual to individual, and from society to society. They also vary over time. An income shock that drives consumption below the current minimum acceptable level will almost always induce a sharp change in savings and investment. That change may eventually be reversed, but only with a lag that depends on the speed of adjustment of consumption expectations.

There is no inequality-related measure of poverty that is appropriate here, even though the social minimum acceptable level of consumption may well be a relative one. Instead the minimum acceptable level of consumption at any moment in time defines a subjective poverty point. Beyond that point the social decision-maker will choose to dissave. Hence the zero savings level of income is regarded as the 'subjective' poverty point for the decision-maker, and dissaving to maintain consumption is taken to indicate that the decision-maker is in 'subjective' poverty. It follows that a decision-maker is in 'subjective poverty' at time t if their consumption rate is greater than one at that time.

Suppose that the consumption rate is required to satisfy $(c_t f(\cdot)) \geq \bar{C}$, where $\bar{C}$ is the subjective poverty point, implying a utility function of the general form $u((c_t f(\cdot)) - \bar{C})$. Suppose further that output is subject to shocks deriving either from environmental, market or political factors, so that $f(\cdot) = f(K_t, z_t R_t \Omega)$, where Ω defines the shocks. To keep things simple, I take Ω to be a shift parameter that affects the productivity of natural capital, and hence output. Take the case where the impact of Ω is negative. Since $df/d\Omega > 0$ by assumption, this will have a negative effect on output, but if $c_t f(\cdot)$ is close to $\bar{C}$ the decision-maker may choose to dissave in the short run. Since dissaving implies that natural capital stocks will be run down, it will be reflected in an increase in the extraction rate beyond the rate of regeneration of those stocks.

Consumption may be written as a function of the consumption and extraction rates. In the short run, it is:

$$C_t = c_t f(\bar{K}_t, z_t \bar{R}_t \Omega)$$

both natural and produced capital stocks being constant. Maintenance of consumption in the presence of a negative shock requires that:

$$\frac{dc_t}{d\Omega}\frac{f(\cdot)}{\bar{R}} = -c_t\left[f_z\Omega\frac{dz_t}{d\Omega} + f_\Omega z_t\right] \tag{9.12}$$

Given that $z^* = \dfrac{f(\cdot)}{\bar{R}}$ in the steady state, this implies that

$$\frac{dc_t}{d\Omega} = -c_t\frac{z_t}{z^*}[f_z\eta + f_\Omega] \tag{9.13}$$

where $\eta = (\Omega/z_t)/(dz_t/d\Omega)$ is the elasticity of the extraction rate with respect to productivity shocks. That is, the decision-maker will choose to increase their consumption rate in response to a negative productivity shock if η is positive. If η is negative they may either increase or decrease their consumption rate, depending on the strength of the productivity shock.

We are particularly interested in decisions made in the neighbourhood of the subjective poverty point. At that point c_t is close to 1 and hence there is little scope for increasing consumption, that is, $dc_t/d\Omega = 0$. In this case maintenance of consumption levels in the face of a negative productivity shock requires an increase in output, which can only occur if natural capital stocks are depleted. Specifically, it requires that $\eta = -(f_\Omega/f_z)$, that is, that the elasticity of the extraction rate with respect to productivity shocks is equal to the negative of the ratio of the marginal productivity of extraction to the shocks. Decision-makers who are unable to increase consumption by reducing savings will increase the rate of extraction in proportion to the strength of the shock.

Notice that this does not affect the steady state conditions (9.11), but by changing the rate at which natural capital stocks are run down to meet a binding consumption constraint, it can affect which long-run equilibrium the system will converge on.

DISCUSSION

The preceding sections have made two points. The first is that under quite reasonable assumptions (depensatory or critically depensatory growth of natural capital stocks) there exist at least two equilibrium values for natural capital stocks. One of these is characterized by high levels of productivity and resilience to output shocks, the other is characterized by low levels of productivity and resilience to output shocks. Which equilibrium the system converges on depends on the initial values of those stocks. Put another way, in the case where there are two equilibria, the system can converge on either a resilient or robust environmentally productive state or on a vulnerable degraded state. Which state holds in any given case depends on the initial values of capital stocks relative to a critical value – the Skiba point.

The second point is that initial values of natural capital stocks may be sensitive to short-run decisions to maintain consumption. Decision-makers who are unable to meet their minimum subsistence requirements by reducing savings, may do so by drawing down natural capital stocks – by consuming those stocks at rates greater than the optimal rate. By reducing stocks to meet a currently binding consumption constraint, decision-makers may cause the system to converge on a low-productivity, vulnerable equilibrium state.

There are two effects at work. The first is the impact of a productivity shock on the critical value of natural capital – the Skiba point. If the effect of a shock is to reduce the productivity or regeneration rate of natural assets, then the Skiba point will be shifted to the right. That is, the size of the stocks at which the system converges on the low-level equilibrium will increase. The second is the impact of the shock on the yields offered at the system equilibria. These will be lower for both the high-level (Koopmans) and low-level equilibria. These effects are illustrated in Figure 9.3.

In real economy-environment systems the steady-state effect of current changes in stocks may not be immediately apparent. Whether the poverty-induced changes in stocks cause the system to converge on a new and different equilibrium will take time to become clear. Nevertheless at least some developments are suggestive. The incidence of dissaving in poor countries has become much clearer since the development of the World Bank's genuine savings index (latterly adjusted net savings). These indices take at least some account of changes in environmental stocks. Using these data, Dasgupta (2001) considered the evidence on what he calls genuine investment in both South Asia and Sub-Saharan Africa in the last third of the 20th century. He showed average levels of dissaving in this period that varied between 0.1 percent in India and 3.4 percent in Africa. The implications of this for the future well-being of people in those regions are hard to overlook. Sub-Saharan Africa is estimated to have lost around half of its wealth in the years between 1965 and 1997, much of it in the form of environmental assets.

Disinvestment in natural resources may involve not only the substitution of high-yielding produced assets for low-yielding natural assets, but also the drawing down of natural assets to meet the consumption needs of people in 'subjective' poverty. The point being made in this chapter is that where the stock of natural assets is reduced below a critical minimum, the system may converge on a new equilibrium characterized by both lower productivity and lower resilience to external shocks. However this only occurs if the reduction in assets

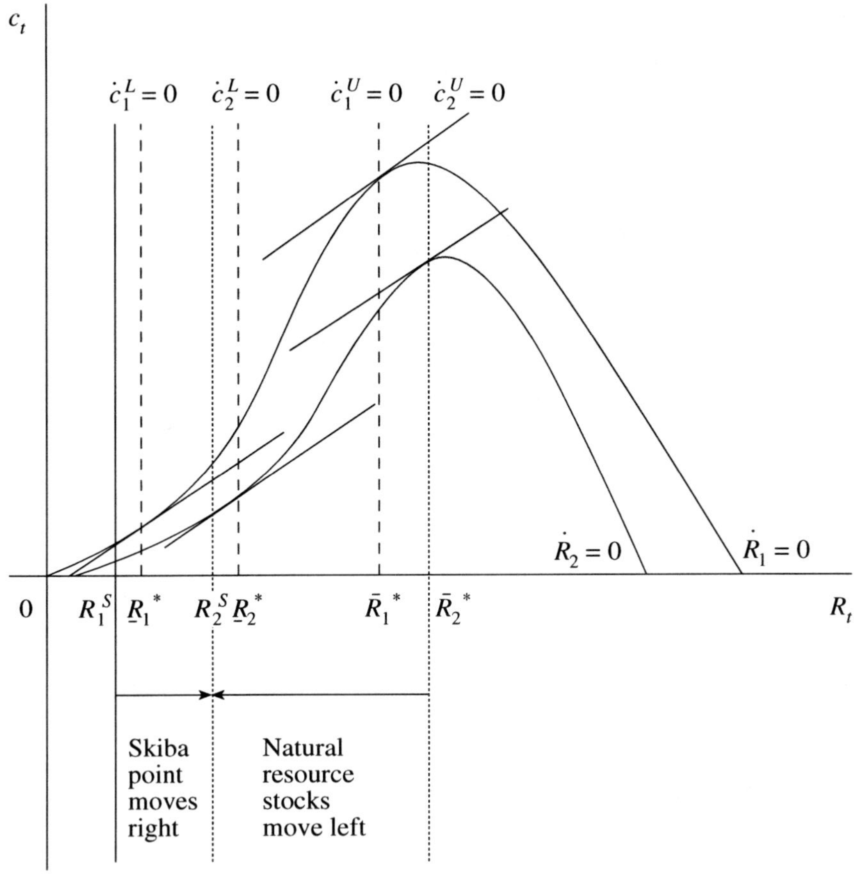

Figure 9.3 The impact of productivity shocks on the optimal stock of natural capital: depensatory growth

takes the system past the Skiba point. Since poverty may be implicated in the decision to reduce stocks, this offers one explanation for the apparently ambivalent empirical relationship between poverty and environmental degradation.

NOTE

* I am indebted to Buz Brock for discussions on this problem, and to participants at the Griffin Festschrift for comments on an earlier version of the chapter.

REFERENCES

Barbier, E.B. (1997), 'The environmental Kuznets curve', *Environment and Development Economics*, **2**, 341–58.

Bartolini, S. and L. Bonatti (2002), 'Negative externalities as a cause of growth', working paper, Dipartimento di Economia Politica, University of Siena.

Brock, W.A. and A.G. Malliaris (1989), *Differential Equations, Stability and Chaos in Dynamic Economics*, Amsterdam: North Holland.

Daily, G. (1997), *Nature's Services: Societal Dependence on Natural Systems*, Washington, DC: Island Press.

Dasgupta, P. (1993), *An Inquiry into Well-being and Destitution*, Oxford: Oxford University Press.

Dasgupta, P. (2001), *Human Well-Being and the Natural Environment*, Oxford: Oxford University Press.

Drewnowski, J. (1977), 'Poverty: its meaning and measurement', *Development and Challenge*, **8**, 183–208.

Duraiappah, A. (1996), 'Poverty and environmental degradation: a literature review and analysis', CREED working paper series 8, IIED, London.

Ekborn, A. and J. Bojo (1999), 'Poverty and environment: evidence of links and integration into country assistance strategy process', discussion paper 4, Environment Group, Africa region, World Bank, Washington, DC.

Hamilton, K. (2000), 'Sustaining economic welfare: estimating changes in per capita wealth', policy research working paper 2498, World Bank, Washington, DC.

Hamilton, K. and M. Clemens (1999), 'Genuine savings rates in developing countries', *World Bank Economic Review*, **13**, 333–56.

Heath, J. and H. Binswanger (1996), 'Natural resource degradation effects of poverty and population growth are largely policy induced: the case of Colombia', *Environment and Development Economics*, **1** (1), 65–84.

Holden, S.T., B. Shiferaw and M. Wik (1998), 'Poverty, market imperfections and time preferences', *Environment and Development Economics*, **3** (1), 105–30.

Lopez, R. (1992), 'Environmental degradation and economic openness in LDCs: the poverty linkage', *American Journal of Agricultural Economics*, **74**, 1138–45.

Markandya, A. (2000), 'Poverty, environment and development', in A. Rose and L. Gabel, *Frontiers of Environmental Economics*, Cheltenham, UK and Northampton, MA, USA: Edward Elgar Publishing.

Markandya, A. (2002), 'Poverty alleviation, environment and sustainable development: implications for the management of natural capital', discussion paper, World Bank, Washington, DC.

Perrings, C. (1989), 'An optimal path to extinction? Poverty and resource degradation in the open agrarian economy', *Journal of Development Economics*, **30**, 1–24.

PART IV

Globalization and Inequality

10. Globalization and the transition to egalitarian development*

Robert Pollin

Keith Griffin is one of the giants of economics in our time. His writings on egalitarian development are of course prodigious and highly influential. But what sets him apart from even other leading thinkers in this field is his focus not simply on what should be done to advance an egalitarian development path, but also the specific means through which a more equal society that is also sustainable might actually be achieved. This should not be surprising, since many of Griffin's most important works emerged out of specific projects in which he was advising governments throughout the world on precisely the question of how to advance a workable transition toward egalitarian development. *The Transition to Egalitarian Development* (co-authored with Jeffrey James, 1981) was the title of just one of his many works reflecting this set of concerns and approach to research.

I have been absorbing the strong force field emanating from Keith Griffin since we first became colleagues at the University of California, Riverside in 1988. As a political economist of the left, I always assumed part of my job description was to think about what might be realistic strategies for moving capitalist societies from where they are today to where we would like them to be in the not-too-distant future. I confess to having at times felt frustration by the relative lack of attention among like-minded colleagues to this issue. Keith Griffin ponders this and related matters – the 'how to get from here to there' questions – every day he walks into his office. You can't work in the same building as Keith and miss this central fact of his professional existence.

Providing coherent answers to such questions has become decidedly more challenging during our contemporary historical epoch, known variously as 'the era of globalization', 'the era of neoliberalism', or some combination of the two. Keith Griffin, characteristically, has accepted this challenge. Just since the time when we became colleagues in 1988, Keith has led advising missions to Bolivia, Mongolia, Uzbekistan, Vietnam and Kazakhstan, and has published substantial research works drawing from these engagements. Advising national governments in our current era cannot be done without spending lots of time contemplating the effects of globalization. Having been with Keith in Bolivia,

I saw first-hand that even progressive governments – or maybe especially progressive governments – have become disoriented in their approach to policy due to what they perceive as the constraints on them imposed by globalization. Griffin has also regularly opened a wider lens in his observations and analysis on globalization, combining his first-hand knowledge of how economies actually operate with a sweeping array of economic, social, historical and cultural insights.[1]

In this chapter, I attempt to synthesize these various features of the Griffin approach to doing economics to excavate the question of globalization. Specifically, within the context of our contemporary historical epoch, I wish to explore what I take to be *the* basic Griffin question – how can we advance a transition to egalitarian development within the context of globalization? Considering this question in its full scope entails, by definition, examining the global economy as a whole. Obviously one cannot hope to touch on even a small fraction of the significant issues flowing from this topic within a single chapter, and I do not pretend to try. In fact, while the scope of this chapter is wide, my ambition remains relatively modest – to generate some usable perspectives, leading to concrete policy ideas, that might be more difficult to perceive through approaches that are more narrowly focused. Moreover I will offer somewhat more detailed observations on conditions in developing countries, an emphasis which is clearly in keeping with a volume in honor of Professor Griffin.

We begin with what I take to be the single most important fact about the contemporary pattern of global economic integration. This is that it is being guided by a predominant commitment to neoliberal economic policies throughout the world. Such policies include more openness to trade and foreign direct investment, fewer government regulations of financial markets and institutions and other sectors, and a substantially reduced role for macroeconomic policy management. How one assesses the implications of this process of neoliberal globalization depends on the analytic perspective from which one approaches the question. The majority of mainstream economists regard neoliberal globalization as a fundamentally benign process. Of course, such a view follows logically from a broader perspective that holds that the operation of free markets in a capitalist economy generates efficiency, a stable macroeconomic environment and as close an approximation to a fair distribution of income as is likely to be attained. But from the left dissident traditions in economics, one would begin from a premise that neoliberal globalization is likely to engender systemic unemployment, increasing disparities in income and wealth, and greater macroeconomic instability, even while it may still promote market competition and greater efficiency in some areas.

The chapter proceeds by first discussing the term 'globalization' itself. Moving onward, the chapter is structured around three overarching problems which have emerged in this era of neoliberal globalization. I term these 'the Marx problem', 'the Keynes problem', and 'the Polanyi problem'. The Marx problem refers to the expansion of what Marx termed the 'reserve army of labor', which has resulted from a range of structural changes and policy responses in the era of globalization. The Keynes problem is that highly liquid financial markets, such as those that have emerged on a global scale in our current era, are prone to bouts of speculation and instability. Financial instability, in turn, is frequently transmitted into the real economy, creating severe cyclical volatility in incomes and employment. The Polanyi problem concerns the ability of non-market forces to engender norms of social solidarity that can serve as effective counterweights to the competitive imperatives of a free-market economy.

In structuring the chapter in this way, I hope to show how the array of problems due to neoliberal globalization are interrelated. This simple point can become obscured when one separately considers for example trade policy, foreign direct investment, and financial markets; or, for that matter, the specific practices of the International Monetary Fund, World Bank or World Trade Organization. I will argue that the fundamental problems with for example liberalizing trade do not stem from the expansion of trade itself. They rather result from the fact that in the current policy environment, trade opening has led to growth in the reserve army of labor, and thus a shift in bargaining power that favors employers over workers. In addition, for many developing economies, the revenues generated by tariffs had been a significant fraction of total government revenues. In these cases, trade opening has therefore effectively meant cuts in government spending on social services, that is, exacerbating a country's Polanyi problem. And still again: proponents of neoliberal globalization hold that opening financial markets creates benefits parallel to those of trade expansion. I would rather argue that effective regulations of financial flows – that is, addressing the Keynes problem – are a precondition for attaining the possible benefits from trade opening.

WHAT IS GLOBALIZATION?

The answer is not obvious. The major technical innovations in communications and transportation technologies have reduced the transaction costs of maintaining effective economic links on a global scale. Moreover the collapse of the Soviet system eliminated this challenge to capitalist hegemony, even though the governments professing to Communism had long since abandoned any serious claim to a democratic, egalitarian alternative to free market capitalism. The result, in any case, is that huge areas of the world economy were now open to capitalism to a degree unprecedented in generations.

Neoliberalism has been the guiding ideological and policy framework within which capitalism has spread in the contemporary epoch. In turn, it is because capitalism spread within the neoliberal framework that most discussions of globalization hold that the power of nation-states to influence economic activity is eroding as economies become more integrated, while the power of business and market forces is correspondingly rising. It is true that the power of nation-states has eroded while those of business and the market have increased. But this is only because such a shift in relative power between the state, business and the market is a completely explicit consequence of the ascendant neoliberal policy agenda.

Corresponding with the shift in the global policy regime in the contemporary epoch has been the emergence of crucial new patterns in global economic activity. In particular, two such patterns stand out: the rise in manufacturing capacity in less developed economies; and the exponential growth in gross financial market trading across borders and in foreign exchange markets. These two developments could not have occurred without the advances of our time in communications and transportation technology. But to understand their economic impact, it is illuminating, in my view, to consider them within the context of the Marx, Keynes and Polanyi problems, and the ascendancy of neoliberal economic policy – the task to which we now turn.

THE MARX PROBLEM

Levels of employment and compensation – the most basic determinants of well-being for the majority of the world's population – are established through various processes of bargaining between workers and employers. Marx argued that, in general, workers have less bargaining power than employers in labor markets because they do not own their own means of production. But Marx also stressed that workers' bargaining power diminishes further when unemployment and underemployment are high, since that means that employed workers can be readily replaced by the reserve army outside the factory gates. Some variation of Marx's basic observation has been restated innumerable times in the professional literature, including recent work on NAIRU and the so-called 'wage curve'.[2] Understanding this relationship is central to grasping the broad effects of neoliberal globalization on working people in both the global North and South.

Workers in the North

The era of globalization has been characterized by a sharp decline in the economic fortunes of the majority of lower-paid workers in the leading industrialized countries. The trend is manifested through declining wages and growing inequality in the United States, and persistently high unemployment in Europe.[3]

How does the 'reserve army of labor' theory help illuminate this trend? The basic point is quite straightforward: the dynamics of the reserve army effect in high-wage economies changes when firms operating in low-wage economies can produce export-competitive manufactured products. In this situation, the potential size of the reserve army necessarily expands to also include both the unemployed and, even more to the point, employed but low-paid workers in the developing economies. As such, the capitalists in the advanced economies have gained an additional bargaining advantage in wage-setting negotiations. This is because firms can now credibly claim that their own relatively high labor costs will threaten their export markets and increase import competition from low-wage competitors. In addition, the firms in high-wage economies whose operations are not tied to a specific location can credibly threaten to move to low-wage economies if costs in their current locations appear too high. The crucial issue here is not that firms actually leave their existing high-wage location but that they can brandish a credible threat to exit.[4]

Moreover, what makes such threats credible is not the rise of low-wage countries' manufacturing capacity alone. Rather it is that given the rise in export competitiveness among low-wage countries, the governments of the advanced economies have not acted to counter the increased bargaining power accruing to capitalists. Quite the contrary – by pursuing the deregulation of labor markets and abandoning employment-targeted macroeconomic policies, the governments of the advanced economies have only strengthened further the relative bargaining power of capital over labor.

Bronfenbrenner (1996) has conducted the most directly relevant study of how threat effects *per se* have influenced labor negotiations. She reports the results of a survey between 1993 and 1995, which showed that 50 percent of all firms and 65 percent of manufacturing firms that were targets of union organizing campaigns threatened to close their shops and relocate if the workers voted to unionize. Though only 12 percent of those firms that ended up unionized did then carry through on their threat to relocate, workers nevertheless found the threats credible. In particular, in cases where firms did make threats to shut down or relocate, unions lost a significantly larger percentage of elections.

Workers in the South

If one follows the factor price equalization theory, it should not be surprising that the well-being of Northern workers should fall as neoliberal globalization proceeds. That is, wages should go down in rich countries while rising in poor countries as rich and poor countries become more closely integrated.[5]

Global integration should therefore be offering a decided benefit to Southern workers – that their wages would rise toward the level of Northern workers. However to reach this conclusion about upward wage tendencies in the South, the factor price equalization model makes two crucial assumptions: that both the rich and poor countries operate at full employment and that they utilize identical production technologies. In reality, neither of these assumptions corresponds to reality. Rather, most developing countries have abundant numbers of people – perhaps the majority of the adult labor force – who are underemployed in some form or another. In terms of technologies, both in manufacturing and agriculture, most developing economies have employed significantly less advanced production methods than those in rich countries during the period in which they have opened their economies.

Relaxing these assumptions of the factor price equalization model means that the impact of increased integration in developing countries becomes contingent on the labor market and technological conditions in these countries as they interact with the ascendant neoliberal policy regime.[6]

Migration from Agriculture

Beginning with the early literature on development economics in the 1950s, economists such as Nurske (1953) and Lewis (1955) argued that less developed economies operate with large supplies of 'surplus labor' or 'disguised unemployment' in the rural sectors. Nurske and Lewis held that these conditions offered an opportunity for less developed economies – that is, that workers could be transferred from agricultural to non-agricultural employment without having to sacrifice agricultural output. Rather, the movement of labor into non-agricultural activities would be a key element enabling non-agricultural output to rise.

Non-agricultural output has generally risen dramatically in developing countries since the Second World War. But the migration out of agriculture then created a new problem: that the supply of labor from agriculture was exceeding the demand, initially in urban areas, then increasingly in rural non-farm sectors as well. This has produced a long-run source of downward pressure on wages in developing countries.

This tendency has accelerated under conditions of neoliberal globalization, resulting from the interaction of several factors. First, the reduction or elimination of tariffs on agricultural products has enabled cheap imported grains and other agricultural products to capture an increasing share of the developing countries' markets. Agricultural producers in developing countries have also shifted their own target markets, as the most lucrative activities have become exporting fresh fruits and vegetables as well as wood and wood products to North American, European and Japanese markets. This development favors large-scale, capital-intensive agriculture. Finally, neoliberal policies have brought reductions, if not outright elimination, of agricultural subsidies to smallholders.[7]

Growth of Rural Non-Farm Labor

For the past 25 years, the most important growing tendency among smallholders in the third world has been to join the rural non-farm labor market rather than entering the urban labor pool. According to studies by Reardon and various co-authors (1998, 2001), rural non-farm labor employment in the 1990s accounted for between 35 and 45 percent of rural incomes in Latin America, Asia and Africa, exceeding incomes from self-employment, farm wages and remittances from migrants. Reardon et al. find that there is wide variation in the types of jobs falling within this category and the corresponding wages paid for them. They include traditional activities such as crop transport, grain milling or production of so-called 'Z-goods' such as baskets or mats. They also include domestic employment in rising tourist areas or rural middle class housing communities for commuters, as well as production of modern non-farm goods, using modern production and financing methods and higher-skilled labor.

Given this wide range of job types, the largest variables affecting wages are workers' educational attainment level and the level of rural infrastructure. Because neoliberal policies have entailed cuts in public sector expenditures, including in education and infrastructure, these cuts in turn hold back the growth of better-paying non-farm rural jobs.[8]

Labor Market Effects of Export-Led Manufacturing

Following the Heckscher–Ohlin framework, one would expect labor-intensive jobs to be transferred from the high-wage to low-wage countries as trade expands. And while the share of manufacturing exports from developing countries has risen dramatically, this has not generally translated into more manufacturing employment in developing countries.

Thus, according to the WTO, the share of developing economies in world manufacturing goods exports rose from 11.2 percent in 1980 to 24.8 percent in 1999. However this growth in manufacturing exports has been concentrated in 13 developing countries – Argentina, Brazil, China, Hong Kong China, India, Indonesia, Malaysia, Mexico, the Philippines, Singapore, South Korea, Taiwan China and Thailand.[9]

But even among these countries, employment in manufacturing has not generally grown. Using aggregated national data from UNIDO for example, we observe that growth in manufacturing employment between 1985 and 1998 averaged 9 percent for Malaysia, 5.8 percent for China and 4.4 percent for Chile, but –2.2 percent for Brazil, –2.1 percent for Argentina, –0.5 percent for Mexico and –0.3 percent for Taiwan.

Ghosh (2002) has argued that three factors explain the lack of manufacturing job growth in developing countries.[10] The first is the 'fallacy of composition' in export expansion. That is, while an export-led growth strategy may be perfectly viable for some subset of developing economies, when all developing countries attempt the same strategy, increasing competition for the same export markets, many countries are likely to fail. This point had long been recognized in considering countries whose exports were mostly primary products. However many proponents of export-led growth held that opportunities for success would increase substantially when developing countries were able to diversify their export offerings to include manufactured products. But experience since the early 1980s has contradicted this view: it now appears true that competition does indeed limit the number of countries that can succeed by emphasizing exports as their primary growth engine.

The second factor is a 'substitution effect' within the developing countries' own domestic markets. Many of the countries that have been working to develop export-competitive manufacturing sectors already had large-scale manufacturing sectors in operation, though these earlier-vintage manufacturing sectors concentrated on producing for their domestic markets. This is most clearly the case among the large Latin American economies – Mexico, Brazil and Argentina – whose industrialization strategy through the 1970s was built around an import-substitution model. The liberalization of trade policies has therefore led to two results in these countries: an expansion of their exporting capacity, but a corresponding increase in the penetration of their domestic markets by imports.

This substitution effect also creates the conditions for a third, 'productivity effect', as manufacturing shifts from focusing on domestic markets to exports. For developing countries to become successful as exporters they need to compete on the basis of productivity as well as on wage rates. To a large extent, this entails appropriating more capital-intensive, higher-productivity technologies, even if not always the cutting-edge production methods utilized in more advanced economies. Thus the shift from targeting manufacturing production from domestic markets to exports has generated a tendency for labor-shedding among manufacturers in developing countries.

Workers in developing countries employed in the successful exporting firms do generally enjoy a wage premium over the domestic market average, corresponding to the higher rates of both sales and productivity growth at these exporting firms. But even this narrowly targeted premium can be less than would otherwise be the case, given the large and growing pool of underemployed workers both within and outside the formal manufacturing sector. This persistence of underemployed and informal sector workers in developing countries continues to exert downward pressure on overall wage levels in these countries.

THE KEYNES PROBLEM

Systemic Instability and the Case for Financial Regulation

The Keynes problem flows from a fundamental fact about the nature of capitalist economies: that the investment process – the basic activity which is a proximate determinate of an economy's level of income, employment and productivity growth – is unstable because it operates on the basis of uncertainty. As Keynes (1936) famously put it, 'we simply do not know' how profitable a prospective investment project will be. A primary purpose of financial markets is to ameliorate problems due to uncertainty through increasing the liquidity of investments. When financial instruments are freely traded in relatively thick markets, illiquid investments in plant and equipment can be transformed into claims that are convertible into cash or other liquid assets as quickly as the institutional and technological structures permit.

However enhancing the liquidity of assets also tends to create serious problems for the stability of capitalist economies. An initial analysis of these sources of instability was presented forcefully in Keynes's *General Theory*. But this critical literature has also developed widely since Keynes. One important contribution has been that of Robert Schiller (for example 2000), who emphasizes the role of investor psychology, independent of individual firm fundamentals, as a major determinant of stock market prices. Related to Schiller's critique are arguments about the centrality of asymmetric information in financial markets, and specifically the influence exerted by ill-informed 'noise traders'. For example, Shleifer's (2000) presentation of the 'behavioral finance' perspective models financial markets as containing two kinds of traders, fundamental traders and noise traders. But noise traders are not competed out of the market by the fundamental traders in this perspective. This is because arbitrage is risky, costly and therefore limited. For example when stock prices are inflated relative to fundamentals, arbitrageurs who choose to sell short face potential losses from prices moving still higher under the influence of noise traders – that is, their short-selling will not necessarily drive prices down to fundamentals. Thus the actions of noise traders are not merely ephemeral to market activity, but rather exert a sustained influence on price formation.

But a deeper point about Keynesian uncertainly also emerges from this perspective. If noise traders persistently and unpredictably move markets away from fundamentals, it no longer becomes logical for even well-informed traders and professionals to try to trade on the basis of fundamental information. It rather follows that professional traders should proceed, as Keynes argued, to trade by trying to outguess market sentiment, moving ahead of the herd by 'anticipating what average opinion thinks average opinion to be' (1936, p. 156).[11]

Systems of financial regulation

Overall then, according to these critical perspectives, thick but unregulated financial markets operate with substantial degrees of inefficiency and irrationality. The general logic of this Keynesian perspective was the analytic foundation on which the post-Depression and World War systems of financial regulations were constructed. These regulations included the Bretton Woods system of fixed exchange rates and related capital control measures, implemented at the level of domestic economies, to control international capital flows and speculative currency markets.[12] The Glass-Steagall system of domestic financial regulations was established in the United States. The main purpose of these regulations was to create barriers between various segments of the overall financial market, to limit the portfolio options for each market segment and to regulate interest rates.[13] Even more extensive systems of domestic financial regulations operated in most European economies and Japan. Government regulations played a major role in determining the allocation of credit, and thus the level and composition of investment, as government regulators operated in close association with banks and non-financial businesses. The capital markets played a much more limited role in these economies in terms of mobilizing funds, allocating credit and influencing investment decisions.[14]

The demise of financial regulations

These regulatory systems were strongly criticized virtually from the outset by free market proponents. But the emergence of a persistent inflationary environment was more important to the demise of financial regulations than any purely academic critique. Among other difficulties created by inflation were sustaining appropriate exchange rates, managing interest rate ceilings and limiting asset acquisition options for separate segments of financial markets. But within a neoliberal analytic framework, these problems generated by inflation were seen as evidence on behalf of opening markets and minimizing regulations, not the basis for reforming the regulatory environment. This was the basis on which, from the 1970s onward, financial markets globally have been increasingly deregulated.[15]

Dramatic shifts in international financial flows

Since the demise of Bretton Woods and the emergence of deregulated financial markets, there has been an enormous increase in gross flows, that is, the total amount of international lending as well as secondary market trading in stock, bond, foreign exchange and derivative markets. We present some representative data on these trends in Table 10.1.

To begin with, Table 10.1a shows the total amount of funds raised on international financial markets relative to world exports from 1960–97 (I was unable to construct a consistent data series past 1997). For 1960, this figure was only

Table 10.1 The growth of financial market transactions

Table 10.1a Funds raised on international financial markets as % of world exports

1960	1970	1975	1980	1985	1990	1997
0.5	1.8	4.6	5.8	13.5	10.5	26.2

Sources: OECD (1998, 2002); Maddison (1995); IMF (1996); For 1997, Exports from World Trade Organization Annual Report Table A.3; Funds Raised on Capital Markets, OECD Financial Market Trends, February 1998, Table 1, p. 5.

Table 10.1b Cross-border transactions in bonds and equities as % of GDP

	1975–79	1980–84	1985–89	1990–94	1995–99	2000–2002
United States	5.9	13.0	73.5	108.7	183.8	256.7
Japan	3.2	13.9	129.0	82.2	80.6	104.3
Germany	6.9	12.9	51.7	102.5	257.3	474.0
France	–	9.2	34.0	125.5	289.6	419.4
Italy	0.9	1.4	9.4	114.6	518.7	801.6[a]
Canada	4.5	10.4	44.1	123.7	269.5	265.8

Note: [a] Figures for Italy are for 2000–2001 only.

Source: Houben et al. (2004).

Table 10.1c Daily foreign exchange markets turnover as % of total central bank reserves

1977	1980	1983	1986	1989	1992	1995	1998	2001	2004
6.9	21.3	35.0	58.8	82.3	88.4	85.6	90.7	58.7	62.2

Note: Figures for years other than 2004 are end of year. Figure for 2004 is beginning of year.

Source: Felix (1998) for 1977–86. For other years BIS (2005).

0.5 percent. It rises to 1.8 percent by 1970, still prior to the collapse of Bretton Woods. But post-Bretton Woods the ratio rises rapidly in the mid-1970s through the mid-1980s. By 1985, the ratio is 13.5 percent – more than a sevenfold increase over 1970. By 1997, the figure we report is up to 26.2 percent, showing a continuing dramatic rise.[16]

Table 10.1b then shows more detailed breakdown of foreign transaction between 1975 and 2002 in bonds and equities as a percentage of GDP for six OECD countries, including here both secondary trading as well as primary issues. In all six cases, the jump in cross-border flows from 1980 has been spectacular – for example for the United States, the ratio of cross-border transactions to GDP rose from 5.9 percent between 1975 and 1979 to 256.7 percent in 2000–2002. The largest jump was that of Italy, where the ratio rises from 0.9 percent in 1975–79 to 801.6 percent in 2000–2001.

In Table 10.1c we see broadly similar patterns with growth of foreign currency trading. Since the collapse of Bretton Woods in 1973, the rise in currency trading and the gross flows of financial assets across borders is unprecedented. As we see, the ratio of daily foreign exchange turnover relative to the reserves of all central banks rose spectacularly, from 6.9 percent of central bank reserves to 90.7 percent of reserves in 1998. In the aftermath of the 1997–98 Asian financial crisis, central banks have become much more committed to holding foreign exchange, and committing their own resources to achieve this. Thus average foreign reserve holdings for all countries rose by 84 percent between 1998 and 2003. For developing countries, foreign exchange holdings virtually doubled between 1998 and 2003. This shift in central banks' foreign exchange policy is then reflected in the fall in the ratio of daily foreign exchange market turnover to central bank reserves, to 58.7 percent in 2001 and to 62.2 percent in 2004. In these most recent figures, we see one clear indicator of the rising costs that central banks must pay to protect themselves against the risks of financial crises engendered by speculation on foreign exchange markets.

Effects of Financial Deregulation

How have these financial patterns affected economic welfare? We consider this in terms of both short- and long-run effects.

Short-term effects

The rise of short-term financial flows has made economies much more susceptible to financial crises. Among other factors, the very expansion of financial trading makes it more difficult for governments to control the inevitable periods of financial herd behavior. Once a financial crisis has broken out and government must try to neutralize a stampeding financial herd, their capacity to intervene effectively will be smaller when the size of the stampede is relatively large. The logic of this is clear in the case of contemporary foreign exchange markets. Precisely because daily trading on these markets rose from 6.8 percent of central banks' foreign currency reserves in 1977 to roughly 85 percent by the mid-

1990s, central banks had far less capacity to serve as a market-maker to counteract speculative stampedes.[17] Subsequent to the Asian crisis, the central banks then had to nearly double their holdings of foreign exchange to protect themselves against stampedes – and this doubling of foreign exchange holdings established the central banks at still only at roughly the ratio of market turnover to reserves as prevailed in the mid-1980s. The 62.2 percent ratio is still 55 percentage points higher than the 6.9 percent ratio for 1977.

The idea of financial markets becoming increasingly vulnerable to crises is fully consistent with the data since the early 1980s. According to a study published by the IMF itself, nearly three-quarters of the 182 members of the IMF, including a substantial number of developed countries, suffered one or more bouts of banking crises or 'significant banking problems' during 1980–95 (Lindgren et al., 1996). Banking crises, defined in this IMF survey as 'cases where there were runs or other substantial portfolio shifts, collapses of financial firms, or massive government intervention' afflicted 36 countries. 'Significant banking problems', defined as 'extensive unsoundness short of crisis', afflicted another 108. The 1997–98 Asian crisis and its repercussions have since raised these numbers significantly.

Long-term effects

Long-term interest rates Paralleling the explosive post-1970s growth of international capital flows has been the sharp rise of long-term real interest rates. The figures in Table 10.2 on US long-term real rates give an indication of the worldwide pattern. As we see in the table, the ten-year Treasury Bond rate spiked at an average of 5.9 percent between 1980–84, after having ranged between 0.8 and 2.7 percent over the five-year periods falling between 1955 and 1979. The rate does fall in subsequent five-year periods after 1980–84, though by 1995–99, only to a still historically high 4.3 percent. In 2000–2004, the rate then falls to 2.7 percent, which is at the level of 1960–64. But this was due to the Federal Reserve also pushing the Federal Funds Rate to its lowest levels in 50 years, in order to counteract the stock market crash and recession of those years.

Moreover as we see with the next column of the table, the decline in the BAA Corporate Bond rate is far more modest over 2000–2004 than occured with the Treasury Bond rate. Indeed the differential between the BAA rate and the T-Bond rate in this 2000–2004 period, at 2.7 percent, is wider than any previous five-year period since 1955. This indicates that the risk premium in holding bonds of private corporations versus the US government had reached its highest levels in these most recent years, even while the Federal Reserve was aggressively attempting to push real interest rates down.[18]

The deregulation of financial markets has very likely played a major role in pushing real interest rates up and keeping them high, even to the extent of resist-

Table 10.2 Real long-term interest rate in the United States

	10-year Treasury Bond rate – ΔGDP deflator %	BAA Corporate Bond rate – ΔGDP deflator %	BAA Corporate Bond rate – Treasury Bond rate %
1955–59	1.1	2.0	+0.9
1960–64	2.7	3.7	+1.0
1965–69	1.9	2.9	+1.0
1970–74	1.0	2.9	+1.9
1975–79	0.8	2.5	+1.7
1980–84	5.9	8.3	+2.4
1985–89	5.7	7.9	+2.2
1990–94	4.4	6.3	+1.9
1995–99	4.3	6.2	+1.9
2000–04	2.7	5.4	+2.7

Sources: US Federal Reserve Board and Bureau of Economic Analysis.

ing Federal Reserve interventions to push them downward. A recent OECD econometric study (Orr et al., 1995) has calculated that about half the rise of real long-term interest rates in the 1980s was due to financial deregulation. Felix (2001) proposes one causal link:

> Prior to decontrol, when the monetary authorities lowered short-term interest rates to stimulate the economy, the major holders of long-term bonds, notably insurance companies and private pension funds, anticipated, rightly or wrongly, inflationary consequences. However since fiduciary restrictions blocked them from holding stocks, they could merely move funds from longer to shorter-maturity bonds. Capital decontrol gave them the opportunity to move funds instead between home and foreign bond markets in pursuit of higher yields. That pushed up long-term rates, and to a lesser degree, short-term rates as well, and undermined the effort to stimulate the economy by monetary easing. (Felix, 2001, p. 40)

Other factors are also at play, including the trend rise in the demand for credit by households and businesses in the US – that is, rising credit demand – accompanied by the shift in monetary policy in favor of inflation targeting, that is, a tightening of credit supply. Note that these demand and supply considerations operated initially in a period of relatively large government deficits throughout the world, but persisted as the deficits were eliminated – suggesting that the government-deficit 'crowding out' explanation for high real interest rates, at the least, must be placed in a broader analytic context.[19]

Transformation of Macroeconomic Policy Objectives

The increasing size and volatility of deregulated financial markets has led to a profound shift in macroeconomic policy objectives throughout the world. During the Bretton Woods era, macroeconomic policy was concerned with domestic employment as well as financial stability and inflation. But increasingly since the 1970s, macroeconomic policy has been focused on achieving minimal if not zero inflation rates via generally tight, and frequently austere, fiscal and monetary policy regimes.[20] In particular, fiscal policy interventions on behalf of employment expansion have been almost completely abandoned.

To a substantial extent, this shift in macroeconomic policy goals is a reaction to the pressure governments feel to retain the confidence of volatile financial markets.[21] The new macroeconomic policy regime has been most fully formalized through the establishment of the European Monetary Union. Membership of the Union requires abandonment of an active fiscal posture. In terms of monetary management, the bank is committed to maintaining strict inflation targets, even apparently in the face of deflationary forces such as prevailed in 2001. The US has been somewhat less stringent, but primarily because the pressures of the reserve army of labor in the US has dampened upward wage pressure at low unemployment.[22] These same principles have been adopted throughout the developing countries as well, as they accept a macroeconomic regime governed by either dollarization of their currency or a currency board regime.[23]

THE POLANYI PROBLEM

The period in which big government capitalism was built was the aftermath of the 1930s Depression, the Second World War, and the developing worldwide competition with Communist governments. In this context, Karl Polanyi made a forceful case in his classic work *The Great Transformation* (1944) that for market economies to function with some modicum of fairness, they must be embedded in social institutions that effectively promote broadly accepted notions of the common good.

Various social democratic movements within the advanced economies adapted the Polanyi perspective. They argued in favor of government macroeconomic interventions to achieve three basic ends: stabilizing aggregate demand at some reasonable approximation of full employment; creating a financial market environment that is stable and conducive to the efficient allocation of investment funds; and distributing equitably the rewards from high employment, macroeconomnic stability and efficiency in investment allocations. The political ascendancy of these ideas was the basis for a dramatic increase in the government expenditure–GDP ratio throughout Japan, North America and Western Europe.

But the implementation of a social democratic capitalism was never a consensus position. Many sectors of capital opposed efforts to sustain full employment because – as 'the Marx problem' illuminates most forcefully – full employment engenders greater bargaining power for workers in labor markets, even while it also increases the economy's total output of goods and services.[24] Greater worker bargaining power can also create inflationary pressures, and inflation will, in turn, depreciate the value of rentiers' portfolio of assets with nominally fixed values. In addition, market-inhibiting financial regulations limit the capacity of rentiers to both diversify risk and speculate.

Hence it should not be surprising that capitalists and rentiers would utilize their increased bargaining power in labor and financial markets also to change the direction of government policy on behalf of their own ends. The issue here moreover is not deregulation of markets *per se*. Rather it is that markets be deregulated to support the interests of capitalists and rentiers, even as these same groups still benefit greatly from many forms of government support, including investment subsidies, tax concessions and central bank rescue operations during financial crises. At the same time, the deregulation of markets that favor capitalists and rentiers is correspondingly the most powerful regulatory mechanism limiting the demands of workers, in that deregulation has been congruent with the worldwide expansion of the reserve army of labor and the declining capacity of national governments to implement full-employment macroeconomic policies.

Of course changes in the global economic environment have been of major significance in shifting the terms of the Polanyi problem. As we have discussed, the main economic effects of globalization have been through making possible both the rise of export-competitive manufacturing industries in low-wage countries and the explosion of financial market trading levels. These factors in turn create difficulties for maintaining effective government interventions consistent with a broad Polanyi policy agenda. At the same time, these changes in the economic environment do not impose insuperable obstacles to advancing effective alternatives to neoliberalism. Quite the contrary: taking the full measure of the difficulties they impose is actually the first step toward advancing a viable alternative agenda. The intellectual challenge is therefore to advance new policy regimes that are able to transcend the real constraints imposed by globalization – that is to say, to recapture momentum, in the sense of Keith Griffin, toward a transition to egalitarian development.

Elements of an Alternative Policy Framework

Maintaining perspective on international cooperation

Given that the problems at hand are global, it is perhaps inevitable that we initially focus attention on policy measures that offer similarly global scope.

Measures to promote international policy coordination clearly fall within this category of proposals. An important example of such a proposal is the plan advanced by Eatwell and Taylor (2000) for a new Global Financial Authority. However the failings of the existing policy framework are by no means due to a lack of institutions and policies supporting global economic cooperation. After all, the IMF, World Bank and WTO already operate on the basis of international cooperation. The problem is not the lack of international cooperation *per se*, but that these institutions promote cooperation on behalf of neoliberalism. The need therefore is not simply to create another such transnational institution, but to build a viable international constituency for an egalitarian alternative to neoliberalism.

Features of an alternative agenda

I concentrate here on only three interrelated policy areas: (1) financial market regulation; (2) employment-targeted macroeconomic policies; and (3) labor market regulation. I also offer brief observations on a broader range of policy questions, including trade policy, industrial policy and foreign direct investment, and redistributionist welfare-state policies. But as I will try to show, employment policies along with regulations of financial and labor markets are best suited to provide the foundation of a new egalitarian policy agenda.

The logic of our foregoing discussion suggests that we begin this policy discussion in the area of financial markets. This is because the explosion of financial market trading and corresponding increase in financial market volatility has led to the shift in the aims of macroeconomic policy away from employment targeting. If an effective set of financial market regulations can be constructed, this will allow for macroeconomic policy to return to the goal of employment targeting while also maintaining control over inflationary pressures. Having macroeconomic policy concerned with employment targeting will thus create a stronger foundation on which to construct effective labor market regulations.

Financial market regulation Three basic principles should guide the formulation of a new financial market regulatory regime. Firstly, the regulatory environment should be consistent in the way that it affects all intermediaries and markets; in other words, following D'Arista and Schlesinger (1993), that policy should engender an upward leveling of the regulatory environment. Such an approach minimizes opportunities for rent-seeking through exploiting regulatory differences among market segments. A consistent regulatory structure is also easier to design, implement and enforce. The second principle is that, as much as possible, regulations should work through altering market prices and incentives rather than establishing hard limits on market activity. This is a point that Keith Griffin has long emphasized – to achieve the benefits of regulations while also maintaining market flexibility to the greatest possible extent. The third principle is the promotion of financial market activities in which social rates of return exceed private rates. The US Glass–Steagall system for example heavily supported the social goal of financing of individual family housing, through limiting the assets of savings and loan institutions to mortgage loans.

This is not to say that determining social rates of return is always straightforward. But one clear choice would be to weight heavily the benefits accruing through financial stability itself. Thus any new regulatory environment should seek to limit the immediate sources of instability – herd behavior, the contagion effects of market trends, and the spillover effects from financial market activity to the broader economy.

Two specific policy measures that are consistent with all three of these broad principles are asset-based reserve requirements and security transaction excise taxes. Asset-based reserve requirements would include Basel-type capital adequacy requirements, margin requirements on stock trading, and requirements limiting the composition of loans, such as had applied to savings and loans under the Glass-Steagall system. When they operate properly, such measures enable regulators to establish differential carrying costs to financial institutions according to the quality of the assets in their portfolio. Thus if financial market stability is the social outcome sought by such measures, then loans from regulated intermediaries that finance speculative trading would carry higher reserve or margin requirements. The same technique is capable of promoting other goals as well, as was the case under Glass-Steagall with individual family housing.

Securities transaction excise taxes, such as the so-called 'Tobin tax' on foreign exchange markets, are an efficient way of raising the costs of short-term speculative trading in financial markets, as opposed to trading for the purpose of long-term asset holding. Following the principle that regulations should be consistent across market segments, the tax should be imposed not simply on foreign exchange markets, as with Tobin's initial proposal, but consistently across all markets.

The idea of the tax is that it allows the market to screen out speculative from more stable financial flows. This is because a small tax on a security transaction – for example a 0.5 percent tax on equity trades – would create a negligible burden on asset owners who intend to hold their asset for the long term. However if asset owners purchase a new stock with the intention of selling it at a profit in the short term, the 0.5 percent tax would be imposed on each trade, and would thus constitute a significant burden.

Proposals for these taxes have faced substantial criticism in recent years, in particular around the point that imposing them necessarily creates serious market distortions and thereby new opportunities for rent-seeking. But in fact, such measures can be implemented in a workable fashion across financial market segments.[25]

Employment-targeted macroeconomic policy It is well known that in a purely demand-constrained economy, it is not difficult to induce an employment-targeted expansion by deploying standard fiscal and monetary tools. But economies are rarely constrained strictly by demand, especially within a globally integrated economic environment. Depending on the country, an array of additional constraints can limit the expansionary impulse of a demand-centered policy intervention, such that the initial expansion of employment and output will not be sustainable. The most general such constraints include the effects of expansion on inflation, interest rates and exchange rates. They also include the dissipation of the force of an expansion through import, saving and what we call speculative leakages, this being the unproductive trading of existing assets rather than the creation of new productive assets. Let us focus here on two of the most serious such constraints – import leakages and inflation.

In terms of import leakages, it is useful to consider this question within two contexts. The first is international coordination of expansion. Clearly, if coordination is effectively executed, then the problem of import leakages should be minimized. But even in the absence of coordinated expansion, import leakages can be significantly reduced by paying careful attention to the output composition of expansion. An expansion of domestic demand can be led by private consumption, private investment, public consumption or public investment. Of these a public investment-led expansion is best suited to minimize import leakage since the first round of expansionary spending is conducted entirely by the government itself. Well-executed public investment expenditures will also promote longer-term productivity growth, and are therefore an efficient means of expanding aggregate supply as well as aggregate demand.[26]

In terms of inflation, Epstein (2000) and Bruno and Easterly (1998), among others, have shown that short of hyperinflationary situations, inflation does not inhibit economic growth. Indeed according to both Epstein and Bruno, increases in inflation are more consistently correlated with higher growth rates. But in a positive growth environment, inflation alters the distribution of wealth and income. In part, these distributional changes are unpredictable, since they depend on a country's system of indexation and the relative rates at which different sectors of society are able to achieve nominal income gains. Still, a broadly predictable distributional change of inflation is that it will bring wealth and income losses for those holding assets that are nominally fixed in value. Such losses would therefore tend to be concentrated among rentiers more than other social groups. This in turn explains the strong opposition of 'the bond market' to signs of inflation.

Labor market regulations Assuming that a sustainable high-employment regime can be effectively promoted through the appropriate combination of financial market regulations and employment-targeted macro policies, the point of labor market regulations will be to enable working people to share in the benefits of financial stability and growth. The labor market regulations that are of central importance operate along three dimensions: workplace conditions, including standards of cleanliness and safety; the rights of workers to associate, grieve and organize; and the establishment of decent minimum standards for wages and benefits.

As a first principle, the single most effective form of social protection for workers is a tight labor market. However tight labor markets are not a sufficient condition for providing an equitable sharing of the benefits of growth. Moreover labor market regulations must also contribute to dampening inflationary pressures, as was the case with the Swedish model of minimizing frictional unemployment through labor market policies. Such issues obviously need to be addressed.

Advanced Economies

United States The inadequacy of labor market tightness as a guarantor of equitable labor market outcomes was made clear during the experience with the last full business cycle in the US, 1991–2000. The unemployment rate did fall sharply over this period, and without setting off a cycle of accelerating inflation. Despite this, wage inequality also increased and the average wage stagnated through 1996. Even after four years of wage increases from 1997 to 2000, the average real wage by 2000 remained 10 percent below the peak of 1973.[27] For the gains from such growth to be more equitably shared will entail a shift in the institutional setting of wage bargaining – including higher minimum wages, and more generally, a more supportive political and legal environment in which workers can collectively advance their interests.

Europe The widely accepted premise in Europe is that excessive labor market regulations already exist. Indeed from this perspective, reducing these regulations – that is, increasing 'labor market flexibility' – is the only viable solution to Europe's unemployment problems (for example, Bean, 1994; Siebert, 1997). But as Glyn and Salverda (2000), among others, show, employment protection legislation, the generosity of minimum wages and unemployment benefits are all without discernible impact on employment rate differences across OECD countries. The suggestion flowing from this research is that European workers need not relinquish the gains they have won over the past two generations in the area of regulations. Renovations of the existing regulatory systems are no doubt in order in many cases. But as a general matter, European labor market regulations have achieved standards from which other regions of the world can profitably learn.

Developing countries Here of course a separate set of issues becomes important because of the large number of workers employed in informal activities where, by definition, regulations governing workplace conditions, workers' rights of association and minimum wages either do not exist or, if they exist, are routinely ignored. Thus in addition to producing a regulatory environment that enhances workplace conditions, ensures a reasonable bargaining environment and establishes a decent minimum wage floor, the aim of labor market regulations in developing countries should be to broaden the reach of formal sector employment itself.

Of course the purpose for labor market regulations in developing countries is controversial, given the facts of mass poverty and underemployment. Even prohibitions on child labor have been challenged by serious analysts (for example Basu, 1999), since the alternative to legal employment opportunities for children may be even less acceptable, including the drugs trade or prostitution. More generally, increasing labor regulations should induce corresponding increases in labor costs, which can in turn weaken export competitiveness. In a series of econometric exercises, Rodrik (1996) has found that an index number proxying for labor standards does indeed vary positively with labor costs.

But recent research I have done with two colleagues (Pollin et al., 2004) has posed a more direct question as regards the relationship between labor costs and employment – that is, what is the relationship, by country, between real wage and employment growth in the global apparel industry? The apparel industry is an important case to study here, since among manufacturing industries, its low fixed costs promote a high degree of capital mobility. Our regression analysis finds no statistically significant relationship at all between real wage and employment growth, either through examining a sample of 45 OECD and non-OECD countries, or through narrowing the sample to 27 non-OECD countries alone.

These conclusions were based on a series of bivariate regressions, so they are not sufficiently well specified to explain why no relationship exists between real wage and employment growth. But they do enable us to conclude that, both in advanced and developing economies, other factors can dominate over wage rates alone in establishing a viable apparel manufacturing industry. This in turn implies that labor market regulations, which collectively will yield rising labor costs, do not necessarily entail a loss of viable manufacturing industries, even in a highly mobile sector such as apparel.

Broader Policy Implications

There is a one simple point that I wish to stress here – that the context within which one considers trade, industrial policy, foreign direct investment and the welfare state will be substantially changed within the macroeconomic and regulatory environment that I have sketched as against a neoliberal policy regime. This is the process through which a transition to egalitarian development advances outward from its foundation. This point can be seen clearly in the crucial case of trade policy. A first point that emerges from the foregoing discussion is that trade opening and financial market liberalization should not be treated in parallel fashion. Rather, what becomes clear within our alternative framework is that tight regulation of speculative financial flows is a necessary precondition for the gains from trade opening to be sustainable. Open trading is persistently disrupted and ultimately becomes unsustainable when financial markets, including foreign exchange markets, fluctuate heavily and experience regular crises.

Moreover the welfare losses to workers from trade opening that we have described under the Marx problem would not occur to nearly the same extent in our alternative policy framework. This is because, in both the North and the South, active employment policies and labor market regulations would operate to support the welfare of working people. These would act as direct forms of social protection that would almost always be more effective than trade policy at raising the welfare of the majority. At best, trade policy is an indirect and inefficient means of providing social protections.

A second issue with trade is the extent to which countries should stress export promotion as a primary growth engine. The results that we report in 'the Marx problem' section of the chapter show that export promotion policies have not led to broad gains in employment among developing countries. We would also not expect these patterns to change substantially in the future. This does not mean that developing countries should abandon efforts at export promotion. But it does follow that the case for expanding domestic markets through higher levels of employment at rising wages should return as a viable feature of development policy. Indeed considering export promotion and domestic market expansion as incompatible alternatives is the most serious error here. The stress should be on maintaining a viable employment environment, while also promoting higher productivity through active industrial policies. Both trade and foreign direct investment can play important roles in this broader policy framework, but they need not be seen as the dominant focus of policy.

Finally, independently of other considerations regarding trade policy, there continues to be an important argument for maintaining tariffs in the case of developing countries. Perhaps the single most neglected issue regarding trade liberalization has been its impact on the fiscal revenues of developing countries, and hence on the governing capacity of the state for these countries. Rao (1999) has shown that for low- and middle-income countries trade taxes provide a major share of overall tax revenue, frequently being the government's largest single source of revenue. But trade liberalization has meant that revenues from trade taxes have fallen substantially. Thus for low-income countries, trade tax revenues constituted 40.8 percent of total revenue from 1970 to 1975. This figure then falls steadily, such that by 1991–96 it constitutes 32.2 percent of total revenue. Rao goes on to explore the difficulties low- and lower-middle income countries face in successfully generating alternative sources of revenue. The result has been that trade liberalization has led to significant declines in total tax revenues, and thus a squeeze on government expenditures.

CONCLUSION

Let me simply restate the basic arguments of the chapter. They are:

1. The contemporary period of globalization is historically unique. It has resulted in part through technological breakthroughs and the demise of Soviet-style Communism. But it is more fundamentally the result of the prevailing neoliberal policy regime within which the impact of new technologies, and the transition away from Soviet Communism, have been experienced.
2. Neoliberal policies do promote competitiveness and micro-efficiency under certain situations. But they also lead to the deepening of the Marx, Keynes and Polanyi problems in the contemporary global economy, in both the global North and the global South.
3. Alternatives to neoliberalism are not just desirable but also feasible. That is to say, transitions to egalitarian development, in both the global North and South, are within our grasp now. They begin with a careful rethinking of financial and labor market regulations and a reconstruction of employment-targeted macroeconomic policies. Once these key features of a new policy regime are in place, the terms under which we examine trade opening, foreign direct investment, industrial policy and the welfare state should all change substantially. In particular, the severe difficulties that frequently emerge in these policy areas under the prevailing neoliberal regime should be substantially ameliorated under the alternative policy framework sketched here.

NOTES

* I wish to thank James Heintz and Andong Zhu for their extremely able assistance and Jerry Epstein for the long and detailed discussions we have had on the topic of this chapter and for his careful reading of the chapter itself. I have also benefited from discussions of the chapter at the April 2004 Festschrift conference in honor of Keith Griffin, at the Political Economy Research Institute, University of Massachusetts, Amherst.

1. As a sampling of Griffin's more general writings on globalization, see (1994, 1997a, 1997b).
2. See for example Blanchflower and Oswald (1995), Layard et al. (1991) and Pollin (1998a).
3. See Mishel et al. (2000) and Glyn (1995) for reviews of some basic evidence on these trends.
4. This same point is developed, if from a different analytic framework, in Rodrik (1997).
5. I recognize that a wide range of economists do not consider this a realistic model (for example Bhagwati and Dehejia 1994). But it is still useful because – as with the Arrow–Debreau model of general equilibrium – it enables one to pursue a more systematic analysis through examining the ways in which the assumptions of the model need to be relaxed.
6. Larudee (1998) presents an important demonstration of this point as regarding Mexico and the United States.

7. These trends are described in various essays in Bryceson et al. (2000).
8. At the same time, slowing the development of rural infrastructures does also, ironically, create a countertendency, in that it slows the rate at which imports and domestic products from urban areas achieve a dominant position in rural areas.
9. The figures from this and the next paragraph are reported in Ghosh (2002).
10. Alarcon and Zepeda (1998) present evidence focused on the Mexican manufacturing industry which supports these same points.
11. See Crotty (1994) for a contemporary perspective on this question.
12. Panic (1995) provides a useful brief overview of the initial design of the Bretton Woods system.
13. Essays in Dymski et al. (1993) describe the structure and evolution of the Glass-Steagall system.
14. These financial structures are described in Zysman (1983), Pollin (1995) and Grabel (1997).
15. See Schaberg (2000) for institutional and econometric discussions of the decline of financial regulatory systems.
16. But even this 26.2 percent figure for 1997 is a conservative estimate, in that, for purposes of comparability across the full period, we exclude the category 'uncommitted facilities', as reported by the OECD for this year. Had we included these 'uncommitted' as well as the 'committed facilities' in our total for funds raised, the ratio of funds raised to exports for 1997 would be about 30 percent.
17. Felix (1998, 2001) considers this issue in some detail.
18. Pollin (2003), pp. 88–91 provides more detail on the divergence between the Federal Funds rate and the private market rates from 2000 to 2002.
19. Pollin (1997) provides a framework for exploring these demand and supply shifts.
20. Epstein (2000) provides an analytic survey of the literature on this topic, especially as focused on monetary policy.
21. This view was recently lent support by former Federal Reserve vice-chair Alan Blinder (1998), who writes, 'So far I have spoken about (central bank) independence from the rest of government … this sort of independence is what people seem to have in mind when they talk about independent central banks … But there is another type of independence that, while just as important in my view, is rarely discussed: independence from the financial markets … my point is … that delivering the policies that markets expect – or indeed demand – may lead to very poor policy. This danger is greater now than ever, I believe, because the currently prevailing view of financial markets among central bankers is one of deep respect. The broad, deep, fluid markets are seen as repositories of enormous power and wisdom. In my personal view, the power is beyond dispute, but the wisdom is somewhat suspect' (pp. 60–62).
22. This issue is discussed in some detail in Pollin (2003).
23. Some recent literature on this issue includes Santiprabhob (1997) and Grabel (2000).
24. The classic modern statement of this problem is by Kalecki (1971).
25. Pollin et al. (2003) surveys the literature on securities transaction taxes and offers a design proposal that would allow the tax to operate neutrally across segments of the financial services industry. Ul Haq et al. (1996) is a useful collection on tax as it would apply within foreign exchange markets only.
26. Pollin (1998b) reviews the relevant literature on public investment and expansionary policy. Much of this essay was inspired by work I did with Keith Griffin in Bolivia in the early 1990s. Griffin designed a public-investment led expansionary program for Bolivia focusing on the rural sector that was viable at both a macro- and micro-level – since it increased micro-efficiency while also expanding employment and jobs.
27. Mishel et al. (2000) provide the relevant evidence on these trends.

REFERENCES

Alarcon, Diana and Eduardo Zepeda (1998), 'Employment trends in the Mexican manufacturing sector', *North American Journal of Economics and Finance* (9), 125–45.

Bank for International Settlements (BIS) (2005), *BIS Triennial Central Bank Survey of Foreign Exchange and Derivatives Market Activity in April 2004*, Basel: BIS.

Basu, Kaushik (1999), 'Child labor: cause, consequences, and cure, with remarks on international labor standards', *Journal of Economic Literataure*, **37** (3), 1083–119.

Bean, Charles R. (1994), 'European unemployment: a survey', *Journal of Economic Literature*, **32** (2), 573–619.

Bhagwati, Jagdish and Vivek Dehejia (1994), 'Freer trade and wages of the unskilled: is Marx striking again?', in Jaghish Bhagwati and Marvin H. Kosters (eds), *Trade and Wages: Leveling Wages Down?* Washington, DC: American Enterprise Institute.

Blanchflower, David G. and Andrew J. Oswald (1995), 'An introduction to the wage curve', *Journal of Economic Perspectives*, **9** (3), 153–67.

Blinder, Alan (1998), *Central Banking in Theory and Practice*, Cambridge, MA: MIT Press.

Bronfenbrenner, Kate (1996), 'The effects of plant closing or threat of plant closing on the right of workers to organize', report to the US Department of Labor, September.

Bruno, Michael and William Easterly (1998), 'Inflation crises and long-run growth', *Journal of Monetary Economics*, **41** (1), 3–26.

Bryceson, Deborah, Cristobal Kay and Jos Mooij (2000), *Disappearing Peasantries? Rural Labour in Africa, Asia, and Latin America*, London: Intermediate Technology Publications.

Crotty, James (1994), 'Are Keynesian uncertainty and macrotheory compatible? Conventional decision making, institutional structures, and conditional stability in Keynesian macromodels', in Gary Dymski and Robert Pollin (eds), *New Perspectives in Monetary Macroeconomics: Explorations in the Tradition of Hyman P. Minsky*, Ann Arbor, MI: University of Michigan Press, pp. 105–42.

D'Arista, Jane and Tom Schlesinger (1993), 'The parallel banking system', in Gary Dymski, Gerald Epstein and Robert Pollin (1993), *Transforming the US Financial System: Equity and Efficiency for the 21st Century*, Armonk, NY: M.E. Sharpe, pp. 157–99.

Dymski, Gary, Gerald Epstein and Robert Pollin (1993), *Transforming the US Financial System: Equity and Efficiency for the 21st Century*, Armonk, NY: M.E. Sharpe.

Eatwell, John and Lance Taylor (2000), *Global Finance at Risk: The Case for International Regulation*, New York: New Press.

Epstein, Gerald (2000), 'Myth, mendacity and mischief in the theory and practice of central banking', manuscript, University of Massachusetts-Amherst Political Economy Research Institute.

Felix, David (1998), 'Asia and the crisis of financial globalization', in Dean Baker, Gerald Epstein and Robert Pollin (eds), *Globalization and Progressive Economic Policy*, Cambridge: Cambridge University Press, pp. 163–91.

Felix, David (2001), 'Why international capital mobility should be curbed, and how it could be done,' paper prepared for the International Confederation of Free Trade Unions (ICFTU), Brussels, Belgium.

Ghosh, Jayati (2002), 'Exporting jobs or watching them disappear? Relocation, employment and accumulation in the world economy', in Jayati Ghosh and C.P. Chandrasekhar (eds), *Work and Well-Being in the Age of Finance*, New Delhi: Tulika Books, pp. 99–119.

Glyn, Andrew (1995), 'The assessment: unemployment and inequality,' *Oxford Review of Economic Policy*, **11** (1), pp. 1–25.
Glyn, Andrew and Wiermer Salverda (2000), 'Does wage flexibility really create jobs?', *Challenge*, January–February, pp. 32–43.
Grabel, Ilene (1997), 'Savings, investment, and functional efficiency: a comparative examination of national financial complexes', in Robert Pollin (ed.), *The Macroeconomics of Saving, Finance, and Investment*, Ann Arbor, MI: University of Michigan Press, pp. 251–98.
Grabel, Ilene (2000), 'The political economy of "policy credibility": the new classical macroeconomics and the remaking of emerging economies', *Cambridge Journal of Economics*, **24** (1), pp. 1–19.
Griffin, Keith (1994), 'Regulating world markets in a liberal global economy', working paper no 94-32, Department of Economics, University of California-Riverside.
Griffin, Keith (1997a), 'Culture, human development and economic growth', occasional paper series on culture and development, New York: United Nations Research Institute for Social Development.
Griffin, Keith (1997b), 'Globalization and development cooperation: a reformer's agenda', in Albert Berry, Roy Culpeper and Frances Stewart (eds), *Global Goverance and Development Fifty Years After Bretton Woods*, London: Macmillan.
Griffin, Keith and Jeffrey James (1981), *The Transition to Egalitarian Development: Economic Policies for Structural Change in the Third World*, London: Macmillan.
Houben, Aerdt, Jan Kakes and Garry Schinasi (2004), 'Toward a framework for safeguarding financial stability', International Monetary Fund working paper no 04/101, Washington, DC.
International Monetary Fund (IMF) (1996), *World Economic Outlook (October)*, Washington, DC: IMF.
International Monetary Fund (IMF) (2004), *International Financial Statistics*, on CD-ROM, Washington, DC: IMF.
Kalecki, Michal (1971), 'Political aspects of full employment', in Michal Kalecki, *Selected Essays on the Dynamics of the Capitalist Economy*, Cambridge: Cambridge University Press, pp. 138–45.
Keynes, John Maynard (1936), *The General Theory of Employment, Interest, and Money*, New York: Harcourt Brace & World.
Larudee, Mehrene (1998), 'Integration and income distribution under the North American Free Trade Agreement: the experience of Mexico', in Dean Baker, Gerald Epstein, and Robert Pollin (eds), *Globalization and Progressive Economic Policy*, Cambridge: Cambridge University Press, pp. 273–92.
Layard, Richard, Stephen Nickell and Richard Jackman (1991), *Unemployment: Macroeconomic Performance and the Labour Market*, Oxford: Oxford University Press.
Lewis, W.A. (1955), 'Economic development with unlimited supplies of labour', *Manchester School of Economic and Social Studies Bulletin*, **22**, 139–92.
Lindgren, Carl-Johan, Gilliam Garcia and Matthew Saal (1996), *Bank Soundness and Macroeconomic Policy*, Washington, DC: International Monetary Fund.
Maddison, Angus (1995), *Monitoring the World Economy, 1982–1992*, Paris: OECD.
Mishel, Lawrence, Jared Bernstein and John Schmitt (2000), *The State of Working America*, Washington, DC: Economic Policy Institute.
Nurske, Ragnar (1953), *Problems of Capital Formation in Underdeveloped Countries*, Oxford: Oxford University Press.
Organisation for Economic Co-operation and Development (OECD) (1998), *Financial Market Trends (February)*, Paris: OECD.

Organisation for Economic Co-operation and Development (OECD) (2000), *International Capital Market Statistics*, Paris: OECD.

Orr, Adrian, Malcolm Edey and Ketil Hviding (1995), 'Real long-term interest rates: the evidence from pooled time-series', OECD economic studies no 25, Paris.

Panic, Mica (1995), 'The Bretton Woods System: concept and practice', in Jonathan Michie and John Grieve Smith (eds), *Managing the Global Economy*, Oxford: Oxford University Press, pp. 37–54.

Polanyi, Karl (1944), *The Great Transformation*, Boston, MA: Beacon Press.

Pollin, Robert (1995), 'Financial structure and egalitarian economic policy', *New Left Review*, **214** (November–December), 26–61.

Pollin, Robert (1997), 'Financial intermediation and the variability of the saving constraint', in Robert Pollin (ed.), *The Macroeconomics of Saving, Finance, and Investment*, Ann Arbor, MI: University of Michigan Press, pp. 309–66.

Pollin, Robert (1998a), 'The "reserve army of unemployed" and the "natural rate of unemployment": can Marx, Kalecki, Friedman, and Wall Street all be wrong?' *Review of Radical Political Economics*, Summer, 1–13.

Pollin, Robert (1998b), 'Can domestic expansiony policies succeed in a globally integrated environment? An examination of alternatives', in Dean Baker, Gerald Epstein and Robert Pollin (eds), *Globalization and Progressive Economic Policy*, Cambridge: Cambridge University Press, pp. 433–60.

Pollin, Robert (2003), *Contours of Descent: US Economic Fractures and the Landscape of Global Austerity*, London: Verso Press.

Pollin, Robert, Dean Baker and Marc Schaberg (2003), 'Securities transaction taxes for US financial markets', *Eastern Economic Journal*, Fall, 527–59.

Pollin, Robert, Justine Burns and James Heintz (2004), 'Global apparel production and sweatshop labor: can raising retail prices finance living wages?', *Cambridge Journal of Economics*, **28** (2), 153–71.

Rao, Mohan (1999), 'Globalization and the fiscal autonomy of the state', background paper for the Human Development Report, United Nations Development Program, New York.

Reardon, Thomas, Julio Berdegue and German Escobar (2001), 'Rural nonfarm employment and incomes in Latin America: overview and policy implications', *World Development* **29** (3), 395–409.

Reardon, Thomas, K. Stamoulis, A. Balisacan, M.E. Cruz, J. Berdegue and B. Banks (1998), 'Rural nonfarm income in developing countries', special chapter in *The State of Food and Agriculture 1998*, Rome: Food and Agricultural Organization of the United Nations, pp. 283–356.

Rodrik, Dani (1996), 'Labor standards in international trade: do they matter and what do we do about them?' in Robert Z. Lawrence, Dani Rodrik and John Whalley (eds), *Emerging Agenda for Global Trade: High Stakes for Developing Countries*, Overseas Development Council essay no 20, Washington, DC: Johns Hopkins University Press.

Rodrik, Dani (1997), *Has Globalization Gone Too Far?*, Washington, DC: Institute for International Economics.

Santiprabhob, V. (1997), 'Bank soundness and currency board arrangements: issues and experience', IMF working paper on policy analysis and assessment, no. 11.

Schaberg, Marc (2000), *Globalisation and the Erosion of National Financial Systems: Is Declining Autonomy Inevitable?*, Cheltenham, UK and Northampton, MA, USA: Edward Elgar Publishing.

Schiller, Robert J. (2000), *Irrational Exuberance*, Princeton, NJ: Princeton University Press.

Shleifer, Andrei (2000), *Inefficient Markets: An Introduction to Behavioral Finance*, New York: Oxford University Press.

Siebert, Horst (1997), 'Labor market rigidities: at the root of unemployment in Europe', *Journal of Economic Perspectives*, **11** (3), 37–54.

Ul Haq, Mahbub, Inge Kaul and Isabelle Grunberg (1996), *The Tobin Tax: Coping with Financial Volatility*, New York: Oxford University Press.

World Trade Organization (WTO) (1998), *World Trade Organization Annual Report*, Geneva: WTO.

Zysman, John (1983), *Governments, Markets and Growth*, Ithaca, NY: Cornell University Press.

11. Gender equality, public finance and globalization

Diane Elson

INTRODUCTION

> Global inequalities in the distribution of income, wealth, power and influence are enormous and the spread of rapid and cheap global communications has increased the awareness of hundreds of millions of people of widespread injustice and the unfairness of the global economic and political system. Increasingly it is recognised that equity is a global public good. (Griffin, 2003, p. 800)

This chapter considers a particular dimension of inequality: the inequality between women and men, and boys and girls. It considers the interrelation between, on the one hand, attempts to make public finance more gender-equitable, and on the other, the fiscal squeeze produced by some aspects of globalization.

The Beijing Platform for Action, agreed at the UN Fourth World Conference for Women in 1995, specifically endorsed measures to 'engender' government budgets, calling in Paragraph 345 for:

> the integration of a gender perspective in budgetary decisions on policies and programmes, as well as adequate financing of specific programmes for securing equality between women and men.

Since the mid-1990s, a series of gender budget initiatives (GBIs), in both the South and North, have sought to improve the distribution, adequacy and impact of government budgets at national, regional and local levels, and to secure greater transparency in the use of public money, and greater accountability to women as citizens. The spread of GBIs has itself been an example of globalization, in this case the globalization of action for gender justice, facilitated by email, internet and air travel and supported by international foundations and international development cooperation funds.

But, it may be argued, GBIs have begun to engage with public finance just at the time when governments, especially in the South, have less and less control over public finance decisions, due to other aspects of globalization. Globalization of trade, investment and finance puts pressure on government to reduce tax revenues and reduce public expenditure, even as it creates a need for more investment in public goods to counteract inequality and insecurity.

This chapter considers the weaknesses and strengths of GBIs as they seek to promote gender equality in the diminished national fiscal space, and discusses the changes in global governance that are needed if efforts to make public finance more gender-equitable are to be fruitful.

GENDER AND PUBLIC FINANCE: SOME POINTS OF DEPARTURE

The impetus for advocates for gender equality to focus on government budgets has come from a concern that government budgets have not been designed and implemented in ways that promote gender equality. There has been concern that governments have not been backing their gender equality policies with the funding necessary to implement them, that when they have cut back on expenditure, cuts have fallen disproportionately on programmes of importance to women, and that when they have restructured taxation, they have done so in ways that disproportionately and regressively increase women's tax contribution, through the introduction of sales taxes like value-added tax (VAT).

Feminist analysis of the macroeconomic dimensions of public finance (for instance Elson and Cagatay, 2000) suggests that neither the neoliberal nor the Keynesian approach is wholly adequate from the point of view of gender equality. The neoliberal approach tends to result in deflationary bias and commoditization or privatization bias, resulting in outcomes such as: unemployment, 'informalization' of paid work, inadequate public services and low levels of social protection. The Keynesian (and other heterodox approaches) are preferable to the neoliberal approach, but they tend to be marked by implicit or explicit 'male breadwinner bias', in which priority is given to men's employment, as they are assumed to be the breadwinners, and women are treated as dependents of men, their access to public services and social protection conditioned by their relations to men. Neither approach takes into account the unpaid work required to sustain families and communities, work which is disproportionately done by women. Because of this, both approaches are likely to result in underinvestment in the public services that women require in order to achieve a more equal balance between time spent in production and social reproduction, and in underinvestment in forms of social protection that recognize women as autonomous citizens, with claims in their own right.

Feminist macroeconomists consider that the Keynesian approach is however superior, because it incorporates more 'fiscal space': that is, it allows more government discretion about how to manage public finance, both in terms of the general levels of tax and spend, and in terms of how the deficit or surplus is managed. Within that enlarged fiscal space, advocates for gender equality (and for all other types of social equality) have more room for manoeuvre.

Given the current systems of gender relations prevailing in the world today, each method of raising revenue and spending money is likely to have gender-differentiated implications. These can be revealed by additional analysis, bringing further information (such as knowledge of existing patterns of inequality in households, markets and businesses) into play. Banerjee (2003) provides some examples for the case of economies in South Asia. For instance if a rise in VAT leads to a rise in the price of commercial fuels used for cooking (like kerosene), then there is likely to be a disproportionate effect on women. Poor families are likely to reduce their purchase of commercial fuel and make more use of fuels that they can acquire without money payment from the subsistence economy, such as animal dung and wood. However gathering and preparing this fuel is disproportionately done by women, who pay an invisible price in terms of additional workload. If the state introduces user fees for primary education, then in a context in which families prioritize educating sons over educating daughters, there will be a disproportionate negative impact on the education of girls.

Various 'tools' have been developed that can be used to conduct various forms of gender budget analysis to reveal more of their gender impacts (see for example Elson, 1998; Budlender and Sharp, 1998; UNIFEM, 2002).

GENDER BUDGET INITIATIVES: SOME EXAMPLES OF PRACTICE

The pioneers in taking action were the 'femocrats' in the government of Australia in the mid-1980s. Feminists came into public office in considerable numbers and persuaded the Labour government to launch an annual Women's Budget Statement, issued as part of the federal budget papers for the first time in 1987 (Sawer, 2002). This lengthy document (of about 300 pages) attempted to examine the whole budget, tax as well as expenditure, for the likely implications for women in Australia (Sharp and Broomhill, 2002).

The gender focus on Australian budgets was promoted by gender equality advocates who had become officials and ministers. They had three goals: to raise awareness within government of the gender impact of the budget and the policies funded; to make governments accountable for their commitments to gender equality; and to bring about changes to budgets and the policies they fund to improve the socio-economic status of women. Sharp and Broomhill (2002) judge that there was some success in achieving each of these goals. They point out that as a result of the Women's Budget, a tax rebate paid primarily to men for dependent spouses was replaced with a cash payment for child care responsibilities to the full-time (usually female) carers of children. However successes were limited by political factors and by the adverse economic situation of Australia in the early 1990s, which led to the introduction of neoliberal economic policies, including expenditure cutbacks. The Office of Status of Women was not able to persuade the Ministry of Finance to review these policies even if they seemed likely to have an adverse impact on women. The election of a neoliberal government in the mid-1990s led to a suspension of the production of Women's Budget Statements at the federal level, though the practice was continued in some of the states and territories. In 2001 the Australian Labour Party committed itself to the reintroduction of the Women's Budget Statement if it returned to government, but failed to win the elections.

Women in South Africa drew upon the Australian example to develop their own Women's Budget Initiative (WBI), which originated in 1994 through a coalition of civil society activists and parliamentarians (Govender, 2002). Debbie Budlender, who coordinates the WBI analysis, notes that the term 'women's budget' may be something of a misnomer (Budlender, 2000a). The WBI does not advocate a separate budget for women. It is a form of policy monitoring and audit and is used to inform parliamentarians so that they are able to understand better the gender implications of the government budgets, and to exercise their parliamentary scrutiny function more effectively.

The standard method employed is to take the government's policy framework sector by sector and go through the following steps: (1) review gender issues in the sector; (2) analyse the appropriateness of the policy framework; (3) examine the extent to which the allocation of resources reflects a serious commitment to the policy goals; (4) examine how the resources have actually been utilized (For example how many male and female members of the population have benefited and at what cost); and (5) assess the longer-term impacts on male and female members of the population, identifying to what extent their lives have improved.

As well as producing an annual volume of technical analysis, the South African WBI produces popular handbooks in a number of languages for use in workshops with the women for whom it is advocating. It is engaged in a long-term process of capacity building so that there is a well-informed demand for budgets that deliver the promises of the South African constitution. It has succeeded in influencing the design of particular programmes, such as the reform of child benefit. However its well-informed analysis and passionate advocacy has not dented the determination of the South African Ministry of Finance to pursue a neoliberal economic policy, in which trade liberalization has resulted in the loss of thousands of women's jobs in the textile and garments industry, and in which a deflationary bias in fiscal and monetary policy has prevented the creation of adequate numbers of new jobs.

The Australian and South African examples were among the inspirations for a Commonwealth Secretariat initiative (to which I was an advisor) to promote the use of gender budget analysis by governments as a response to the challenges of economic restructuring. The Commonwealth Secretariat decided to prioritize expenditure, and a set of tools which might be used for gender analysis of government expenditure was put together (Hewitt and Mukhopadyay, 2002). Beginning in 1997, the Commonwealth Secretariat supported five Commonwealth governments in undertaking some gender analysis of the expenditure and services of selected ministries. (The governments were those in South Africa, Sri Lanka, Barbados, Fiji Islands, and St Kitts and Nevis.) A notable feature of this initiative was the leadership role of the Ministry of Finance in each government. Some useful analysis was carried out but it proved difficult to get sustained commitment from the Ministries of Finance in the five countries to institutionalize the analysis and to use it to improve their budgets, polices and programmes.

Since 2000, in a growing range of countries, North as well as South, governments have come to see gender budget analysis as a potential tool for mainstreaming gender in their policies and programmes. For instance in Europe there are government initiatives of varying scope and sustainability: at the national level in France, Belgium, the Nordic countries, Ireland and UK, and at the regional level in Scotland, the Basque country and Emilia Romagna. In Asia, some work has begun in India, Nepal and Malaysia. In Africa, Kenya, Malawi, Rwanda, Mozambique and Mauritius are among the governments that have done some gender analysis of their budgets. In Latin America, Chile has introduced gender analysis into the process by which departments bid for funds from the national budgets, while in Mexico analysis has been done of the budgets of the Ministry of Social Development and of Health. There is a tendency for these initiatives to focus on the narrower questions of distribution by sex of the benefits of particular programmes, rather than on the adequacy of the levels of expenditure, and the appropriateness of the mix and scale of revenues measures.

In some countries, the lead has been taken by gender equality advocates, who have often gone on to develop collaborative relations with governments and parliaments. For example in 1997 a civil society organization (CSO), the Tanzania Gender Networking Programme (TGNP), began to analyse the Tanzanian budget using the same approach as the South African WBI. The aim was:

> to examine the national budgeting process from a civil society perspective to see how public resources are allocated in national and local budgets and to assess how this allocation impacts women and other groups, such as youth and poor men … the exercise seeks to lay the foundation of an effective consensus-building campaign to influence the public, policy-makers, legislators and government officials on the neces-

> sity of increasing resources towards programmes to benefit women and other disadvantaged members of society. (Rusimbi, 2002)

Later the Swedish International Development Agency began funding a parallel exercise in the Ministry of Finance, and subsequently TGNP was brought in as a consultant to the government, to conduct training based on its research, and to develop guidelines for gender mainstreaming. The 2000/2001 Budget Guidelines mandated all ministries to prepare their budget with gender mainstreaming objectives in mind. TGNP has also been invited to contribute to the processes that Tanzania must undergo in order to get debt relief and additional funding from the World Bank, such as the Public Financial Reform Management Programme, the Public Expenditure Review and the production of a Poverty Reduction Strategy Paper. TGNP has expressed dissatisfaction at the limitations of these processes, which leave undisturbed the neoliberal policy framework.

In Mexico, civil society organizations have also been active (Hofbauer, 2002). Gender analysis of the allocations for the women's reproductive health services budget was initiated in 1999 by Foro, a network of women's organizations, and one of the network members, Equidad de Genero (a CSO working to develop the capacities of women elected to public office), began conducting public finance workshops for women leaders. In 2000 Equidad joined forces with Fundar, a think-tank devoted to applied budget research, in a joint project which began by analysing the gender dimensions of anti-poverty programmes. The election of a new government in 2000 opened up the opportunity for collaborative work with some government departments, especially the Ministry of Health which commissioned the publication of a handbook on gender-sensitive budgeting for the health sector. The Minister of Health expressed a commitment:

> to developing a methodology for the gender-sensitive formulation of the sectoral budgets ... in order to progressively achieve their institutionalization toward the end of the current administration. (Hofbauer, 2002, p. 93)

However the implementation of this was hampered by expenditure cutbacks ordered by the Ministry of Finance in 2002.

One important aspect of the GBI in Mexico has been its links, through Fundar, with an international network of civil society budget initiatives focusing on transparency, accountability and the alleviation of poverty. This network is facilitated by the International Budget Project – established by the Center on Budget and Policy Priorities, a watchdog organization in Washington, DC – and financially supported by the Ford Foundation. The first network conference in 1997 was attended by 50 people from 14 countries. The third conference had 100 participants from 24 countries (Krafchik, 2002). It has grown up side by side with the spread of GBIs, and reflects a widespread and growing concern with fiscal democracy (see www.internationalbudget.org).

In some parts of Latin America progressive mayors initiated participatory budgeting processes in the 1990s, in which citizens could play a greater role in determining the investment priorities of their town. The best known internationally is Porto Alegre in Brazil, but there are other examples in Brazil (for example San Andre), Peru (Villa El Salvador), Ecuador (Cuenca), Uruguay (Guyana) and Venezuela (Montevideo). In Peru and Ecuador, women's organizations wanted to strengthen their voice in these processes and in 2001 turned to UNIFEM (United Nations Development Fund for Women) for support in conducting research and training (Vargas-Valente, 2002; Pearl, 2002). A gender analysis was conducted of the budget of Villa El Salvador, developing new tools to look at patterns of spending, budget processes and the contribution made by women's unpaid work to the delivery of municipal services. The mayor elected in 2003 has made a commitment to incorporate some of the findings and recommendations into the reform of the participatory budget process. NGOs central to the organization of the participatory process have agreed to include a gender perspective into the training they conduct for the participatory budget committees.

India does not have participatory budgets on the Latin American model (except in the state of Kerala, which has something comparable) but it does have decentralization of funding for some types of economic and social development to local councils, on which 33 per cent of seats are reserved for women. The reservation of seats for women, which was introduced in 1993, brought 1 million women into elected office for the first time. However they are often excluded from an active role in the preparation and implementation of budgets, which is seen as the province of men. In the state of Karnataka, the Women's Information and Resource Centre is working (with some support from UNIFEM) to enable women elected as representatives on local councils to understand the budget process, decide their priorities and organize to transform budgets to better meet women's needs (Jain, 2002; Karnataka Women's Information and Resource Centre, 2002). A problem faced by these and other GBIs at the local level in Latin America, Asia and Africa is the devolution of responsibilities to local government, without adequate funding to discharge them.

To summarize the experience of GBIs: by 2002, up to 50 countries in all parts of the world, North as well as South, had hosted some kind of gender budget initiative (Budlender and Hewitt, 2002, p. 8). There is no one template: GBIs have taken place at all levels of government, involving regional and local government budgets as well as national budgets. Moreover a multiplicity of actors have been involved: government ministers and officials (especially women's ministries, sometimes Ministries of Finance), parliamentarians, policy research NGOs, gender equality CSOs and academics (Budlender et al., 2002; Budlender and Hewitt, 2002; UNIFEM, 2002).

However some of these GBIs amounted to no more than a sensitization workshop while others are dormant and a few have come to an end. GBIs have often been supported in the South by development cooperation agencies, leading to worries that they are donor-driven rather than the outcome of a demand by women in the South for greater accountability of their governments to them (Budlender, 2000a). The most effective GBIs have produced some institutionalization of gender equality concerns in one or more stages of the budget cycle in one or more ministries, or resulted in an ongoing public scrutiny of the budget from a gender equality perspective. There is an informal global network between GBI activists who email regularly and meet at regional and international workshops. UNIFEM organizes a GBI on-line discussion and a website (www.gender-budgets.org).

Debbie Budlender (2002, p. 123) summarizes effectiveness in the organization of GBIs by referring to the 'triangle of players': progressive elected politicians, effective government institutions staffed with well-trained officials, and active and well-informed coalitions of NGOs. Effective and sustainable GBIs are generally based on the interaction of all three.

Rhonda Sharp, adviser to the South Australian GBI, points to a different triangle (Sharp, 2002, p. 88), a 'triangle of goals': raise awareness and understanding of gender issues and the impacts of budgets and policies; make governments accountable for their budgetary and policy commitments; and change and refine government budgets and policies to promote gender equality. She also points to a hierarchy between these goals, with the achievement of the first being necessary for the achievement of the second, and the achievement of the first two being necessary for the achievement of the third. In her assessment, there are many examples of success in achieving the first two goals, though fewer in achieving the third.

There are two key obstacles to achieving the third goal. The first is lack of sufficient commitment to gender equality. As Pregs Govender, former chair of the Parliamentary Committee on the Improvement of the Quality of Life and Status of Women in South Africa, points out, a government's budget reflects its priorities. An end to discrimination against women and the promotion of women's empowerment is not necessarily high on the list of priorities, despite lip-service about gender mainstreaming. Creating a budget that is gender-equitable and supports the advancement of women generally means a change in priorities, and there are often strong forces opposed to this. The second obstacle is the constraint on public finance caused by profit-led globalization. This issue is addressed in the rest of the chapter.

PROFIT-LED GLOBALIZATION AND PUBLIC FINANCE

Profit-led globalization entails the reduction of barriers to the mobility of finance and goods and services across national borders. It takes place through reductions of tariffs and quotas on imports; reductions of controls on multinational corporations; and reductions of controls on inflows and outflows of money invested in stocks and shares. As Griffin (2003) points out, it is a profoundly asymmetric globalization, since barriers to the movement of low-skilled labour have been maintained and in some cases strengthened.

New technology facilitates the mobility but it is policy decisions by governments that reduce or abolish controls. Since the mid-1970s, governments all around the world have decided to maintain controls on the mobility of labour and reduce controls over the mobility of capital. Some governments, mainly in the rich countries of the North, have freely chosen to do this (for example the UK government under Mrs Thatcher). Many governments, mainly in the South and East, have done this in order to obtain loans from international financial institutions, both public and private. A highly unequal system of global governance has been created, with three key components: the IMF, the World Bank and the WTO (Khor, 2003). Though in formal terms the WTO operates a one-country-one-vote system, in reality this is vitiated by 'green room' deals in which the mercantilism of the rich has tended to triumph.

Neoliberal economic analysis argues that such policies will bring benefits to countries in terms of growth, employment and poverty reduction. For many governments there were short-term benefits in terms of an inflow of capital which financed budget and balance-of-payments deficits, and a growth of exports, often creating more paid work for women. But these short-term benefits had a cost: subsequent unexpected debt burdens when interest rates rose much more than expected in the 1980s; loss of jobs in industries out-competed by imports; volatility, insecurity and financial crisis, when short-term capital left even faster than it had arrived. The result has been stagnation and growing poverty in the weakest economies (especially in Africa), and growing inequality within and between countries. Feminist scholarship has documented how poor women have particularly borne these costs (for a discussion of the literature see Rai, 2002).

The capacity of governments to use public expenditure to combat poverty, inequality and insecurity has been weakened by what has become known as the fiscal squeeze (Grunberg, 1998). Cagatay (2002) summarizes the key aspects of this. The capacity of governments to raise many forms of revenue has been reduced. Trade liberalization cuts import duties and export taxes, key sources of revenue in many poor countries. Competition to attract multinational corporations and their highly paid executives leads to cuts in corporation and capital gains taxes; tax holidays and other exemptions; and to cuts in top rates of income tax. Development cooperation grants have fallen as trade is supposed to replace aid. Governments have been encourage or pressured into turning to sales taxes like VAT to raise revenue, but such taxes fall most heavily on poor people and worsen the distribution of income. Revenue has also been raised through the sale of public enterprises and other public assets, but this only gives a one-time boost to revenue, and may result in costs for services, like water, that poor people cannot afford. Charges have also been introduced for public services like education and health, worsening the access of poor people, especially poor women and girls.

With revenue limited and debt burdens rising, the pressure has been on governments to make their budgets sustainable by cutting back on expenditure. This pressure has come from the public international financial institutions like the IMF and the World Bank, and also from private investors, who have seen budget deficits as harbingers of inflation, signals that the value of their assets would be eroded. Initiatives to address the debt problems of poor countries, such as the Highly Indebted Poor Countries (HIPC) initiative, have failed to provide much relief, and access to them is conditional on the continuing implementation of neoliberal economic policies. There is no global 'lender of last resort' and higher-income countries which run into financial crisis are forced by the IMF to cut back sharply on expenditure, thus turning a financial crisis into a recession (Stiglitz, 2002). In order to build a reputation for 'sound finance' in financial markets, many governments have enacted legislation (such as balanced budget laws) that severely limit the fiscal space (Bakker, 2002). The size of government budgets is now disciplined by financial institutions rather than the votes of citizens (Bakker, 2002; Elson and Cagatay, 2000). Moreover the ways that governments can spend the revenues they have raised is becoming more and more constrained by the ever-widening remit of WTO agreements, which stretch beyond trade to encompass government subsidies and procurement policies.

Most GBIs have not yet directly analysed the impacts of profit-led globalization on the fiscal space because they have focused primarily on the expenditure side of the budget, particularly on the social sectors such as health, education and poverty reduction programmes. Most of them have not yet considered the revenue side of the budget or the macroeconomic dimensions of the budget (the issue of the appropriate deficit or surplus and the aggregate levels of revenue and expenditure).

An exception is the South African WBI which has analysed the gender dimensions of taxation in the context of globalization in its budget report in 2000. In this report, Smith documents the dramatic shift in the composition of revenue from direct taxes in the period since 1988–89 away from corporate taxes to personal taxes (mainly income tax). In 1988–89 personal taxes accounted for 30 per cent of total tax revenue, while corporate taxes accounted for 22 per cent. By 1998–99, personal taxes accounted for 42 per cent, while corporate taxes accounted for only 13 per cent of total tax revenue (Smith, 2000, p. 8). The lowering of corporate taxes has been a key element in the South African government's Growth, Employment and Redistribution (GEAR) strategy, which aims to achieve growth and employment creation through exports and private sector investment. It has been complemented by trade liberalization. In the 2002 report of the WBI, it is reported that by 1999–2000 customs duties accounted for only 2.5 percent of government revenue, whereas in neighbouring Swaziland and Lesotho, they accounted for half of government revenue (Goldman, 2000, pp. 11–12). The GEAR strategy was adopted without any pressure from the World Bank or IMF, to which South Africa has few debts. Rather it was a response to the worries of foreign investors following a sharp fall in the value of the rand caused by an outflow of short-term capital. It does not seem to have worked: 'on the whole many more jobs have been lost in the South African economy since 1996 than those created' (Smith 2000, p. 19). The clothing and textile industry has been particularly hard hit by job losses, predominantly among women, as South Africa lowered tariffs on clothing and textiles faster and to lower levels than required under the WTO (Goldman, 2000, p. 16).

Total revenue in South Africa was projected to fall in relation to gross domestic product from 32.2 per cent in 1997–98 to 30.7 per cent in 2001–2002. The WBI report points to the loss this represents to programmes which would benefit women (Budlender, 2000b, p. 3). The report does not directly challenge the GEAR (perhaps because the government has so far been totally impervious to the widespread criticism of this strategy). But it does call for an end to reductions in corporate taxation, additional efforts to end widespread evasion and avoidance of taxes and import duties, and a system for conducting gender-aware employment impact assessments of trade agreements.

Poor, highly indebted countries have far less room for manoeuvre than South Africa, and are not free to determine their own trade, fiscal and monetary policies but must adopt neoliberal globalization policies required by the IMF and World Bank. The GBIs in some of them have produced critiques of these policies. For instance in Tanzania the TGNP has consistently stressed the need to challenge such policies, arguing that they result in 'limited room for government to support development that is gender-sensitive and owned by the people' (Rusimbi, 2002, p. 125).

In Nepal a gender budget audit produced by the Institute for Integrated Development Studies (IIDS) concluded that:

> The impact of the marked shift in budgetary polices since mid-1980s toward a more open economy and a minimalist state has not been gender friendly in general. (IIDS, 2002, p. 74)

As in South Africa, the tax system has been restructured to promote private investment, with corporate taxes reduced from 50 per cent to between 20 and 30 per cent, the maximum income tax rate reduced from 45 per cent to 25 per cent, and import duties from an average of 25 per cent to an average of 10 per cent. The ratio of government revenue to GDP has been rising, but in 2001 was still only 12.5 per cent , and the growth of revenue was unable to keep pace with expenditure, which stood at 20.3 per cent of GNP in 2001. There has been some expansion of export-oriented businesses but women have benefited very little from these while they have been hard hit by withdrawal of subsidies (another neoliberal pro-globalization policy) on food and fertilizers. The livelihoods of women farmers have become precarious because of competition from subsidized products from India and other countries. The report argues that there is a lack of measures to reconcile the social needs of the citizens of Nepal, especially those of poor women, and the integration of Nepal into a globalized economy. Nearly 60 per cent of the development expenditure of Nepal is financed by foreign aid, and the report calls for more foreign aid to be oriented to sectors such as income-generating activities for women, and services such as basic education, literacy, primary health care and drinking water. Donors are criticized for focusing on opening up the economy for international capital, and not meeting the promises about levels of aid made in UN forums. The report recognizes that Nepal cannot survive by itself in isolation from the global economy, but criticizes the government of Nepal for not making the process of integration in the global economy 'more gender-sensitive and human'.

ENLARGING FISCAL SPACE AND CREATING FISCAL DEMOCRACY

To achieve budgets which are more effective in promoting gender equality, there needs to be both more fiscal space, and a more democratic process for determining the use of that space. This requires action at both international and national levels. As a UN report on human development and trade points out:

> The international regime cannot and should not be blamed for government failures to design appropriate policies. But it can and should be accountable for restricting government choices and opportunities – or for channelling them in inappropriate directions. (UNDP, 2003, p. 63)

At the international level, we need a system of global governance that does not restrict the ability of governments to raise higher levels of revenue in a more equitable way, and that does not limit their ability to use fiscal policy to cushion their societies against economic shocks.

In the realm of trade, this means a fundamental reshaping of the WTO, so that its rules operate fairly. It requires that poor countries which raise a substantial portion of their revenue from trade taxes should not be pushed into precipitate reduction of tariffs and export taxes, and that WTO agreements should not constrain the way that governments spend public money. As the UN report on trade and human development puts it:

> Trade rules must allow for diverse national institutions and standards ... citizens of different countries have different preferences for the role of government regulation or provision of social welfare. (UNDP, 2003, p. 67)

In the realm of international finance, this means cancellation of debts of the Highly Indebted Poor Countries; no pressure from the IMF for countries to liberalize capital markets to permit financial investors to move money freely across borders; no pressure from the IMF for countries hit by financial crises to severely cut back on public expenditure; and the introduction of new systems for dealing with financial crises (Stiglitz, 2002; Singh and Zammit, 2000).

In the realm of international direct investment, it means no expansion of WTO rules to cover investment, competition and government procurement. Such an expansion would lock countries into a system with gives multinational corporations even greater rights to operate in all countries free from all but minimum regulation. It would severely limit the ability of government to pursue social objectives through their procurement policies (such as affirmative action to give contracts to small businesses owned by disadvantaged groups), since foreign firms and local firms would have to be treated in exactly the same way (Khor, 2003, p. 539).

It means looking at ways of reinvigorating public provision of finance for development through developing global taxation and redistribution schemes. One possibility is to introduce a tax on international currency transactions (the Tobin Tax, originally proposed by Nobel prize-winning American economist, James Tobin) and redistribute the proceeds to finance universal public provisioning of basic social services and gender-equitable social protection schemes (Cagatay, 2002, p. 19). Another is the scheme advocated by Griffin and McKinley (1996) whereby funds would be raised by a compulsory progressive tax on the national income of rich countries and distributed automatically to poor countries, in accordance with their per capita income.

There are many civil society groups, including women's groups, campaigning for all of these kinds of changes in international governance. More links need to be built between them and GBIs:

> ... in the context of globalisation, fiscal policy cannot be rendered gender-equitable or broadly equitable at the national or local levels alone. It is also necessary to address these concerns at the international level and to ensure that there is coherence between the international dimensions of policy and advocacy and the national and local ones ... This can be accomplished through greater dialogue between a) feminists who are involved in national or local budget initiatives and those who do advocacy at the international level; b) between feminists and other groups who focus on democratising macroeconomics polices (such as those who focus on pro-poor budgets or other types of progressive macroeconomic policy-making ... and c) between feminists involved in budget initiatives in the South and the North. (Cagatay, 2002, p. 19)

An important way to build these links is for GBIs to extend their scrutiny to the Ministries of Finance and Trade and Industry (as the South African WBI has done); and for GBIs in the North to extend their scrutiny to the development cooperation budgets of their countries.

It is however important to remember that within the limited fiscal space left by profit-led globalization, governments can and do make choices; and often these choices are not consistent with gender-equality goals. The IMF and the World Bank do not dictate where the cuts should fall. Governments make these decisions.

For example in Mexico, cutbacks in public expenditure introduced by both the Zedillo government and the Fox government have tended to fall more heavily on programmes of direct importance to women (Colinas, 2003). In 1998–2000 the Zedillo government made cuts in response to a fall in the price of oil (which reduced government revenue from the Mexican oil industry). The Ministry of Finance announced that the cuts would fall on the National Electricity Commission, PEMEX (the state-owned oil company) and the Department of Communications and Transport. In fact the cuts actually fell on the Ministry of Social Affairs, the Ministry of Health and the Ministry of Education. The Fox government, whose election in 2000 ended a long period of *de facto* one-party rule, also made cuts. In 2002 the Ministry of Finance gave assurances that programmes specifically targeting women would not be cut, but there were cuts in anti-poverty programmes, resulting in fewer resources for nutrition, basic housing, temporary employment programmes and community services. The budgets of the Attorney-General, the Ministry of National Defence, the Ministry of the Navy and the Ministry of Public Security were not cut. The budgets of Ministries of Health and of Education were cut, as was that of the Mexican Social Security Institute.

Mexican women have been fighting back. In September 2002, the Commission on Gender Equality of the federal Chamber of Deputies hosted a public meeting on gender and budgets attended by women from Mexican groups working on gender analysis of budgets, officials from a variety of ministries and some international GBI advocates.

In subsequent negotiations on the 2003 budget, the Commission succeed in getting increases in the amounts proposed by the government: for instance an increase of 100 million pesos for the reproductive health programme (an increase of 40 per cent on the original proposal). Other programmes for which funding allocations were increased include a programme to reduce maternal mortality (from almost 50 million pesos to 75 million pesos), a programme for women in agriculture (from just over 50 million pesos to 200 million pesos), and a programme for immigrant women (from almost 2 million pesos to 6 million pesos). In addition it was agreed that all government entities will be required to introduce evaluation mechanisms that incorporate the objective of reducing gender inequality (Colinas, 2003). Now the challenge is to ensure that the increased allocations are transformed into activities that have a positive impact on Mexican women. Mexico is not yet anywhere near the point when the whole budget is formulated in a gender-equitable way, but some Mexican women are now using the available fiscal space to struggle to achieve budgetary allocations for public policies that offer prospect of some real gains for Mexican women, especially poor women.

To transform government budget-making so that it is fully consistent with gender equality and the empowerment of women requires the creation of fiscal democracy, a system in which budget processes are transparent, accountable and participatory, and in which every type of citizen has an equal voice (Bakker, 2002). In most countries, rich and poor, this is far from being achieved. Even if there is no secrecy about budget allocations and no misappropriation of funds, powerful interest groups connected to the rich elite tend to dominate the setting of priorities, winning tax concessions and expenditure on programmes important to them.

Four aspects of fiscal democracy are identified by Norton and Elson (2002, pp. 47–8): governance of budgets by elected representatives; government officials holding consultations with the public; governments sharing decision-making on budget formulation and execution with citizens; citizens holding statutory entitlements to public services, backed up by mechanisms of redress. Goetz and Jenkins (2002) stress the importance of participatory auditing, to ensure that decisions are actually carried out, and that the people who were supposed to benefit, actually do benefit. Both sets of authors stress that for formal structures of fiscal democracy to be democratic in practice, there must be active engagement of well-informed and well-organized citizens. Goetz and Jenkins find that although the state of Kerala in India has introduced an impressive formal structure of fiscal democracy, women have not yet been able to exercise an equal voice within it. They attribute this to the lack of autonomous organizations of women.

CONCLUSIONS

Profit-led globalization puts strong limits on what can be achieved by attempts to turn government budgets into instruments for gender equality, but ministers of finance still have important areas of discretion in the way they raise revenue and spend it. GBIs have the potential to be significant actors in the struggle to enlarge the fiscal space and make it more democratic. To achieve this, they will need to make alliances with other initiatives, both those working on transforming globalization, and those working on transforming budgets; and they will need to focus attention not only on the budgets of those ministries that seem most immediately relevant to women, but also on the budgets and policies of the Ministries of Finance, Trade and Industry. They will need to advocate for systems of public finance that redistribute not only internally, but also internationally.

REFERENCES

Bakker, Isabella (2002), 'Fiscal policy, accountability and voice: the example of gender responsive budget initiatives', Human Development Report Office occasional paper, New York: UNDP.

Banerjee, Nirmala (2003), 'What is gender budgeting? Public policies from women's perspective in the Indian context', in the Follow the Money series, South Asia no. 1, New Delhi: United Nations Development Fund for Women.

Budlender, Debbie (2000a), 'The political economy of women's budgets in the South', *World Development*, **28** (7), 1365–78.

Budlender, Debbie (2000b), 'Introduction', *The Women's Budget Series, 2000 Issue*, Cape Town: IDASA.

Budlender, Debbie (2002), 'A global assessment of gender responsive budget initiatives', in Debbie Budlender and Guy Hewitt (eds), *Gender Budgets Make More Cents*, London: Commonwealth Secretariat, pp. 83–164.

Budlender, Debbie and Guy Hewitt (eds) (2002), *Gender Budgets Make More Cents*, London: Commonwealth Secretariat.

Budlender, Debbie and Rhonda Sharp (1998), *How to Do a Gender-Sensitive Budget Analysis: Contemporary Research and Practice*, London: Commonwealth Secretariat.

Budlender, Debbie, Diane Elson, Guy Hewitt and Tanni Mukhopadhyay (2002), *Gender Budgets Make Cents*, London: Commonwealth Secretariat.

Cagatay, Nilufer (2002), 'Gender budgets and beyond: feminist fiscal policy in the context of globalisation', paper presented at the conference of the Association for Women's Rights in Development, Guadalajara, Mexico.

Colinas, Maria de Lourdes (2003), 'Gender, budgets and development planning in Mexico', MA dissertation, Department of Sociology, University of Essex.

Elson, Diane (1998), 'Integrating gender issues into national budgetary polices and procedures: some policy options', *Journal of International Development*, **10**, 929–41.

Elson, Diane (2002), 'Gender responsive budget initiatives', in *Gender Budget Initiatives. Strategies, Concepts, Experiences*, New York: United Nations Development Fund for Women.

Elson, Diane and Nilufer Cagatay (2000), 'The social content of macroeconomic policies', *World Development*, **28** (7), 1347–63.

Goetz, Anne-Marie and Robin Jenkins (2002), 'Accountability to women in development spending-experiments in service delivery audits at the local level', Brighton: Institute of Development Studies.

Goldman, Tanya (2000), 'Customs and excise paper', *The Women's Budget Series 2000 Issue*, Cape Town: IDASA.

Govender, Pregs (2002), 'Lessons from practice: the role of parliament in South Africa's women's budget', in *Gender Budget Initiatives. Strategies, Concepts, Experiences*, New York: United Nations Development Fund for Women.

Griffin, Keith (2003), 'Economic globalization and institutions of global governance', *Development and Change*, **34** (5), 789–807.

Griffin, Keith and Terry McKinley (1996), 'Development cooperation in the twenty-first century: suggestions for a new framework', *Indian Journal of Applied Economics*, **5** (4), 161–82.

Grunberg, Isabelle (1998), 'Double jeopardy: globalization, liberalization and the fiscal squeeze', *World Development*, **26** (4), 591–605.

Hewitt, Guy and Tanni Mukhopadhyay (2002), 'Promoting gender equality through public expenditure', in Debbie Budlender, Diane Elson, Guy Hewitt and Tanni Mukhopadhyay (eds), *Gender Budgets Make More Cents*, London: Commonwealth Secretariat, pp. 49–81.

Hofbauer, H. (2002), 'Mexico: collaborating with a wide range of actors', in Debbie Budlender and Guy Hewitt (eds), *Gender Budgets Make More Cents*, London: Commonwealth Secretariat, pp. 84–97.

Institute for Integrated Development Studies – IIDS (2002), *Gender Budget Audit Nepal*, Kathmandu: IIDS.

Jain, Devaki (2002), 'Building budgets from below', in *Gender Budget Initiatives. Strategies, Concepts, Experiences*, New York: United Nations Development Fund for Women.

Karnataka Women's Information and Resource Centre (2002), *Building Budgets from Below*, Bangalore: Karnataka Women's Information and Resource Centre.

Khor, Martin (2003), 'Globalisation, global governance and the dilemmas of development', in Ha-Joon Chang (ed.), *Rethinking Development Economics*, London: Anthem Press, pp. 521–44.

Krafchik, Warren (2002), 'Can civil society add value to budget decision-making?', in *Gender Budget Initiatives. Strategies, Concepts, Experiences*, New York: United Nations Development Fund for Women.

Norton, Andy and Diane Elson (2002), *What's Behind the Budget? Politics, Rights and Accountability in the Budget Process*, London: Overseas Development Institute.

Pearl, Rebecca (2002), 'The Andean region: a multi-country programme', in Debbie Budlender and Guy Hewitt (eds), *Gender Budgets Make More Cents*, London: Commonwealth Secretariat, pp. 23–42.

Rai, Shirin (2002), *Gender and the Political Economy of Development*, Cambridge: Polity Press.

Rusimbi, Mary (2002), 'Mainstreaming gender into policy, planning and budgeting in Tanzania', in *Gender Budget Initiatives. Strategies, Concepts, Experiences*, New York: United Nations Development Fund for Women.

Sawer, Marian (2002), 'Australia; the mandarin approach to gender budgets', in Debbie Budlender and Guy Hewitt (eds.), *Gender Budgets Make More Cents*, London: Commonwealth Secretariat, pp. 43–64.

Sharp, Rhonda (2002), 'Moving forward: multiple strategies and guiding goals', in *Gender Budget Initiatives. Strategies, Concepts, Experiences*, New York: United Nations Development Fund for Women.

Sharp, Rhonda and Ray Broomhill (2002), 'Budgeting for equality: the Australian experience', *Feminist Economics*, **8** (1), 25–47.

Singh, Ajit and Anne Zammitt (2000), 'International capital flows: identifying the gender dimension', *World Development*, **28** (7), 1249–68.

Smith, Terence (2000), 'Women and tax in South Africa', in *The Women's Budget Series 2000 Issue*, Capetown: IDASA.

Stiglitz, Joseph (2002), *Globalisation and its Discontents*, New York: W.W. Norton.

United Nations Development Programme (UNDP) (2003), *Making Global Trade Work For People*, London: Earthscan.

United Nations Fund for Women (UNIFEM) (2002), *Gender Budget Initiatives. Strategies, Concepts and Experiences*, New York: United Nations Development Fund for Women.

Vargas-Valente, Virginia (2002), 'Municipal budgets and democratic governance in the Andean region', in *Gender Budget Initiatives. Strategies, Concepts, Experiences*, New York: United Nations Development Fund for Women.

12. Class transition in the age of globalization: examples from the rural sectors in India and Kenya

Anjan Chakrabarti, Stephen Cullenberg and Mwangi wa Gĩthĩnji

Thirty years ago Keith Griffin published his influential book *The Political Economy of Agrarian Change* where he analyzed the economic, social and political consequences of the 'green revolution' in Asia and Latin America. The powerful and controversial conclusion that Griffin reached in his study was that the green revolution, rather than having an unambiguous positive effect on reducing malnutrition or increased agricultural production, resulted instead in increased inequality and the polarization of classes.

This analysis was stunning and controversial because it challenged what many felt were the overwhelming salutary effects of the green revolution, arguably the most important phenomenon affecting the development process at the time. Today for many it is 'globalization' that has replaced the green revolution as the driving force for growth, the reduction in inequality and the eradication of poverty. In recent work, Griffin has challenged this oversimplification as well.

We want to argue that one of most important innovations that Griffin made in his *The Political Economy of Agrarian Change* is not only the controversial policy implications his study produced, but a methodological and analytical innovation that is central to the complexity and multifaceted nature of his investigation. It is central not only to his methodology but also to the conclusions of increased inequality and the polarization of classes. Rather than theorize on the economy, or more precisely the rural economy, as a homogeneous space occupied by peasants, or peasants and landlords, Griffin recognized a multitude of institutional and class arrangements whereby those living and working in rural areas produce and reproduce their conditions of existence.

Thus for Griffin the relationship between tenure arrangements, land ownership and risk-bearing is a complicated one:

> The three basic types of tenure arrangements are owner-operation, sharecropping and fixed rental or leasehold systems. An owner-operator hires labour for a fixed wage,

> organizes production himself, bears all risks and reaps all profits. Under this system the workers essentially become a rural proletariat. Sharecropping is an alternative arrangement, whereby the landlord and tenant share the costs, risks and profits, not necessarily equally, of course. Both parties to the contract typically have a role to play in the decision-making process. Under the leasehold system, in contrast, the landlord usually bears no risk and becomes a pure rentier; the tenant assumes all risks, makes all decisions and reaps the profits, if any. The tenant in effect becomes a small entrepreneur.
>
> It is important to note that there is no necessary connection between ownership of land, entrepreneurship and risk taking. He who makes the decisions, bears most of the risk, but he who bears the risk need not own the land. Thus the extent to which the peasant is able to make many of the decisions which affect his well-being depends upon the type of contract he is able to negotiate with the landlord.
>
> Even the three basic tenure forms allow landlords and peasants to adopt a variety of roles – agricultural worker, share-tenant, leaseholder, owner-operator, rentier, and crop-sharing landlord. Moreover, most of these roles can be found within any given locality and, indeed, many individuals will combine roles. For example, an individual may be simultaneously, or alternatively, a sharecropper, an owner-operator and a wage labourer. Thus even in the simple rural community we have described, social differences are rather blurred; there is no sharp class differentiation. (1974, pp. 23–4)

It is this last paragraph which we wish to develop in the rest of this chapter. There are three points which we especially wish to emphasize: (1) rural society is not a homogenous space but one where class distinctions overlap and contradictory class positions often coexist; (2) the categories of landlords and peasants need to be unpacked as they hide as much as they reveal; (3) individuals may hold, or households may consist of, a number of different class positions simultaneously.

Thus development and transition in rural society will not likely move in an unambiguously 'progressive' direction but will have uneven and contradictory effects on the different class institutions in rural society. Just as the green revolution in the 1970s produced such complex and contradictory effects, so too do we see the process of globalization changing the class landscape of rural society in complex and contradictory ways. The focus of the rest of this chapter is to use a disaggregated Marxian theory of class and a decentered notion of transition to provide an analysis of the changing class landscapes of rural India and Kenya in this age of globalization.

CLASS DIFFERENTIATION AND THE ECONOMY

We will analyze the agrarian economy and its transition from a Marxian class perspective, a perspective that as Griffin pointed out, must be able to differentiate and disaggregate the agrarian economy in order to capture its full complexity. Traditionally, Marxian economics has understood the idea of transition most commonly as a once-and-for-all macro shift in the mode of production (the economy) and the subsequent changes in the 'complex social totality', including the political and ideological realms of society. In contrast, we deploy a disaggregated, micro-focused concept of transition (first developed by Chakrabarti and Cullenberg, 2003), which explicitly theorizes changes in distinct types of class processes as well as changes in the forms of class processes themselves.[1]

In order to see the potential multifaceted class nature of society, we use the idea of class sets to define specific types of class processes (Cullenberg, 1992; Chakrabarti and Cullenberg, 2001). This framework of class sets is a useful way to see the disaggregated class nature of society and the complexity involved in the process of transition. We identify different class sets in terms of the appro-

Table 12.1 *Class sets*

	Surplus labor appropriation	Worker remuneration	Output distribution
1	A	W	C
2	A	W	NC
3	A	NW	C
4	A	NW	NC
5	N	W	C
6	N	W	NC
7	N	NW	C
8	N	NW	NC
9	S	W	C
10	S	W	NC
11	S	NW	C
12	S	NW	NC

Notes:
A = all[1], N = none[2], S = shared[3], W = wage, NW = non-wage, C = commodity, NC = non-commodity

1. 'A' is the form of appropriation whereby the performer of surplus labor is able to exclude all others from the process of appropriation and therefore appropriates the surplus labor completely and individually. That is, the direct producer appropriates the surplus labor at the individual level. Class structures that fall under the class sets with 'a' are called independent or ancient class structures.
2. 'N' refers to a form of appropriation whereby the performers of surplus labor are able to excluded themselves from the process of any appropriation. That is, none of the surplus labor is appropriated by the direct producers. Class structures that resemble class sets with 'n' are exploitative class structures.
3. 'S' refers to a form of appropriation whereby all performers of surplus labor are able to share in its appropriation, and therefore no one is being either completely excluded from appropriation or can exclude others. Class structures that resemble class sets with 's' are communal class structures.

priation of surplus labor and its relation to the manner of the remuneration to workers (either as wage, W, or non-wage, NW), and the distribution of output (either as commodity, C or non-commodity, NC). The combination of the different possibilities among the three gives us 12 different class sets (Table 12.1).[2]

The first four class sets refer to individual appropriation, sets 5–8 refer to exploitative appropriation and sets 9–12 refer to shared appropriation.[3] At any point in time, all these distinct class sets could coexist within a society. Each of these class sets in turn depends upon other economic (including other class sets) and non-economic conditions of existence whose articulated existence is what we call the class structure of an economy.[4] The distinct conditions of existence and the contradictions involved with these class sets could further differentiate them into a more variegated set of class structures, each distinct from the other.[5] In that case transition, resulting from changes in the conditions of existence of the class sets, refers to not only the changes in class structures of the firms from one class set to another (for example from set 4 to set 5) but it must also address itself to changes within class structures (that is, while remaining as set 5, the class structure could undergo a change in its form, for example, a living wage law could decrease the rate of exploitation). Contrary to the approach in traditional Marxism, we analyze transition by considering the distinctive micro changes taking place on a plateau of ever-changing, uneven and disaggregated class structures.

The overall point we are making is that any society, disaggregated in terms of class sets, is heterogeneous in its structure and the deployment of this class set framework helps us see the complex configuration of change to the class structures of any society. That is, the definition of these class sets implies a multitude of class structures that could fit any of these 12 forms of appropriation. Because of this complex nature of society, the contemporary transition process in any society resulting from the liberalization policies and globalization process should be theorized in terms of an uneven, disaggregated and complex series of changes in the types and forms of class structures. We now turn to a detailed analysis of class transition in the rural sectors of two different countries, India and Kenya.

INDIAN AGRICULTURE: A CLASS JOURNEY INTO THE MATERIALIZING GLOBAL ORDER

In 2000 the government of India introduced a new agricultural policy (NAP) that set out policies to put Indian agriculture on a global footing. To put the birth of NAP in the proper context, the government of India in its Vision for 2020 summarizes what it calls India's Stages of Agricultural Development:

1. *Pre-Green Revolution* Boost in productivity growth of coarse grains and pulses per unit of land.
2. *Green Revolution* Expansion of area and rapid growth in productivity of wheat and rice, made possible by widespread adoption of improved varieties, expansion of agricultural research, demonstration and education, and investment in irrigation, supported by establishment of a national infrastructure to produce and supply inputs and to warehouse, distribute and market outputs.
3. *Post-Green Revolution* Continued growth in productivity through intensification of chemical and labor inputs, followed by a gradual deceleration in productivity growth. Expansion of area under maize, cotton, sugarcane, and oilseeds.
4. *Commercialization* Further diversification of cropping patterns from low value to high value crops such as fruits, vegetables, flowers and other horticulture crops for domestic consumption, processing and export. (Planning Commission, 2002)

We want to displace this technologist description of the evolution of Indian agriculture to the social terrain through a class analysis of the type we have already elaborated. The pre-green revolution stage was part and parcel of the Nehru–Mahanalobis development plan that decided not to disturb the traditional basis of agriculture, rooted as it was in various non-capitalist class sets. In the plan, this agricultural sector was understood to provide excess labor (traditional agriculture was presumed to have zero marginal productivity or marginal productivity less than the workers in the cities) and plentiful food to the poor including industrial workers, thereby keeping real wages low, allowing higher industrial profits, higher savings and hence higher capital accumulation. The Nehru–Mahanalobis plan thus envisaged the role of traditional agriculture as feeding industry-led capitalist development by supplying labor and food.

The green revolution was a response to the consecutive droughts in the mid-1960s which produced extreme food shortages and high inflation, thereby shaking the foundation of the Nehru–Mahanalobis plan. Instead of trying to change the socio-economic foundation of rural India, the green revolution focused on increasing agricultural production through productivity increases. The green revolution saw tremendous increases in agricultural production in a few geographical areas and its effect was especially pertinent in North-West India where wheat, which was experimented with more than any other crops, remained the major crop. Another far-reaching effect of the green revolution and the adoption of capital-intensive production was the beginning of the process of consolidation of land and the emergence of a new group of rich and powerful farmers. This consolidation coincided with the commercialization of Indian agriculture and the sustained rise of capitalist farming, at least in the areas of the green revolution. While not its self-professed goal, the green revolution helped initiate a certain class transition of the agrarian society, which Keith Griffin in his work captured so profoundly.

With the adoption of capital-intensive techniques, deepening commercialization and capitalist farming spreading to some other parts of India, another bout of increased agricultural output occurred in the 1980s. This constituted one phase of India's so-called post-Green revolution period. In all these decades the consolidation of land and commercialization of Indian agriculture were only deepening, at least in the areas of capitalist farming. In other areas, further fragmentation of land holdings was also materializing due to factors we shall touch upon later. In fact, the consolidation of land in certain areas and the fragmentation of land holdings went hand in hand, thereby changing the property landscape of agricultural land in contradictory directions. As we shall see later, the NAP fully appreciates and tries to internalize this contradiction.

In class terms, one can visualize the class transition from the pre-green revolution phase to this post-green revolution phase as a transition from a mainly non-capitalist traditional agrarian economy to an agrarian economy that is an articulation of the non-capitalist traditional agriculture and expanding circuits of local capital. The new economic policies (NEP), which began in 1991, are the other phase of the so-called post-Green revolution which started another round of change in Indian agriculture, even though the 1990s witnessed low agricultural growth. The NEP inaugurated a transition process that attempts to create a complex agrarian economy comprised of non-capitalist traditional agriculture, circuits of local capital and circuits of global capital. India's ongoing integration to the circuits of global capital and its changing relations with non-capitalist traditional agriculture and circuits of local capital will take up the rest of this section.

The NEP looks at the ongoing Indian transition towards a new society in terms of a 'big bang' progressive move to a free market capitalist economy integrated into the global order. Among other things, the NEP called for a series of reforms to free the economy from the controls that the state had so far enjoyed over various sectors of the economy. Importantly though, the formulation of the NEP which targeted reforms in industry, finance, trade and state sectors left out agriculture from its reform discourse. However the reforms in other sectors, especially the state sector, considerably affected the agricultural sector.

As part of the NEP and the new orientation of the state, the government was determined to reduce its fiscal deficit sharply, principally its revenue deficit. This involved sharp cuts in transfer payments and government purchases. Since fertilizer subsidies, input subsidies (especially for water and electricity), interest subsidies, administrative price supports, easy loan guarantees and many other services by the government provided critical conditions for existence in the agricultural class sector, cuts in these led to the reduction in the existing subsumed and non-class revenues of agricultural class sets. This threatened the very process of the reproduction of the existing agricultural class enterprises in cases where the reduction in revenue from these effects outweighs the increase in revenue coming from increased, if at all, output prices or output quantities. Additionally, due to withdrawal or at best reduction in activities rendered previously by government agencies, these farms or rural enterprises may now have to access the open market and pay a higher amount of subsumed class payment to (alternative or the same) agencies carrying out processes that secure those particular conditions of existence of the fundamental class process. Reduction in the subsumed class revenue and non-class revenue, and a higher subsumed and non-class payment, created crises in numerous agricultural class sets. One can predict that the effect of the changes in the state policies towards agriculture will have a much stronger effect on small and marginal agricultural class enterprises, most of whom have few assets to overcome such a crisis and sustain the reproduction of their respective enterprises without government support.

The government's response to the above criticism has been to argue that the removal of various agriculture-related controls, including subsidies as required by the WTO, will drive up the international prices for agricultural products, thereby benefiting farmers and agro-industry from India who enjoy comparative advantage in these products. Also, due to international competition, Indian agricultural farms will be forced to upgrade their technological capability and become competitive. Because of higher agricultural prices along with higher profit opportunities and a better economic environment, private investments would flood in, further facilitating growth in agriculture that in turn will produce a demand-driven growth in industry, and so a virtuous cycle would materialize (Gulati, 1998, p. 130). Thus we are told that the integration of the Indian agrarian class sets into the circuits of the global capital will create a new era of growth and prosperity. It is against this background of the NEP-driven transition process that in July 2000, the government of India introduced a new national agricultural policy (NAP) which telescopes the fourth stage of commercialization of the government of India document.

The new NAP aims to achieve a 4 percent per annum growth rate in the agricultural sector and integrate India into the global order. While Indian agriculture has slowly but surely been moving towards an integration with the circuits of global capital, the NAP actively seeks to direct the transition of Indian agriculture with the help of the following:

> Indian agriculture is characterized by pre-dominance of small and marginal farmers. Institutional reforms will be so pursued as to channelize their energies for achieving greater productivity and production. The approach to rural development and land reforms will focus on the following areas:

1. Consolidation of holdings all over the country on the pattern of north-western states;
2. Redistribution of ceiling surplus lands and waste lands among the landless farmers, unemployed youth with initial start up capital;
3. Tenancy reforms to recognize the rights of the tenants and share croppers;
4. Development of lease markets for increasing the size of the holdings by making legal provisions for giving private lands on lease for cultivation and agri business;
5. Updating and improvement of land records, computerization and issue of land passbooks to the farmers; and
6. Recognition of women's rights on land. (Government of India, 2000–01, pp. 122)

We will consider the above policy recommendations from a class perspective and try to reveal exactly the ongoing and possible impact of these recommendations on the transition of Indian agriculture. In this context, we argue that point 2 is moot, points 3 and 6 are difficult to implement and point 5 open to manipulation. Points 1 and 4 are however serious interventions.

Point 2 is moot because there is hardly any cultivable land left to be distributed. Paradoxically this is accepted by no less than the Ministry of Finance, another important department of the Government of India, which says that:

> The country has thus reached a plateau in so far as the area devoted to foodgrains production is concerned. Any increase in foodgrains production in the country has therefore, to come through increase in productivity. (Government of India, 2000–01, p. 153)

Not only is the option of redistribution of land limited, but the average holding of land is under further pressure due to growing population, the breakdown of the joint family system, the decline of handicrafts and village industries which had previously absorbed a large segment of non-agricultural artisans, the laws of inheritance which say that all sons and daughters are entitled to equal shares of the ancestral property, and finally the rural indebtedness and indigenous moneylenders who by appropriating land help deepen the process of fragmentation.

Point 3 is simply difficult to implement under the existing socio-economic scenario. The problem of tenants *vis-à-vis* the landlords was first recognized after independence and a tenancy reform was enacted that instituted three measures: (1) regulation of rent, (2) security of tenure, and (3) conferment of ownership rights on tenants. However the economic aspect of tenancy was constituted by political and cultural processes that meant a historic alliance in India between the capitalists and the rural power brokers (landlords, moneylenders and so on) through the medium of the state, and also that the rural power balance would not be disturbed (see Chakrabarti and Cullenberg, 2003). With the balance of political power still left intact, the fate of the tenancy reform can be anticipated except for a few other places including West Bengal and Kerala that saw interventions through Communist movements. This is the reason why tenancy reform is still on the agenda of the NAP. But if the reasons for the failure of the old tenancy reforms are not addressed, then it is not at all clear as to why and how any new tenancy reform will be successful.

Point 6 pertains to gender rights. Innumerable studies have pointed to the deplorable state of gender relations in agrarian India. The dominated and exploited position of women is critical to the existing reproduction of agrarian society, including its economic reproduction. The question of women's rights is not simply a matter of legal justice as the NAP suggests, but pertains to an ethical position concerning gender relations in India's agrarian society. Establishing the rights of women preliminarily and primarily calls for overturning patriarchal relationships that to begin with deny women rights, including rights over land. This entails attacking the social fabric of the existing agrarian Indian society, hardly something the NAP or its policy-makers have in mind. To highlight this lacuna, assume that the rights of women over land are legally established. Given the existing social position of women in agrarian society, one can imagine a host of different outcomes. While women will legally own the land, following the social right guaranteed by cultural processes the man of the household or alternatively some male relatives might appropriate the surplus and exploit the women. Thus the fruits of land and labor will remain with the man even if the property lies with the women. This manner of appropriation in turn constitutes and solidifies further the gender processes that is tilted against women, which means that one needs to address the issue of appropriation in order to produce a beneficial and guaranteed change in gender relations. Take another possibility. Since leasing is to be made legal under the NAP, the socially weaker position of the woman may compel her to lease out to other farmers who are not women. This she may do because she is being coerced to do so, or her class enterprise has run into a state of crisis, or she may have fallen into debt, or she may not have the capacity to cultivate, and so on. All in all, the rights of women over land cannot be separated from the question of rights of women within the agrarian society, something which the NAP does not recognize.

Point 5 pertains to written documents and records, including that over land. With half of the rural population illiterate and the grip of existing power brokers strongly entrenched, one can imagine the space for manipulation. In fact, attempts at recordation are not new but, as even the different organs of the government of India admit, these have failed due to their effective manipulation in favor of the existing power brokers. Again, without fundamental change in the agrarian structure, the question remains: why should what failed then succeed now?

The only substantial points are 1 and 4. These complement one another and constitute the relevant institutional reforms that are designed to solve the problem of small and marginal lands and those of stagnating production and productivity. Consolidation of land in the North West pattern will see the emergence of large farms and hence the application of a capital-intensive form of production enabling an increase in production and productivity. This would allow India to face what the NAP calls the 'challenges arising out of economic liberalization and globalization' (Government of India, 2000–2001, p. 169) and the desired growth rate in excess of 4 percent.

Elsewhere in the NAP, agriculturalists are exhorted to encourage contract farming and land leasing arrangements to allow accelerated technology transfer, capital inflows and assured markets for crop production, especially oilseeds, cotton and horticultural crops. Lease markets will be developed for increasing the size of holdings, and legal provisions will be made for giving private land in lease for cultivation and agro-business

With average land holdings less than 2 hectares and worked upon by mostly non-capitalist enterprises using labor-intensive technologies that have low productivity, the goal of the Indian policy-makers is itself a technical problem. Moreover with a large segment of such non-capitalist, small-size production systems driven not by profit but simply by basic needs, the goal of such farmers and the goal of the policy-makers do not match. While small and marginal lands are means to achieve the basic needs for these farmers, the policy-makers see the small and marginal lands as part of the problem in achieving the projected growth and meeting the challenges of liberalization and globalization. To account for this problem, the clear policy for consolidating land and its leasing is designed to increase the size of land, and pass it into the hands of enterprises that invariably in this case would be capitalist enterprises, and in a globalized terrain, ideally global capitalist enterprises.

The other interesting case is the leasing of land for agri-business. We are already seeing the branching out of foreign-based MNCs such as Pepsico, Cargill and so on, as well as local-based MNCs. These are essentially enterprises which enter with considerable financial and market power. One can visualize different patterns emerging. For example these global capitalist enterprises could lease the land themselves, cultivate with wage laborers and sell the produce, domestically and abroad. Or local farmers with consolidated land could, using wage laborers, cultivate, say, mangos, using wage laborers that then would be sold to MNCs like Pepsico, which would create processed food with them. Thus the local class enterprise and Pepsico global class enterprise would become vertically integrated.

This local class enterprise could be a capitalist one or could be one of a number of non-capitalist class enterprises, including so-called family-based peasant class enterprises whereby the head of the family – typically a male member – appropriates the surplus produce. Feudal, communal, ancient and slave types of agricultural class sets (using bonded labor) could now be forced into a process of transition, by either becoming commodity producers accessing domestic as well as export markets or to sell the produce to MNCs like Pepsico for the purpose of food processing, or by leasing out land, preferably to the global capitalist enterprises. Overall, after the NAP these various class sets would be facing severe pressure to undergo a change in their class structure, thereby providing a different meaning to the Indian class configuration and of the transition of its society.

What about the input market, that is, the linkage of agriculture to industry? While farm machineries needed for mechanization provide the usual linkages, what is especially significant in the NAP is the use of biotechnology including 'bio-mass, organic and inorganic fertilizers, and controlled use of agro chemicals through integrated nutrients and pest management (INM and IPM)' (Government of India, 2000–2001, p. 169). Notwithstanding the furious debate on its effect on land, biodiversity and basic needs of small and marginal farmers, MNCs such as Hindustan Lever, Cargill, Seedtech International, HI-Bred International, Sandoz, Monsanto and so on have already entered the seed market which normally also involves the sale of fertilizers and pesticides. With the government determined to cut down on its fertilizer subsidies, the changing pattern of inputs in Indian agriculture is an ongoing process. The replacement of organic inputs by marketable inputs produced by industry points to an ongoing and yet deepening process of commercialization of Indian agriculture, and one which small and marginal farmers can hardly sustain.

All these different possibilities analyzed from a class perspective tell us that not only is the Indian agrarian economy disaggregated into multifaceted class sets, but also that the individuals are classified as occupying multiple class and non-class processes by virtue of their personification of class processes. The NAP with its clear vision of trying to achieve a commercialized agriculture is bent on transforming the Indian agrarian society into a homogenous space characterized by capitalist class sets, preferably of a globally capitalist type for commercial production in the domestic and global market and sensitive to instruments of productivity. It is seeking a transformation of agrarian discourse from basic need to profit and growth. Non-capitalist independent, feudal, local capitalist and communal-type agrarian class sets are being reconfigured into large capitalist enterprises fit to compete in the materializing global order. Alternatively, like the decentralized home system that forms the world of informal sectors, they are reconstrued as the abundant repository of the providers of food or land (through leasing) which the capitalist enterprises as well as the subsumed enterprises such as trading or merchant enterprises can then use to garner high profit for certain subsumed classes. Or, given the vast ensemble of non-capitalist existence that thrives in Indian agrarian society, we will end up perhaps, as in the urban areas, creating super-enclaves of global capital. What happens to the large population living with basic needs in the rural areas, large numbers of whom under the NAP are definitely going to be impoverished and dislocated as a result of this process of consolidation of land and commercialization, is quite another matter.

TRANSITION IN RURAL KENYA

The question of rural transition and globalization in modern Kenya is an old one, dating back at least to the turn of the twentieth century. After completion of the Ugandan railroad at the beginning of twentieth century, the colonial government began reforming Kenyan agriculture with the introduction of cash crops and settler farming. The Ugandan railroad ran through the heart of Kenya's richest agricultural district. The aim of the government was to create capitalist farmers (initially both African and European) who would be linked to the global markets through the railroad and the port of Mombasa. In creating capitalist farmers the government expected that the colony would be able to pay for its own administration without recourse to funds from the home country. The initial stages may be interpreted as having mixed success. African cash crop farmers, while having smaller holdings than European settlers, prospered in the period that accompanied a worldwide boom in the prices of primary goods from the late 1910s through the 1920s. European settlers, while profitable, found it hard going. This was primarily due to their lack of skill in tropical agriculture. As long as Africans had equal opportunity to grow and sell their own crops there was little incentive for African farmers to work on European farms. To deal with this situation a series of government acts on native labor, taxation, the selling of cash crops and land were enacted in the 1920s. These laws limited or banned African participation in the cash crop market, limited access to land, introduced the Passbook system and forced all Africans to pay taxes in colonial currency. The impact of this was the creation of a labor force for both the capitalist agricultural sector and the nascent trade and rudimentary manufacturing sectors in the urban parts of the economy.

However unlike the classical transformation of agrarian society as described by Marx in *Capital*, there was not a complete transformation of rural African households to either small farmer 'peasant' households or worker households in Kenya. Due to the limited employment possibilities and the need to control the movements of African populations for political reasons, what emerged was a hybrid system in which African rural households had individuals who participated in one or more different types of productive and class activities. To supply labor to the capitalist sector, often the head of household would work in a capitalist enterprise (farm or firm) while other members engaged in other activities such as subsistence farming, or small-scale artisanship, or the gathering of wild products.

The stress and inequalities caused by this system, plus lessons learned from the Second World War and the promotion of the Atlantic Charter led to the development of the post-Second World War independence movement at the center of which was the Kenya Land and Freedom Army. Part of the colonial government response to the tensions was the Swynnerton Plan, which attempted to create an African capitalist farmer class who would be vested in the system, and whose success would be an example to the other Africans. The fundamentals of the Swynnerton Plan, which included consolidation of holdings and a shift to an Anglo-Saxon private property regime, along with some redistribution of land to Africans, became part of the first independent government's agricultural policy.

The results of this attempt at transition have been debated within Africanist circles over the last 30 years and are often referred to as the Nairobi debates. Elsewhere we (Gĩthĩnji 2000, Gĩthĩnji and Cullenberg, 2003) have engaged in this debate and pointed out the shortcomings of these approaches, namely the use of a teleological view of history and transition which employs the broad conceptual categories of undifferentiated peasants, workers and capitalists.

In this section of the chapter we apply the theoretical work of Cullenberg and Chakrabarti and our earlier empirical work to address questions that Griffin (1974, 1976) has long had an interest in, namely the heterogeneity of the rural population, the relationship of class to poverty, the issue of land concentration and inequality, and the extent to which there exists sufficient common interest to allow for political organization among the rural poor.

We have in previous work (Gĩthĩnji 2000, Gĩthĩnji and Cullenberg, 2003) established an alternative picture of the Kenyan countryside using methodology developed by Cullenberg (1992). Due to the limitations of the data we use, and in order to replicate the theoretical categories of Chakrabarti and Cullenberg (2001) we have to make a number of assumptions in our class categorizations. Our data set contains information on form of payment, that is, wage versus non-wage, job classification including industrial sector of activity, and whether one works on a family farm or not, and whether one heads an enterprise and employs people. In our first round of estimations we focus on individuals and their primary occupations.

We begin by establishing the form of payment that people receive. This is fairly simple as we have information on wage and non-wage income. All individuals reporting wage earning are classified as wageworkers, whereas those receiving non-wage payments are classified as such. A large number of individuals however do not report earnings but report an industrial sector and the time spent working. Because in rural Kenya one would expect the vast majority of the population to work on family farms or enterprises, we classify individuals who report neither wages nor non-wage income and are family farm workers as recipients of non-wage income. We also assume that the form of output distribution for them is non-commodity as most of their output is in the form of produce from subsistence farms.

We assume the form of surplus labor appropriation for this group to be shared.[6] For our purposes here household production is an example of a communal class set.[7] For individuals who report activity in other sectors of production but no wage income, we assume since these are all commodity-producing sectors that they are remunerated by non-wage earnings and the output is distributed as a commodity. Where these individuals do not employ any other labor we classify them as independent appropriators of the surplus labor performed. Where they do employ labor we classify them as participating in an exploitative process. We also classify all other individuals who receive a wage as participants in the exploitative class process. These individuals are also classified as being in a process where the output is distributed as a commodity. Individuals who do not report any income we classify as being in one of the processes where the output is distributed as a non-commodity.

In the Kenyan case the following would be examples of processes to be found among the various class sets (see Table 12.2). Individual appropriation of all surplus would be composed of those engaged in artisanal production such as wood carving, charcoal production and repair shops who distribute their output as a commodity These would be classified in set 3. The other major independent producers include individuals dependent on natural resource production such as honey collecting, hunting and the collection of other forest products who may

Table 12.2 Percentage of individuals and households in rural Kenya by class set

Class sets	Surplus labor appropriation	Labor remuneration	Output distribution	% of individuals	% of households
Independent					
1	A	W	C	0	0
2	A	W	NC	0	0
3	A	NW	C	6.78	21.51
4	A	NW	NC	10.8	29.07
Exploitative					
5	N	W	C	36.01	55.16
6	N	W	NC	0	0
7	N	NW	C	3.15	10.57
8	N	NW	NC	0.23	0.67
Communal					
9	S	W	C	0.35	4.33
10	S	W	NC	0	0
11	S	NW	C	17.49	55.87
12	S	NW	NC	25.09	25.44

Source: Gĩthĩnji and Cullenberg (2003).

exchange their production for other goods or use it to supplement farm production. The 'exploitative' group of class sets has the most varied forms of organization. Class set 5 or 7 for example could include the typical capitalist firm employing wage labor and selling output as a commodity, a government cooperative or farm, either a cash crop farm or cooperative that employs labor. In class set 8 one may find various forms of sharecropping arrangements. The 'communal' class sets in the Kenyan case would be dominated by household production and artisanal cooperatives.

Our basic results from this new description of the rural household were:

1. We confirmed that rural households were indeed heterogeneous. Of the 12 categories seven had populations that amounted to at least 4 percent of the total number of households.
2. Households had individuals who participated in different class sets. In all instances there was a larger number of households represented than individuals, meaning that individuals in any class set are spread out amongst a large number of households. This was confirmed by an actual count of the number of class sets found within each household (see Table 12.3). Over 60 per cent of all households had individuals engaged in more than one class set, and indeed a small number of households have individuals participating in as many as six or seven class sets.
3. Of specific interest to the description of rural Kenyans we found that households that engage in the independent class set were a substantial part of the population. While only a little over 17 percent of the population participated in these processes they were found in 43 percent of the households (see Table 12.4). This means that close to half of all rural households have an individual engaged in independent class sets. Any attempt to politically organize rural Kenyans would need to take this portion of the population into account. Because of the entry point used by previous students of the Kenyan countryside, these are activities that have been ignored in the attempts to describe a countryside inhabited by an undifferentiated peasantry, workers and capitalists.

Table 12.3 Total number of class sets with rural Kenyan households

Total number of class processes occurring within a household	% of households
1	37.0
2	34.1
3	17.4
More than 3	9.5

Table 12.4 Percentage of individuals and households in rural Kenya by class set categories

Class sets	% of individuals	% of households
Independent	17.58	43.00
Exploitative	39.39	60.24
Communal	42.93	72.54

Source: Gĩthĩnji and Cullenberg (2003).

We also established that rather than being separate households, there was a huge overlap between households that were in exploitative processes, and those in communal processes. In a sense we did not have as one might expect large numbers of separate workers, as peasant or capitalist households, but a mix of combinations of people involved in the different class processes.

Our findings allow us to comment on one of Griffin's concerns – that is, the possibility of organizing around common interests. The heterogeneity of households suggests that organizing around class interests is complicated by the fact that individuals reside in households that are not homogeneous. The extent that class interests of individuals within households may be antagonistic will therefore limit organization based purely on specific class interests. We would argue that this is one of the reasons why organizations on the left that have conceived the countryside in an orthodox manner – assuming the existence of an undifferentiated peasantry, workers and capitalists – have had a hard time organizing rural populations. The problem being that in organizing around class as a noun, one is likely to suggest options that are amenable to individuals within those class processes in a household, but antagonistic to others in the same household. Organizations such as Partido Trabaja have been successful with rural voters precisely because they have eschewed a narrow class (as a noun)-based organizing.

Griffin (1974, 1976), as we have noted earlier, is interested in the degree of inequality and the relationship of inequality to the social structure. Presented in Table 12.5 are calculations of household and per capita income as well as average size of land holdings across different class sets.

Our findings again point to the complexity of the rural countryside. As one would find in most orthodox development literature, households that are engaged as exploiters in the capitalist class process earn the highest household income easily doubling the average rural figure of 28 000 Kenyan shillings. Households on the other end of the exploitative process earn close to the average. While households that participate in the exploitative process via contribution of wage labor have incomes close to the average households, those that are in the inde-

Table 12.5 *Income and farm size by class set in rural Kenya*

Class sets	Surplus labor appropriation	Labor remuneration	Output distribution	% of individuals	% of households	Average household income (KShs)	Per capita income (KShs)	Average farm size (acres)
Independent								
1	A	W	C	0	0	–	–	–
2	A	W	NC	0	0	–	–	–
3	A	NW	C	6.78	21.51	29408	5749	6.2
4	A	NW	NC	10.8	29.07	25859	4734	7.5
Exploitative								
5	N	W	C	36.01	55.16	28054	5316	6.9
6	N	W	NC	0	0	–	–	–
7	N	NW	C	3.15	10.57	63619	10750	8.1
8	N	NW	NC	0.23	0.67	33672	7393	19
Communal								
9	S	W	C	0.35	4.33	28426	5837	4.3
10	S	W	NC	0	0	–	–	–
11	S	NW	C	17.49	55.87	29490	5760	6.3
12	S	NW	NC	25.09	25.44	30293	5549	7.9

Source: Gîthînji and Cullenberg (2003).

pendent set 4 have the lowest average income. Past descriptions of rural Kenya have again ignored this fact. Class sets 11 and 12 – communal class sets – while not rich have average household incomes that are slightly above that of both the independent producers and the worker households.

Average incomes however are heavily dependent on distribution and obscure many salient facts. In Table 12.6 we present calculations of the head count ratio and the poverty gap as a way to further explore the relationship between class sets and well-being. The head count ratio for our population is 62 per cent, while our poverty gap is 60 per cent. Our last column in the table is the difference between the poverty gap of all poor households not in the specific class set we are examining, and that of the set we are examining. This column tells us by what average percentage of the poverty line the per capita average income of the poor not in our reference class set would have to change to be equal to the average income of the poor in our reference class set. For example say the poverty gap of class set 1 was 54 per cent and the poverty gap of all the poor not in class set 1 was 60 per cent; our third column would be the difference which is 6 per cent. This would mean that that the average income of the all the poor not in class set 1 would have to go up by 6 per cent of the poverty line in order for class set 1 to have the same poverty gap as the rest of the population of the poor. Where the number is positive, the average poor household in the reference set has an income that is above that of poor households outside the reference set, and vice versa when negative.

By the head count measure the class sets with the most poverty in actual numbers are the communal class sets 11 and 12, the exploitative set 5 and two independent sets 3 and 4. What is clear from this basic result is that poverty is spread out fairly evenly across the different class sets. An interesting fact is that despite having incomes that are twice the nearest group, class set 7, which is made up of households that employ wage labor, has fairly high levels of poverty as denoted by the head count figure of 41 per cent.

The poverty gap illustrates a number of interesting things that have hitherto been ignored in the literature. The first is that the poor among the worker households (set 5) do not suffer from the deepest poverty. In fact their depth of poverty is about the same as that of their employers (set 7). In both of these groups households are an average of 18 percent closer to the poverty line than all other poor households. For communal households the fact that average incomes are relatively high and the measures of poverty are also relatively high suggests that contrary to popular opinion households are fairly unequal within this group. A similar case holds for capitalist households (class set 7) where you have extremely high income and substantial amounts of poverty.

Beyond our discussions of poverty, what is clear from our disaggregation is that with the exception of the capitalist households (class set 7) and the independent class set 4, most average incomes are around the average rural income.

Table 12.6 Head count and poverty gap measure by class sets in rural Kenya

Class sets	Surplus labor appropriation	Labor remuneration	Output distribution	% of households	Head count (%)	Poverty gap (%)	Poverty gap of all poor minus poverty gap of class set
Independent							
1	A	W	C	0	–	–	
2	A	W	NC	0	–	–	
3	A	NW	C	21.51	55	52	8
4	A	NW	NC	29.07	64	54	6
Exploitative							
5	N	W	C	55.16	53	51	18
6	N	W	NC	0	–	–	–
7	N	NW	C	10.57	41	51	18
8	N	NW	NC	0.67	85	93	–33
Communal							
9	S	W	C	4.33	50	45	11
10	S	W	NC	0	–	–	–
11	S	NW	C	55.87	65	58	2
12	S	NW	NC	25.44	59	60	0

It suggests that as one would expect, the diversification of class processes within a household has an equalizing impact across households. This claim is buttressed by an examination of households that specialize in just one class set. We find that these households on average have an income substantially below the rural average. This surprisingly includes households that are purely capitalist exploiters. The average household income for the households that specialize ran from 18 309 Kenya shillings for households solely engaged in communal processes, to 25 043 Kenya shillings for households engaged in exploitative capitalist processes. The average for the non-specialist households is 32 051 Kenya shillings. These households (non-specialist) also tend to have larger land holdings than the specialist households.

How does one explain this diversification? We think that this diversification is a result of the stress undergone by households during transition periods. Due to the inherent risk of specializing in a context of low levels of capital and savings, households opt for diversification. This diversification means that the impacts of process such as globalizations are sometimes muted or amplified depending on the degree of diversification and the relation of each class process and industrial sector to the global markets.

An example of a group that may be differentially impacted by global markets are female-headed households, whose income is a product of both class and the non-class processes associated with differentiation based on sex. As we noted earlier, the Kenyan colonial experience and particularly the modernization of agriculture are not only part of a transition process but part of the globalization process. The modernization of Kenyan agriculture (which is analogous to the green revolution – though more scientifically rudimentary) was associated with the construction of the Uganda railway and the introduction of cash crops, and a nascent industrial sector. The organization of labor that came out of this social formation depended, as we noted earlier, on migrant male labor that worked within the capitalist process but resided away from their own households. This arrangement which remained after independence has resulted in a high number of female-headed households in Kenya specifically, and more generally in Africa. We now briefly turn our attention to these households.

Slightly over 30 per cent of Kenyan rural households are female-headed. Of this group approximately 50 percent are *de jure* female-headed households in that they are the result of divorce or death of a husband, or are single female-headed households. The other 50 percent are *de facto* female-headed in that they are part of a married household in which the husband's place of residence is at his place of work, which is not in the same location as where his family lives.

An examination of the class processes that these households participate in suggests that these households are internally not as diversified as other households (see Table 12.7).

Table 12.7 Total number of class sets with rural Kenyan female-headed households

Total number of class processes occurring within a household	% of households
1	50.0
2	28.8
3	13.3
More than 3	7.4

It is immediately clear that female-headed households are not as diversified as male-headed. For female-headed households only 50 percent have more than one class set within a household as compared to the 63 percent for all rural (male and female) households.

Female-headed households, apart from being less diverse, are also more likely to be found in the class sets with greatest poverty, namely class sets 11 and 12, and much less likely to be found in class set 5.

In general the class sets that they participate in and the lack of diversification are consistent with the lower incomes that these households receive. In Table 12.8 we present the average incomes plus the ratio to male-headed households. The pattern of the distribution of income remains very similar to that found in the general population, with one clear exception. Whereas in the general population the lowest income class sets are class set 5, which contains wage workers, and class set 4, which contains individuals participating in the dependent class process, among female-headed households the lowest average incomes are among class set 12, a communal set. Because it is often assumed that the *de facto* female-headed households have a male earning high income in the modern sector, it is thought that these households would employ more wage labor. The assumption is that the missing male would have an income high enough to obtain a replacement on the farm given the gap between pay in the modern sector and the rural sector. This would suggest that there would be higher participation by women in class set 7. However our examination of the participation in different class sets as pointed out earlier suggests that female-headed households engage in the different class sets in roughly the same proportion as does the general population. In fact in class set 7 the percentage of female households is the same as that found in the overall population. This is important to note as it means that these households might be stressed directly by the two processes of globalization and transition in a manner different from other households. Because participants in the modern sector are more connected to global markets and the resulting competition, as globalization proceeds, companies have at-

Table 12.8 Income and farm size for female-headed households by class set in rural Kenya

Class sets	Surplus labor appropriation	Labor remuneration	Output distribution	% of households in total population	% of female headed households	Average household income (KShs) (ratio to male %)	Per capita income (KShs) (ratio to male %)	Average farm size (acres) (ratio to male %)
Independent								
1	A	W	C	0	–	–	–	–
2	A	W	NC	0	–	–	–	–
3	A	NW	C	21.51	28	19 908 (60)	4 241 (67)	4.8 (70)
4	A	NW	NC	29.07	25	19 500 (70)	3 657 (71)	6 (81)
Exploitative								
5	N	W	C	55.16	22	18 945 (62)	3 721 (65)	6.2 (87)
6	N	W	NC	0	–	–	–	–
7	N	NW	C	10.57	30	32 286 (42)	6 335 (50)	7.4 (87)
8	N	NW	NC	0.67	60	9 354 (13)	1 910 (12)	17 (340)
Communal								
9	S	W	C	4.33	22	12 006 (36)	2 828 (42)	3.8 (95)
10	S	W	NC	0	–	–	–	–
11	S	NW	C	55.87	39	19 989 (56)	4 382 (66)	5.1 (74)
12	S	NW	NC	25.44	22	17 467 (51)	3 634 (60)	6.9 (60)

Source: Gîthînji and Cullenberg (2003).

tempted to keep costs low by keeping their wages low. Lower wages for the male migrant who in the Kenyan case is likely to be employed in this sector also affects the rural household by the possible fall in the amount of remittances sent back to the rural household.

In the last few pages we have attempted to show how a different kind of Marxian class analysis can illuminate different aspects of transition in a rural economy. We have shown that contrary to more orthodox approaches, and more consistent with Griffin's approach, the countryside is made up of households that are varied in terms of participation in class sets and which individually have participants in different class sets. We have argued that this state of affairs leads to possibly antagonistic class positions within households, making organizing the rural population a more complex undertaking than is hitherto imagined in the orthodox literature. We have also shown how complicated the relationship is between the distribution of income and the class sets. Rather than having an extreme polarization across class sets we find that there is often as much if not more polarization within households participating in different class sets. Our findings also highlight the independent class set, a portion of the population that has been ignored in the Kenyan literature on rural transition. Finally our approach allows us to examine the interaction of class processes and a non-class process, namely gender, and the possible impact of globalization on female-headed households.

CONCLUSION

> The diversity of tenure and class relationships we have described above seems to be common in many countries of monsoon Asia. We shall argue below, however, that as a result of the technical changes that are presently occurring in several tropical regions the tenure system will tend to become simplified and class relationships will tend to become polarized. Landowners will increasingly become owner-operators or agro-businessmen and the peasantry will tend to be reduced to the status of agricultural workers who no longer perform any entrepreneurial functions. (Griffin, 1974, p. 25)

Thus, despite the diversity of class relationships, Griffin argued that the impact of the green revolution would eventually simplify class relationships, an argument that harkens back to Marx and Engels's claim in the *Communist Manifesto* that class struggle in capitalism was increasingly a struggle between two great classes, the proletariat and the bourgeoisie. Today commentators on globalization have made the same claim about the potential impact of globalization. In contrast however, our analyses of India and Kenya suggest that the multiplicity of class sets is not disappearing even though there may be an increased polarization of other dimensions such as income. History in our approach does not unfold rapidly and teleologically as is often suggested by students of the transition process, but rather in a slow, complex wandering way. In many ways the call made by Amilcar Cabral to re-examine the nature of class in developing countries is particularly apt:

> Those who assert – and in our view rightly – that the motive force of history is the class struggle, would certainly agree to re-examining this assertion to make it more precise and give it wider application, if they had a deeper knowledge of the essential characteristics of some of the colonized peoples (dominated by imperialism). In fact, in the general evolution of mankind and each of the peoples in the human groups of which it is composed, classes appear neither as a generalized and simultaneous phenomenon throughout all these groups, nor as a finished, perfect and spontaneous whole. (Cabral 1979)

NOTES

1. Marxist theory understands class not as a homogenous group of social actors (that is, as a noun) but as a process (that is, as an adjective). Class process comprises of the performance, appropriation, distribution and receipt of surplus labor. For convenience, the process of performance and appropriation of surplus labor is defined as fundamental class process (FCP), and its distribution and receipt as subsumed class process (SCP). FCP and SCP exist as overdetermined. Importantly for our purpose in this chapter, SCP provides various conditions of existence for FCP to materialize against which the authorities running the enterprise provide subsumed class payments to the holders of these subsumed class processes. Indeed what are subsumed class payments are for the holder subsumed class revenues. For example in a capitalist enterprise, merchants (trading companies), moneylenders (banks), the state, and managers among others, provide various conditions of existence by activating processes that enable the procreation of the performance and appropriation of surplus labor. They are paid against these activities with payments shown as subsumed class revenues in their account book.
2. The specification of these class sets does not directly include processes of property, power or income distribution. These are non-class processes whose specific constitution of a class set creates a further differentiation in terms of a multiplicity of uniquely constituted class structures.
3. The concept of class sets is similar to the concept of fundamental class process first introduced by Resnick and Wolff (1987) insofar as we differentiate class sets by the manner in which surplus labor is appropriated. The difference from Resnick and Wolff is in terms of the exact taxonomies being put forward. The class sets approach allows a finer differentiation of distinct modes of appropriation than does the concept of class process as developed by Resnick and Wolff.
4. The relationship between class process, class enterprise and class set is close. Class set which contains the aspect of appropriation of surplus labor (an element of FCP) definitionally excludes but stands overdetermined by performance of surplus labor as well as the SCP, that is, the distribution and receipt of the appropriated surplus labor. Class enterprise, on the other hand, encompasses all these class processes as well as other non-class processes that belong to an enterprise which is involved in class activities. By virtue of its definitional root in exploitation, class set is used to differentiate the exploitative and non-exploitative class processes into various types that could be located and named. Thus every class enterprise belongs to a class set by virtue of the manner of appropriation (exploitative, non-exploitative or self-exploitative). These enterprises are typically grouped into industry, agriculture, household and state. In this context, Resnick and Wolff (2001) ask us to rethink the existence of global enterprise from a class

standpoint. A global capitalist agriculture enterprise in India (IN), for example, would have the following class equation to contend with:

$$\Sigma SV_i^{IN} + \Sigma SSCR_i^{IN} + \Sigma NCR_i^{IN} = \Sigma SSCP_{IN}^k + \Sigma X_{IN}^k + \Sigma Y_{IN}^k \quad \text{(a)}$$

where, SV = Surplus value produced and appropriated by the enterprise;

$\Sigma SSCR$ = Subsumed class revenue;
ΣNCR = Non-class revenue;
$\Sigma SSCP$ = Sum of subsumed class payments;
ΣX = Sum of payments made to secure SSCR;
ΣY = Sum of payments made to secure NCR.

The left-hand side of equation (a) represents the revenue side of the enterprise while the right-hand side is the expenditure required to reproduce the conditions of existence of the components in the revenue side. $\Sigma SSCP$ reflect subsumed class payments made by the enterprise to ensure the flow of SV. Indeed, much of the Marxian tradition focuses only on this truncated version of the class analytic equation. $\Sigma SSCR$ captures the subsumed class revenues of the enterprise, that is, any revenue it generates from its occupation of subsumed class positions with respect to other firms. It might include returns such as dividends, ground rents, merchant fees and so on. Reproduction of these subsumed revenue class positions, in turn, requires expenditure or payments for those social positions which will ensure the reproduction of $\Sigma SSCR$. Such payments are gathered around ΣX. Similarly, ΣNCR stands for all non-class revenues earned by the enterprise, such as return on loans advanced to productive laborers. ΣY stands for the expenditure or payments required to reproduce the conditions of existence of ΣNCR. In order to bring out the global dimension of an enterprise, we use the subscript i in the left-hand side to index the various global locations from where the revenues are drawn and the superscript k in the right-hand side as capturing the global locations of expenditure. If the global locations i and j are in fact reduced to one specific country or region, that is, $i = j$, then that enterprise is a local or national enterprise and not a global enterprise. From a class perspective, an enterprise or class structure is a complex body that encompasses a wide array of variegated activities – class (fundamental and subsumed) and non-class – under the two headings of revenue and expenditure. The stocks and flows encapsulated under 'revenue' and 'expenditure' together (over)determine the span and function of the enterprise.

5. The exact number of delineated class sets will depend on the details, purpose and context of a particular analysis. There is no pre-given number which is always and everywhere correct. Therefore if one considers other relations to appropriation such as corvee labor or profit-sharing schemes, the class sets would be further differentiated. This only goes to show the depth of the micro or disaggregated nature of class-based society. This is in direct contrast to the orthodox Marxian concept of social totality signified by a specific, uniform mode of production.
6. While one can have exploitation within a family farm, we assume that it is shared because at this point we do not have information on how the proceeds are actually divided. This assumption is consistent with most narrative descriptions of the Kenyan family farm.
7. We are well aware that household production may be exploitative, say in a patriarchal household. At this point we have no way of differentiating between households in which production is exploitative and those that are not and we assume for simplification that they are not.

BIBLIOGRAPHY

Babu, Mohammed (1981), *African Socialism or Socialist Africa?*, London: Zed Books.
Cabral, Amilcar (1979), 'The weapon of theory', in *Unity and Struggle*, New York: Monthly Review Press.

Chakrabarti, Anjan and Stephen Cullenberg (2001), 'Transition and development in India: a decentered Marxist approach', in Kathie Gibson et al. (eds), *Class: The Last Post-modern Frontier*.
Chakrabarti, Anjan and Stephen Cullenberg (2003), *Transition and Development in India*, New York: Routledge.
Chege, Michael (1987), 'The political economy of agrarian change in central Kenya', in M. Schatzberg (ed.), *Political Economy of Kenya*, New York: Praeger.
Cowen, Michael (1981), 'The agrarian problem', *Review of African Political Economy*, **20**, 57–73.
Cullenberg, Stephen (1992), 'Socialism's burden: toward a "thin" definition of socialism', *Rethinking Marxism*, **5** (2), pp. 64–83.
de Janvry, Alain (1981), *The Agrarian Question and Reformism in Latin America*, Baltimore, MD: Johns Hopkins University Press.
Dobb, Maurice (1964), *Studies in the Development of Capitalism*, New York: International Publishers Company.
Gĩthĩnji, Mwangi wa (2000), *Ten Millionaires and Ten Million Beggars*, Aldershot: Ashgate Publishing.
Gĩthĩnji, Mwangi wa and Stephen Cullenberg (2003), 'Deconstructing the peasantry: class and development in rural Kenya', *Review of Critical Sociology*, **29** (1), 67–88.
Government of India (2000–01), *National Agricultural Policy*, Indian Department of Agriculture and Cooperation annual report, Government of India publications.
Griffin, Keith B. (1974), *The Political Economy of Agrarian Change*, Cambridge, MA: Harvard University Press.
Griffin, Keith B. (1976), *Land Concentration and Poverty*, Guildford: Mcmillan.
Gulati, A. (1998), 'Indian agriculture in an open economy: will it prosper?', in I.J. Ahluwalia and I. Little (eds), *India's Economic Reforms and Development: Essays for Manmohan Singh*, Oxford: Oxford University Press.
Hilton, Rodney, et al. (1976), *The Transition From Feudalism to Capitalism*, London: NLB.
Hunt, Diana (1984), *The Impending Crisis in Kenya*, Brookfield, VT: Gower.
Kautsky, Karl (1988), *The Agrarian Question*, two vols, translated by Pete Burgess London: Zwan Publishers.
Kenya Government (1966), *Statistical Abstract*, Nairobi: Government Printers.
Kenya Government, (1976), *Statistical Abstract*, Nairobi: Government Printers.
Kenya Government (1980), *The National Sample Survey and Evaluation Programme 1980/84*, Nairobi: Ministry of Economic Planning and Development.
Kenya Government (1988), *Rural Labour Force Survey, 1988 Survey and Enumerators Manual*, Nairobi: Ministry of Planning and National Development.
Kitching, Gavin (1980), *Class and Economic Change in Kenya*, New Haven, CT: Yale University Press.
Kitching, Gavin (1985), 'Politics, method and evidence in the "Kenya Debate"', in H. Bernstein and B. Campbell (eds), *Contradictions of Accumulation in Africa*, London: Sage Publications.
Lenin, Vladimir I. (1977), *The Development of Capitalism in Russia*, Moscow: Progress Publishers.
Leo, Christopher (1989), *Land and Class in Kenya*, Harare: Nehanda Publishers.
Leys, Colin (1975), *Underdevelopment in Kenya*, Berkeley, CA: University of California Press.
Mao Tse-Tung (1965), *Selected Works, Volume I*, Beijing: Foreign Language Press.
Marx, Karl (1990), *Capital*, volume I, London: Penguin Classics.

Marx, Karl and Frederick Engels (1998), *The Communist Manifesto*, New York: Verso Press.

Ministry of Finance (2001), *Economic Survey, 2000–2001*, Government of India Publication.

Ng'ang'a Mukaru (1981), 'What is happening to the Kenyan peasantry?', *Review of African Political Economy*, **20**, 7–16.

Njonjo, Apollo (1981), 'The Kenya peasantry: a reassessment', *Review of African Political Economy*, **20**, 27–40.

Nyongo, Anyang (1981a) 'The development of a middle peasantry in Nyanza', *Review of African Political Economy*, **20**, 108–20.

Nyongo, Anyang (1981b) 'What "The Friends of the Peasants" are and how they pose the question of the peasantry', *Review of African Political Economy*, **20**, 17–26.

Oman, C. and G. Wignaraja (1991), *The Post War Evolution of Development Thinking*, New York: St. Martin's Press.

Pattanaik, Utsa (ed.) (1990), *Agrarian Relations and Accumulations*, Delhi: Oxford University Press.

Planning Commission (2002), *Report of the Committee on India Vision 2020*, Government of India publication.

Resnick, Stephen A. and Richard D. Wolff (1987), *Knowledge and Class*, Chicago: University of Chicago Press.

Resnick, Stephen A. and Richard D. Wolff (2001), 'Empire and class analysis', *Rethinking Marxism*, **13** (3–4).

Spivak, Gayatri (1999), *A Critique of Post Colonial Reason*, Cambridge, MA: Harvard University Press.

Steenson, Gary (1978), *Karl Kautsky: Marxism in the Classical Years*, Pittsburgh, PA: University of Pittsburgh Press.

Tiffen, Mary, Michael Mortimore and Francis Gichuki (1994), *More People, Less Erosion: Environmental Recovery in Kenya*, New York: John Wiley & Sons.

Wolff, Richard (1974), *The Economics of Colonialism: Britain and Kenya, 1870–1930*, New Haven, CT: Yale University Press.

13. What will become of the welfare state?

Victor D. Lippit

Among the various forms of contemporary capitalism, the 'welfare state' has become most firmly entrenched in continental Europe. The welfare state is based on a broad social consensus favoring relative equality and the assurance of access to the basic requirements for a decent living standard for the entire population. This implies access to health care and sufficient income to provide decent food, housing and other basic requirements. Retirees are assured of adequate pensions, and those who lose income due to unemployment, disability or the death of the main breadwinner are also eligible for regular payments. In addition, in much of Europe, the welfare state implies access to education and child care, and such benefits as parental leave to care for newborns, young children or sick children.

Since the early 1990s, the welfare state has come under increasing challenge. There are a number of reasons for this, ranging from the intensification of internal contradictions within the welfare state itself to demographic changes, medical advances, globalization and technological change. The challenges confronting social democracy or the welfare state threaten to undermine the most humane form of capitalism the world has managed to produce. In addition to the welfare state, the other primary forms are the state-led capitalism of East Asia (for which Japan and South Korea are the primary prototypes, with China beginning to follow a similar path), and the 'harsh' capitalism of the Anglo-American (especially American) variety. Under 'harsh' capitalism, policy tends to be driven by market ideologues. That is, there is broad public acceptance of the idea that people get paid what they are 'worth' (according to the dictates of market forces), and that redistributive taxation undermines fairness (people should be able to retain what they earn) and incentives. The social attitudes supporting harsh, market-driven capitalism in America are reflected in the fact that in 2003 some 46 million people (15.2 percent of the population) were permitted to go without health insurance (*Wall Street Journal*, 1 July 2004, p. D4) and 17.6 percent of children to grow up in poverty (US Census Bureau cited in *Press-Enterprise*, 27 August 2004, p. A1), despite living in the wealthiest country the world has ever seen.

My concern in this chapter is especially to examine the way in which globalization and technological change are undermining the welfare state model of capitalism (they are also undermining state-led capitalism, but that is not my focus here), and tending to make it more akin to its harsh capitalist cousin on the other side of the Atlantic. Besides considering the evidence for the existence of severe pressures, I will turn in the conclusion not to particular policy palliatives, but to consideration of how policy issues might be approached. Addressing the challenge to the welfare state and the issues it raises for public policy are in keeping with a volume organized to honor Keith Griffin's consistently humane concerns and scholarship.

INTERNAL CONTRADICTIONS IN THE WELFARE STATE

The initial impetus for the provision of welfare often begins with the observation that individuals are not, for the most part, responsible for the various calamities to which they are susceptible. If people happen to fall ill or become victims of recessions or accidents, or lose employment as a result of industrial change, there is often limited scope for individuals and families to protect themselves. If people consider themselves part of a national community, they may consider it quite natural to provide for the victims of misfortune. For those societies in which relative equality is a widely held value moreover, or where it is considered unacceptable to allow poverty and misery to exist in a society that provides ample means to eliminate them, it is quite natural to support various forms of public assistance to those who are less fortunate.

Once redistributive welfare policies become established however, people's behavior tends to adapt to the new institutions. In the United States for example, income support for mothers with dependent children was initially motivated, in large part, by the feeling that they should not be punished because the (male) family breadwinner had died or abandoned the family. Over time however it appears that some young women were motivated to have children out of wedlock by the knowledge that they could receive financial support from the state to live in their own apartments if they did so. Thus former Surgeon-General Joycelyn Elders frequently referred to a 1988 survey in which 87 percent of unwed teen mothers in the US said that their babies' births were 'intended' (*Wall Street Journal*, 9 February 1994).

To consider another example, in Sweden there is a tradition of a strong work ethic. It was broadly assumed that those without jobs were largely the victims of circumstance. When laws were created to pay those out of work for days missed due to illness, the incentives to stay out longer than necessary increased greatly. In the early 1990s, Swedish workers were eligible to receive some 60 percent of their basic salaries for the first three days of work missed due to illness, and about 90 percent for subsequent days. Under these conditions, absenteeism among younger workers came to exceed that among older workers by 50 percent (Angresano, 1996, p. 321). By encouraging such adaptive behavior, welfare support tends to become vastly more expensive over time, and to undermine the social consensus that typically underlies the initial legislation. As the assumptions about why people are unable to be self-supporting shift, support for the welfare state erodes. In this way, institutionalized welfare programs tend to bring about changes in behavior that invalidate the initial assumptions upon which the welfare programs were based, an internal contradiction that is widespread in the welfare state. Other factors however are likely to prove still more significant in challenging the welfare state.

DEMOGRAPHIC CHANGE AND MEDICAL ADVANCES

The rising costs of the welfare state are based on much more than adaptive behavior on the part of welfare recipients. If the cost of old-age pensions and public health care, two of the most expensive components of welfare-state spending, is taken into account, then the impact of demographic change and medical advances comes to the fore. With regard to demographic change, the ageing of the populations in the industrialized countries and the decrease in their fertility rates play an especially prominent role. The impact is especially severe since all of these countries have essentially been on a pay-as-you-go retirement program. Under such programs, no real assets are set aside by the state to provide for retirement by those currently in the labor force. Rather, each generation pays taxes (generally payroll taxes) that are then transferred by the government to the existing retirees. When the existing generation of workers has retired, its pension and social security needs are supposed to be met through taxes on the next generation of workers.

The problem for such schemes arises when the ratio of those who are currently employed to those who are retired diminishes dramatically, something that is certain to happen to a greater or lesser extent in the coming decades throughout the industrialized world. In Europe as a whole, there are currently about three workers per retiree; within 30 years there are likely to be 1.5 workers per retiree (*The Economist*, 27 September 2004, p. 15). This implies that for current benefits to be maintained, the payroll taxes devoted to pension support will have to be doubled. Since payroll taxes covering all forms of welfare benefits are already very high (in Germany they are more than 42 percent of gross wages, half each paid by employer and employee), it is questionable whether much higher taxes are feasible. It is not just a matter of whether future employees and employers would be willing to pay them, but the already strong incentives to locate new jobs outside of Germany or other high-tax states would be immensely intensified, and the incentives to replace live workers with automated production would be increased as well. Any loss of jobs these consequences could be expected to bring about would require even higher taxes on those remaining in the labor force.

Pay-as-you-go (PAYG) retirement schemes are inherently unsound, since the most basic accounting principles suggest that if a worker earns a retirement benefit by working in a particular year, funds should be set aside in that same year to fund the eventual benefit (the funds need not be equal to the full benefit, since some return on the funds set aside can be assumed). Indeed in the United States corporations are now required to fund their defined benefit programs – it is only the state that gets away with improper behavior in this respect. When public pensions were initially begun however, there were so many taxpayers and so few beneficiaries that the various countries did not have to face up to the future problems they were creating. When Bismarck introduced the PAYG scheme in Germany in 1889, the retirement age was 70 and the average life expectancy was 48 (*The Economist*, 27 September 2004, p. 70). Similarly, when social security was introduced during the New Deal in the United States (in the 1930s), the ratio of taxpayers to beneficiaries was extremely high. Falling birth rates and rising life expectancies have since changed circumstances rather dramatically.

In the European Union, between 1960 and 1965, the overall birth rate was 2.7 children per woman, higher than the 2.1 required to maintain the size of the population. By 1995, the ratio had fallen to 1.5 children per woman (*The Economist*, 27 September 2004, p. 70). In 2000, the average fertility rate for German women was 1.36 children, higher in the EU only than Spain's 1.25 and Italy's 1.26; these are countries increasingly dominated by 'dinkies' (double-income, no children; *The Economist*, 6 December 2000, p. 47). The problem of declining fertility and eventually population is still more serious in Japan, where 'official demographers now say that Japan's population will peak at 127 million in 2006 and *halve* to 64 million by the end of the century' (*Financial Times*, 20 March 2004, p. W1).

Countries with ageing populations whose retirement is supported by public PAYG pension schemes face serious, unavoidable welfare problems. A few countries, most notably Chile, followed by several other countries in Latin America, have instituted dedicated retirement schemes under which 10 percent of earnings must be saved. The transition to such schemes is made more difficult in the West because they imply that the current generation of workers would have to pay for both their own retirement and the pensions of those who are already retired. The problem is not that reform is impossible, but that the longer it is delayed, the more costly and difficult it becomes. And by and large, with moderate qualifications to be discussed below, the political will to address the problems of pension and welfare reform has been lacking.

It is not only the problem of pensions that challenges the welfare provisions of continental European countries. The advance of medical science is also raising costs dramatically, creating a further drain on state budgets. This has both direct effects – higher costs of hospitalization, drugs and so forth – and indirect ones: an ageing population with longer life expectancies due to medical progress consumes a disproportionate amount of health care spending (besides adding to the pension deficit). In the United States, health care spending in 2003 is estimated at $1.7 trillion, more than 15 percent of GDP (*Wall Street Journal*, 12 February 2004, p. D2). Spending increased by 9.3 percent in 2002, 7.8 percent in 2003 and is expected to grow faster than GDP for the next ten years, reaching $3.4 trillion by 2013, more than 18 percent of GDP. While there is some inflation in these figures, much of the increase is reflected in the cost of new medicines and procedures. With the rise of biotechnology, moreover, which promises the development of targeted medicines through enhanced understanding of disease mechanisms (as well as an era of personalized medicine based on individual genetic characteristics that knowledge of the human genome will make possible), the advances in medical science may well accelerate, with commensurate increases in cost.

Like Germany's, France's public health care system is supported by some of the world's heaviest payroll taxes, but it nevertheless ran a deficit of about $12 billion in 2003, and its costs are rising at some 6.4 percent annually (*Business Week*, 13 October 2003, p. 60). The French government had planned to introduce cost-cutting reforms in late 2003, but put them off until late 2004 in the face of widespread opposition. In Sweden the health care system was ranked as the best among OECD countries in a *British Medical Journal* study of December 2003, but as is true elsewhere in Europe, the system has entered a state of crisis. Hospitals have been closing wards and laying off staff, and telling patients to turn to the private sector for some surgeries. Although access to health care is seen as a basic right, the government has begun to ration procedures for which it will pay, and some newspapers have begun to publish price lists for private treatment. Since 1998, health care costs in Sweden have been rising by 8 percent per year (*Los Angeles Times*, 7 December 2003, p. C4). The financial problems in European health care systems, it should be noted, have emerged despite the fact that price controls on medicines keep their cost some 60 percent below US levels (*The Economist*, 31 January 2004, p. 59). The increase in health costs associated especially with advances in medical science, then, combines with the pensions pressure created by an ageing population and rising dependency ratio of retirees to workers to intensify fiscal pressures on the European welfare state.

GLOBALIZATION, TECHNOLOGICAL CHANGE AND THE WELFARE STATE

While capitalism has been global from its outset, as Immanuel Wallerstein (1979) has argued, the nature of globalization today is qualitatively different from what it has been in the past. The revolution in information and communications technology (ICT) especially has facilitated the rise of international supply chains and international outsourcing. Multinational or transnational corporations (MNCs or TNCs) have found it increasingly easy to locate their production facilities in low-cost countries, or to contract work out to those countries to minimize their costs of production. The ICT revolution, together with improvements in transport, has made it more feasible to track more precisely the status of overseas material goods production to ensure timely deliveries. Further, types of work that would not previously have been outsourced abroad, such as software projects and call centers, are increasingly being sent abroad to India and elsewhere.

Although labor costs are of greater or lesser importance for the many firms capable of international outsourcing, they are just one of the costs that must be taken into consideration. Taxes must also be considered, both at the corporate and the personal level. The welfare states of continental Europe depend on high levels of taxation to fund their social benefit programs. Personal and corporate income taxes, payroll taxes, value-added taxes, and in some cases even wealth taxes play a role. When taxes are much higher than those charged abroad, an incentive is created above and beyond labor-cost differentials to move work abroad. And even when work is not moved abroad, strong incentives are created to substitute capital for labor in the production process. This also contributes to keeping new hiring down and to rising unemployment rates, especially among the young. Taken together, the set of incentives created by globalization and technological change tends to deprive the welfare states of the tax revenues necessary to fund their various social benefits.

International mobility exists at an individual level moreover, as well as at the corporate level. Younger people with strong qualifications especially may be tempted to work in locations with lower tax rates. The 'traditional' brain drain has been from less developed countries to more developed ones. The new brain drain however also includes people within the industrialized world seeking to locate in lower-tax countries. To attract the most qualified personnel, this creates an added incentive for corporations to expand their operations in lower-tax locales. Thus in the early 1990s, Germany was hoping to have Frankfurt compete with London as the financial center of the new Europe, but in recent years Germany's largest banks have been cutting employment in Germany in favor of expanding employment in London, with foreign banks (such as Spain's Santander) making similar moves (*Wall Street Journal*, 11 July 2003, p. A7).

The international wage and tax competition promises to increase, with the European Union having expanded by ten nations in May 2004, including eight countries in Eastern and Central Europe. Relatively low flat personal income taxes have been widely adopted in the region, with Russia and Ukraine at 13 percent, the Slovak Republic at 19 percent, Estonia at 26 percent, Lithuania at 33 percent, and Latvia at 25 percent (*Wall Street Journal*, 19 January 2004, p. A12). Bulgaria, Romania and Georgia are all considering flat taxes as well.

The problem of high taxes and labor costs is intensified by another aspect of contemporary globalization: the intensification of competition. In the middle of the twentieth century, a great deal of corporate behavior could be described as 'satisficing' rather than profit maximizing; many companies were able to survive and prosper without being low-cost producers. As the economies of Japan and Europe were rebuilt following the devastation of the Second World War, however, global competition began to intensify. In the US, companies like Chrysler were able to survive only with the aid of a federal government bail-out. As globalization intensified at the end of the century, including the rise of China to become the 'workshop of the world' – much like England had been in the eighteenth century – companies that failed to take advantage of every possible means of cost-reduction became increasingly at risk. Competition is no longer merely national but increasingly global, and companies that fail to take every possible advantage of cost reducing opportunities are subject to failure.

It is within this context that traditional measures of assuring popular welfare have become increasingly problematic. In the case of Germany for example, when firms lay off employees they are required to start with those most able to find alternative employment. This is mandated by the *Kundigungsshutz* or job protection law, which has been little changed since the 1950s (*Business Week*, 17 February 2004, p. 47). In effect, that means that firms often are required to lay off their most able employees first, while retaining those who are least productive. A recent proposed reform would have increased the exempt firms with five or fewer employees to include those with 20 or fewer, but opposition to the reform forced a cutback to exempt only firms with ten or fewer employees.

The difficulty of firing workers throughout Europe has made firms extremely hesitant to employ new workers. Hiring someone in his or her early twenties might mean an employment commitment lasting as long as 40 years. Since firms have difficulty estimating their outlooks for more than a few years, most are hesitant in the extreme to make such long-term commitments. It is within this context that while the unemployment rate in France is about 9.6 percent overall, the unemployment rate for those under 25 is 21 percent (*The Economist*, 10 January 2004, p. 44). Thus legislation meant to protect workers from arbitrary firing has, paradoxically, slowed the rate of new hiring and contributed to sluggish economic performance throughout continental Europe. In general, the Continental commitment to income, job and health security has come under increasing challenge as globalization and technological change lead to heightened competition.

SLUGGISH ECONOMIC PERFORMANCE IN CONTINENTAL EUROPE

One might expect the various problems affecting the welfare-state economies of continental Europe to be reflected in weak economic performance, growing difficulties in maintaining the array of benefits to which people have become accustomed, and intensifying pressures for reform. This has indeed been the case despite the adoption of a common currency, the euro, which might have been expected to give the participating economies a meaningful boost. The stability and growth pact, which penalizes those euro-zone countries maintaining budget deficits in excess of 3 percent of GDP per year, has also played a role in the poor economic performance, especially since the concentration of control over the region's interest rates in the European Central Bank (ECB) deprives individual countries of monetary policy tools to stimulate their economies; the ECB's interest rate policies depend on the rate of inflation in the euro-area as a whole, which (as of mid-2004) remained in excess of its 2 percent target, so that individual countries like Germany experiencing stagnation and low inflation have had to live with interest rates higher than their domestic conditions warranted. Despite the loss of control over monetary policy associated with economic integration however, it is clear that deeper economic difficulties derive from structural problems associated with the existence of the welfare state.

It is not the welfare state alone that has created these problems. Rather, it is the high levels of social spending that take place in the context of an increasingly competitive global economy on the one hand, and the rising costs associated with an ageing population and medical advances on the other, with additional burdens created by adaptive behavior that adds to the cost of welfare provisions. In addition to the examples of adaptive behavior cited above, the increase in those receiving disability benefits in the Netherlands is also a case in point. Although the Netherlands has made more concerted reform efforts than the larger economies at the heart of the Continent, given the remaining difficulties of firing workers, some companies have been putting unwanted workers on disability. Thus in the Netherlands 13.5 percent of the labor force is classified as sick or disabled, and the proportion is expected to rise to 15 percent by 2006 (*Wall Street Journal*, 18 July 2003, p. A14). The challenge to the welfare state then is created by the interaction of multiple factors leading to rising costs and declining competitiveness. The expected outcome is sluggish economic performance, and that indeed has been the case over the past decade. Table 13.1 compares average annual European and US GDP growth rates between 1995 and 2002.

Table 13.1 Average annual growth rates, 1995–2002

Ireland*	7.6%	Britain	2.8%
Finland	4.0%	Sweden	2.7%
Greece	3.6%	France	2.4%
Spain	3.4%	Austria	2.2%
US	3.3%	Belgium	2.2%
Portugal**	3.0%	Italy	1.6%
Netherlands	2.8%	Germany	1.4%

Notes:
* 1998–2002
** 1996–2002

Source: *Business Week*, 17 February 2003, p. 51.

Although the overall figures in Table 13.1 do not appear disastrous at first sight, several factors must be taken into account when evaluating their significance. Firstly, the major countries and/or those with the most extensive social welfare programs tend to be among the weakest performers (note in particular the placing of Germany, Italy and France). Secondly, some of the smaller countries on the periphery of the Continent have been reform leaders (such as Ireland and Finland). And thirdly, the creation of the euro as a common currency created an economic reform imperative for countries wishing to join the euro-zone, leading to more balanced budgets, curtailment of national debt and so forth, resulting in a number of cases in stronger economic performance than might otherwise have been achieved.

Relative productivity performance may give deeper insight into the problems Europe is experiencing. In the European Union, output per labor hour in the 1995–2000 period grew at 1.42 percent per year, compared to the 1.97 percent in the US. In the three years to the third quarter of 2003, the gap widened as American productivity growth moved up to 2.5 percent, with Europe's slowing to 0.89 percent (Becker, 2003, p. 22). Germany, at one time the most vigorous of Europe's economies and influencing economic performance throughout the Continent by virtue of its size – the unified Germany accounts for about one-third of European GDP – is now contributing to the economic weakening of the entire Continent. More significantly, countries with sharply rising demands on their social welfare systems cannot afford to be lagging economically. In the absence of reform, unsustainable tax increases would be required to finance existing benefits, putting the entire welfare-state project at risk. Fortunately, reform options do exist.

ECONOMIC REFORM IN EUROPE

The central issue of economic reform in Europe is finding a way to restore competitiveness and financial viability while sidestepping the pressures generated to emulate the 'harsh', market-driven capitalism that characterizes the United States. These pressures, as I have indicated, include the internal contradictions that welfare systems tend to create, and the problems generated by ageing populations and advances in medical science. All of these are intensified moreover by the forces of globalization and technological change, which have made contemporary capitalism much more price competitive than its mid-twentieth century counterpart. Since capital, both financial and real, can move more readily than ever before to low-labor-cost and/or low-tax sites, and since individuals can choose to live and work in low-tax locations, the economic foundations for the welfare state have been seriously undermined. Given these conditions, full recognition of the need for reform – and the political will to carry it out – are necessary if the best elements of the more humane form of capitalism that has emerged in Europe are to be preserved. Fortunately there have been experiments with reform in various parts of Europe, and both France's Agenda 2006 and Germany's Agenda 2010 reflect a genuine if belated understanding that reform is necessary.

In France and Germany, a 35-hour work week is fairly standard. The 35-hour week was mandated in France in the late 1990s and supported by (false) arguments that with a fixed amount of work available, a shorter week would assure higher employment (similar arguments have been used by German unions since the late 1970s). Since the French legislation mandated no reduction in weekly pay along with the shorter hours, the hourly payments rose, making France less competitive (it created other problems as well, since with doctors, nurses and other health care personnel working shorter hours, health care services had to be curtailed even while costs rose). High labor costs in both France and Germany contribute to high unemployment, which in August 2004 was about 9.6 percent in France and 10.6 percent in Germany. French and German workers do work less than those in other countries, and if the choice is simply one between work and leisure, there is obviously no imperative in favor of work. Table 13.2 indicates the hours of work in various countries.

When French and German workers work about 20 percent fewer hours per year than their American counterparts, they are not the ones, for the most part, who bear the burden of their choice. Rather, with labor costs high, their companies become less competitive and less willing to create new jobs. This results in the high unemployment and especially the high youth unemployment already noted. It also means that the full array of social services financed by the payroll tax – pensions, unemployment insurance and health care – is deprived of adequate financing. The real choice then is not whether workers prefer higher

Table 13.2 Average hours worked per person employed in 2002

Germany	1444
France	1459
Britain	1707
Japan (2001)	1809
US	1815

Sources: *Business Week*, 27 October 2003, p. 58; *Wall Street Journal*, 30 January 2004, p. A10.

income or more leisure, but whether they are entitled to both at the expense of those members of the population who face unemployment, reduced health care and lower pension benefits.

The French government is seeking to reduce welfare benefits for unemployed workers who turn down jobs. At present, unemployed workers are eligible to receive 75 percent of their most recent salary for as long as two years on the condition that they register as job-seekers. The problem with this system is that they can turn down job offers without losing any benefits (a leading French union has said that the proposed reform is unacceptable since it would force workers to accept jobs unsuited to their qualifications; *Wall Street Journal*, 21 November 2003, p. A10).

The welfare reform issues that confront continental Europe then are fairly straightforward, although there is some evidence that the German population is ahead of its French counterpart in recognizing the inevitability and indeed the urgency of economic reform. This may reflect in part Germany's higher export share in GDP, and a correspondingly greater willingness of German companies to shift jobs abroad for the sake of competitiveness, a willingness that may be further enhanced by the proximity of the eight Eastern European countries that joined the European Union in May 2004.

Although relatively modest in the aggregate, the December 2003 reforms (part of the Agenda 2010) agreed to in Germany by the Social Democrats and the Christian Democratic opposition represent the most substantial changes to the country's economic framework since the Second World War (*Wall Street Journal*, 16 December 2003). The reforms involved:

1. bringing forward tax cuts valued at some $19 billion to 2004;
2. requiring the unemployed to accept jobs paying less than union wages or lose benefits;
3. easing protection against lay-offs in firms with fewer than ten employees (versus five previously);
4. toughening criteria for receiving social benefits.

The opposition and the corporate sector had also hoped to give more flexibility to the bargaining process by allowing firms to bargain individually with unions, rather than rely on industry- or region-wide bargaining; this would allow bargaining to adjust to situations where the lack of competitiveness might require the closure of entire plants. The reform agreement gave unions and employer groups a year to figure out on their own how to make the system more flexible, with further government action a possibility if no progress is made.

In both France and Germany, modest efforts are under way to increase the retirement age. In France, a reform passed in 2003 requires public sector employees to work as long as private sector workers, 40 years, to qualify for full pensions (they could previously qualify after 37.5 years; *The Economist*, 18 October 2003, pp. 49–51). In both Germany and France however the pensions remain, for the most part, pay-as-you-go systems.

Reform remains however an especially difficult project in France. In the mid-1990s, Prime Minister Alain Juppe was forced to retreat after a series of paralyzing strikes and protests. The 2003 reform by Prime Minister Raffarin was cut back to the pension change indicated in the face of opposition to his proposals for health care reforms, the consideration of which had to be postponed. It is of interest that in Germany only 35 percent of the population believes that comprehensive social protection is possible without high contributions, as opposed to 53 percent with that belief ten years ago, and that 70 percent of the population agrees that reforms are necessary (ibid). In France, by contrast, only 51 percent believe that the government should continue with reforms.

Other types of reforms have been under consideration or have been implemented in these two countries as well as elsewhere in Europe. In Germany, the ageing population issue will be addressed in part with new initiatives to encourage families to have children and women to enter the labor force. Although family support was 2.7 percent of GDP in 1998, about three-quarters of the public support took the form of direct benefits and tax breaks rather than child-care support. Child-care facilities in Western Germany are often poor or non-existent. Thus the government plans to spend 1.5 billion euros on child care after 2005 and to invest 4 billion euros in all-day schools (most pre-schools are now half-day) over the next four years (*The Economist*, 6 December 2003, p. 47).

In Denmark, a reform package included higher indirect taxes and a cut in entitlements, with more public resources devoted to higher education and research and development; GDP growth in Denmark was 2.6 percent between 1994 and 2003 compared to Germany's 1.4 percent (*Business Week*, 17 November 2003, p. 58). In Sweden and the Netherlands (as well as in New Zealand and the state of Oregon), health care reform includes an attempt to ration health care by considering the cost–benefit ranking of various procedures and medicines to determine which ones will be publicly covered (*Los Angeles Times*, 7 December

2003, p. C4). Under a corporatist agreement in the Netherlands during the 1980s, unions agreed to limit wage demands, government to limit taxes and corporate costs, and companies to hire more workers and consult with unions on major staffing decisions (*Wall Street Journal*, 8 July 2003, p. A14). In addition, regulations limiting part-time work have been eased. The system appeared to work well in good times, with economic growth in the late 1990s exceeding 3 percent compared to a European average of 2.5 percent. During and after the 2001 downturn, however, the Dutch economy has struggled with sub-par growth.

THE FUTURE OF THE EUROPEAN SOCIAL MARKET ECONOMY

Attitudes toward economic reform in Europe are changing slowly, but they are changing. What is at stake is whether the European social market economy or welfare state will survive – in anything like the form it has thus far assumed. The pressures that will be confronting it over the coming decades are extremely powerful, with internal contradictions, ageing populations and the revolutionary transformation of medicine promising to raise the costs of existing systems significantly. The pressures created by these changes are further intensified by the interacting impacts of globalization and technological change, which increasingly force firms throughout the capitalist world to focus on competitiveness and maximizing shareholder value as opposed to focusing on the welfare of their entire community of stakeholders.

Under capitalism as it exists in the world today, the prevailing forces of global competition promote the harsh, market-driven type of American capitalism at the expense of Europe's social market economy. If the latter, more humane form of capitalism is to be preserved – hopefully until post-capitalist society arrives – the need for flexibility and reform must be recognized. In the absence of flexibility and reform, the capacity of states to maintain their social welfare commitments cannot be sustained, and the threat of breakdown cannot be dismissed.

SELECTED BIBLIOGRAPHY

Angresano, James (1996), *Comparative Economics*, 2nd edn, Upper Saddle River, NJ: Prentice-Hall.

Becker, Gary (2003), 'A little German reform would go a long way', *Business Week*, 1 December.

The Economist (2003), 'State pensions in Europe', 27 September.

Farrell, Diana (2004), 'How Germany can win from offshoring', *McKinsey Quarterly*, 7 November, accessed on line.

Farrell, Diana, Heino Fassbender, Thomas Kneip, Stephan Kriesel and Eric Labaye (2004), 'Reviving French and German productivity', *McKinsey Quarterly*, 17 November, accessed on line.
Ferrera, Maurizio and Martin Rhodes (2000), *Recasting European Welfare States*, London: Frank Cass.
Gilbert, Neil (1983), *Capitalism and the Welfare State*, New Haven, CT: Yale University Press.
Gilbert, Neil (2002), *Transformation of the Welfare State*, Oxford: Oxford University Press.
Goodin, Robert E., Bruce Headey, Ruud Muffels and Henk-Jan Dirven (1999), *The Real Worlds of Welfare Capitalism*, Cambridge: Cambridge University Press.
Greve, Bent (ed.) (1996), *Comparative Welfare Systems*, New York: St Martin's Press.
Kautto, Mikko, Matti Heikkila, Bjorn Hvinden, Staffan Marklund and Niels Ploug (eds) (1999), *Nordic Social Policy*, London: Routledge.
Mishra, Ramesh (1999), *Globalization and the Welfare State*, Cheltenham, UK and Northampton, MA, USA: Edward Elgar Publishing.
Rachman, Gideon (2004), 'Outgrowing the union: a survey of the European Union', *The Economist*, 25 September.
Schmidt, Vivien A. (2002), *The Futures of European Capitalism*, Oxford: Oxford University Press.
Sodersten, Bo (ed.) (2004), *Globalization and the Welfare State*, Basingstoke: Palgrave Macmillan.
Swenson, Peter A. (2002), *Capitalists against Markets*, Oxford: Oxford University Press.
Wallerstein, Immanuel (1979), *The Capitalist World-Economy*, Cambridge: Cambridge University Press.

PART V

Strategies for Reducing Poverty and Inequality

14. The structure and distribution of personal income and poverty reduction: a case study of Bangladesh during the 1990s

Azizur Rahman Khan and Binayak Sen[1]

INTRODUCTION

Despite its moderate growth performance, Bangladesh has experienced major changes in the structure of employment and income in the recent past, especially in rural areas where most of the people live. The inequality in the distribution of income has also steadily increased. The purpose of this chapter is to use the household-level data from the three surveys during the 1990s – the Household Expenditure Surveys (HES) of 1991–92 and 1995–96 and the Household Income and Expenditure Survey (HIES) of 2000, all carried out by the Bangladesh Bureau of Statistics (BBS) – to make comparable estimates of personal income for rural and urban Bangladesh, including its source, and to estimate the indices of inequality in the distribution of personal income, along with that of its sources. The study illustrates the nature and the sources of rising inequality that has often characterized the growth and structural change of developing countries in recent decades. It also shows the effect that a change in income distribution makes on the impact of economic growth on poverty reduction.

STRUCTURE AND COMPOSITION OF INCOME

Income is classified into six major sources while certain elements, not belonging to any of the six sources, are lumped together in a residual category of 'other income'. These sources of income are as follows:

1. Income from farming (return to farm enterprise, owned land, family labour and other owned assets);

2. wages and salaries (further classified into agricultural wage, non-agricultural wage and non-agricultural 'salary');[2]
3. income from non-farm enterprises (sometimes loosely referred to as 'entrepreneurial' income or 'profit' for brevity, but representing returns to enterprise, family labour and owned assets;
4. property income (rent, interest and dividends on assets);
5. remittances and transfers (for 2000 further classified into domestic, presumably private, cash remittances; private cash remittances from abroad; and all other private and public gifts, subsidies and transfers);
6. rental value of owner-occupied housing;
7. other income.

Income estimates of this study differ from the official estimates made by the BBS. The main source of the difference is the exclusion from the definition of this study of a number of capital receipts – for example revenue from sale of assets; withdrawal of working capital, savings deposits and provident funds; receipts from repayment of loans made in the past; and possibly some borrowing – that are included in the official BBS definition of income.[3]

Change in Composition of Rural Income

Table 14.1 shows per capita rural personal income and its sources at current prices for each of the three years. The most important change that has taken place over the decade is the decline in the relative importance of agricultural production activities as a source of income for rural households. Rural household income derived from agriculture may be said to consist of three distinct types of factor payment: profits, wages and rent. Together these sources accounted for 53 per cent of personal income in 1991–92, whence it fell to 47 per cent in 1995–96 and to just below 35 per cent in 2000.

Among the three kinds of factor payments for agricultural activities, there was a steady rise in the share of wages in total agricultural income, from about 20 per cent at the beginning of the decade to about 30 per cent at the end. 'Profits' (income from farming) fell steadily and sharply, from 78 per cent to 60 per cent. Rents rose quite sharply, from less than 2 per cent of total agricultural factor income in 1991–92 to about 10 per cent in 2000. Among the reasons behind the rise in the share of rent is a steady rise in the incidence of tenancy, for which evidence is cited later. As a proportion of per capita rural income from all sources, agricultural 'profits' (farm income) fell even more sharply, its share being halved over the period under review. As a proportion of all rural income, agricultural wages remained roughly unchanged while rents rose.

Factor payments from non-agricultural production activities – 'profits', wages and salaries – together rose from about a quarter of rural income in 1991–92 to

Table 14.1 Per capita annual income of rural households (current taka)

	1991–92		1995–96		2000	
	Amount	%	Amount	%	Amount	%
Income from farming	2794.57	41.44	2656.59	35.04	2189.58	20.92
Crop production	...	...	...	...	1674.96	16.01
Livestock	...	...	...	...	153.36	1.47
Fishery	...	...	...	...	169.61	1.62
Forestry	...	...	...	...	191.65	1.83
Wages and salaries	1372.23	20.35	1870.16	24.66	3261.85	31.17
Agricultural wage	732.41	10.86	838.39	11.06	1076.78	10.29
Non-agricultural wage	285.43	4.23	488.46	6.44	766.77	7.33
Non-agricultural 'salary'	354.39	5.25	543.31	7.17	1418.31	13.55
Non-farm enterprise	1034.04	15.33	1448.32	19.10	2031.52	19.41
Property income	59.79	0.89	103.73	1.37	429.02	4.10
Rent from land	...	...	...	...	357.22	3.41
Return to other assets	...	...	...	...	71.81	0.69
Remittances and transfer	735.00	10.90	724.71	9.56	1273.42	12.17
Domestic remittance	...	...	...	...	348.13	3.33
Foreign remittances	...	...	...	...	788.06	7.53
Other transfers	...	...	...	...	137.24	1.31
Rental value of housing	522.10	7.74	425.37	5.61	481.91	4.61
Other income	226.57	3.36	353.75	4.67	797.05	7.62
Total income	6744.30	100.00	7582.63	100.00	10464.35	100.00

40 per cent in 2000. They represent handicrafts, other manufacturing and services in private, non-governmental (NGO) and public sectors, although information is not available on their composition by sector or type of ownership. As a proportion of total factor payments for non-agricultural activities, 'profits' fell, wages changed very little and salaries rose, especially sharply during the late 1990s. As a proportion of all rural income, non-farm 'profits' rose, as did wages. There was a dramatic rise in salaries as a proportion of total rural income, from about 5 per cent in 1991–92 to nearly 14 per cent in 2000. This almost certainly indicates a change in composition of non-agricultural enterprises in favour of service activities, including public and non-governmental organizations.

Factor payments from all agricultural and non-agricultural production activities together account for approximately 80 per cent of all rural personal income throughout the period. The largest of the remaining components is transfers including cash remittances. There was a small rise in this source of income, as a proportion of total, over the decade. By 2000, the only year for which such information is available, cash remittances made by Bangladeshi migrant workers abroad came of be the largest component of these transfers, amounting to almost 8 per cent of rural income. Domestic cash remittances amounted to just over 3 per cent of income. Other transfers, including net transfers made by the public sector, remained small.

Rental value of housing as a proportion of income was not only small to begin with but also fell over the period, as did its absolute value. Considering that practically all rural housing is owner-occupied, this is an indication of the declining average housing condition in rural Bangladesh.[4]

Change in Composition of Urban Income

Compared to that in rural areas, the change in the composition of urban personal income has been less dramatic and less clear (Table 14.2). Factor income received from non-agricultural production activities – 'profit', wage and salary – has accounted for nearly two-thirds of all personal income in the second half of the decade under review, rising from 59 per cent in 1991–92. Unfortunately this diverse category, encompassing all industries, services, public administration and non-governmental voluntary activities, cannot be further disaggregated. As a proportion of total factor earnings from non-farm production, 'profits' went up from 48 per cent in 1991–92 to 57 per cent in 1995–96, but fell sharply thereafter to less than 44 per cent of the total, perhaps indicating fluctuations in the profitability of non-farm activities or changing shares of production and non-production activities or both. As a proportion of total factor earnings in non-farm enterprises, wages fell and salaries, after falling between 1991–92 and 1995–96, rose sharply thereafter. As a proportion of total urban personal income, 'profits' rose between 1991–92 and 1995–96, but fell thereafter to the same level in 2000 as in 1991–92; wages fell; and salaries rose, especially sharply during the late 1990s. These changes indicate that there was a rise in the proportion of salaried employment (public administration and 'not directly productive' services) in the non-farm sector during the late 1990s.

Factor returns to farming fell drastically over the period, indicating a decline in the extent of agricultural production activities that takes place within the geographical boundary of urban areas (due perhaps to a change in the pattern of urban land use).

Transfers and remittances show no trend as a proportion of income and were about 10 per cent of all personal income at the beginning and the end of the period under review. Cash remittances are less important in urban areas than in

Table 14.2 Per capita annual income of urban households (current taka)

	1991–92		1995–96		2000	
	Amount	%	Amount	%	Amount	%
Income from farming	643.25	6.09	860.57	5.80	499.20	2.41
Wages and salaries	3862.29	36.55	5320.64	35.84	7877.52	38.02
Non-agricultural wage	1058.00	10.01	1204.16	8.11	1662.95	8.03
Non-agricultural salary	2155.74	20.40	3043.06	20.50	6029.67	29.11
Other wage	648.54	6.14	1073.43	7.23	184.90	0.89
Non-farm enterprise	3003.30	28.42	5597.56	37.70	5962.47	28.78
Property income	396.95	3.76	507.62	3.42	1647.21	7.95
Rent from land	...	...	...	...	329.55	1.59
Return to other assets	...	...	...	...	1317.66	6.36
Remittances and transfer	979.01	9.27	1068.52	7.20	2092.05	10.10
Domestic remittance	...	...	...	...	399.30	1.93
Foreign remittance	...	...	...	...	808.00	3.90
Other transfers	...	...	...	...	884.75	4.27
Rental value of housing	970.73	9.19	1006.64	6.78	1328.50	6.41
Other income	710.33	6.72	484.47	3.26	1309.96	6.32
Total income	10565.86	100.00	14846.01	100.00	20716.91	100.00

rural areas as a proportion of all transfers, although their absolute per capita level is a little higher. Per capita foreign cash remittance received by an urban household is also a little higher than per capita foreign remittance received by a rural household. The same is true of domestic cash remittance. Quite unlike that in rural areas, non-remittance transfers constitute the largest component of income from transfers and remittances in urban areas.

Income from property increased sharply as a proportion of urban income, all of it taking place in the late 1990s, to reach 8 per cent of the total in 2000. Rent from land, almost certainly representing the earnings of absentee landowners, is a small proportion of urban personal income, but per capita rent received by the urban population is almost as high as per capita rent received by the rural population. Return to non-land assets represents most of the personal income derived from property.[5]

Finally, rental value of housing, as a proportion of urban income, fell significantly over the period and there was little increase in its per capita absolute level in real terms. If the estimates are accurate, then one must conclude that despite the comparative boom in upper-income urban housing construction in major cities, the average housing condition for the urban population showed little improvement, unless there was a major shift in favor of rented as compared to owned accommodation, for which little evidence exists.

Change in Urban–Rural Inequality

Per capita urban personal income, as a multiple of per capita rural personal income, increased from 1.57 in 1991–92 to 1.96 in 1995–96. There was a further small rise in urban–rural inequality by the year 2000 when the ratio rose to 1.98. Urban–rural inequality in Bangladesh thus reached a level since the middle of the 1990s which is completely out of line with long-term historical levels. Between the mid-1960s and the mid-1980s this ratio ranged between 1.33 and 1.59.[6] As shown below, this was a major source of the increase in national inequality, quite apart from stimulating migration and urbanization which have arguably reached undesirable proportions in Bangladesh.

THE DISTRIBUTION OF INCOME

Measuring Income Distribution: the Index of Inequality

This chapter uses the Gini ratio and the 'pseudo-Gini' or 'concentration' ratios to measure the distribution of income and to decompose it into its sources. The method of measuring them may be summarized as follows. Households are ranked in ascending order of per capita income. They are then divided into ten decile groups of population and the shares of each decile group in total income and income from each of the different sources are calculated. Plotting cumulative shares of total income for the cumulative deciles of population, one gets the Lorenz distribution of income. For the i-th component of income, one can similarly derive a 'pseudo-Lorenz distribution' in which cumulative shares of the i-th source of income are plotted against the cumulative deciles of population in which the latter is obtained from a ranking of individuals according to per capita overall income rather than per capita income from the i-th source. As the Gini ratio is estimated from the Lorenz distribution of income, so is the 'pseudo-Gini ratio' or the 'concentration ratio' for the i-th source of income estimated from the pseudo-Lorenz distribution of the i-th income component. The Gini ratio is the weighted average of the concentration ratios of the components of income where the weights are the shares of the respective components in total income:[7]

$$G = \sum_{i=1}^{n} q_i C_i$$

where,
G = Gini ratio of total income;
q_i = the ratio of the i-th source of income to total income; and
C_i = the pseudo-Gini or concentration ratio (hereafter the concentration ratio) for the i-th source of income.

A component of income having a concentration ratio that is greater (smaller) than the Gini ratio is said to be 'disequalizing' (equalizing); relatively high proportions of it accrue to the higher (lower) income groups. A change in the Gini ratio over time can be caused by two distinct kinds of changes: a change in the composition of income between equalizing and disequalizing categories; and a change in the concentration ratio, the degree of inequality in distribution, of an individual source of income. The Gini ratio falls (rises) over time when (1) an equalizing component of income becomes more (less) equalizing or a disequalizing component becomes less (more) disequalizing; and/or when (2) equalizing (disequalizing) components are income-elastic, that is, they increase at a faster rate than total income.

Rural Income Inequality and its Sources

Over the decade, the inequality in the distribution of rural income, as measured by the Gini ratio, increased steadily from 0.276 in 1991–92 to 0.310 in 1995–96 and 0.356 in 2000 (Table 14.3). Growth and distribution of a handful of sources of income – non-farm enterprise, salary from non-farm employment, remittances from abroad; and property income – accounted for much of the increase in the rural Gini ratio over the period under review. Both the shares of income and the concentration ratios of these sources increased steadily over the decade. Together these sources accounted for 45 per cent of income in 2000, probably twice their share of total income at the beginning of the decade.

Non-farm entrepreneurial income, the largest of these components, was an equalizing source of income in the beginning. It became mildly disequalizing by the middle of the 1990s and strongly disequalizing by 2000. Non-agricultural salary, another type of factor income derived from the non-farm sector and the next most important of these sources, also became more disequalizing over the decade.

Direct evidence on the change in the income share and distributional impact of foreign remittance is available only for 2000 when it had become the most disequalizing component of income. Indirect evidence from macroeconomic

Table 14.3 Rural income shares and inequality indices

	Share of total income (%) ($100q_i$)			Gini/concentration ratio (C_i or G)		
	1991–92	1995–96	2000	1991–92	1995–96	2000
Farm income	41.44	35.03	20.92	0.332	0.338	0.347
Crop farming	...	...	16.01	...	...	0.349
Livestock	...	...	1.47	...	...	0.236
Fishing	...	...	1.62	...	...	0.397
Forestry	...	...	1.83	...	...	0.367
Wage	20.34	24.67	31.17	0.090	0.141	0.208
Agricultural wage	10.86	11.06	10.29	−0.113	−0.078	−0.147
Non-agricultural wage	4.23	6.44	7.33	0.138	0.126	0.071
Non-agricultural 'salary'	5.25	7.17	13.55	0.472	0.492	0.551
Non-farm enterprise	15.33	19.10	19.41	0.224	0.329	0.477
Property income	0.89	1.37	4.10	0.552	0.572	0.558
Rent from land	...	...	3.41	...	...	0.560
Rent from other assets	...	...	0.69	...	...	0.551
Remittances and transfer	10.90	9.56	12.17	0.364	0.599	0.552
Domestic remittances	...	...	3.33	...	...	0.394
Foreign remittances	...	...	7.53	...	...	0.707
Other transfers	...	...	1.31	...	...	0.064
Rental value of housing	7.74	5.61	4.61	0.351	0.276	0.300
Other income	3.36	4.67	7.62	0.393	0.281	0.286
Total income	100.00	100.00	100.00	0.276	0.310	0.356

Notes: q_i = the share of the i-th component of total income; C_i = the concentration ratio of the i-th source of income; and G = the Gini ratio of income distribution. Column totals, values shown in the 'Total income' row, do not always add exactly up to the amounts shown due to rounding error.

data suggests that it has been growing as a proportion of income.[8] Domestic remittance is mildly disequalizing and a much smaller proportion of income than foreign remittance.

Income from property has increased sharply. Much of it consists of rent for land, the rapid growth in which should largely be attributed to the sharp rise in the ratio of land rented out by the larger landowners, a phenomenon that may have helped make income from farming a relatively (that is, relative to the distribution of overall income) equalizing component of income over time. Over time return from non-land assets has also emerged as a source of income and it is likely to grow as the market for irrigation water and other farm equipments continues to expand. Both components of property income are fairly strongly disequalizing.

In contrast, two sources of income, farm income and wages, came to exert an equalizing effect on the distribution of income by the end of the decade under review. Farming was a moderately disequalizing source of income in 1991–92. By the mid-1990s its concentration ratio rose slightly but it came to have a much milder disequalizing effect on distribution because the concentration ratio of all other sources of income taken together increased much more. By the end of the decade, the concentration ratio of this source of income increased further; but, because of the sharp rise in the concentration ratios of the rest of income sources, it became an equalizing source of income; that is, its numerical value fell below the numerical value of the Gini ratio. As a proportion of total income, farm income has however fallen rapidly.

Wages have always been strongly equalizing, agricultural wages being more strongly equalizing than non-agricultural wages.[9] The share of agricultural wages in total income has stagnated while the share of non-agricultural wages has increased modestly.

Thus increased rural inequality has mainly been due to four disequalizing components of income that have grown much faster than overall income. This effect has been aggravated by the increase in the disequalizing effect of these components over the decade. The equalizing components of income have grown at a slower rate than overall income.

Are these trends likely to continue in the future? Or can public action arrest them? Consider first the possibility of reducing the shares of the disequalizing sources and/or increasing the shares of the equalizing sources of income. High GDP-elasticity of non-farm enterprise and non-agricultural salaries is a necessary and desirable attribute of economic growth. A high GDP-elasticity of foreign remittances similarly helps economic growth.

The increasing share of rent in income must be seen in the overall context of the rather complex agricultural transformation experienced by Bangladesh during the period under review. Some of the features and consequences of this transformation are summarized in Table 14.4. Between 1991–92 and 2000, the distribution of landownership became more unequal but the distribution of operational landholding became more equal. The Gini ratio of landownership remained unchanged at 0.649 between 1991–92 and 1995–96 while the concentration ratio of landholding, with individuals ranked according to per capita landownership, fell from 0.529 to 0.466. Comparable estimates for 2000 are somewhat problematic because the HIES recorded no entry for land for about a third of the households. Since these households show no income from farming, this may simply signify that a third of rural households quit farming altogether between 1995–96 and 2000.[10] If these

Table 14.4 Access to land in rural Bangladesh

	1991–92	1995–96	2000
Gini ratio of landownership	0.649	0.649	0.765 (0.682)
Concentration ratio of operational landholding (individuals ranked by per capita landownership)	0.529	0.466	0.471 (0.223)
Concentration ratio of landownership (individuals ranked by per capita income)	0.360	0.368	0.372
Concentration ratio of operational landholding (individuals ranked by per capita income)	0.320	0.270	0.192

Note: Figures in parentheses for 2000 refer to estimates based on the exclusion from the sample of those households for which there is no entry for land. See the text for further explanation.

households are included in calculations, as owning and operating no land, then the Gini ratio of landownership turns out to have risen to 0.765 while the concentration ratio of landholding still remains as low as 0.471. If the estimates exclude the households that show no landownership or landholding, the Gini ratio of landownership turns out to be 0.682 while the concentration ratio of landholding falls dramatically to 0.223. Thus while the distribution of landownership almost certainly became more unequal over the period under review, the distribution of access to operational landholding became more equal. The latter change must have led to an improvement in the distribution of income from farming; the effect of increased tenancy was to increase the equality of access to land which has made the distribution of farm income more equalizing (less disequalizing) over time. A concomitant of the increased incidence of tenancy was of course the sharp rise in the share of rent, a disequalizing source, in total income. To this extent the process also has a disequalizing component.

The last two items of Table 14.4 provide a glimpse into the overall effect of the process of increased access to land through a rise in the incidence of tenancy. Distribution of landownership among different income groups has remained roughly unchanged in a period of rising inequality in the distribution of income, possibly indicating that the inequality of landownership has not been a major impetus to increasing inequality. Distribution of access to landholding among different income groups has become dramatically more equal, indicating that access to land has become decreasingly associated with income inequality.

The effect of a fall in the incidence of tenancy, and the consequent fall in the income share of rent, on overall distribution will depend on the process through which the fall occurs. If an egalitarian land reform redistributes land among the farming households, the income share of rent will fall along with a widening of households' access to land. This will undoubtedly improve the distribution of income. If the larger landowners are induced to resume self-cultivation, prompted say by an attempt at tenancy reform, income share of rent will fall along with a reduction in access to land. The overall effect on the distribution of income may quite easily be adverse. In the absence of the political feasibility of land reform, it makes sense to strengthen the forces behind the change in the agrarian structure that has widened the access of the farming households to land as a method of improving the distribution of income, even though it results in a rise in the income share of rent, which worsens the distribution of income.

It thus seems that the option of putting a brake on inequality by reducing the growth of the disequalizing sources of income is not particularly attractive. The income from some of these sources – for example non-farm enterprise – will grow rapidly as an integral part of the process of growth. A decline in the growth of income from some other of these sources will either harm economic welfare (as is likely to be the case with foreign remittances) or unleash forces of inequality elsewhere (as is likely to be the case with the reduction in the growth of rent, induced by an ill-conceived tenancy reform).

What about the possibility of increasing the growth rate of income from the equalizing components? A low GDP-elasticity of farm income, following from a low GDP-elasticity of agriculture itself, may seem inevitable. It is nevertheless questionable if the kind of rapid fall in the share of farm income that occurred during the 1990s is entirely inevitable or desirable. During much of the decade, especially until about 1996, crop agriculture had a very low rate of growth. This is the outcome of complex forces that have been at work. On the one hand there seems to be a good deal of unsatisfied domestic demand for food which is not translated into effective demand due to the lack of purchasing power on the part of the hungry poor, thereby resulting in a low relative price and a lack of incentive for production of the overwhelmingly dominant staple, rice. This would seem to suggest that overcoming structural impediments to the emergence of the poor as producers of food – lack of access to land and other resources on their part – would be the way to have a faster, poverty-alleviating growth of crop production. On the other hand, substantial imports of rice and other agricultural products have taken place in recent years under the auspices of private traders, which may be interpreted as an indication that at the margin Bangladesh agriculture no longer has comparative advantage in staple food production. This conflicting evidence needs to be resolved by careful research.[11]

In the above, we have only considered the possibility of changing the incremental composition of personal income, so as to preserve or increase the share of equalizing components, as a way of containing a rise in inequality. And yet for rural Bangladesh it was not the change in the composition of income, but the increased inequality in the distribution of given components, that explains a larger proportion of the total rise in inequality. This is seen by comparing what the Gini ratio would have been in 2000 if income shares were as in 1991–92 while the concentration ratios had changed to what they actually were in 2000 – $\Sigma q_{i91/92}C_{i2000} = 0.331$ – with what the Gini ratio would have been in 2000 if income shares had changed to what they were in 2000 while concentration ratios had remained the same as in 1991–92[12] – $\Sigma q_{i2000}C_{i91/92} = 0.288$. Thus the containment of inequality must focus on containing the rising inequality of the distribution of specific components of income. Needless to say, the impact of this is greater if the rise in inequality is contained for the more income-elastic components of income.

Can anything be done to make the GDP-elastic components of income less (more) disequalizing (equalizing)? Rapid growth of the non-farm rural sector is rightly looked upon as a major element of development policy in Bangladesh. In 2000 non-farm entrepreneurial income, salary and wage together contributed two-fifths of household income. On available evidence, the notion that it is also a source of egalitarian growth must be rejected. Even after counting the effect of the distribution of wages and salaries generated by non-farm enterprises, the overall concentration ratio for all factor income generated by the sector is 0.428, indicating a highly disequalizing overall effect on income distribution. The principal focus of income distribution policy in Bangladesh must be on this sector to find ways of increasing the share of the poorer households in factor income from this sector by augmenting their access to capital, technology, skills and market.

As noted earlier, income remittances, especially those from abroad, made an increasing contribution to inequality because of their rising share of income and high concentration ratio. Attention instead should be focused on providing inducements to channel these resources into productive and labour-intensive investment that would have a positive impact on income distribution.

Urban Income Inequality and its Sources

Urban inequality increased steadily during the decade (Table 14.5); the Gini ratio increased from 0.327 in 1991–92 to 0.389 in 1995–96 and 0.437 in 2000. Urban inequality has been consistently higher than rural inequality.

The largest source of urban income consists of non-farm wages and salaries, their contribution exceeding 37 per cent of total income by the end of the decade.[13] As in rural Bangladesh, wages have a strongly equalizing effect on urban income distribution while salaries have a strongly disequalizing effect.[14]

Wages have become increasingly equalizing over the decade, the weighted average concentration ratio of farm and non-farm wages becoming –0.198 by the end of the decade. Their equalizing influence on overall distribution was

Table 14.5 Urban income shares and inequality indices

	Share of total income (%) $(100q_i)$			Gini/concentration ratio (C_i or G)		
	1991–92	1995–96	2000	1991–92	1995–96	2000
Farm income	6.09	5.80	2.41	0.115	0.226	0.220
Wage/salary	36.55	35.84	38.02	0.276	0.266	0.304
Non-agric. wage	10.01	8.11	8.03	0.087	0.030	–0.182
Non-agric. 'salary'	20.40	20.50	29.11	0.406	0.421	0.458
Other wage	6.14	7.23	0.89	0.157	0.092	–0.345
Non-farm enterprise	28.42	37.70	28.78	0.306	0.464	0.503
Property income	3.76	3.42	7.95	0.643	0.644	0.643
Rent from land	...	...	1.59	...	...	0.509
Other rental income	...	...	6.36	...	...	0.676
Remittance and transfer	9.27	7.20	10.10	0.427	0.581	0.616
Domestic remittance	...	...	1.93	...	...	0.305
Foreign remittance	...	...	3.90	...	...	0.593
Other transfer	...	...	4.27	...	...	0.777
Rental value of housing	9.19	6.78	6.41	0.434	0.410	0.488
Other income	6.72	3.26	6.32	0.424	0.442	0.417
Total income	100.00	100.00	100.00	0.327	0.389	0.437

Notes: See note to Table 14.4 for an explanation of the notation. Due to error in rounding, the sums of the components do not always exactly match the totals.

however blunted by their declining share of total income. An expansion in wage employment, leading to a rise in the share of wages in total income, would have the strongest possible equalizing effect on urban income distribution.

Salary income, representing the earnings of all those in regular employment in public and private enterprises and NGOs, reached a much higher proportion of total income in 2000 than in the earlier years. Its concentration ratio has also increased over time although, as a multiple of the Gini ratio, it has fallen over time, indicating a relative weakening of its disequalizing effect.

Non-farm entrepreneurial income was the largest single source of income except in 2000 when it was a close second to salary as an income component. By 2000, its share of total income reverted back to what it was at the beginning of the decade. Its concentration ratio rose sharply over the decade. Its proportionate contribution to overall inequality – the product of its income share and the concentration ratio expressed as a percentage of the Gini ratio – increased between 1991–92 and 1995–96, but fell thereafter.

Property income, land rent and income from assets had a high concentration ratio throughout the period and their share of total income rose sharply, thereby substantially increasing their contribution to overall inequality.

Transfer income, gifts (other transfer) and foreign remittance, were strongly disequalizing, the former far more so than the latter. Domestic remittances were the smallest of the transfer components and strongly equalizing. Overall, remittances and transfers were highly and increasingly disequalizing and their share of total income at the end of the decade was a little higher than what it was at the beginning of the decade.

As in the case of rural Bangladesh, public policy can make few meaningful interventions to alter the disequalizing effect of income from transfer and remittances (except by resorting to redistributive public transfer whose prospects are limited) and assets. The containment of urban inequality must therefore focus on salary and 'entrepreneurial' income from non-farm enterprise (both disequalizing) and wages (strongly equalizing). One would expect variations in these components to be closely related because they all represent factor payments from non-farm enterprises. That is not the case. Between 1991–92 and 1995–96 non-farm entrepreneurial income rose sharply while wages and salaries changed little. Between 1995–96 and 2000 there was a sharp rise in the share of salaries in total income while the share of non-farm entrepreneurial income fell and the share of wages remained unchanged. This might have been due to a change in the composition of enterprises, indicating a rise in the proportion of those with a high incidence of salaried employment, possibly even a rise in the proportion of not directly productive enterprises relative to directly productive enterprises.

If non-farm enterprises consist of industries and services that are appropriately labour-intensive, that is, intensive in wage labour, then the equalizing effect of the growth in wage income will offset the disequalizing effect of the growth in entrepreneurial income from them. If however the growth of non-farm enterprises is concentrated in skilled labour-intensive and/or white collar-labour-intensive activities – for example information technology, financial institutions and consultancy firms – then there will be a rapid growth in salary income which will exacerbate the disequalizing effect of the growth of entrepreneurial income.

Which of the above types of enterprises should grow faster is a matter to be guided by broader considerations of social profitability, of which their distributional consequence is one of many elements. To pursue the objective of improved distributional outcome the attention of public policy would need to focus on the reduction of the concentration ratios of salary income and income from non-farm enterprises. This would require a widening of access of members of the labour force to education and skills, and the access of small and micro entrepreneurs to credit, technology and markets.

Just as in the case of rural areas, it is the change in the distribution of specific components of income that explains a larger part of the change in the urban Gini ratio than does the change in the composition of income, although the difference in the contribution of the two is smaller in urban areas than in rural areas. Had the composition of urban income in 2000 been the same as in 1991–92 while the concentration ratios were what they actually were in 2000, the Gini ratio would have been 0.365. In comparison, it would have been 0.357 if the composition of income were what it actually was in 2000 while the concentration ratios had remained unchanged at their 1991–92 levels.

Overall National Inequality and its Sources[15]

Inequality in Bangladesh as a whole increased steadily throughout the decade; the overall Gini ratio increased from 0.303 in 1991–92 to 0.359 in 1995–96 and 0.405 in 2000 (Table 14.6). In explaining the sources of this increase, the first important point that deserves to be noted relates to the two memo items shown in the table. Throughout the period, rural income has been strongly equalizing and urban income has been strongly disequalizing in the context of the overall distribution of income for Bangladesh. This simply reflects the fact that the recipients of rural income (urban income) rank relatively low (high) in the overall income distribution scale for Bangladesh. A rise in the ratio of average urban income to average rural income therefore increases the Gini ratio for Bangladesh as a whole even when the distributions within rural and urban areas remain unchanged. The proportionately higher increase in the Gini ratio for Bangladesh between 1991–92 and 1995–96 than between 1995–96 and 2000 was largely due to a much sharper rise in urban–rural inequality over the former period than over the latter period.

Only four of all the specific sources of income have an equalizing effect on the distribution of income. These are: farm income, agricultural wages, non-agricultural wages and domestic remittances. For the first three, estimates of concentration ratios are available for each period and they indicate that their equalizing effect became stronger over time, dramatically so for wages, especially agricultural wages. Their share of total income has however fallen over time, from nearly a half of all personal income to less than a third. Thus in the overall Bangladesh context too, the equalizing components of income have been highly income-inelastic.

Broadly speaking, the income sources that are disequalizing in the rural and urban economies are also disequalizing in the overall national context. They are: property income (income from return to non-land assets being much more

Table 14.6 Income shares and inequality indices for Bangladesh as a whole

	Share of total income (%) ($100q_i$)			Gini/concentration ratio (C_i or G)		
	1991–92	1995–96	2000	1991–92	1995–96	2000
Memo items:						
Total rural income	71.89	68.22	64.00	0.196	0.213	0.250
Total urban income	28.11	31.78	36.00	0.578	0.672	0.680
Farm income	31.50	25.74	14.11	0.261	0.261	0.262
Wage/salary	24.09	27.13	33.90	0.222	0.261	0.300
Agricultural wage	8.72	8.76	6.98	–0.140	–0.081	–0.233
Non-agric. wage	5.86	6.97	7.65	0.230	0.179	0.064
Non-agric. 'salary'	9.51	11.40	19.27	0.549	0.575	0.587
Non-farm enterprise	19.01	25.01	23.00	0.319	0.462	0.519
Property income	1.69	2.02	5.37	0.674	0.663	0.654
Rent from land	...	...	2.65	...	...	0.530
Other rental income	...	...	2.72	...	...	0.773
Remittance and transfer	10.44	8.81	11.69	0.371	0.590	0.570
Domestic remittance	...	...	2.85	...	...	0.370
Foreign remittance	...	...	6.46	...	...	0.675
Other transfer	...	...	2.38	...	...	0.522
Rental value of housing	8.15	5.98	5.28	0.390	0.362	0.424
Other income	5.09	5.30	6.65	0.483	0.319	0.337
Total income	100.00	100.00	100.00	0.303	0.359	0.405

Notes: See note to Table 14.4 for an explanation of the notation. Due to errors in rounding, the sums of the components do not always exactly match the totals.

disequalizing than any other component of income); foreign remittances and other transfers; non-farm enterprises; and non-agricultural salary. There was a large increase in their income share over the period, from around 38 per cent in 1991–92 to more than 55 per cent in 2000. Thus for Bangladesh as a whole too, the disequalizing sources of income are highly income-elastic.

The additional dimension that is worth noting is that the income-inelastic and equalizing sources of income are rural-intensive (that is, a very high proportion of income from those sources accrues to rural households) whereas the income-elastic and disequalizing sources of income are urban-intensive (that is, a very high proportion of income from those sources accrues to urban households). This again highlights the point noted above, that an increase in the ratio of urban income to rural income leads to a rise in overall inequality of income distribution for Bangladesh, even if the distribution within rural and urban areas each remains unchanged.

Unlike rural and urban areas, for the nation as a whole the change in the composition of income has been a more important determinant of change in inequality than the change in the distribution of specific components. For the year 2000 the Gini ratio would have been 0.343 if the composition of income were the same as in 1991–92 while concentration ratios were as they actually were in 2000. The Gini ratio for 2000 would have been 0.356 if concentration ratios were the same as in 1991–92 while the composition of income was what it actually was in 2000.

Changes in Nominal and Real Income Distributions

Change in income distribution over time is usually measured, as in this chapter, by comparing distributions of income at current prices over time. Change in the distribution of real income can however differ from change in the distribution of nominal income if the price indices are different for the bundles of goods on which different income groups spend their income. A change in nominal income distribution does not represent the change in the distribution of welfare accurately if price indices for different income groups change at different rates. Despite the obvious validity of this argument, actual estimates continue to be based on nominal income distribution for the simple reason that the estimation of price indices for different income groups is usually beyond the capacity of statistical authorities and researchers.

While practical obstacles to the estimation of the change in the distribution of real income are overwhelming, it is still useful to ask if there are reasons to believe that the change in real income distribution has been significantly different from the change in nominal income distribution. Indeed it seems likely that changes in real and nominal distributions have diverged. Over the decade under review, the price of the most important food grain, rice, fell relative to general prices. Expenditure on rice accounts for a higher proportion of income for the poorer income groups than for the richer income groups. Other things being equal, this would mean a slower increase in the income–expenditure deflator for the poorer households than for the richer households.

It is impossible to judge the magnitude of the effect of the above phenomenon on the change in real income distribution. Furthermore it is possible that there have been offsetting price changes, a faster rise in the prices of certain things (for example, fuel for the poor) that feature more prominently in the budget of the poor. It is nevertheless important to note that by itself the less-than-average rate of rise in the price of rice has had a moderating effect on the adverse change in the distribution of income. It is also interesting to note that this makes the Bangladesh experience asymmetrical to the experience in much of the developing world, where the greater integration with the world economy often led to a rise in the relative price of basic food grains.

IMPLICATIONS FOR POVERTY REDUCTION

The adverse effect that rising inequality had on the goal of poverty reduction is illustrated by Table 14.7. This exercise is primarily illustrative. Hence no attempt is made to estimate poverty lines independently. Instead the poverty lines used in the recent interim poverty reduction strategy paper (IPRSP: see Government of Bangladesh, Economic Relations Division, 2003) have been used. Unlike the

Table 14.7 Poverty in Bangladesh: facts and a counterfactual

	Rural			Urban		
	1991/92	1995/96	2000	1991/92	1995/96	2000
	Actual					
Headcount	46.95	52.77	45.19	30.22	31.05	25.27
Proportionate poverty gap	13.10	16.45	14.32	7.77	8.51	7.09
Weighted poverty gap	5.06	6.96	6.39	2.88	3.09	2.76
	Assuming 1991/92 Lorenz distribution for all the years					
Headcount	46.95	49.14	35.95	30.22	21.55	10.88
Proportionate poverty gap	13.10	14.03	8.92	7.77	4.95	2.14
Weighted poverty gap	5.06	5.50	3.17	2.88	1.71	0.69

Notes: Headcount is the ratio of the number of persons with income below the poverty line to total population. Proportionate poverty gap is the product of the average income gap of the poor times the headcount ratio. Weighted poverty gap is the average of the squares of all proportionate poverty gap, the latter being defined as the ratio of income shortfall from poverty line to poverty line, and the average calculated over the entire population with the proportionate poverty gap for the non-poor is assumed to be zero. For fuller description of these three widely-used indices of poverty, see Fields (2001).

These estimates were made by combining the decile distribution data for income with the poverty lines used in the IPRSP. Computations were made by using a program developed at the World Bank which fits a parametric Lorenz distribution to the decile distribution data and finds the values of the three measures of poverty by juxtaposing the poverty line and average income against that distribution. The program also gives the Gini ratios from the fitted parametric Lorenz distribution. These, as expected, are slightly higher than our estimates (see Note 14 for an explanation) and are not reported.

IPRSP and the practice adopted by certain other agencies, including the World Bank, poverty estimates are based on income rather than expenditure distribution (that is, the estimates refer to headcounts and other characteristics of individuals who have incomes below the poverty lines).[16]

The first three rows of the table show three different dimensions of the actual performance in poverty reduction. The headcount index simply shows the proportion of population in poverty. The proportionate poverty gap (PPG) is the product of the headcount index and the average income gap of the poor relative to the poverty line. If this index rises at a faster rate (or falls at a slower rate) than the headcount index, then it must be concluded that the poor have become poorer on average. The weighted poverty gap (WPG) shows the distribution of income among the poor. A faster rise in this index than in the headcount shows that the distribution of income among the poor has been getting worse.[17]

In rural areas, despite a 15 per cent increase in real per capita personal income, the headcount rate of poverty declined only a little and the absolute number of population in poverty actually rose from 43 million in 1991–92 to 48.5 million in 2000. Worse still, the average poverty gap increased and the distribution of income among the poor became worse as indicated by the fact that the improvement in PPG was less than that in headcount and the improvement in WPG was lower still.[18]

Urban population had a 45 per cent increase in real per capita personal income. The performance in poverty reduction was better in urban areas than in rural areas. There was nearly a 5 percentage point (16 per cent) reduction in the headcount rate of poverty even though the absolute number of population in poverty increased from 6.5 million in 1991–92 to 7.1 million in 2000. Another interesting point to note is that all three indices of urban poverty worsened between 1991–92 and 1995–96 despite a decent 16 per cent (3.7 per cent per year) increase in per capita real income.[19]

The last three rows of the table show the counterfactual: the poverty outcome in the hypothetical case of the growth in per capita income being exactly what it was but the inequality in the distribution in income remaining the same as in 1991–92. All three indices of poverty would have been dramatically more favourable. By 2000 the proportion of population in poverty would have declined to 36 per cent in rural areas (as compared to the actual of 45 per cent) and a mere 11 per cent in urban areas (as compared to the actual of more than 25 per cent). Furthermore average income gap of both the rural and urban poor would have declined. While actual indices of urban poverty went up between 1991–92 and 1995–96, they would have fallen significantly in the counterfactual case. Rural poverty over that period would have increased – an outcome of the estimated fall in rural per capita income over the period about which the authors of this chapter remain somewhat sceptical – but this increase would be far smaller

(2 percentage points) than what the estimate of actual increase (of 6 percentage points) in the headcount index shows.

For Bangladesh as a whole 49.5 million people – 43.8 per cent – were income poor in 1991–92. Estimates of actual poverty show that in 2000 there were 52.6 million poor – a 6.4 per cent increase in absolute number – or 40.8 per cent of the population – a 3 percentage point decline in the headcount rate. Had the distribution of income remained unchanged over the period, the outcome would have been dramatically different: the absolute number of people in poverty would have fallen to 39.3 million – a 20.6 per cent decline in the absolute number – or 30.5 per cent of the population – a 13.3 percentage point decline. At this rate of annual average decline in the headcount rate (1.56 percentage points per year), the total decline in the headcount rate over a 15-year period would have been more than 23 percentage points, which would have better than the equivalent of the millennium goal of halving the rate of poverty over a 15-year period.

The conclusion that clearly stands out is that the rapid increase in inequality has robbed Bangladesh of more than three-quarters of the potential decline in the headcount index of poverty over the period under review (an actual decline of 3 percentage points as compared to a potential decline of 13.3 percentage points). The pursuit of the millennium goal of poverty reduction must put as much emphasis on containing the rise in inequality as on promoting growth.

CONCLUDING COMMENTS

The last decade of the twentieth century was marked by a steady and rapid increase in inequality of income distribution in Bangladesh. One of the consequences of this was that the reduction in the headcount rate of income poverty was less than a quarter of what would have been achieved if the distribution of income remained unchanged at its level in 1991–92. The remaining three-quarters of the potential poverty reduction were lost because of rising inequality.

Distribution of income will not stop getting worse on its own. A continuation of the past trend will however make it impossible to attain anything like the millennium goal of reducing the incidence of poverty by a half by the year 2015. Trusting that growth alone can accomplish the task of poverty reduction, while permitting 'leakage' by way of continued increase in inequality, is a costly strategy to pursue. Public policy must therefore address the task of containing inequality.

As often said above, inequality can be contained by: (1) a change in the composition of income in favour of the equalizing components (reducing the share of the disequalizing components); and (2) by making individual components of income more equalizing (less disequalizing). Options in pursuit of a change in the composition of income should be limited to seeking to increase the share of wages in factor income and the share of the rural population in total income. Any attempt to shift the share of incremental income from the other disequalizing sources to the other equalizing sources would have to confront natural laws of economic growth and efficiency. The remaining focus of income distribution policy must be on reducing the disequalizing effect of individual components of income. It is the non-farm production sectors, which incorporate some of the most disequalizing components of factor income as well as provide the best hope for increasing the shares of the most equalizing components, where these changes need to be sought. Public policy could seek to influence the growth of these sectors in the following four ways to help contain inequality:

1. Make adjustments in incentives, within the limits dictated by considerations of efficiency, to promote low-skilled labour-intensive activities which would result in an increase in the share of wages in total factor income.
2. Improve the access to salaried employment by widening the access to skill acquisition.
3. Strengthen the existing programmes of making 'entrepreneurial income' in non-farm activities more accessible to the small and micro entrepreneurs by improving their access to capital, skill, technology and market.
4. Improve the share of the rural society in total public resources to promote both worthwhile farming and non-farm activities while taking special care to make rural non-farm activities less disequalizing (that is, by adhering to policies (1), (2) and (3) above).

Direct fiscal redistribution has so far had an insignificant role in Bangladesh. The HIES 2000 however provides evidence that the existing programmes have been highly successful: redistributive programmes like Vulnerable Group Feeding, Food for Education and Vulnerable Group Development have by and large succeeded in reaching the poor. While these components accounted for a miniscule 0.25 per cent of rural income, they had a strongly equalizing distribution. Less than 16 per cent of these resources leaked out to the top three deciles. The concentration ratio for this source of income was highly negative. Apparently not even the much-maligned corrupt administration has prevented these resources from reaching the poor. There is a strong case for considering an expansion in these programmes by increasing the pitifully low tax burden on the rich.

NOTES

1. The authors are very grateful to Shanker Chandra Saha, who helped with computations, and to Keith Griffin, Mahabub Hossain and a number of other colleagues who helped with comments and ideas. There is a certain overlap of ideas and arguments in this chapter with those in a paper by Khan, titled 'Rising Inequality in Bangladesh: An Analysis of Sources and Policies for Containment', presented at the World Bank/Dhaka University Bureau of Economic Research Conference held in Dhaka on 25–27 June 2003.
2. The distinction between wages and salaries is explicitly made only in HIES 2000 while the preceding surveys adopt a classification of wages from casual and regular employment. Not much is said in HIES 2000 about the distinction between wages and salaries except that wage-earning workers are paid daily or weekly while salaried workers are paid monthly. According to this principle it seemed reasonable to surmise that wage from regular employment shown in HES 1991–92 and 1995–96 is comparable with salaries shown in HIES 2000. Following the same logic, wage from casual employment in 1991–92 and 1995–96 is assumed comparable with wages in 2000. By and large 'wage-earners' seem to represent blue-collar workers with relatively low or no skills while 'salaried workers' include white-collar employees and/or workers with higher skills. The real significance of the distinction between the two, demonstrated later, is that wages largely accrue to low-income households while salaries are mostly appropriated by high-income households.
3. See Khan and Sen (2001) for further details on the difference between income definitions adopted in this study and in official BBS estimates.
4. It should however be noted that this component of income is an imputed value based on the estimated value of housing. It is hard to know how housing values are estimated by the HES/HIES given the near absence of a housing market in rural Bangladesh.
5. Return to physical assets employed in farming and non-farm production enterprises is not included in this component but is lumped together with 'profits' (income from farming and non-farm enterprise).
6. See Khan and Hossain (1989), p. 150.
7. The Lorenz distribution in our case consists of ten discontinuous segments of linear approximations of the true Lorenz distribution which is continuous. This means that our estimates of Gini ratio would be slightly smaller than what they would be if calculated either from the entire set of unit record data or the Lorenz distribution actually fitted to the data. For the application of this method of decomposing the Gini ratio, see Fei et al. (1978); Fields (1980) and Kakwani (1980, 1986). Fields (1980) is a useful source for further explanation of the method and for references to other applications of this kind of decomposition of the Gini ratio. Also see Khan and Sen (2001) for an application of the method to the data from HES 1991–92 and 1995–96.
8. Government of Bangladesh (Economic Advisor to the Ministry of Finance) (2003), p. 205 shows that the annual rate of increase in nominal inflow of remittance per person in Bangladesh was close to 13 per cent between 1991–92 and 1999–2000. Between 1991–92 and 2000, the annual increase in per capita nominal personal income was 5.3 per cent for rural Bangladesh and about 8.2 per cent for urban Bangladesh.
9. For 1991–92 and 1995–96 agricultural wages consist of wages in both casual and regular employment. As noted earlier, unlike regular wages in non-farm enterprise, that in agriculture is fairly strongly equalizing and hence has not been classified separately as 'salary'.
10. There are other possibilities as well, for example the possibility that the surveys prior to 2000 included homestead land in the definition of landownership or landholding while the HIES 2000 did not. Perhaps some combination of these factors explains the change in 2000 compared to earlier years.
11. Imports of rice in recent years may have received impetus from a number of temporary circumstances, notably the appreciation of Bangladesh taka *vis-à-vis* the currencies of major exporters (for example Thailand whose currency depreciated sharply in the aftermath of the Asian crisis) and the alleged dumping by India which faced the problem of large public stocks of rice, the consequence of an unrealistically high support price policy pursued by the government.

12. The comparison is based on the most detailed classification of sources of income which is available for the two periods. Sub-categories of farm, property and transfer income are excluded.
13. Farm wages accounted for less than 1 per cent of income in 2000. In the earlier years farm wages were larger, together all wages and salaries accounting for approximately 36 per cent of income.
14. As in the case of rural Bangladesh, for urban areas too there is a possible problem of comparability over time for salary income: for 2000 this is an explicit category in the HIES while for the earlier years we treated the earnings from regular employment, as opposed to casual employment, as salary.
15. The first step in estimating inequality for Bangladesh as a whole is to combine the samples for the rural and urban HES/HIES in such a way that the overall sample for Bangladesh properly represents the shares of rural and urban population. In the actual surveys, the proportion of rural population is much smaller than their proportion in total population. To make the national sample for Bangladesh reflect the shares of actual rural and urban population, subsamples of appropriate size were drawn from the rural samples of the BBS and added to the original rural and urban samples. Of the total number of persons included in the surveys, the rural sample represents 67 per cent in 1991–92 and 68 per cent in 1995–96 and 2000. The actual proportion of population living in rural areas was about 80 per cent according to the 1991 population census and is estimated to have fallen to about 78 per cent by 2000. We augmented the rural sample so that, in the final sample for Bangladesh as a whole, the proportion of rural population is 81 per cent in 1991–92 and 1995–96 and 78 per cent in 2000. The use of the same 81 per cent share of rural population for 1991–92 and 1995–96 is at the cost of ignoring the fall in the proportion of rural population between the two years in order to benefit from the advantage that this simplified the procedure of augmenting the rural sample by just counting each household in the original BBS rural sample twice. By 2000 this procedure would have resulted in a more serious distortion. For that year 3318 rural households were randomly drawn from and added to the BBS rural sample of 5040 households which, adding the 2400 urban households from the BBS sample, formed the national sample of 10758 households. This resulted in a 78 per cent share of the rural people (not households) in the total number of people in the augmented national sample.
16. This is the logical thing to do in this chapter which is about the distribution of income. In Bangladesh poverty estimates are often based on consumption, rather than income, indicators. This is the case for the estimates made by both the IPRSP and the World Bank (World Bank, 2003). The argument that is made in defense of consumption is that it is a better indicator of 'permanent' income – the present value of income expected over the longer-term future – than current income, which is apt to be disproportionately affected by short-term fluctuations. For a poor country like Bangladesh however, one can think of sensible arguments in defence of income as the desirable indicator of poverty. For the poor households current consumption is often achieved by resorting to survival mechanisms – for example sale of assets and incurring of debt – which can not be sustained in the long run. The present chapter does not intend to get involved in this controversy, or in many others that concern the determination of an appropriate poverty line and related issues of measuring change in the incidence of poverty. It merely tries to demonstrate the effect of a change in income distribution on the rate of poverty reduction. Although this is being illustrated by using income as the indicator to measure poverty, the argument applies to poverty measured with reference to consumption as well when similar changes in the distribution of consumption occur. The poverty lines in this chapter are the same as that in the IPRSP. They consist of the cost of a food bundle that provides 2122 kcalories per person per day and adds to that the actually observed non-food expenditure of a typical individual located at the food-poverty line. Poverty estimates based on consumption expenditure show very different changes over time because consumption expenditure estimates for 1995 are out of line with income estimates. See Khan and Sen (2001).
17. It is worth noting that even if there was indeed a difference between the real and nominal income distributions, it would not bias the estimate of headcount poverty over time because the poverty line is adjusted by a CPI for the households at the poverty threshold. It would however bias the estimates of PPG and WPG if the CPIs for different levels of poverty differ.

18. We are ignoring the highly unfavourable change in all the three indices for 1995–96 because of the possible problem with the income measure for that year. See note 19.
19. Poverty estimates reported in the IPRSP, based on per capita consumption, are quite different from the above. Poverty reduction was found by the IPRSP to be very significant between 1991–92 and 1995–96 for both rural and urban areas and very little between 1995–96 and 2000. Indeed urban poverty is found to have increased between 1995–96 and 2000. For the entire period, the decline in consumption poverty as estimated in the IPRSP is faster than the decline in our estimates of income poverty. The chapter does not have space to resolve these differences. In general, the differences are due to two factors: 1) a difference between the rate of growth in per capita consumption in IPRSP and the per capita income in this chapter, and 2) a difference in the rate of change in consumption irregularity in IPRSP and income inequality in this chapter.

REFERENCES

Bangladesh Bureau of Statistics (BBS) (1995), *Household Expenditure Survey 1991–92*, Dhaka: BBS.

Bangladesh Bureau of Statistics (BBS) (1998), *Household Expenditure Survey, 1995–96*, Dhaka: BBS.

Bangladesh Bureau of Statistics (BBS) (2003), *Household Income-Expenditure Survey 2000*, Dhaka: BBS.

Fei, John C.H., Gustav Ranis and S.W.Y. Kuo (1978), 'Growth and the family distribution of income by factor components', *Quarterly Journal of Economics*, February.

Fields, Gary S. (1980), *Poverty, Inequality and Development*, Cambridge: Cambridge University Press.

Fields, Gary S. (2001), *Distribution and Development, A New Look at the Developing World*, Cambridge and London: MIT Press.

Government of Bangladesh (GOB) Economic Advisor to the Ministry of Finance (2003), *Bangladesh Economic Survey 2003*, Dhaka: GOB.

Government of Bangladesh (GOB) Economic Relations Division, Ministry of Finance (2003), *Bangladesh: A National Strategy for Economic Growth, Poverty Reduction and Social Development*, Dhaka: GOB.

Kakwani, Nanak (1980), *Income Inequality and Poverty: Methods of Estimation and Policy Applications*, Oxford and New York: Oxford University Press.

Kakwani, Nanak (1986), *Analysing Redistribution Policies: A Study Using Australian Data*, Cambridge: Cambridge University Press.

Khan, A.R. and M. Hossain (1989), *The Strategy of Development in Bangladesh*, London: Macmillan.

Khan, A.R. and B. Sen (2001), 'Inequality and its sources in Bangladesh, 1991/92 to 1995/96: an analysis based on household expenditure surveys', *Bangladesh Development Studies,* March.

Sen, Binayak (1998), 'Politics of poverty alleviation', in Centre for Policy Dialogue, *Crisis in Governance: A Review of Bangladesh's Development 1997*, Dhaka: University Press Limited.

World Bank (2003), *Poverty in Bangladesh, Building on Progress*, Dhaka: World Bank.

15. Poverty as injustice: refocusing the policy agenda

Rehman Sobhan

THE ARGUMENT: THE SOURCES OF INJUSTICE

This chapter argues that structural injustice remains the source of poverty and exclusion. This recognition of structural concerns is yet to be incorporated into the reform agendas of the developing world. This chapter is designed to address the structural sources of poverty and injustice with a view to refocusing the policy agenda which has driven national policy-making as well the programmes of international financial institutions. Its aim is to initiate an exploration for a more relevant agenda of structural reforms where the primary mission will be to correct injustice through incorporating the excluded into the mainstream of development.

The Structural Dimensions of Poverty

A decade ago the World Bank was arguing that rapid growth was the best solution for eradicating poverty. A commitment to growth-sustaining policy reforms, inspired by the Washington Consensus, backed by temporary safety nets for those who were possible victims of such growth, was expected to reduce the proportion of those living in poverty. Needless to say, the success story of the Asian Tigers, as well as Chile, provided the substantive foundations of this hypothesis. A decade later, in the *World Development Report 2000*, the World Bank has come to terms with the proposition that policy reforms were not enough to alleviate let alone eradicate poverty. Structural concerns, of a rather more basic nature than the structural adjustments demanded by the Washington Consensus, were recognized as central to the design of policy reforms. It is arguable that this recognition by agencies such as the World Bank of structural concerns as a source of poverty has contributed little to transform the policy discourse. The new agenda for poverty focused on the contemporary, near-universal initiatives across the developing countries (DCs), to prepare Poverty Reduction Strategy Papers (PRSP), appears to have been designed to keep them eligible for aid from the Bretton Woods Institutions (BWI), the World Bank and IMF. As a result the PRSPs across the world look remarkably similar in their essentially astructural design and remain wedded to the macro-economic policy model which was integral to the reform programmes initiated by the BWI in the 1980s. This approach to poverty alleviation is no more likely to bear fruit than an earlier generation of policy reforms. Setting targets under the Millennium Development Goals is no substitute for initiating a process of structural change to correct the injustice of poverty.

The assumptions underlying this structuralist perspective on poverty recognizes that neither targeting of development resources to the poor, nor the promotion of growth, are likely to resolve the problem of poverty. The poor are embedded in certain inherited structural arrangements such as insufficient access to productive assets as well as human resources, unequal capacity to participate in both domestic and global markets, and undemocratic access to political power. These structural features of poverty reinforce each other to effectively exclude the poor from participating in the benefits of development or the opportunities provided by more open markets. In such a system even targeted programmes of poverty alleviation carry transaction costs due to the institutional structures which mediate the delivery of resources to the poor.

It is not enough however to recognize the salience of structural issues in the poverty discourse without addressing the political economy which underlies the structural features of a society. Poverty originates in the unequal command over both economic and political resources within the society and the unjust nature of a social order which perpetuates these inequities. We may term these inequities as structural injustice. Such injustice remains pervasive in most societies exposed to endemic poverty. Any credible agenda to eradicate poverty must seek to correct the structural injustices which perpetuate poverty. The main areas of structural injustice may be addressed in relation to:

- productive assets
- markets
- human development
- governance.

It would be appropriate to add the injustice of asymmetrical globalization to the above themes. However the theme of globalization needs to be addressed as an issue in its own right. Responding to the unequal and immiserizing incidence of globalization on countries and social groups around the world merits separate discussion.

Unequal access to assets

In all countries faced with endemic poverty, and indeed in many middle-income countries, inequitable access to wealth and knowledge disempower the poor from participating competitively in the market place. Indeed the market itself, as it operates in the real world rather than in text books, is designed to compromise the opportunities on offer to the poor. In most societies, with a substantial proportion of the population living in poverty, the poor have insufficient access to land, water and water bodies. Where they access such resources they do so under exploitative tenancy arrangements.

Such inequities in title and access to agrarian assets do not derive from the competitive play of the market but from the injustices of history, and therefore lack moral as well as social legitimacy. Such an inequitable access to productive assets in the rural economy also tends to be inefficient because small farmers have proven to be both more productive, as well as more likely to spend most of their income derived from their meagre assets in stimulating secondary activity in the rural economy. Where there is a dichotomy between the owners of land and the actual tiller of the land, this serves as a disincentive to investment of capital, as well as to more productive effort on the land.

Unequal participation in the market

Within the prevailing property structures of society, the rural poor in particular remain disconnected from the more dynamic sectors of the market, particularly where there is scope for benefiting from the opportunities provided by globalization. The fast-growing sectors of economic activity tend to be located within the urban economy, where the principal agents of production tend to be the urban elite, who own the corporate assets which underwrite the faster-growing sectors of the economy. Even in the export-oriented rural economy, in those areas linked with the more dynamic agro-processing sector, a major part of the profits, in the chain of value addition, accrue to those classes who control corporate wealth.

The rural poor therefore interface with the dynamic sectors of the economy only as producers and wage earners, at the lowest end of the production and marketing chain, where they sell their produce and labour under severely adverse conditions. This leaves the rural poor with little opportunity for sharing in the opportunities provided by the market economy for value addition to their labours.

Unequal access to human development

Low productivity remains an important source of income poverty. Higher income and ownership of wealth remains closely correlated to higher levels of education. Low productivity thus originates in insufficient access to education and technology. However a more serious problem facing the poor, in many developing countries, lies in the growing disparity in the quality of education which divides the rural and urban areas as well as the majority of the people from a much narrower elite. In such societies today, the principal inequity in the education sector is manifested in the growing divide between a better-educated elite with access to private as well as foreign education, and the poor who remain condemned to remain captives within an insufficiently funded and poorly governed public education system supplemented by poor-quality private or denominational schools. In an increasingly knowledge-based global economy, which is driving the IT revolution, inequitable access to quality education, relevant to the dynamics of the market, could emerge as the principal deprivation of the rural poor.

Insufficient and inequitable access to health care is also compounding the inequities in education. The dominant problem in most developing countries is not the complete absence of health care, but the incapacity of the public health care systems to deliver quality health care or for the market to meet the needs of the poor. Ill-provisioned public and private health services expose the poor to a life of insecurity, where earning opportunities can be disrupted by episodes of ill health. Poor health and nutrition can undermine both individual as well as national productivity and can influence the lifetime opportunities of the poor. In contrast, a small elite who are positioned to avail of private and even foreign health care enjoy first-world health standards. This growing disparity between the health status of the elite and the poor in such countries is inherently unjust because it denies all citizens equal chances of living a healthy life and compromises their capacity to compete in the market place.

Unjust governance

This inequitable and unjust social and economic universe is compounded by a system of unjust governance which discriminates against the poor and effectively disenfranchises them from the political benefits of a democratic process. The poor, where they are not directly oppressed by the machinery of state, remain underserved by available public services. Where such services are at all accessible to the poor, they pay high transaction costs for these services. The agencies of law enforcement insufficiently protect the poor and frequently oppress them for personal gain as well as on behalf of the elite. The judicial system denies the poor elementary justice, due both to the social biases of most third world judiciaries, and the more general lack of opportunities facing the poor, such as the inability to receive adequate legal representation.

In such a social universe the poor remain tyrannized by state as well as money power, and have to seek the protection of their oppressors within a system of patron–client relationships which perpetuates the prevailing hierarchies of power. Where the democratic process has been renewed, often after long episodes of autocratic rule, the poor are denied adequate access to representation in the systems of democratic governance from the local to the national level. Representative institutions tend to be monopolized by the affluent and socially powerful who then use their electoral office to enhance their wealth and thereby perpetuate their hold over power. In such an inequitable and politically unjust environment, the benefits of democracy remain the privilege of the elite supported by small collectives of sectional power.

POLICY INTERVENTIONS TO CORRECT STRUCTURAL INJUSTICE

In the second part of this chapter we address the issue of policy interventions, at the macro level needed to confront the issue of structural injustice. This discussion addresses the issue of correcting injustice through empowerment of the poor, by strengthening their capacity to participate in a market economy and democratic polity. The proposed policy interventions are structured under the following heads:

- Expanding the ownership and control of the poor over productive assets.
- Enhancing their access to a knowledge-based society.
- Strengthening the capacity of the poor to compete in the market place.
- Redesigning budgetary policy to deliver public resources to the poor.
- Restructuring monetary policy to deliver credit and provide savings instruments to the poor.
- Designing institutions for the poor.
- Empowering the poor.

The subsequent discussion is largely suggestive and is designed to initially stimulate debate as a prelude to designing more substantive policy proposals.

Expanding the Ownership and Control of the Rural Poor over Productive Assets

The principal assets available to the rural poor tend to be land and water. The reservations of some scholars and international agencies about confiscatory land reform remain open to challenge, largely because the prevailing title to such land, in most developing countries, is grounded in unjust and often illegitimately acquired title to such land. However we need to recognize that the correlation of political forces to underwrite a radical agrarian reform is not present in too many countries today. If such a coalition could be put in place it is arguable that a radical reform, which could transform the political economy of rural society, would not only help to end rural poverty but could also dynamize the economies as well as democratize the polities of many third world countries.

Whilst social revolution may not be round the corner there is no reason why we cannot explore agrarian reforms which are politically feasible as well as economically sustainable. Within such a perspective, four areas of agrarian reform could be considered:

- Transforming tenancy rights into either ownership rights for the tenant or through right of permanent tenancy;
- redistribution of ownership of uncultivated land;
- giving title to lands and water courses owned by the state;
- correcting injustice in the system of land administration.

Transfer of tenancy rights into permanent leaseholds has already been implemented in the agrarian reforms of the Philippines in the 1970s and 1980s and in the state of West Bengal in India, under Operation Barga. The operative issue here is to give those who actually cultivate the land, a direct stake in the land. Without legal title to ownership or tenancy of land the cultivator retains little incentive to invest in the land, and is unable to use land as collateral to access the credit market. The first principles of both market and institutional economics would therefore suggest that some form of agrarian reform remains part of an unaddressed agenda of economic reforms. We therefore need to explore why the World Bank has not applied aid conditionalities in the service of agrarian reform whilst it has never hesitated in pressurizing aid-dependent third world governments to enforce changes in property rights through privatization of SOEs or promoting decollectivization of farms in the transitional economies.

There are obviously significant socio-political problems which need to be addressed within particular countries, which remain specific to the design of such agrarian reforms, particularly where land remains a source of power within rural society. Here substantive work is needed in at least some identifiable countries where introduction of agrarian reforms can immediately lead to positive gains for the landless or land-poor at relatively limited political cost. Initially such work may focus on:

1. A few countries where tenancy reforms could be introduced. This should indicate the resources needed to either buy up lands under tenant farming or to compensate owners who would be willing to surrender permanent leasehold rights on the land.
2. Countries and areas where sizeable amounts of untenanted and uncultivated land remain available. In such countries a comprehensive rather than project-related strategy for transferring land not directly under productive use to the ownership of small farmers, should be worked out. The financial,

legal, social and political implications of such a reform process should be spelt out.

3. Countries where the system of land administration is both inefficient as well as corrupt and is used by rural elites to erode the properly rights of the weak. Here programmes may be designed to reform and simplify the land administration so that this can be made transparent and serviceable to the weaker members of society.
4. Studies in a selection of countries exposed to high rural poverty to comprehensively identify scope for policy interventions in the following areas:

   - Distribution of public lands, as well as rights over water bodies in the public domain which could be assigned exclusively to the poor.
   - Distribution of forest lands in the public domain, and lands alongside public roads and water bodies, for community development through groups of the poor.

What is suggested here is a conscious departure from the donor-designed project approach towards a national macro-programme which identifies available productive assets for distribution to the poor. Such an exercise should work out the modalities, as well as estimate the costs of the transfer, spell out the institutional arrangements to sustain such transfers, indicate provisions for credit, technological support and marketing arrangements, and finally estimate the social and political implications of the process of asset transfer. Such a series of exercises at mapping reform opportunities at the national and global level, backed by a process of social advocacy could be used to build a national constituency for reform. This would put a major issue of structural reform, with far-reaching implications for empowering the rural poor, before national legislatures as well as the global development community, who could then be encouraged to seek to mobilize funding as well as political support to underwrite such a reform process.

Enhancing Access to Human Resources

In the area of human development, courtesy of the pioneering work of scholars such as Amartya Sen and visionaries such as Mahbub ul Haq, human development (HD) is already recognized as a mainstream concern of the development agenda. As a result, in most DCs budget allocation and GDP ratios for HD in many developing countries have shown some improvement as have HD indicators. Today some MDG goals for HD across the globe remain within the realm of possibility. However such quantitative gains in HD budgets and goals have done little to bridge the growing societal divide within the education and health care system of many of these countries. The interventions proposed in this chapter thus move beyond quantitative target-setting by placing emphasis on democratizing access to education and health care by enhancing the quality of HD services directed to the deprived.

Such an agenda for human development would move beyond ensuring education or health for all, which should remain on every agenda. The priority for the next decade should move towards substantially enhancing investment for the purpose of upgrading the quality and governance of schools and health care facilities serving low-income groups to a level where they do not feel disadvantaged compared to the expensively educated members of society. Such a goal carries formidable implications as to costs and governance. What may therefore be more feasible is a phased series of investments in upgrading these public facilities so that the budgetary impact and governance problems could be more easily absorbed. At the same time, within the next five to ten years, the graduates of such a process of quality enhancement efforts should be seen to be competing for university places with the elite, endowed with a no less robust state of health than the children of the elite. The spectacle of the children of the poor rising to positions of professional, economic and political influence will itself have an empowering effect on the poor to demand more rapid democratization of opportunities for human capacity development.

Until public services in the health sector can be brought to a competitive level with better-quality private services, public resources should be channelled to establishing a system of health, disability and old-age insurance for the poor to enable them also to access private health care. A number of countries in the DCs offer some form of insurance coverage through public and private programmes but these facilities in most countries have a rather narrow coverage. This system needs to be substantially expanded, through collaboration between the state, private sector and possibly non-governmental organizations (NGOs). A similar system of public scholarships should be targeted to the children of the poor to access private education, where the better-endowed private institutions and also the more elite-oriented publicly funded state institutions should be encouraged to set aside a proportion of places for those living in poverty.

The knowledge revolution is now being brought within the reach of the poor by advances in telecommunications. Formidable opportunities are being opened up in the area of distance learning and telemedicine, for urban standards of education, medical diagnosis and prescription to be delivered to the most remote villages. Here major investments to build the infrastructure to take the IT revolution to the villages, remains a major goal of public and global development policy. Grameenphone in Bangladesh remains an important example of how poor rural women can be brought into the communications revolution as both providers and users of IT services. In similar vein, the direction of R&D agendas, at the global level, to not only address the concerns of the poor, as in the case of HIV-AIDS, but to develop technologies for the rural poor, merit urgent attention. The related global public goods debate needs to be taken forward so that global development aid can be directed to delivering such goods to the poor across the world.

Strengthening the Capacity of the Poor to Compete in the Market Place

Market-based institutions for the poor

The capacity of the poor to operate on more equal turns in the market place depends in considerable measure on their capacity for collective action. The weakness of the poor in the market place originates in their isolation. Here investment in institutions, whether sponsored by NGOs or representing collective action by the poor, in the form of marketing cooperatives or corporate bodies of the poor, need to be imaginatively conceived and developed.

Since the developing world is littered with the debris of captured, corrupted or failed cooperatives, directing collectives of the poor into such a risk-prone area as the market should not be underestimated. However the issue remains to invest the poor with the capacity to develop the financial and organizational strength to sell their products and services, at a time and in a market which offers them the best terms, rather than to sell their produce out of distress or the need to subsist. Such a perspective would demand interventions in the macro-credit market to underwrite such marketing ventures as well as the deployment of professional management skills to assist the poor in participating in the market place.

It should be kept in mind that commercial managers are professionals who can be hired in the market place and can be provided with incentives for good performance by collectives of the poor no less than corporate enterprises. The task ahead would be to empower the poor to draw upon such professionals without feeling socially intimidated by their own hired employees. Conversely such a process should encourage the emergence of a socially motivated class of managers who would not necessarily remain undercompensated, and who could specialize in serving such organizations of the poor which have dared to venture into the market place. International development agencies can be persuaded to underwrite initially some credit support as well as management inputs for such commercial organizations of the poor. But in the final analysis such ventures must be sustained in the market place.

Adding value to the labour of the poor

Many NGOs around the world are already providing marketing services to the poor, for particular commodities, in particular markets. However the best service that can be provided is to help the poor to add value to their labours by moving upmarket through either agro-processing or providing inputs to the corporate sector. The pioneering role of Amul Dairy in India, and more recently BRAC in Bangladesh, in enabling small dairy farmers, or just poor households who own a cow, to become part of a milk processing chain, allows the poor to share in the profits from selling pasteurized milk or cheese in the metropolitan market. Similarly Grameen Bank's initiative to support rural handloom weavers to upgrade their product to provide Grameencheck fabrics, as inputs to Bangladesh's leading export industry of ready-made garments, provides significant new opportunities for value addition to the labours of the poor, rural-based weavers.

Such initiatives could be taken one step further, by financially empowering the vast body of small farmers servicing the private agro-processing sector, as well as handloom weavers, to become equity stakeholders in the upstream enterprises which add value to their produce or labour. Tobacco, cotton, sugar cane and jute growers, servicing export-oriented corporate bodies, could be brought together as corporate bodies or as members of a dedicated mutual fund, to acquire a stake in these private corporate bodies engaged in the task of value addition. This marriage between the small farmer and the downstream agro-processor could also be promoted by local civil society organizations and consummated through a dowry provided by both multilateral and bilateral funding agencies to organized groups of small farmers to buy into such ventures.

At the global level, better use needs to be made of such organizations as the Fair Trade Movement (FTM), which carry the produce of poor farmers and craft artisans into the retail markets of the developed world. The FTM remains a commendable initiative in cutting out global market enterprises who normally appropriate much of the value addition in the market chain for primary produce. However such micro-producers in the DCs usually tend to be linked to the FTM through locally based small commercial enterprises or NGOs who serve as intermediaries between local producers and the global market. If the FTM remains committed to its objective of maximizing the retention of value addition with the primary producers, it should begin by encouraging its client base of small businesses in the DCs, who reach out to small producers, to transform their suppliers or artisans into shareholders of the local business enterprises. Where feasible, the artisans should form their own corporate enterprises or cooperatives to empower themselves to deal directly with the FTM. At the same time, the FTM should consider incorporating itself and providing an equity stake in such a formidable global corporate enterprise to the small farmers and artisans whose products are being sold in the supermarkets of the developed world. The emergence of such a global corporation of and for the small and the weak primary producers would do much not just to build global solidarity amongst the deprived, but also to transform this into market power. There is no reason why the Fair Trade Movement could not aspire to emerge as the Lever Brothers of the poor.

Redesigning Budgetary Policy to Deliver Public Resources to the Poor

Restructuring the budget

In its present configuration, budgetary policy aggregates public expenditure programmes without setting any explicit goal to serve the poor, who tend to remain marginalized in the budgetary concerns of most developing countries. In the absence of any explicit structuring of the budget to serve the poor, most budgets contain a plethora of projects and programmes ostensibly targeted to the poor. In many least-developed countries (LDCs) such pro-poor programmes tend to be underwritten by a variety of aid donors. A not insignificant part of the expenditure targeted to the poor does not reach them, due to high transaction and delivery costs which enrich the non-poor or expatriate consultants.

Much of this misdirection of public expenditure is concealed under opaque budgetary practices which make it impossible to identify the share of the budget directly reaching the poor or to estimate its outcomes on the circumstance of the poor. In this respect, targeted aid programmes are no less likely to carry high transaction costs, with poor outcomes and weak sustainability.

Any serious attempt to dedicate public expenditure budgets to the concerns of the poor should be transparently structured to identify clearly not just projects explicitly targeted to the poor, but also resources delivered to and directly impacting on their lives. A number of such efforts, usually at the level of civil society, have attempted every year to restructure the national budget in order to isolate its contribution towards poverty eradication. The pro-poor budgeting exercises in Porto Allegre, Brazil, have acquired global recognition. However most other such efforts remain under-resourced, some carry unresolved conceptual problems and most such initiatives tend to exercise insufficient leverage for persuading finance ministers to calibrate their budgets more carefully to reach the poor. Nor have like-minded donors been any more successful than civil society, in spite of many efforts at promoting budgetary reform through the provision of technical assistance in making national budgets more transparent in defining their impact or delivering public resources to the poor.

Inducting the poor into the budgetary process

Apart from targeting public expenditure to the poor, the more serious limitation of the budgetary process lies in the absence of consultation with the poor. A quite disproportionate amount of time is spent consulting business leaders and economists on budget design. Much less, if any, effort is invested in consulting the poor about what they expect from the budgetary process. Some consultative exercises, often at donors' initiative, have tended to produce some rather self-conscious exercises where the sponsors end up hearing what they want to hear. A number of civil society initiatives to consult the poor have yielded more promising results. However unless such efforts are institutionalized and can serve to influence policy-makers, they degenerate into episodic exercises in providing some catharsis for the grievances of the poor.

Ideally it is governments who should reach out to the poor whose votes elect them to office. Such an effort should not however manifest itself as a pro-forma, pre-budget exercise in bureaucratic tourism of some rural areas, but should be institutionalized into the structures of governance. The consultative process each year should be preceded by a process whereby the concerns of the poor are systematically recorded and reviewed by the budget-makers before they embark on their annual consultative encounters with the poor.

All such efforts at making budgets more transparent and consulting the poor will be meaningless if they do not end up reprioritizing public expenditures to put resources into those sectors that serve the poor. This process will have to precede the task of ensuring that allocated resources actually reach the poor. However redirecting budget priorities is not a zero-sum game and the political economy of a society needs to be taken into account in any discussion on the budget. If the poor are to compete with the defence forces to influence the allocative choices of the Finance Ministry, they will need to collectively empower themselves to compete in the political arena rather than to depend exclusively on the social conscience of the policy-makers.

Fiscal policy

The instruments of fiscal policy in many developing countries are usually not designed to address the concerns of the poor. It must therefore be recognized that fiscal systems can also be redesigned to do more than provide incentives for business enterprises and relief to the poor. The poor are also producers of goods and services and remain sensitive to the incentives offered by a well-designed fiscal policy. The instruments of direct as well as indirect taxation need to be calibrated to make better use of their distributive and poverty-reducing power. Fiscal specialists should be invited to join hands with poverty specialists to rethink the design and mechanisms for formulating a fiscal policy which can better serve the needs of the poor.

Restructuring Monetary Policy

Taking micro-credit out of the ghetto

Nowhere is there a greater need for developing a macro perspective for poverty eradication than in the area of monetary policy. The instruments of monetary policy appear to be exclusively targeted towards ensuring macro-economic stability, moderating inflation and meeting the credit needs of the corporate sector. The financial needs of the poor, once left to the informal sector, have now been segregated in the micro-credit market. This apartheid within the monetary system remains a major anomaly in the global development discourse.

The micro-credit movement has, in many ways, revolutionized the banking system of many countries such as Bangladesh by moving a large segment of the rural population from the informal to the formal capital market through access to institutional credit. In Bangladesh 15 million poor borrowers, mostly women, have graduated from the informal money market into organized banking, where recognition of their innate sense of fiduciary responsibility for repaying loans and making regular savings has been institutionalized. These numbers are comparable to those who participate in the commercial banking system. No less important, the micro-credit system has established the creditworthiness of the poor and laid to rest the myth that only men of property should be eligible to access the institutional banking system.

It is not intended here to discuss the merits and limitations of micro-credit or to suggest that it is the panacea for poverty eradication. Indeed it could be argued that by its very nature, micro-credit can never aspire to eradicate poverty since it only addresses one component of the various markets which condition the lives of the rural poor. It is arguable that by locking the poor into the micro-credit system, based on the fiduciary responsibility of the household, they have been excluded from participating in the macro-economy, have been isolated from collective action and condemned to live on the fringes of the poverty line. It is therefore not surprising that countries with the most substantive exposure to micro-credit remain mired in poverty. This caveat on the limits of micro-credit remains without prejudice to the enormous contribution of micro-credit in alleviating poverty and distress, as well as enhancing the self-worth of the poor.

Regrettably, few finance ministers in the developing world have registered the crucial lessons from the micro-credit revolution that the poor are bankable and creditworthy. The logic of this discovery would be to enable micro-credit organizations to graduate into corporate banks or financial enterprises, owned by the poor. This indeed is the path followed by Grameen Bank which is a corporate body with over 2 million shareholders, composed mostly of poor women, who are also the clientele of the bank. Bangladesh, and indeed a number of other developing countries, are ready to sustain many more such banks, owned by the poor and serving the poor. Given the high level of non-performing loans in the regular banking system of Bangladesh, the fact that Grameen Bank, with a credit volume comparable to the largest commercial banks, can limit its portfolio of non-performing loans in the range of 5 per cent, demonstrates that it has the capacity to operate as a competitive commercial bank, whilst serving the needs of the poor. There is today no reason why such organizations of the maturity of Grameen Bank, with such a consistent record of debt recovery, should not graduate into the macro-finance system by accessing the deposits of the public and even marketing their assets at the global level, through such financial instruments as securitization which are in widespread use in more advanced financial systems.

Restructuring financial services to serve the poor

If Grameen Bank can move upmarket, there is no reason why commercial banks should not redirect their loan portfolios to the poor on account of their creditworthiness, particularly in an environment when many of their largest commercial borrowers remain habitual defaulters. This is not to suggest that commercial bankers have to immediately move out of their air-conditioned offices and visit each client in their village home, as is the practice with the micro-credit organizations. A number of commercial banks in South Asia are already using NGOs and even community-based organizations to retail banking services to the poor. Such organizations which reach out to the grassroots are uniquely equipped to link the urban-centric financial institutions to the wider concourse of the poor. Commercial banks can use these grassroots institutions to adjust their perspective as well as their portfolios to the market opportunities provided by the poor, who remain highly bankable and yet are deprived of the wide range of services that they need.

Corporate banks may be more inclined to do this if the government were to incorporate such a redirection of banking services into the design of financial sector reforms. The World Bank has for many years been promoting financial sector reforms across the developing world to correct distortions ostensibly attributed to public policy failures. Regrettably there is no evidence of any recognition by the World Bank of the most glaring market failure in the financial system, which deprives millions of potentially creditworthy customers of financial services. Nor has there been any serious effort in the various BWI-induced reform processes to restructure the macro-financial system to deliver financial services to the poor on grounds of both market efficiency and alleviating poverty.

Mutual funds for the poor

Apart from the issue of redesigning monetary policy to deliver credit to the poor, the monetary system also needs to put in place a much wider spectrum of financial instruments which can serve to mobilize the savings of the poor. An organization such as Grameen Bank has accumulated Tk. 10 billion (about $187 million) in savings from its 2.3 million members. All these savings remain on deposit with Grameen Bank and are used for further lending to its members. Savings mobilized by other NGOs in Bangladesh, as well as by individual households, indicate that the poor remain formidable savers. In India, a large number of small community organizations in Andhra Pradesh state have in aggregate accumulated savings of around $180 million which remain on deposit with the banks.

The monetary system needs to design special financial instruments to attract these micro-savings into the corporate sector, particularly where it can be structured to serve the poor. Again, Grameen Bank has taken the initiative in launching the first Mutual Fund of the poor, where it is providing opportunities for investing a small fraction (Tk.150 million) of the savings of its members in a managed, close-end, Mutual Fund which would invest its portfolio in the corporate sector. The potential of this experiment has to be tested within the small, rather unstable capital market of Bangladesh.

Whatever may be the fate of the Grameen Fund, the concept of mutual funds for the poor provides a significant institutional mechanism to move the poor out of the village economy and into the more dynamic corporate sector, to a stage where a significant share of corporate wealth could be owned by the poor. The savings of the poor can not only augment the savings base but also broaden the investment capacity of the economy, whilst transforming the poorest rural household into stakeholders in the process of national economic growth.

The channelling of the savings of the poor into corporate investments should be matched by the channelling of urban savings to finance the corporate as well as micro-credit needs of the poor. An integrated monetary system is a two-way street where financial intermediation by the banks should be able to channel the savings of the rich to underwrite the investment needs and creative capacity of the poor. Within such a perspective, credit from the commercial banks should also be made available to organizations of the poor to leverage their investments in the corporate sector.

Such an integrated financial system carries obvious risks associated with the nature of the market mechanism, as well as the probity of the corporate sector, which will demand special safeguards to protect the interests of the poor. But unless these opportunities for linking the poor to the corporate sector are explored through widening the horizons of monetary policy, the poor will remain permanent captives in the ghetto of the micro-economy.

Expanding the stakes of the poor

The Mutual Fund is but one institutional mechanism to link the poor to the corporate sector. The underlying premise of the Mutual Fund is the notion of creating possibilities for the poor to own corporate assets. We have already identified the opportunities for linking the farmers to the agro-processing corporate sector by giving them an equity stake in such enterprises. At the same time, the agro-corporations should be motivated to invest in improving the productivity and capacities of their rural partners.

Financial policy could also be restructured to ensure that all assets, from urban land to real estate development, from banks to corporate trading houses, could be redesigned to accommodate the poor as equity partners. The two institutional instruments to make this possible remain the mutual fund and the need for private limited companies to transform themselves into public limited companies. Here monetary and fiscal policy can provide incentives to encourage the corporatization of private wealth along with the reservation of space for equity ownership of this wealth by the poor.

It may be suggested that the opportunities for democratizing ownership of corporate wealth should not be limited to the rural poor but could be extended to workers, to own shares in the enterprises where they work. The 1.2 million women, mostly from the rural areas, who earn monthly wages of around $30 and provide the substantive value addition in Bangladesh's principal export of ready-made garments, are no less deserving of being made stakeholders in the most dynamic sector of the economy, than are the rural poor. Similarly workers in banana, sugarcane or palm oil plantations could be given an equity stake in the enterprises where they work.

Institutions of the Poor

Collective action by the poor

The poor survive as individuals with no institutional persona. The primary task of building institutions for the poor should be to enable them to rediscover their collective identity. The forging of such a collective identity does not however develop out of abstract notions of identity, but is likely to emerge out of a process of collective action. Such collective action tends to be constructed around particular social actions or through shared participation in pursuit of economic gain. Here, if the poor are to be mobilized for collective action, special institutions of the poor may need to be constructed. Two such institutional arrangements are discussed below.

Corporations of the poor

Over the last two decades the NGOs have come to play a growing role in most developing countries, principally as delivery agents, contracted by donors to deliver certain services targeted to the poor. Whilst we may argue about their institutional efficacy, systems of accountability and even cost-effectiveness, it is generally accepted that NGOs tend to be more effective in delivering resources directly to the poor than the machinery of state. It has however been argued that the emergence of the NGOs as aid contractors keeps them heavily dependent on aid. This external dependence is increasingly compromising the role of NGOs as social mobilizers and advocates of the poor.

It is suggested that the long-term sustainability of the NGO, as a financially autonomous institution of civil society, lies in its reinvention as a corporation of the poor. The future of NGOs as social institutions lies in their ability to use their institutional capacity, which has extended into rural communities across the world, thereby giving them direct access to vast numbers of the poor, to use this reach to link the poor to the market. This can be done through transforming NGOs into corporations of the poor, where their micro-beneficiaries are transformed into the owners of a corporate NGO. Through such a measure, the individual weakness of the poor could be aggregated into the legally recognized power of the many. Initially only a small number of NGOs would have the organizational capacity and resources to evolve into nationally competitive corporate bodies. However smaller NGOs can also evolve into more modest corporate entities. Even a single village-based NGO could evolve into a small enterprise which could mobilize the poor to own the village pond, build and maintain rural roads, or trade in commodities produced or consumed by the poor.

This suggested reconfiguration of the NGOs would also make them accountable to their myriad owners. Such an institutional transformation could lay to rest the critique of NGOs that they are accountable only to their donors and perpetuate the patron–client system which they were designed to challenge. An NGO owned by and accountable to 2 million members or even 2000 members could emerge as a socially powerful organization at the national or local level with no less social legitimacy than a representative institution.

Community-based organizations of the poor

The NGOs are not the only agency for forging collective solidarity within the poor. Community-based or self-help organizations of the poor, co-operatives and activity-based organizations, which bring groups of the poor together, should aspire to forge an institutional identity. A total of 6991 community-based organizations (CBOs), covering 132 000 households, have been organized in six countries of South Asia under the South Asian Programme of Poverty Alleviation (SAPAP) jointly to undertake savings and investment. In Pakistan, the National Rural Support Project has organized 11 000 community organizations with 241 000 members to participate in similar community actions in their village. In the state of Andhra Pradesh the World Bank is assisting a programme for reducing poverty which plans the social mobilization of 5 million of the rural poor in CBOs to collectively participate in economic activity.

Corporatizing these CBOs will provide the legal foundations for collective action, to enable these bodies of the poor to access credit, enter into contractual relationships and deal with international organizations. The precise legal persona of these corporations may vary from limited liability companies, with the poor as equity owners, to co-operatives with the poor as partner members. But the common feature of all such corporate entities of the poor is that they must operate in the market place and generate income rather than limiting themselves to surviving as savings and loan associations.

Empowering the Poor

The entire process of building a collective identity for the poor through specially constructed institutions derives from the need for the poor to claim a place in society which is more commensurate with their numbers. The poor remain disempowered because they are isolated. Bring them together, and they emerge as a major force in the economy, in society and eventually in the political arena. Incorporating the poor, around opportunities for collective economic benefit, may invest them with a sustainable sense of solidarity which may not have been possible through more episodic participation in various class actions. However in the final analysis it is only when the poor are sitting in the representative institutions of the state, in local elective bodies as well as in parliament, that they will be able to ensure that their special concerns will be mainstreamed within the policy-making process.

It is argued that a society populated by a large number of corporate bodies of the poor, bound together by opportunities for economic gain, could aggregate into a powerful political force which could transform the balance of power in many parts of the developing world. This vision however lies in the distant future and we should not tantalize ourselves with the prospect of instant social transformation. The purpose of including the issue of empowering the poor in this chapter is to spell out a broad continuum for policy action. This approach demands a change in perspective from poverty alleviation to poverty eradication through structural change.

It is unlikely that many governments in the developing world would be inclined to rush towards building up institutions of the poor to a point where the balance of power in society could be transformed. Our discussions should thus not be built upon an innocence of the discipline of political economy. Building up the collective power of the poor, whether of 2 million members or 200 members in a village, will challenge existing vested interests at different levels. Any serious discussion of the empowering effect of collective action will therefore have to contextualize the outcome of this process within its given socio-political environment in a country. This recognition of political reality should not however serve as a refuge for business as usual. All social action builds upon testing the limits of commitment and tolerance of state and society. Thus those governments who do have a genuine commitment to eradicate poverty may accommodate some measures of institutional change, as for example by encouraging the emergence of a mutual fund for the poor or promoting community-based organizations. In South Asia for example, most governments have accepted the idea of expanding the coverage of CBOs as an instrument for rural development. But such ideas have to be developed as politically marketable proposals and have to be tested not just on their intellectual merits, but have to mobilize social and political constituencies in their support.

We must furthermore keep in mind that neither the concept of building corporations of the poor nor the mutual fund depend exclusively on the government for their advancement. NGOs are at liberty to reconstruct their corporate identity, as are the poor to organize themselves, though in some countries such a process may require enabling legislation. Here the international development community can help to accelerate such a process of empowering the poor, by redirecting their aid programmes towards both encouraging the emergence of mutual funds as well as enabling corporate bodies of the poor to acquire wealth. This could require provision of resources to support acquisition of land, water bodies, leveraging purchase of shares, building capacity to compete in the market, and enhancing the knowledge base of the poor, particularly to participate in the IT revolution. Indeed all such programmes could themselves derive from a new generation of locally owned structural adjustment reforms, premised on the empowerment of the poor. However such initiatives will depend on whether governments in the developed world, particularly those with an apparently strong commitment to poverty reduction, and international institutions with similar commitments are willing to strike at the roots of poverty, or whether they will remain committed to business as usual.

There is little in this chapter which could be regarded as particularly radical. Neither mutual funds or corporations of the poor should raise the spectre of the barricades. However when such an argument is viewed within a holistic policy framework it does represent a change in the direction of the agenda for poverty eradication, away from narrow programmes of income gain for the poor to their empowerment through collective action for economic gain and social advancement. It is hoped that the ideas articulated in this chapter will encourage more substantive work and public debate on the need for and direction of structural change in developing and transitional societies, which may encourage rethinking among their policy-makers as well as some forward-looking international institutions.

16. Economic policies and poverty reduction in Asia and the Pacific: alternatives to neoliberalism

Terry McKinley

INTRODUCTION

Since the mid-1990s, poverty reduction has emerged as the overriding objective of the international development community. All policies are now evaluated from a poverty reduction perspective as a well as a growth perspective. This is now as true of economic policies as social policies.

Consistent with this approach, the Bretton Woods Institutions require low-income developing countries to formulate Poverty Reduction Strategy Papers (PRSPs) that, among other objectives, would foster 'pro-poor growth'. This is a variant of the 1970s approach of 'growth with equity', but with a sharper focus on those in a society who are most deprived. However the neoliberal, 'equity-blind' economic policies of earlier structural adjustment programmes have been imported into PRSPs with little change, except for the addition of an anti-poverty rhetorical flourish. These policies are, regrettably, neither pro-poor nor even pro-growth.

Consequently PRSPs have been obliged to deploy a broad array of targeted social policies to mitigate the adverse impact of inequality-intensifying, growth-impeding economic policies. Had growth been more 'pro-poor', namely, both more rapid and more equitable in its impact, the extensive PRSP panoply of social policies would not be necessary.

If 'pro-poor growth' should be a primary objective of public policy, how is it defined? The concept incorporates both equity and growth components.[1] UNDP takes the position that if countries are to reach the target of halving extreme income poverty by 2015 (the primary poverty goal of the Millennium Declaration), rapid growth is certainly essential – more rapid, in fact, than the average over 1970–2000. However if growth is more equitable – so that the incomes of the poor grow faster than average – countries have a much better chance of reaching the target.

Hence a strategy of such 'equity-based' growth will need to be rapid enough to significantly improve the 'absolute' condition of the poor and equitable enough to improve their 'relative' position – preferably by achieving equity at the start of the growth process (such as through land reform or universalizing basic education) or by decreasing high inequality over time (such as through pushing up wages by generating widespread employment among low-skilled workers).

'Equity-based' growth can be achieved through a variety of strategies, which obviously depend in part on each country's initial conditions. In general, if growth is to immediately reduce poverty, it should have a pattern that directs resources disproportionately to the sectors in which the poor work (such as small-scale agriculture), the areas in which they live (such as underdeveloped regions) or the factors of production that they possess (such as unskilled labour or land).

Such a pattern of growth is difficult enough to accomplish under normal capitalist patterns of development, but doubly difficult when the governing economic strategy is neoliberal. During the recent period of domination by neoliberal economics, growth has been slow and pro-rich.

In light of these problems, progressive economists have intensified their critical examination of the impact of neoliberal economic policies on growth and poverty reduction. This effort has been motivated by three major concerns: (1) determining, practically, how to achieve 'pro-poor growth'; (2) highlighting the glaring inconsistencies between 'poverty-producing' neoliberal economic policies and the anti-poverty objectives of Poverty Reduction Strategy Papers; and (3) trying to promote a broader and healthier policy dialogue on these issues by helping create a wider range of viable economic options and alternatives.

In order to address these problems, the United Nations Development Programme initiated in early 2002 the Asia-Pacific Regional Programme on the Macroeconomics of Poverty Reduction. This programme has supported studies of eight countries: Bangladesh, Cambodia, China, Indonesia, Mongolia, Nepal, Sri Lanka and Vietnam. Its objective has been to produce policy-oriented research on the impact on poverty of macroeconomic policies (fiscal, monetary and exchange-rate policies) and adjustment policies (financial liberalization, trade liberalization and privatization/deregulation). Related to this agenda, it has also investigated how a country can mobilize the domestic resources (through increased savings, taxation or prudent domestic borrowing) needed to finance a high rate of public and private investment for accelerated economic growth.

Comparative Country Performance

The countries covered by the regional programme vary significantly – such as in terms of size, income level and economic structure. For example China's gross national income was $1131 billion in 2001 while Cambodia's was 3.3 billion and Mongolia's only 1 billion. Income per person in these countries ranges from a low of $1310 in Nepal and $1610 in Bangladesh to $3180 in Sri Lanka and $4020 in China. Some of the countries – China, Mongolia and Vietnam – have been undergoing a transition from a centrally planned economy to a regulated market economy.

China and Vietnam achieved rapid rates of growth in income per capita from 1990 to 2001. China's rate was 8.8 per cent and Vietnam's 6.0 (Table 16.1). However growth in Cambodia, Indonesia and Nepal was much slower, ranging between 2 and 2.5 per cent. Growth slowed down in China and Vietnam during 2000–2001 but picked up in Cambodia. In Mongolia growth was at a standstill while in Sri Lanka it turned negative.

During this period, inflation was not a major problem, except in Mongolia (Table 16.1). The CPI inflation rate for Mongolia during 1990–2001 was about 40 per cent. In Indonesia it was about 14 per cent but for the rest of the countries it was below 10 per cent. During 2000–2001, the inflation rate slowed down in all countries, except in Sri Lanka. Inflation had become very low or negative in several of them. Deflation was a problem in Cambodia (-0.6 inflation rate) and Vietnam (-0.4) while inflation was very close to zero in China and only about 1 per cent in Bangladesh.

Bangladesh, China and Vietnam have had notable success in reducing income poverty during the 1990s. Table 16.1 records progress in poverty reduction based

Table 16.1 Growth, inflation and poverty reduction

	GDP per capita annual growth rate (%) 1990–2001 (2000–2001 in parentheses)	Average annual change in the CPI (%) 1990–2001 (2000–2001 in parentheses)	Share of population that is poor, by national poverty line, (earliest year)	Share of population that is poor, by national poverty line, (latest year)
Bangladesh	3.1 (3.5)	5.1 (1.1)	50 (1991–92)	40 (2000)
Cambodia	2.2 (4.2)	5.3 (–0.6)	39 (1993–94)	36 (1997)
China	8.8 (6.5)	7.6 (0.3)	31.3 (1990)	11.5 (1998)
Indonesia	2.3 (2.0)	13.9 (11.5)	34 (1993)	34 (2000)
Mongolia	–0.2[1] (0.4)	39.0 (8.0)	36.3 (1995)	35.6 (1998)
Nepal	2.4 (2.4)	8.1 (2.8)	40 (1989)	45 (1996)
Sri Lanka	3.6 (–2.8)	9.9 (14.2)	20 (1990–91)	25 (1995–96)
Vietnam	6.0 (5.5)	3.2 (–0.4)	51 (1993)	37 (1998)

Note: 1. estimate.

Sources: World Bank (2003) and UNDP (2003).

on national poverty lines. In Bangladesh, the proportion of the population in poverty declined from 50 per cent in 1991–92 to 40 per cent in 2000. China scored a much more rapid rate of poverty reduction, based on a faster rate of economic growth and supplemented by favourable agricultural terms of trade during the mid-1990s. The proportion of the Chinese population in poverty dropped from about 31 per cent in 1990 to 11.5 per cent in 1998, with most of the progress being registered between 1993 and 1996. In Vietnam, the proportion of the population in poverty declined from 51 per cent to 37 per cent during the relatively short period between 1993 and 1998.

In Cambodia, Indonesia and Mongolia, there was very little progress in reducing income poverty. In Cambodia growth of per capita income was modest during most of the 1990s, and concentrated in urban areas. Because of the setbacks that Indonesia experienced during the Asia Financial Crisis, the level of poverty in 2000 was virtually the same as it was in 1993; during the crisis it had doubled. Mongolia underwent a deep recession in the early 1990s and recovered only slowly thereafter, with little discernible impact on poverty. In Nepal and Sri Lanka poverty appeared to rise during part of the 1990s.

Drawing on the studies of the eight countries covered by the regional programme, this chapter briefly addresses four interrelated issues: (1) the need for investment-led fiscal policy; (2) the impediment of restrictive inflation targeting; (3) the constraint imposed by low public revenue; and (4) the poor record of financial liberalization. The following section examines the four issues.

Hopefully, the policy lessons from the regional programme in the Asia-Pacific can contribute to developing a general outline of a macroeconomic framework that is more aligned with the objective of pro-poor growth and human development. It is evident that the findings of the programme diverge in significant respects from reigning neoliberal orthodoxy.

FOUR INTERRELATED ISSUES

1. Expanding Pro-Poor Public Investment

A major finding of the regional programme – which has been a fairly consistent theme across the country studies – is the need to use fiscal policy more proactively to expand pro-growth and pro-poor public investment. In several countries, capital expenditures are a small percentage of total government expenditures. In South Asia for instance this percentage is only 9 per cent. By contrast, in East and South-East Asia, it is 24 per cent. In Vietnam, in particular, it is 32 per cent.

The country studies generally assume that public investment can, if it is reasonably growth-oriented, have a 'crowding-in' effect on private investment.

Boosting aggregate demand through public investment can have the advantage not only of sparking recovery in a stagnant economy, but also of loosening the supply constraints on long-term growth. However 'crowding-in' cannot automatically be assumed. Public capital expenditures have to be carefully designed as part of a well-conceived pro-growth as well as pro-poor strategy.

The multipliers for expenditures on public investment can be substantial if such investment helps boost the productivity of labour and capital. The higher marginal propensity to consume in developing countries – compared to industrial countries – is an additional factor that can increase these multipliers (Hemming et al., 2002, p. 12). Also the multiplier impact of public investment can be powerful if there is excess capacity in an economy and households are liquidity constrained – as is the case in many developing countries.

The common concern of neoliberal economists has been that increasing public investment will enlarge public deficits and these, in turn, will lead to higher inflation, depreciation of the exchange rate and higher real interest rates. There is little evidence in the literature that public investment crowds out private investment through changes in the interest rate or exchange rate (Hemming et al., 2002, p. 36). Moreover multipliers remain large, and crowding out is minimized, when a moderate monetary expansion accompanies an increase in public investment. As long as deficits are used to finance public investment that expands aggregate supply, the aggregate demand effects should not be unduly inflationary.

Public investment can also be a powerful instrument for the reallocation of public resources to poverty reduction. As part of its National Poverty Alleviation Strategy for example, China has used public investment to channel funds to the poorer western regions of the country, which have been left behind by the economic boom centred in the richer coastal provinces.

In Cambodia, the country study argued that increased public investment is not likely to trigger high inflation since much of the capacity of the economy is underutilized (especially land and labour) and adequate resources can be mobilized through domestic borrowing to finance the investment. Moreover inflation has not been an immediate problem: it was a negative 0.6 per cent in 2000–2001.

While Cambodia has been growing, poverty has not been significantly reduced because, in part, growth has been centred in urban enclaves, based mostly on the exports of garments. Demand expansion, driven by public investment, is needed to generate a broader pattern of growth that can reach rural areas, where most of the poor live.

The picture is very similar in Nepal, where market liberalization has been insufficient to generate dynamism in agriculture, where the majority of the poor work. Deprived of public investment, agricultural growth has barely kept up with the growth of the rural population.

Table 16.2 Investment, savings and external capital

	Gross capital formation as % of GDP 2001 (1990)	Gross domestic savings as % of GDP 2001(1990)	FDI as % of gross capital formation 2001	ODA as % of gross capital formation 2001
Bangladesh	23 (17)	16 (10)	0.7	9.5
Cambodia	18 (8)	10 (2)	18.6	67.1
China	38 (35)	40 (38)	10.1	0.3
Indonesia	17 (31)	26 (32)	–13.2	6.1
Mongolia	30 (38)	14 (9)	20.0	67.5
Nepal	24 (18)	15 (8)	1.4	28.8
Sri Lanka	22 (23)	15 (14)	4.9	9.4
Vietnam	31 (13)	29 (13)	12.9	14.2

Source: World Bank (2003, Tables 4.9, 4.9, 5.2, 6.10).

As a share of GDP, gross capital formation is not very low in either Cambodia or Nepal (Table 16.2). In Cambodia it was 18 per cent in 2001, an increase from a very low 8 per cent in 1990. In Nepal it was 24 per cent in 2001, up from 18 per cent in 1990. However the main problem in these countries is that this investment is not reaching rural areas, where most of the poor are located.

An additional problem is that neither country is generating enough domestic savings to finance its investment. While investment in Cambodia was 18 per cent of GDP in 2001, savings were only 10 per cent (Table 16.2). Similarly, while investment in Nepal were 24 per cent, savings were only 15 per cent. Consequently, in both countries, investment is aid-dependent. In Nepal foreign aid amounted to 29 per cent of gross capital formation in 2001 and in Cambodia a very large 67 per cent.

In Mongolia, the story has been similar. While gross capital formation as a percentage of GDP has been reportedly high, namely, 30 per cent in 2001, domestic savings have been much lower, at 14 per cent. At the same time, official development assistance (ODA) has amounted to over two-thirds of gross capital formation (Table 16.2). ODA and FDI together accounted for almost all of domestic investment. The same is true in Cambodia.

In Indonesia, for roughly a quarter of a century public investment in rural areas helped spread broadly the benefits of growth, even when growth was driven by urban-based manufactured exports in the 1980s. But such capital expenditures have been in decline since Indonesia began liberalizing its economy, especially its financial sector, in the late 1980s. Gross capital formation as a percentage of GDP dropped from 31 per cent in 1990 to 17 per cent in 2001.

Capital expenditures as a share of total government expenditures dropped from 43 per cent in 1990 to 24 per cent in 2000. The growth rate of GDP dropped correspondingly to 3.8 per cent in 1990–2001 (compared to 6.1 per cent during 1980–90). Since the Asia Financial Crisis, growth has remained low, especially in recent years – for example 3.3 per cent in 2001 and 3.7 per cent in 2002.

For Indonesia, the UNDP-supported study calls for a new investment-led growth strategy that can use public investment to leverage Indonesia back onto a higher growth path – instead of relying on the current strategy, which is heavily reliant on attracting foreign capital. In 2001, foreign direct investment made a negative contribution to domestic investment – an indication of the notorious unreliability of foreign sources of capital, certainly since the Asia Financial Crisis.

The financing of the investment advocated by the UNDP-supported study would come from boosting tax revenue back up to the levels of earlier decades. Because of the effect of the balanced-budget multiplier, raising more tax revenue to finance increased public investment could still have a powerful impact on the economy. However these policy recommendations fly in the face of the neoliberal campaign to radically downsize the state.

China and Vietnam have achieved high rates of economic growth, largely due to high rates of investment. In 2001, the share of gross capital formation in GDP was 39 per cent in China and 31 per cent in Vietnam. Both countries have been able to finance most of this investment with domestic savings. In 2001, gross domestic savings were 40 per cent of GDP in China and 29 per cent in Vietnam. In China, ODA has played virtually no role in financing domestic investment, while FDI has financed about one-tenth of it (Table 16.2). In Vietnam, ODA and FDI together have accounted for over one-quarter of domestic investment.

2. Complementing Fiscal Policy with Less Restrictive Inflation Targets

Most of the countries studied by the regional programme have adopted fairly restrictive inflation targets. Monetary policy is customarily geared to achieving an inflation rate in the range of 3–5 per cent.

As a result, several of the countries – even some of the more rapidly growing ones – have recently faced the danger of deflation (a generalized, sustained decline in the price level). This has been the case in Cambodia and Vietnam, where the inflation rates in 2000–2001 respectively were –0.6 per cent and –0.4 per cent (see Table 16.3). During the same years, Bangladesh and China had very low inflation rates: Bangladesh's rate was 1.1 per cent and China's 0.3 per cent.

Only Indonesia and Sri Lanka had inflation rates above 10 per cent (that is, 11.5 per cent and 14.2 per cent respectively). The Sri Lanka study argues that inflation there is driven by cost-push factors, not the growth of high-powered

Table 16.3 Inflation and interest rate

	Average annual change in the CPI (%) 1990–2001 (2000–2001 in parentheses)	Real interest rate (%) 2001
Bangladesh	5.1 (1.1)	14.0
Cambodia	5.3 (–0.6)	19.9
China	7.6 (0.3)	5.8
Indonesia	13.9 (11.5)	5.3
Mongolia	39.0 (8.0)	19.8
Nepal	8.1 (2.8)	4.4
Sri Lanka	9.9 (14.2)	5.5
Vietnam	3.2 (–0.4)	6.6

Source: World Bank, 2003 (Tables 4.14 and 5.7).

money, which is the customary neoliberal explanation. The study claims that monetary policy should target market interest rates (since these pose costs to private corporations), not the money stock. Conventional anti-inflation policies have been attacking the wrong cause of inflation.

The problem of deflation in Asia was compounded by the recent slowdown in the world economy. This is the second time in recent years that deflation has posed a danger. The Asia Financial Crisis prompted the first. The risk of deflation in Asia continues to rise and remains the highest for any region.

In developing countries as a whole, the average inflation rate has declined since the mid-1990s to its lowest level since the 1960s, namely, 4 per cent. In many of them, there is little protection left against the onset of deflation, which could be triggered globally by a significantly large negative demand shock. This is why accommodative monetary policy is appropriate in many countries as the global economy experiences recovery.

In relatively open economies, such as those of Cambodia and Nepal, monetary policy is not an independent instrument. The Cambodian economy is highly dollarized and the Nepalese economy is closely integrated with India's. In Cambodia the target rate of inflation has been 4 per cent. But, as already mentioned, during 1999–2001 deflation was the main problem, not high inflation. Tight monetary policies have been a contributing factor in driving up the real rate of interest, which was almost 20 per cent in 2001 (Table 16.3). Bangladesh faces a similar problem, with a real rate of interest of 14 per cent in 2001. Such high real rates of interest depress the potential for growth.

In countries such as China and Vietnam, where the development strategy largely relies on export-led growth, monetary policy is subservient to maintaining a stable exchange rate. These governments are also concerned about the potentially adverse social and political consequences of high inflation.

Thus these two governments have accorded a high priority to containing inflation. However both countries have recently maintained such restrictive monetary policies that their economies have suffered from deflation. When the government of China sharply reduced central bank lending to state-owned banks in 1998, the general price level fell.

In the late 1990s, the Vietnamese government reigned in the growth of money supply after a spike in the inflation rate (to 10 per cent) in the wake of two financial crises. As a result, deflation emerged in 2000–2001; while the inflation rate edged back up in 2002, it reached only about 4 per cent. Despite the danger of deflation, the government has continued to apply excessively restrictive monetary policies.

The fixation with low inflation, on the part of even relatively successful countries such as China and Vietnam, stems partly from a concern about the potentially destabilizing effects of financial liberalization. No doubt, supply-side factors are also involved. In China, trade liberalization is contributing to low prices, as is the associated excess capacity in some state-owned enterprises and a large pool of surplus labour in rural areas. In response to the problem of deflation, monetary policy has become more accommodating recently and fiscal policy continues to be expansionary.

The danger of deflation is that it can lead to a self-reinforcing downward spiral of prices, profits and incomes, from which it is difficult for policy-makers to extricate an economy. Monetary policy is rendered ineffectual because the economy has sunk into a 'liquidity trap' (a term coined by Keynes). Thus it is better to prevent deflation than try to combat it once it becomes persistent. Once it is entrenched, fiscal policies are more reliable in turning the tide (IMF, 2003).

The neoliberal recommendation to national policy-makers is that they should insist on maintaining inflation rates of 3–5 per cent even though there is little empirical evidence to suggest that inflation rates above that level, or even above 10 per cent, have an adverse effect on growth. For example the fastest period of growth for the Indonesian economy was in the 1970s, when the average annual growth rate of real GDP was 7.7 per cent. During that time, the average annual inflation rate was over 17 per cent. During the period 1990–2001, China had an average inflation rate of almost 8 per cent but still grew at almost 9 per cent. In Sri Lanka, inflation – especially an increase in food prices – has been highest during periods of growth and poverty reduction. An increase in food prices in Sri Lanka's case is likely to have a pro-poor impact on food producers in rural areas.

Although the case studies are reluctant to recommend relaxing inflation targeting too much because of the danger of jeopardizing macroeconomic stability, they also recognize that some degree of inflation will likely accompany a growing economy. This would facilitate the adjustment of relative prices to reallocate resources from unprofitable to profitable sectors. Moreover if monetary policies are excessively restrictive, they can nullify the potential growth stimulus of expansionary fiscal policies. Low inflation is a more reasonable objective after a sustained rate of economic growth has been achieved; trying to maintain low inflation before growth has a chance to take off is likely to throttle an economic expansion.

3. Mobilizing Domestic Resources for Investment

A priority in most of the countries studied is to raise additional public revenue. Many of them have a low revenue–GDP ratio. For example in Bangladesh revenue is only about 10 per cent of GDP and in Cambodia and Nepal it is only 11 per cent (Table 16.4). In several of the countries, such as Bangladesh, China, Indonesia and Sri Lanka, revenue declined from 1990 to 2000. In such circumstances, it is imperative to raise more public resources. But it is also necessary to raise this revenue in a way that will not adversely affect the poor.

Table 16.4 Taxation

	Total revenue as % of GDP 2000 (1990 in parentheses)	Taxes on income, profits and capital gains (% of total revenue) 2000	Taxes on goods and services (% of total revenue) 2000	Taxes on international trade (% of total revenue) 2000
Bangladesh	10.2 (12.0)	11	40	23
Cambodia	11.0 (3.9)	–	–	–
China	15.0 (19.1)[1]	6	75	10
Indonesia	16.0 (18.8)	59	28	3
Mongolia	32.6 (50.6)	12	37	7
Nepal	11.3 (9.0)	17	34	27
Sri Lanka	16.8 (21.4)	13	58	11
Vietnam	21.1 (16.1)[1]	27	34	15

Note: The table does not include non-tax revenue.
[1] Based on UNDP-supported case study.

Sources: ADB (2002 (column 1)); World Bank World Development Indicators (columns 2–4: Table 4.13) (2003); and McKinley (2003).

In developing countries tax revenue as a ratio to GDP is about half the level of industrial countries (that is, 18 per cent versus 38 per cent) (Tanzi and Zee, 2001). As a consequence, many states simply do not command public resources adequate to finance essential economic and social services.

Raising additional revenue is critical to financing a boost in public investment, which can generate accelerated growth. An investment-led pro-poor growth strategy hinges on three financial conditions: (1) mobilizing sufficient revenue for public investment; (2) mobilizing sufficient private savings to finance private investment; and (3) complementing domestic resources with stable inflows of public and private capital. Domestic borrowing by the state can contribute to financing public investment, but only as a complement to revenue mobilization.

Nepal is an example of a country that has limited room for fiscal manoeuvre. Saddled with a low revenue–GDP ratio of 11 per cent, it also faces pressure from donors to maintain low fiscal deficits and refrain from domestic borrowing. Because its value added tax has failed to generate the expected revenue, it has been forced to cut back expenditures. While the share of social services in the budget has been protected, due partly to donor pressure, the expenditures needed for agricultural and rural development, such as irrigation, have suffered. Partly as a result, poverty levels in rural areas remain high.

In Indonesia, the revenue–GDP ratio declined from about 19 per cent in 1990 to 16 per cent in 2000. This has been due in part to the reduction of import tariffs to very low levels. International trade taxes as a whole accounted for only 3 per cent of total current revenue in 2000 (Table 16.4). Hence the country study recommends that the initial financing for increased public investment to stimulate a higher rate of growth come from raising import tariffs across the board by 10 per cent. It also suggests other tax measures, such as reducing exemptions or raising property taxes.

In general, the case studies do not accept the neoliberal assumption that taxes cannot be raised on income and wealth, which are very unequally distributed in many developing countries. In industrial countries, the ratio of income to consumption taxes is more than double that of developing countries (Tanzi and Zee, 2001). In the eight countries reviewed here, consumption taxes significantly exceed income taxes in all cases except one, Indonesia (Table 16.4).

In all cases, consumption taxes also exceed international trade taxes. But in some of the countries studied, revenue has declined because trade liberalization has caused a substantial reduction of trade taxes while consumption taxes, the standard alternative, have not made up the difference. There has been little effort to mobilize additional income taxes. In Sri Lanka, most of the fall in revenue – that is, from 21 per cent of GDP in 1990 to about 17 per cent in 2001 – is accounted for by a fall in receipts from trade taxes. Little has been done to compensate by raising more income taxes.

Part of the problem with income taxes in developing countries is the myriad of exemptions and deductions on such taxes enjoyed by the rich. Closing these loopholes would be part of a broader effort to have the rich pay their fair share of taxes.

Opportunities to tax wealth are often overlooked. Urban property taxes are far too low in most countries, for example. Simply registering urban property – as needs to be done in Indonesia for instance – could help raise a significant amount of funds. Conservative economists often argue that income and wealth taxes are less efficient than consumption taxes, but this claim rests on dubious evidence (Tanzi and Zee, 2001).

In some countries, tax revenue is siphoned off to pay off external debt. The Mongolian government generates every year a current fiscal surplus (current revenue minus current expenditures), but instead of using it to finance public investment, the government is urged by international financial institutions to pay off the external debt (Roy 2001). Servicing public and publicly guaranteed debt eats up about 12 per cent of Mongolia's current revenue. In Nepal this percentage is 13.5 per cent and in Vietnam 17 per cent. In Sri Lanka it is about 20 per cent and in Indonesia over 22 per cent.

In some instances, governments should be allowed additional latitude – through the relaxation of conditionalities – to engage in domestic borrowing, instead of external borrowing, to finance budget deficits. This is the position of the Bangladesh study for example. Since official development assistance has dropped, the budget deficit has risen in recent years. But the study does not believe that financing it with domestic borrowing will run the danger of crowding out private investment – as argued by some conservative economists. Among the major reasons are that, as of 2004, the private sector is already growing healthily and inflation has remained very low (that is, 1.1 per cent in 2000–2001).

In contrast to the fiscal constraints faced by most of the other countries studied, Vietnam has been able to generate a substantial fiscal surplus – measuring about 4–6 per cent of GDP. This surplus has provided the savings for financing public investment.

Between 1992 and 1996, while revenue had collapsed in many other transition economies, Vietnam managed to raise total revenue (tax and non-tax) as a percentage of GDP to 23 per cent (before slightly declining to 21 per cent in 2000). The external debt that Vietnam has incurred has also been used to finance public capital expenditures, which have risen steadily from 5.5 per cent of GDP in 1995 to 10.2 per cent in 2002. As of 2004, Vietnam confronts large potential costs associated with restructuring state-owned enterprises and state banks, but it remains on a fairly stable fiscal path, with significant room left for continuing growth-stimulating and equity-enhancing public investment.

China has had remarkable success in financing a high share of public capital expenditures over a long period. This has been an essential condition for its sustained rapid rate of growth. But the distribution of its total public expenditures remains regressive, with a distinct bias against rural areas.

China's tax system has also been regressive. The 1994 tax reform led for example to a system of fiscal transfers that disproportionately benefited rich regions. Moreover the rural tax burden has been the heaviest for farming households, which account for most of the poor. In effect, China's National Poverty Alleviation Programme is redistributing resources back to poorer regions that the regular functioning of the fiscal system has taken away.

4. Implementing Pro-Poor Financial Reforms

In many of the countries studied, financial liberalization has been one of the most ineffective components of the neoliberal reform agenda. While such liberalization had been heralded as an essential ingredient of pro-growth and pro-poor economic reforms, it appears to have contributed more to destabilizing economies and withdrawing financial services from the poor.

In Bangladesh, while financial liberalization had been designed to lower the real rate of interest, in practice it has led to a higher rate and a widening spread between the deposit and lending rates of interest, hampering both the mobilization of loanable funds and the expansion of lending for private investment. In 2001 the real rate of interest was 14 per cent and the spread between deposit and lending rates was over 7 percentage points. In Cambodia the spread between the two rates was over 12 percentage points in 2001. The interest rate spread is a small but significant barometer of the failure of financial liberalization in these countries.

Another is the increasing inequality in the access to credit. In Cambodia the private banking system is highly concentrated and located mainly in the capital. While liberalization has helped stabilize the economy and has led to financial deepening in urban areas, its benefits have largely bypassed rural areas. Whereas 90 per cent of all deposits and liabilities are dollar-denominated, the great majority of low-income Cambodians, especially in rural areas, carry out transactions in riel, the domestic currency. Therefore devaluation of the riel *vis-à-vis* the dollar widens inequality between rich and poor.

Banks are reluctant to lend in rural areas, where the economy remains relatively stagnant. This reluctance to lend, signalled by a large interest-rate spread, means that the banking system is building up excess reserves (reported to be roughly 3 per cent of GDP) and the economy is paying the price in terms of lost potential for growth.

For Cambodia, the UNDP-supported study stresses the importance of creating an efficient and sustainable rural credit system. For most countries in the Asia-Pacific, this is a major prerequisite for fostering pro-poor growth.

The impact of financial liberalization in Nepal has been similar to that in Cambodia. While financial liberalization has led to the spread of financial institutions and financial deepening (reflected in the increase of credit as a share of GDP to about 46 per cent in 2001), there has been little expansion of credit to rural areas, where poverty is concentrated. The government has in fact withdrawn from rural development banks and phased out priority sector credit programmes that benefited rural development. As a consequence, in rural areas indebtedness is on the rise, in conjunction with growing landlessness.

Micro-finance has been growing in Nepal but is largely donor-driven and has a small capital base. While a valuable tool for stimulating self-employment, micro-finance cannot substitute for a viable rural banking system, which could provide adequate credit to farmers and employment-generating small and medium-sized non-farm enterprises. This is a major lesson drawn from across the country studies.

In China, in contrast to most of the other countries studied, there is indeed a rural banking system, comprised of the Agricultural Bank of China and the rural credit cooperatives. However in the wake of liberalization even these institutions have retrenched their operations, particularly in poor regions, become more cautious in providing loans and demanded more collateral and guarantees. As the largest grassroots source of official finance in rural areas, rural credit cooperatives need however to be expanded and strengthened.

In Sri Lanka, efforts to generate accelerated, pro-poor growth have been hampered because there has been no real source of medium-term or long-term finance for productive private investment since the privatization of two state financial institutions, the Development Finance Corporation of Ceylon and the National Development Bank. The UNDP-supported study argues that contrary to the claims of the advocates of financial liberalization, private financial institutions provide relatively little long-term investment finance. Either retained earnings or state credit institutions usually provide such financing.

While Vietnam has moved to increasingly commercialize its banking system, it has retained some institutions to provide directed credit to priority industries and poor rural households through the Development Assistance Fund (DAF) and the Social Policy Bank. Backed in part by donor resources, the DAF was established in 2000 to provide subsidized state loans for medium- or long-term investments in priority areas, such as infrastructure, export sectors or heavy industry. It is the largest Vietnamese financial institution that channels funds, both domestic and foreign, to investment. In 2002, DAF accounted for about one-quarter of all domestic credit.

With branches in all provinces, the Social Policy Bank provides microfinance to agricultural households and low-income groups, mostly in rural areas. It also gives loans for micro-enterprises and small and medium-sized enterprises. The government of Vietnam uses both the Development Assistance Fund and Social Policy Bank for policy lending and keeps them separate from the commercial banking sector.

In the wake of its mini financial crisis of 1996–97, as well as the Asia Financial Crisis thereafter, Vietnam has tightened up regulation of the financial system. The crisis in 1996–97 arose because of very high domestic interest rates (*vis-à-vis* foreign interest rates) and the liberalization of foreign short-term borrowing (primarily through letters of credit). Guaranteed by state banks, external borrowing was channelled into the speculative real-estate market, causing a speculative bubble in the property market that ended up bursting in 1997.

Because of this experience, the central bank has put strict limits on providing loan guarantees for such short-term external borrowing and has maintained capital controls on short-term capital flows, including those associated with trade credits. Like Vietnam, China has also used controls to protect itself against the volatility of external capital flows. However such measures have not prevented these countries from enjoying a continuing inflow of foreign direct investment, which has been motivated principally by their record of rapid and sustained growth.

There is no conclusive evidence that financial integration with the world economy will enhance a country's rate of economic growth (Prasad et al., 2003). But there is evidence that capital account liberalization is associated with an intensification of some countries' vulnerability to crises. Thus the neoliberal consensus on such liberalization has shifted to a more cautious endorsement, and has tried to place the main blame for volatility on the lack of sound domestic institutions, not on the pro-cyclical nature of external capital flows.

Indonesia represents one of the worst-case scenarios for financial liberalization. Domestic deregulation of its financial sector, beginning in the late 1980s, coupled with a completely open capital account threatened a financial meltdown during the Asia Financial Crisis. In response, the government provided blanket guarantees to foreign and domestic creditors for all deposits and debts.

The government committed itself to the disastrous policy of massively bailing out its banking system by recapitalizing it with government bonds, on which it continues to pay interest and principal. This has drained public resources from vital economic and social services. As a consequence, Indonesia has found itself abruptly reclassified from a rapidly developing 'East Asia Miracle' economy into a seriously indebted low-income country.

Among the general lessons to be drawn from the UNDP-supported country studies are the need for the state to regulate the domestic financial sector, maintain some controls on short-term external capital flows and help build up domestic financial institutions, such as in rural areas, which can provide broad and equitable access to credit and foster long-term productive investment.

CONCLUDING REMARKS

This chapter has presented policy recommendations from eight case studies of the Asia-Pacific Regional Programme on the Macroeconomics of Poverty Reduction. These recommendations chart out elements of a macroeconomic framework that is distinctly different from the neoliberal policy matrix that has dominated economic prescriptions since the early 1980s.

These elements include a more proactive fiscal stance, focused on public investment not only as the basis to foster more rapid growth but also as a mechanism to focus resources on poverty. In this framework, monetary policies play a complementary accommodating role to expansionary fiscal policies. Restrictive inflation targeting is eschewed. In order to finance additional public investment, a more concerted effort would be mounted to mobilize domestic public resources, which are deemed to be too low in many countries to support a pro-poor growth strategy.

Also included in the macroeconomic framework are recommendations for stronger regulation of financial institutions and external short-term capital flows, and the use of state financial institutions to direct credit for both growth-promoting and poverty-reducing purposes.

NOTE

1. For an elaboration of these points, see UNDP (2002).

REFERENCES

Asian Development Bank (ADB) (2002), *Key Indicators of Developing Asian and Pacific Countries*, Manila.

Beresford, Melanie (ed.) (2003), *The Macroeconomics of Poverty Reduction in Cambodia*, New York: United Nations Development Program.

Deraniyagala, Sonali (ed.) (2003), *The Macroeconomics of Poverty Reduction in Nepal*, New York: United Nations Development Program.

Griffin, Keith (ed.) (2003), *Poverty Reduction in Mongolia*, Asia Pacific Press at the Australian National University.

Hemming, Richard, Michael Kell and Selma Mahfouz (2002), 'The effectiveness of fiscal policy in stimulating economic activity – a review of the literature', IMF working paper, WP/02/208, December, International Monetary Fund.

International Monetary Fund (IMF) (2003), 'Deflation: determinants, risks and policy options – findings of an interdepartmental task force', 30 April, International Monetary Fund.

McKinley, Terry (ed.) (2003), 'The macroeconomics of poverty reduction: initial findings of the UNDP Asia-Pacific Regional Programme', UNDP discussion paper, accessed at www.undp.org/poverty/propoor.htm.

Nicholas, Howard (ed.) (2003), *The Macroeconomics of Poverty Reduction in Sri Lanka*, New York: United Nations Development Program.

Osmani, Siddiqur (ed.) (2003), *The Macroeconomics of Poverty Reduction in Bangladesh*, New York: United Nations Development Program.

Prasad, Eswar, Kenneth Rogoff, Shang-Jin Wei and M. Ayhan Kose (2003), 'Effects of financial globalization on developing countries: some empirical evidence', 17 March, International Monetary Fund.

Riskin, Carl (ed.) (2003), *The Macroeconomics of Poverty Reduction in China*, New York: United Nations Development Program.

Roy, Rathin (2001), 'Fiscal policies to complement a poverty reduction strategy for Mongolia', September, University of London School of Oriental and African Studies.

Tanzi, Vito and Howell Zee (2001), 'Tax policies for developing countries', *IMF Economic Issues*, **27** (April).

United Nations Development Program (UNDP) (2002), 'The role of economic policies in poverty reduction', UNDP policy note, accessed at www.undp.org/policy/docs/policynotes/economic-policies-poverty-reduction.doc.

United Nations Development Program (UNDP) (2003), *Human Development Report 2003: Millennium Development Goals: A Compact Among Nations to End Human Poverty*, New York: Oxford University Press.

Weeks, John (ed.) (2003), *The Macroeconomics of Poverty Reduction in Vietnam*, New York: United Nations Development Program.

World Bank (2003), *World Development Indicators 2003*, Washington DC: World Bank.

Appendix: Curriculum vitae for Professor Keith B. Griffin

Name	Keith Broadwell GRIFFIN
Birth	6 November 1938
Citizenship	UK
Degrees	BA Williams College, USA, 1960 BPhil. Oxford, 1962 (Marshall Scholar) DPhil. Oxford, 1965 Hon D Litt. Williams, 1980

Honorary Fellow, Magdalen College, Oxford, 1988

Fellow, American Association for the Advancement of Science, 1997

EXPERIENCE

1988–2004	Distinguished Professor (and Chair, 1988–93), Department of Economics, University of California, Riverside
1965–88	Oxford University: Fellow and Tutor in Economics, Magdalen College (1965–76); Fellow by Special Election (1977–79); Acting Warden/Director (1973 and 1977–78) and Warden/Director, Queen Elizabeth House/Institute of Commonwealth Studies (1978–79)
1979–88	President, Magdalen College, Oxford
2004–2005	Leader, UNDP programme evaluation team in China
2002	Leader, UNDP Mission to Armenia on the Impact of Macroeconomic Policy on Poverty

2001	Leader, UNDP Mission to Mongolia on the Integration of Equity and Poverty Reduction Concerns into Development Strategy
1998	Visiting Fellow, Oxford Centre for Islamic Studies
1998	Consultant to UNDP on the Human Development Report for Europe and the CIS
1997	Leader, ILO Employment and Social Protection Mission to Kazakstan
1997	Leader, UNDP Macroeconomic Policy and Poverty Reduction Mission to Vietnam
1996	Member of UNESCO Culture and Development Steering Committee
1995	Adviser to UNDP on Poverty in Cambodia
1994–95	Member, World Commission on Culture and Development
1994–96	Leader, ILO Social Policy Review Mission to Uzbekistan
1994	Leader, UNDP Poverty Alleviation Mission to Mongolia
1989–91	Economic Adviser to the government of Bolivia
1989, 1991–94	Consultant to UNDP on the *Human Development Report* and on implementing a human development strategy
1988–95	Chairman of the Board, United Nations Research Institute for Social Development
1987–94	Member of United Nations Committee for Development Planning
1986–92	Member of Council, United Nations University; Chairman, Finance and Budget Committee (1988–90)
1986–91	Senior Adviser, OECD Development Centre, Paris

1984–88	Member, Marshall Aid Commemoration Commission
1982	Chief, ILO Employment Advisory Mission to Ethiopia
1978–80	President, Development Studies Association, UK and Ireland
1975–76	Chief, Rural and Urban Employment Policies Branch, International Labour Office
1974	Consultant to the ILO on rural development in Ecuador
1973	Consultant to the World Bank on land reform in Morocco
1971–72	Senior Consultant, United Nations Research Institute for Social Development, on the economic and social implications of the introduction of high-yielding varieties of foodgrains
1968	Adviser to the Inter-American Committee for the Alliance for Progress on the copper expansion programme in Chile
1967	Adviser to FAO/ICO/IBRD World Coffee Study in Guatemala, El Salvador and Colombia
1966	Adviser to the US Agency for International Development on investment allocation in Turkey
1965 and 1970	Research Adviser, Pakistan Institute of Development Economics, Karachi, Pakistan
1963–64	Expert on Agricultural Planning to the Government of Algeria and Acting Chief FAO Mission, Algiers, Algeria
1962–63 and 1964–65	Visiting Professor, Institute of Economics and Planning, University of Chile, Santiago, Chile

LISTINGS, AND MISCELLANEOUS

Listed in *Who's Who* (UK); *Who's Who in America*; *Who's Who in Economics*; *The Writers Directory*; *International Authors and Writers Who's Who*. Entry in Philip Arestis and Malcolm Sawyer (eds), *A Biographical Dictionary of Dissenting Economists*, Edward Elgar Publishing, 1992, 2nd edn, 2001.

Commencement speaker: Williams College, 1980; University of California, Riverside, 1992.

UCR Distinguished Humanist Achievement Lecturer, 2002–2003.

Cecil and Ida Green Visiting Professor, University of British Columbia, 1986. Distinguished Visiting Professor, American University in Cairo, 2001.

Trustee, Islamic Trust (UK), 1985–97; 2000–.

Presenter of a BBC *Horizon* documentary on *A New Green Revolution?*, 1984, which was subsequently analyzed in a book by Roger Silverstone, *Framing Science: The Making of a BBC Documentary*, BFI Publishing, 1985. Participant in a UNESCO/South African Broadcasting Corporation documentary on the World Commission on Culture and Development entitled *From the Tree to the Dugout*, 1996.

PUBLICATIONS

Books and Monographs

Poverty Reduction in Mongolia, editor, Canberra, Australia: Asia Pacific Press, 2003; Mongolian edition, Ulaanbaatar, Mongolia: Amarjargal Foundation, 2002.

Growth, Inequality and Poverty in Armenia, editor, Yerevan, Armenia: UNDP, 2002; published in both English and Armenian.

Studies in Development Strategy and Systemic Transformation, London: Macmillan, 2000; US edition, New York: St Martin's Press, 2000.

Economic Reform in Vietnam, editor, London: Macmillan, 1998; US edition, New York: St Martin's Press, 1998.

Studies in Globalization and Economic Transitions, London: Macmillan, 1996; US edition, New York: St Martin's Press, 1996; Farsi edition, Tehran, Iran: Plan and Budget Organization, Centre for Socio-Economic Documentation and Publication, 1998.

Social Policy and Economic Transformation in Uzbekistan, editor, Geneva: International Labour Office, 1996; Russian edition, ILO, 1997.

New Approaches to Development Cooperation, with Terry McKinley, UNDP, Office of Development Studies discussion paper no 7, New York, 1996. This is a revised version of *A New Framework for Development Cooperation*, UNDP, Human Development Report Office occasional paper no 11, New York, 1994.

Poverty and the Transition to a Market Economy in Mongolia, editor, London: Macmillan, 1995; US edition, New York: St Martin's Press, 1995.

Implementing a Human Development Strategy, with Terry McKinley, London: Macmillan, 1994; US edition, New York: St Martin's Press, 1994; Farsi edition, Tehran, Iran: Plan and Budget Organization, Centre for Socio-Economic Documentation and Publication, 1998.

The Distribution of Income in China, editor, with Zhao Renwei, London: Macmillan, 1993; US edition, New York: St Martin's Press, 1993; Chinese edition, Beijing: Social Sciences Publishing House, 1994.

Globalization and the Developing World, with Azizur Rahman Khan, UNRISD Monograph Series, United Nations Research Institute for Social Development, Geneva, 1992; republished under the same title by UNDP, Human Development Report Office, Occasional Paper No. 2, 1992.

The Economy of Ethiopia, editor, London: Macmillan, 1992; US edition, New York: St Martin's Press, 1992.

Human Development and the International Development Strategy for the 1990s, editor, with John Knight, London: Macmillan, 1990.

Alternative Strategies for Economic Development, London: Macmillan, 1989; US edition, New York: St Martin's Press; French edition, Paris: Economica, 1989; Chinese edition, Beijing: Economic Science Publishing House, 1992, 2nd edition, 1999; Farsi edition, Tehran, Iran: Plan and Budget Organization, Centre for Socio-Economic Documentation and Publication.

World Hunger and the World Economy, London: Macmillan, 1987; US edition, New York: Holmes & Meier.

Institutional Reform and Economic Development in the Chinese Countryside, editor, London: Macmillan, 1984; Chinese edition, Hong Kong: Chinese University Press, 1987.

Growth and Equality in Rural China, with Ashwani Saith, Bangkok, Thailand: Maruzen, for the ILO, 1981.

The Transition to Egalitarian Development, with Jeffrey James, London: Macmillan, 1981; US edition, New York: St Martin's Press.

International Inequality and National Poverty, London: Macmillan, 1978; US edition, New York: Holmes & Meier; Spanish edition, Mexico City, Mexico: Fondo de Cultura Economica, 1984.

Poverty and Landlessness in Rural Asia, editor, with Azizur Rahman Khan, Geneva: ILO, 1977.

Land Concentration and Rural Poverty, London: Macmillan, 1976; US edition, New York: Holmes & Meier; 2nd edition 1981; Spanish edition, Mexico City, Mexico: Fondo de Cultura Economica, 1983.

The Political Economy of Agrarian Change, London: Macmillan, 1974; US edition, Cambridge, MA: Harvard University Press; 2nd edition 1979; Spanish edition, Mexico City, Mexico: Fondo de Cultura Economica, 1982; Hindi edition, Bangalore, India: Macmillan of India, 1983.

The Economic Development of Bangladesh, editor, with E.A.G. Robinson, London: Macmillan, for the International Economic Association, 1974.

The Green Revolution: An Economic Analysis, New York: UNRISD, 1972.

Growth and Inequality in Pakistan, editor, with Azizur Rahman Khan, London: Macmillan, 1972.

Financing Development in Latin America, editor, London: Macmillan, 1971.

Planning Development, with John Enos, London: Addison-Wesley, 1970; Spanish edition, Mexico City, Mexico: Fondo de Cultura Economica, 1975.

Underdevelopment in Spanish America, London: Allen & Unwin, 1969; 2nd edition, 1971; US edition, Cambridge, MA: MIT Press; Spanish edition, Buenos Aires, Argentina: Amorrortu editores, 1972.

Comercio Internacional y Politicas de Desarrollo Economico, with Ricardo Ffrench-Davis, Mexico City, Mexico: Fondo de Cultura Economica, 1967.

Ensayos Sobre Planificación, editor, with Eduardo Garcia, Santiago, Chile: Instituto de Economia y Planificación, 1967.

Articles

'Globalization and global governance: a reply to the debate', *Development and Change*, **35** (5), 2004.

'In defence of Neo-Classical Neo-Populism', with Azizur Rahman Khan and Amy Ickowitz, *Journal of Agrarian Change*, **4** (3), 2004.

'Globalization and culture', in Stephen Cullenberg and Prasanta Pattanaik (eds), *Globalization, Culture and the Limits of the Market: Essays in Economics and Philosophy*, New Delhi: Oxford University Press, 2004; translated into Mallorquín and published in José Luis Groizard Cardosa (ed.), *Globalització i Desenvolupament*, Palma: Universitat de les Illes Balears, 2003.

'Economic globalization and institutions of global governance', *Development and Change*, **34** (5), 2003.

'Confronting human development in Mexico', with Amy Ickowitz, in Kevin Middlebrook and Eduardo Zepeda (eds), *Confronting Development: Assessing Mexico's Economic and Social Policy Challenges*, Stanford University Press, 2003.

'Poverty and the distribution of land', with Azizur Rahman Khan and Amy Ickowitz, *Journal of Agrarian Change*, **2** (3), 2002; also published in V.K. Ramachandran and Madhura Swaminathan (eds), *Agrarian Studies: Essays on Agrarian Relations in Less-Developed Countries*, New Delhi: Tulika Books, 2002; UK edition, London: Zed Books, 2003.

'I Problemi della Povertà e dell' Emarginazione' ('Problems of poverty and marginalization'), in Valerio Castronovo (ed.), *Storia Dell'Economia Mondiale*, vol 6, *Nuovo Equilibri in un Mercato Globale*, Rome: Editori Laterza, 2002; English version published in *Indicators: The Journal of Social Health*, **2** (2), 2003.

'Poverty and land distribution: cases of land reform in Asia', in Horacia R. Morales, Jr. and James Putzel (eds), *Power in the Village: Agrarian Reform, Rural Politics, Institutional Change and Globalization*, Quezon City, Philippines: Project Development Institute and University of the Philippines Press, 2001.

'Trade liberalization and global governance: some observations', in *Democratizing Global Economic Governance: A PERI Symposium*, Political Economy Research Institute working paper no 26, University of Massachusetts, Amherst, 2001.

'The distribution of wealth and the pace of development', with Amy Ickowitz, in Terry McKinley (ed.), *Macroeconomic Policy, Growth and Poverty Reduction*, Basingstoke: Palgrave, 2001; reprinted in G. Raghava Reddy and P. Subrahmanyam (eds), *Dynamics of Sustainable Rural Development*, Delhi: Serials Publications, 2003.

'Macroeconomic reform and employment: an investment-led strategy of structural adjustment in Sub-Saharan Africa', in Terry McKinley (ed.), *Macroeconomic Policies, Growth and Poverty Reduction*, London: Palgrave, 2001.

'Domestic resource mobilization and enterprise development in Sub-Saharan Africa', with Mark Brenner, in Terry McKinley (ed.), *Macroeconomic Policies, Growth and Poverty Reduction*, London: Palgrave, 2001.

'An introduction to human development', in Vassily Kolesov and Terry McKinley (ed.), *Human Development: A Textbook*, Moscow: Human Rights Publishers, 2000; published simultaneously in Russian.

'Discussant: class analysis, individual choice, and economic theory', in Robert Pollin (ed.), *Capitalism, Socialism and Radical Political Economy*, Cheltenham, UK and Northampton, MA, USA: Edward Elgar, 2000.

'Delinking trade, environmental protection and labour standards', *Environment and Development Economics*, 5 (4), 2000.

'The role of the state in transition', in UNDP, *Central Asia 2010*, 1999.

'Globalization and the shape of things to come', *Macalester International*, **7** (Spring), 1999.

'Income distribution in urban China during the period of economic reform and globalization', with Azizur Rahman Khan and Carl Riskin, *American Economic Review*, **89** (2), May 1999; reprinted in Carl Riskin, Zhao Renwei and Li Shi (eds), *China's Retreat from Equality*, Armonk, New York: M.E. Sharpe, 2000.

'Culture and economic growth: a general argument with illustrations from the Islamic world', *Journal of Islamic Studies*, **10** (2), 1999.

'Culture and economic growth: the state and globalization', *Indian Journal of Applied Economics*, **8** (2), 1999; reprinted in Jan Nederveen Pieterse (ed.), *Global Futures: Shaping Globalization*, London: Zed Books, 2000; and in K. Puttaswamaiah (ed.), *John Hicks: His Contributions to Economic Theory and Application*, New Brunswick, NJ and London: Transaction Publishers, 2001.

'Social policy in Kazakstan during the economic transition', *International Journal of Social Economics*, **26** (1/2/3), 1999.

'Economic reform in India: comments on a paper by Prabhat Patnaik and C.P. Chandrasekhar', in Dean Baker, Jerry Epstein and Robert Pollin (eds), *Globalization and Progressive Economic Policy*, Cambridge: Cambridge University Press, 1998; reprinted in Prema-chandra Athukorala (ed.), *The Economic Development of South Asia*, Cheltenham, UK and Northampton, MA, USA, Edward Elgar, vol 1, 2002.

'The end of internal colonialism and autarky in South Africa: comments on a paper by Laurence Harris and Jonathan Michie', in Dean Baker, Jerry Epstein and Robert Pollin (eds), *Globalization and Progressive Economic Policy*, Cambridge: Cambridge University Press, 1998.

'The death and rebirth of international economic cooperation', in Jim Freedman (ed.), *Transforming Development: A Future for Aid*, Toronto: University of Toronto Press, 2000.

'The management of structural adjustment and macroeconomic reform in Vietnam', *Human Systems Management*, **17** (1), 1998.

'Globalization and development cooperation: a reformer's agenda', in Roy Culpeper, Albert Berry and Frances Stewart (eds), *Global Governance and Development Fifty Years After Bretton Woods*, London: Macmillan, 1997.

'Poverty in Uzbekistan: concepts, measurement and policies', *Pakistan Journal of Applied Economics*, **12** (2), 1996.

'Culture, human development and economic growth', UNRISD-UNESCO *Occasional Papers on Culture and Development*, **3**, 1997.

'The state and the economics of cocaine: the case of Bolivia', in Abu Abdullah and Azizur Rahman Khan (eds), *State, Market and Development*, Dhaka: University Press and New Delhi: Oxford University Press, 1996.

'Development cooperation in the twenty-first century: suggestions for a new framework', with Terry McKinley, *Indian Journal of Applied Economics*, **5** (4), 1996.

'Simultaneous versus sequential reform during periods of systemic change: a reply to Laszló Csaba', with Azizur Rahman Khan, *Közgazdasági Szemle*, **42** (July–August), 1995.

'Global prospects for development and human security', *Canadian Journal of Development Studies*, **16** (3), 1995 and 'A reply to Manfred Bienefeld', in the same journal and issue.

'The transition to market guided economies: lessons for Russia and Eastern Europe from the Chinese experience', with Azizur Rahman Khan, in Bernd Magnus and Stephen Cullenberg (eds), *Whither Marxism? Global Crises in International Perspective*, New York and London: Routledge, 1995.

'A new framework for development cooperation', with Terry McKinley, in Üner Kirdar and Leonard Silk (eds), *People: From Impoverishment to Empowerment*, New York and London: New York University Press, 1995.

'A reply to Trevor Lloyd', *Contention*, **3** (3), 1994.

'The Chinese transition to a market-guided economy: the contrast with Russia and Eastern Europe', with Azizur Rahman Khan, *Contention*, **3** (2), 1994; translated into Hungarian and reprinted in *Közgazdasági Szemle*, **41 (May),** 1994.

'The distribution of land in rural China', with Terry McKinley, *Journal of Peasant Studies*, **21** (3), 1993.

'Sources of income inequality in post-reform China', with Azizur Rahman Khan, Carl Riskin and Zhao Renwei, *China Economic Review*, **4** (1), 1993.

'Friction in economics', in Nordal Åkerman (ed.), *The Necessity of Friction*, Heidelberg: Springer/Physica-Verlag, 1993.

'David Gordon on Clintonomics: a comment', *Contention*, **3** (1), 1993.

'Household income and its distribution in China', with Azizur Rahman Khan, Carl Riskin and Zhao Renwei, *China Quarterly*, December 1992.

'Globalization and regionalization: an exploration of issues', in Üner Kirdar (ed.), *Change: Threat or Opportunity?*, New York: United Nations, vol 1, 1992.

'Suggestions for an international development strategy for the 1990s', in A.K. Dutt and K.P. Jameson (eds), *New Directions in Development Economics*, Aldershot, UK and Brookfield, USA: Edward Elgar, 1992.

'The social sciences, academic freedom and professional standards in North America', *Queen's Quarterly*, **98** (4), 1991; translated into Swedish and reprinted in *Tvärsnitt*, **4**, 1992.

'Foreign aid After the Cold War', *Development and Change*, October, 1991; part reprinted in Mark Charlton and Elizabeth Riddell-Dixon (eds), *Readings in International Relations*, Scarborough, ON: Nelson Canada, 1993 and in S.E. Corbridge (ed.), *Development: Critical Concepts in Social Sciences*, New York: Routledge, 1998.

'A comment on "Population growth, economic growth and market economies"', *Contention*, **2** (1), 1992.

'Observations on economic policy in post-revolution Nicaragua', *Review of Radical Political Economics*, **20** (2–3), 1988.

'Thinking about development – the longer view', *Development: Journal of the Society for International Development*, **2/3**, 1988.

'Human development: the case for renewed emphasis', with John Knight, *Journal of Development Planning*, **19**, 1989; reprinted in Khadija Haq and Üner Kirdar (eds), *Development for People: Goals and Strategies for the Year 2000*, North South Roundtable/UNDP, 1989 and in Charles Wilber and Kenneth Jameson (eds), *The Political Economy of Development and Underdevelopment*, New York: McGraw-Hill, 5th edn, 1992.

'Monetarism', *Journal of Business Administration*, **18** (1–2), 1988–89.

'Socialist strategies of development', (in Chinese, translated by Wang Weidong), *Administrative World*, in two parts, **5**, September 1988 and **6**, November 1988.

'Toward a cooperative settlement of the debt problem', *Finance and Development*, June 1988. A slightly revised version was printed as 'Would default on the international debt be in the common interest of the North and South?' in *The External Debt, Development and International Cooperation* (proceedings of a conference in Lima, Peru, 25–29 January 1988), Paris: L'Harmattan, 1988.

'Development in historical context', *Journal of Business Administration*, **17** (1–2), 1987–88.

'Industrialisation: different approaches and case studies', *Revista de Analisis Economico*, **2** (2), 1987.

'World hunger and the world economy'; 'The economic crisis in Ethiopia'; and 'The Chinese economy after Mao': in W. Ladd Hollist and F. LaMond Tullis (eds), *Pursuing Food Security: Strategies and Obstacles in Africa, Asia, Latin America and the Middle East*, Lynne Rienner, 1987.

'Doubts about aid', IDS *Bulletin*, April 1986.

'Rural development in an arid region: Xinjiang', *Third World Quarterly*, July 1986.

'Communal land tenure systems and their role in rural development', in Sanjaya Lall and Frances Stewart (eds), *Theory and Reality in Development*, Macmillan, 1986.

'Problems of agricultural development in socialist Ethiopia: an overview and a suggested strategy', with Roger Hay, *Journal of Peasant Studies*, October 1985.

'Radical analyses of imperialism, the Third World and the transition to socialism: a survey article', with John Gurley, *Journal of Economic Literature*, September 1985.

'Rural poverty in Asia: analysis and policy alternatives', in Rizwanul Islam (ed.), *Strategies for Alleviating Poverty in Rural Asia*, ILO/ARTEP, 1985.

'On misreading development economics', *Third World Quarterly*, April 1984.

'Managing the transition to egalitarian development', with Jeffrey James, in Samir Amin (ed.), *Human Resources, Employment and Development, Vol. 5: Developing Countries*, Macmillan for the IEA, 1984.
'Income differentials in rural China: comment', *China Quarterly*, December 1982.
'Institutional change and income distribution in the Chinese countryside', with Kimberley Griffin, *Oxford Bulletin of Economics and Statistics*, August, 1983; reprinted in Chi-Keung and Joseph C.H. Chai (eds), *Development and Distribution in China*, Centre of Asian Studies, University of Hong Kong, 1985.
'The pattern of income inequality in rural China', with Ashwani Saith, *Oxford Economic Papers*, March 1982.
'Private production and income distribution in a Chinese commune', with Alison Ansell and Roger Hay, *Food Policy*, February 1982.
'Rural poverty and development alternatives in South and Southeast Asia: some policy issues', with Ajit Ghose, *Development and Change*, October 1980.
'Growth and impoverishment in the rural areas of Asia', with the assistance of Ajit Kumar Ghose, *World Development*, April/May 1979; reprinted in *Regional Development Dialogue*, Autumn 1981, in R.P. Misra (ed.), *Rural Development: National Policies and Experiences*, Maruzen, 1981, and in Charles K. Wilber (ed.), *The Political Economy of Development and Underdevelopment*, Random House, 4th edn, 1988.
'Problems of transition to egalitarian development', with Jeffrey James, *The Manchester School*, September 1979.
'Poverty in the Third World: ugly facts and fancy models', with Azizur Rahman Khan, *World Development*, March 1978; reprinted in H. Alavi and T. Shanin (eds), *Introduction to the Sociology of Developing Societies*, Macmillan, 1982.
'Economic development in a changing world', *World Development*, March 1981.
'Increasing poverty and changing ideas about development strategies', *Development and Change*, October 1977.
'Efficiency, equality and accumulation in rural China: notes on the Chinese system of incentives', *World Development*, May 1978; reprinted in J. Unger (ed.), *Chinese Rural Institutions and the Question of Transferability*, Oxford: Pergamon Press, 1980.
'The roots of underdevelopment: reflections on the Chinese experience', *Modern China*, July 1978; reprinted in P.C.C. Huang (ed.), *The Development of Underdevelopment in China*, New York: M.E. Sharpe, 1980.
'Labor utilization in rice production: comments on the paper', in IRRI, *Economic Consequences of New Rice Technology in Asia*, Los Banos, Philippines, 1978.

'Multinational corporations and basic needs development', *Development and Change*, January 1977.
'On the emigration of the peasantry', *World Development*, May 1976.
'Income inequality and land redistribution in Morocco', *Bangladesh Development Studies*, July 1975.
'The international transmission of inequality', *World Development*, March 1974.
'Policy options for rural development', *Oxford Bulletin of Economics and Statistics*, November 1973; edited version reprinted in Edgar O. Edwards (ed.), *Employment in Developing Nations*, Columbia University Press, 1974.
'Agrarian policy: the political and economic context', *World Development*, November 1973.
'The effect of aid and other resource transfers on savings and growth in less-developed countries: a comment', *Economic Journal*, September 1973.
'Pearson and the political economy of aid', in T.J. Byres (ed.), *Foreign Resources and Economic Development*, London: Cass Publishing, 1972.
'An assessment of development in Taiwan', *World Development*, June 1973.
'Reflections on Latin American development', *Oxford Economic Papers*, March 1966; reprinted in C.T. Nisbet (ed.), *Latin America: Problems in Economic Development*, New York: Free Press, 1969; and in N.T. Uphoff and W.F. Ilchman (eds), *The Political Economy of Development*, 1972.
'Latin American development: further thoughts', *Oxford Economic Papers*, March 1968; reprinted in C.T. Nisbet (ed.), *Latin America: Problems in Economic Development*, New York: Free Press, 1969.
'Coffee and the economic development of Colombia', *Bulletin of the Oxford University Institute of Economics and Statistics*, May 1968.
'Reform and diversification in a coffee economy: the case of Guatemala', in P.P. Streeten (ed.), *Unfashionable Economics*, London: Weidenfeld and Nicolson, 1970.
'Algerian agriculture in transition', *Bulletin of the Oxford University Institute of Economics and Statistics*, November 1965; reprinted in I.W. Zartman (ed.), *Man, State and Society in the Contemporary Maghrib*, 1973.
'Foreign assistance: objectives and consequences', with John Enos, *Economic Development and Cultural Change*, April 1970; translated and reprinted in Mexico, *Trimestre Economico*, 1973.
'Foreign assistance: objectives and consequences: a reply to our critics', *Economic Development and Cultural Change*, October 1971; and 'An example of the attribution problem: rejoinder to Over', in same journal, July 1975: both with John Enos.
'Foreign capital, domestic savings and economic development', *Bulletin of the Oxford University Institute of Economics and Statistics*, 1970; and 'Reply', in same journal, 1971; original article reprinted in Peter Burnell and Oliver

Morrissey (eds), *Foreign Aid in the New Global Economy*, Cheltenham, UK and Northampton, MA, USA: Edward Elgar, 2004.

'Choice, institutions and technology: an economist's impressions', in M.M.R. Freeman (ed.), *Intermediate Adaptation in Newfoundland and the Arctic*, Institute of Social and Economic Research, St John's, Newfoundland, 1969.

'An evaluation of Pakistan's third five year plan', with Bruce Glassburner, *Journal of Development Studies*, July 1966.

'Customs unions and Latin American integration', *Journal of Common Market Studies*, with Ricardo Ffrench-Davis, 1965.

'Planificación nacional e integración economica regional en America Latina', with Rodolfo Hoffmann, in *Simposio, Integración Economica*, Institute of Economics and Planning, Santiago, Chile, 1965.

'Financing development plans in Pakistan', *Pakistan Development Review*, Winter 1965; reprinted in Keith Griffin and Azizur Rahman Khan (ed.), *Studies on the Strategy and Technique of Development Planning*, Karachi, Pakistan: Pakistan Institute of Development Economics, 1969.

'Asian economic development', *Pakistan Development Review*, 1966.

'El capital extranjero y el desarrollo', with Ricardo Ffrench-Davis, *Revista Economia*, 1964.

'The potential benefits of Latin American integration', *Inter-American Economic Affairs*, Spring 1964.

'Economic approach to planning education: a criticism', with Carlos Hurtado, *Economic Weekly*, 14 November 1964.

'Algunas reflexiones sobre el model Tinbergen-Correa de planificación de la Educación', with Carlos Hurtado, *El Trimestre Economico*, 1964.

'Comercio Internacional y Modelos de Crecimiento a Largo Plazo', with Ricardo Ffrench-Davis, *Desarrollo Economico*, 1964.

'Comercio internacional y politicas de desarrollo economico', with Ricardo Ffrench-Davis, *Cuadernos de Economia*, 1964.

'El crecimiento mundial y la distribución de la liquidez', with Juan Braun, *Revista Economia*, 1962–3.

'Inflación y devaluación', *Revista Economia*, 1963.

'A note on wages, prices and unemployment', *Bulletin of the Oxford University Institute of Economics and Statistics*, 1962.

'Structural disequilibrium in an underdeveloped economy', *Economic Weekly*, 1 April 1961.

'Inflation in underdeveloped countries: not a monetary phenomenon', *Economic Weekly*, special number, July 1961.

'Inflation: its cause and control', *Economic Weekly*, 25 November 1961.

Index